Yen Press

ZOO

THE GRAPHIC NOVEL

JAMES PATTERSON
MICHAEL LEDWIDGE

ART AND ADAPTATION BY
ANDY MACDONALD

Zoo: The Graphic Novel

Art and Adaptation:
Andy MacDonald

Lettering: AndWorld Design

This book is a work of fiction. Names, characters, places, and incidents are the product of the author's imagination or are used fictitiously. Any resemblance to actual events, locales, or persons, living or dead, is coincidental.

Yen Press
Hachette Book Group
237 Park Avenue
New York, NY 10017

www.HachetteBookGroup.com
www.YenPress.com

Yen Press is an imprint of Hachette Book Group, Inc. The Yen Press name and logo are trademarks of Hachette Book Group, Inc.

First Edition: November 2012

ISBN: 978-0-316-12760-8

10 9 8 7 6 5 4 3 2 1

WOR

Printed in the United States of America

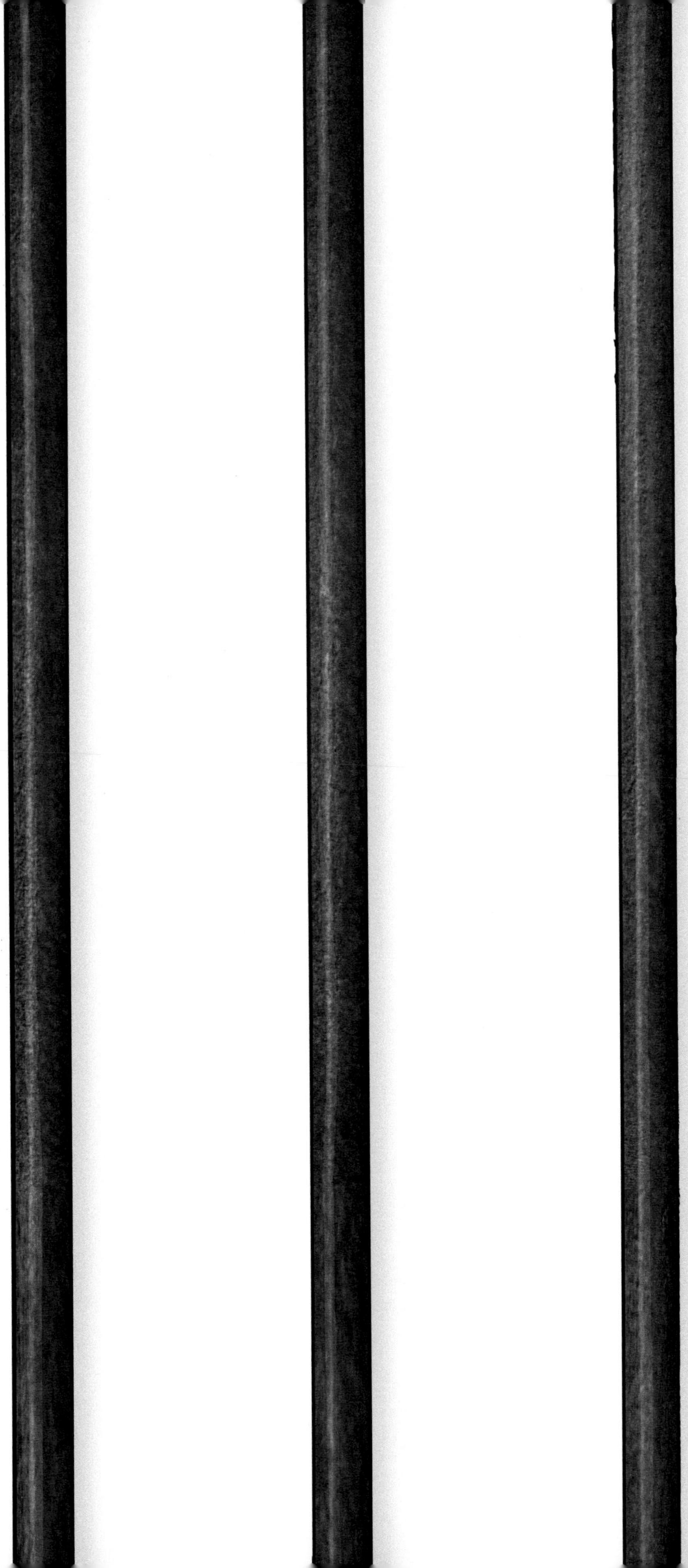

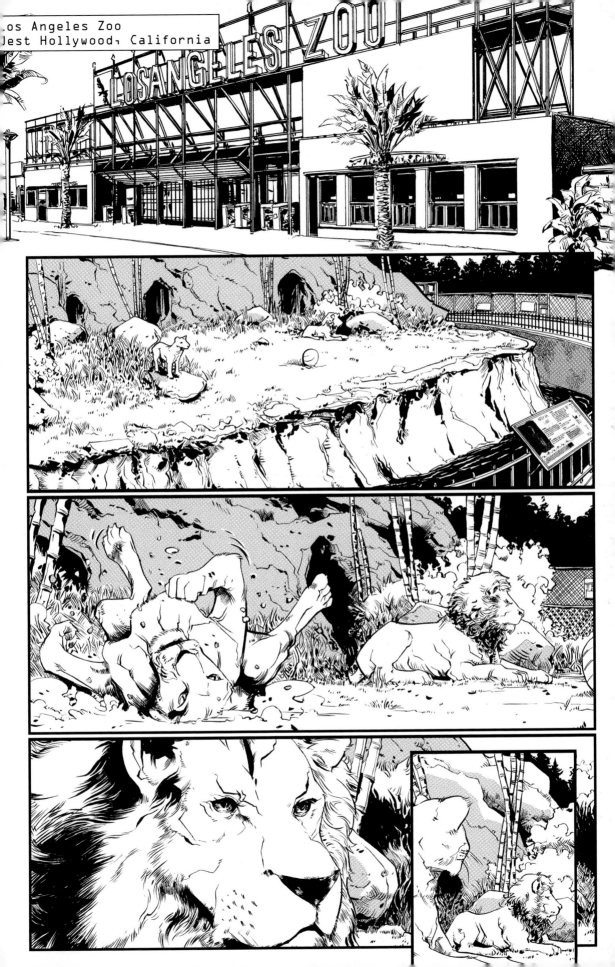

Los Angeles Zoo
West Hollywood, California

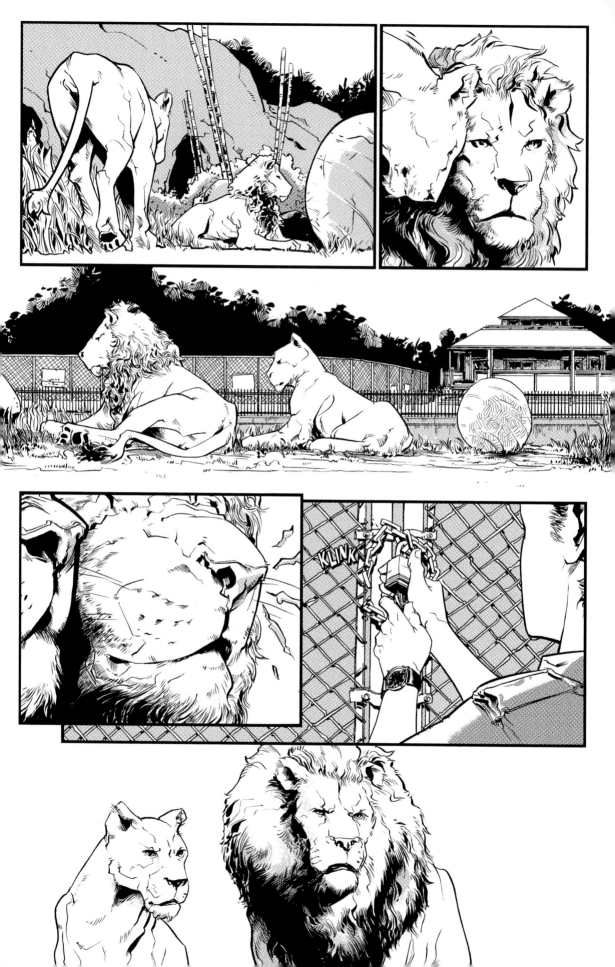

KLINK

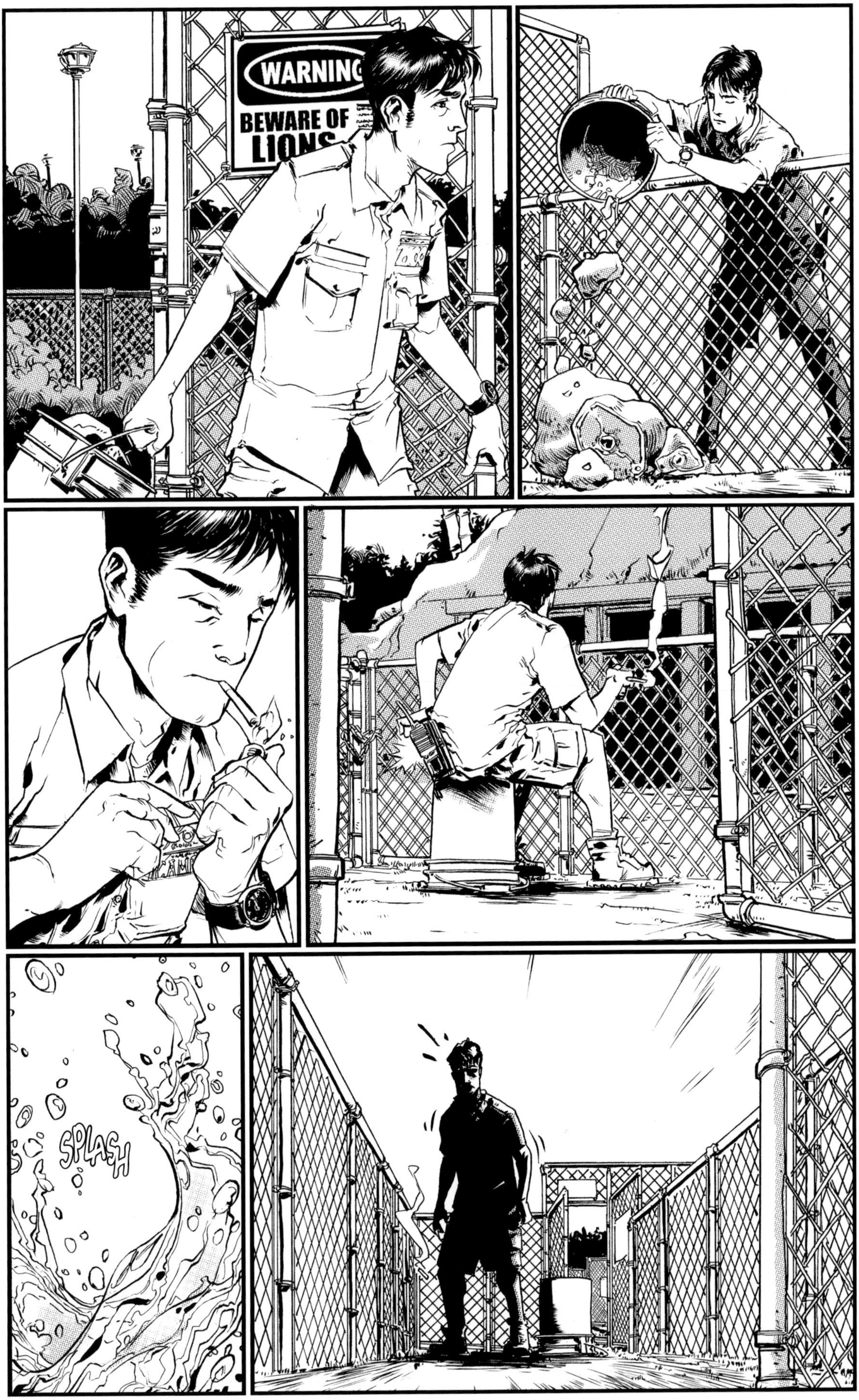
WARNING
BEWARE OF
LIONS
SPLASH

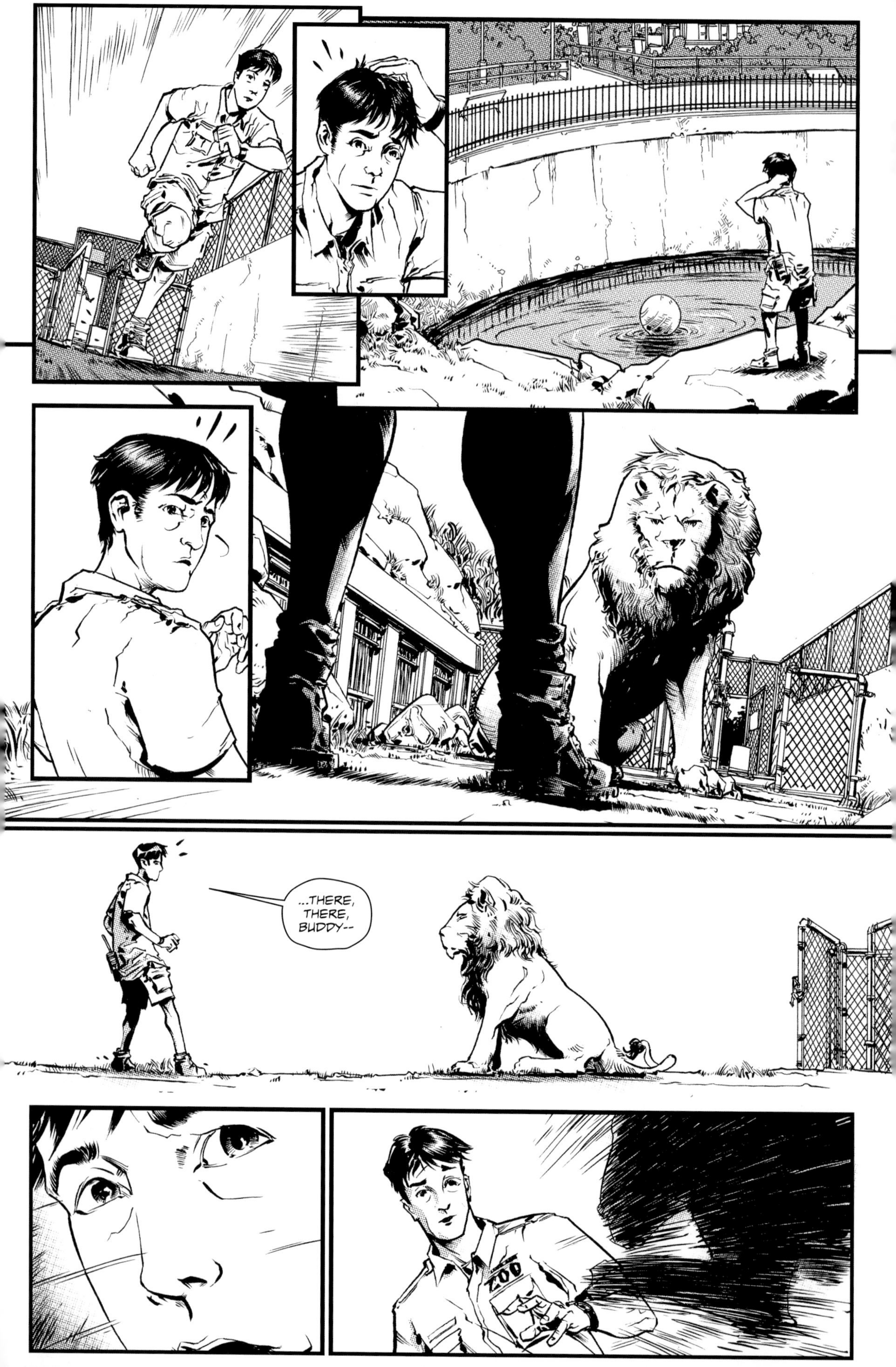
...THERE, THERE, BUDDY--
ZOO

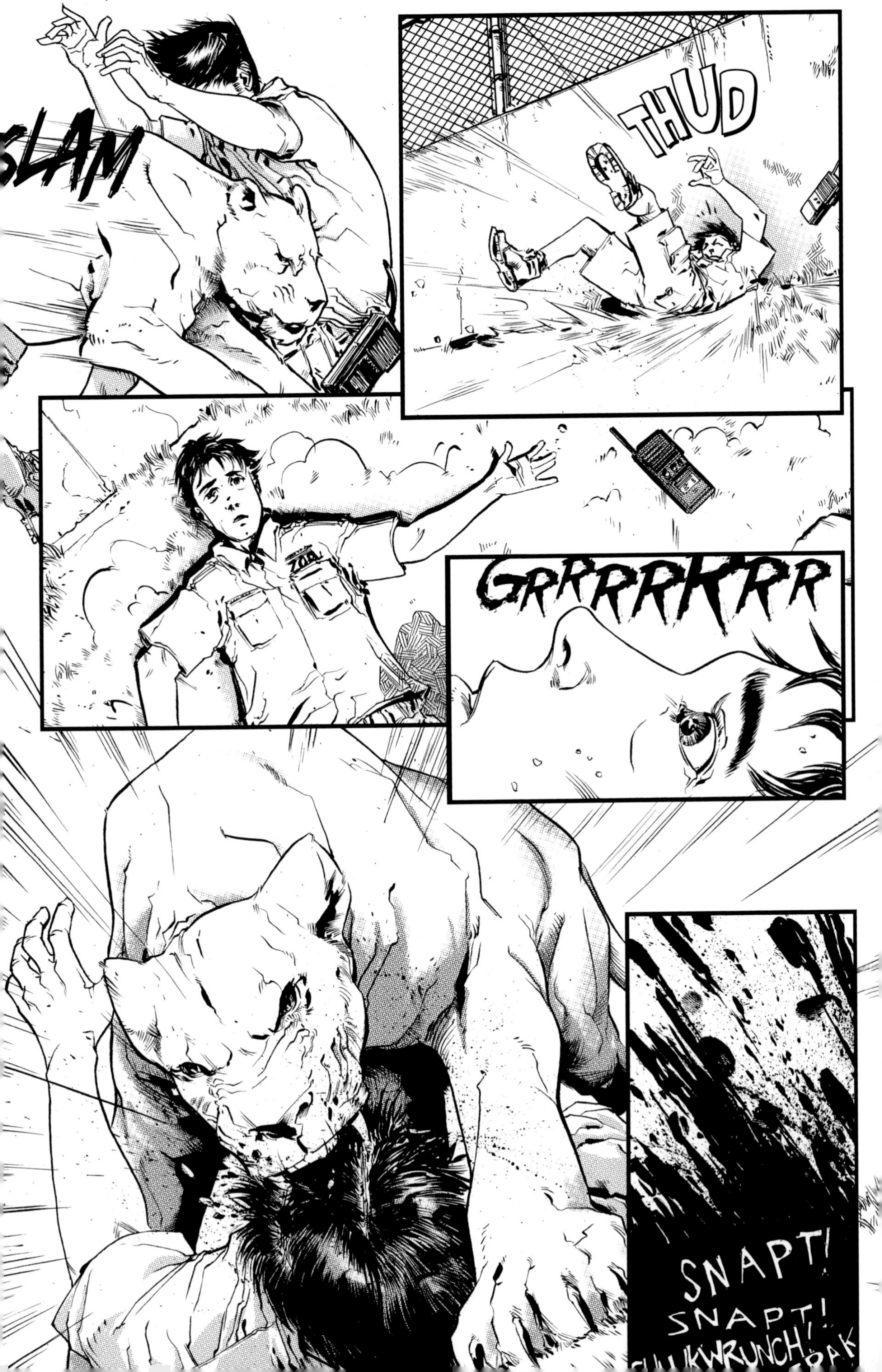
SLAM
THUD
ZOO
GRRRRRRR
SNAPT!
SNAPT!

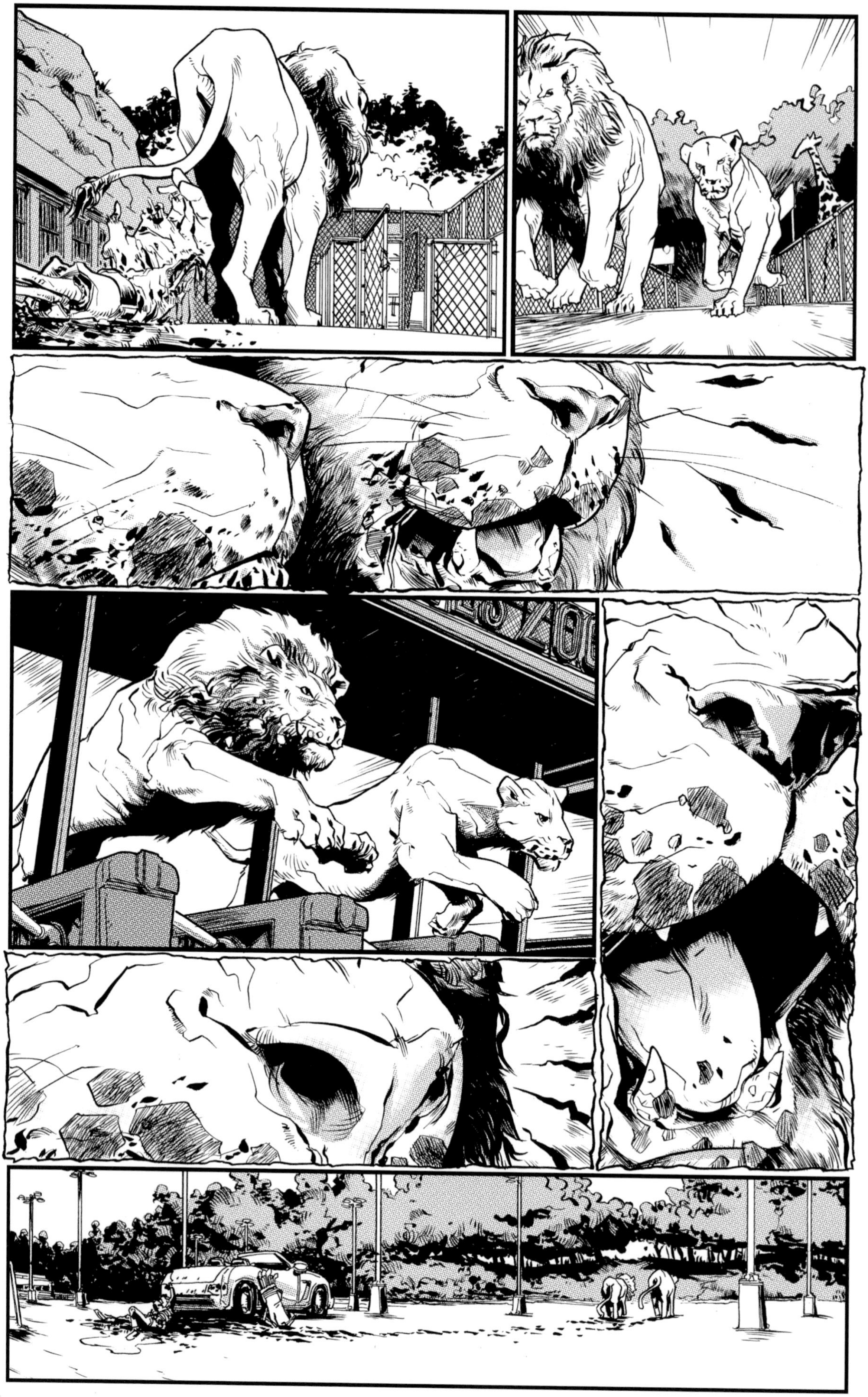

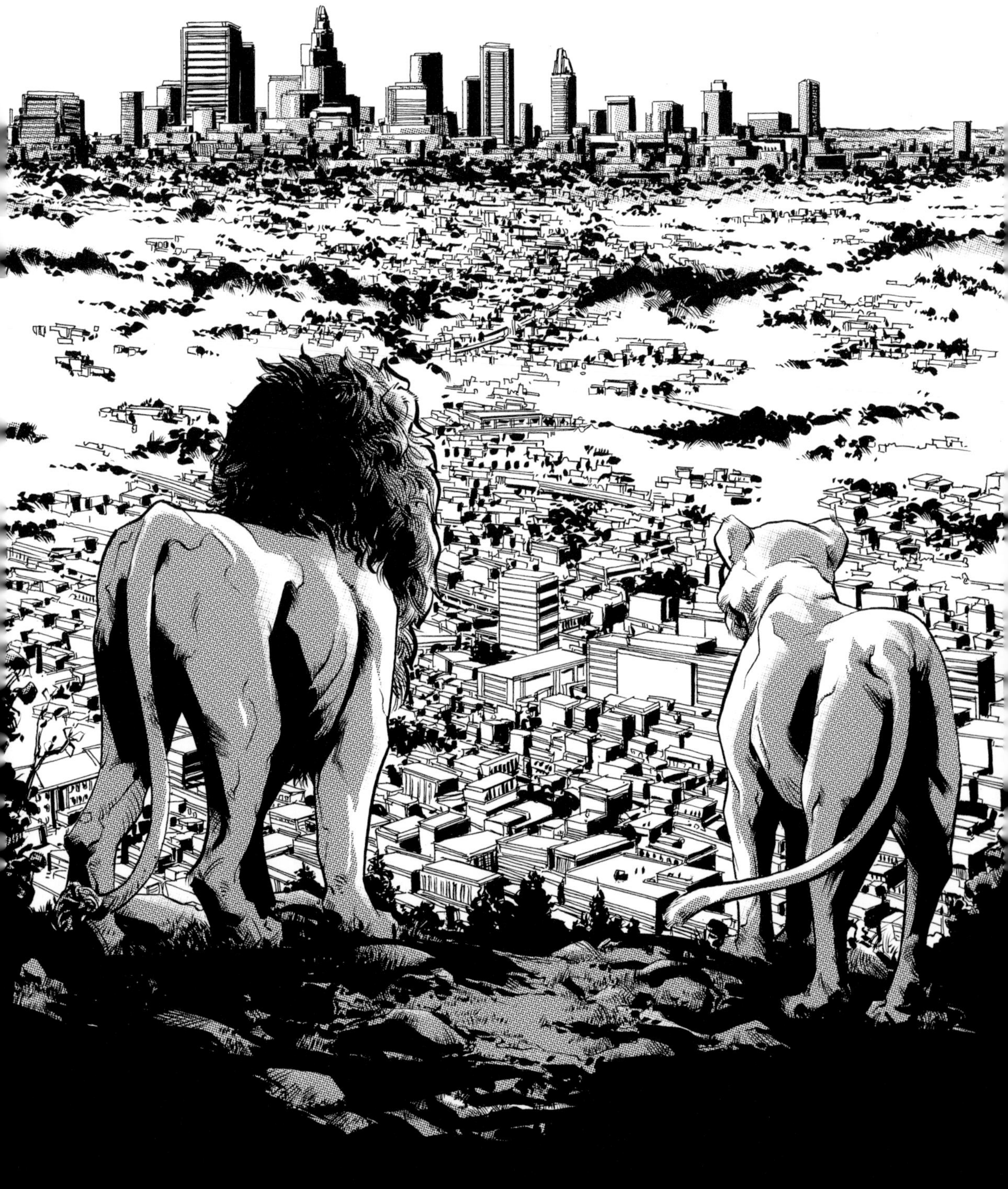

ZOO

THE GRAPHIC NOVEL

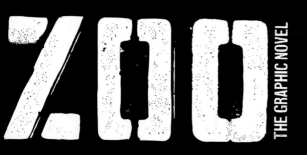

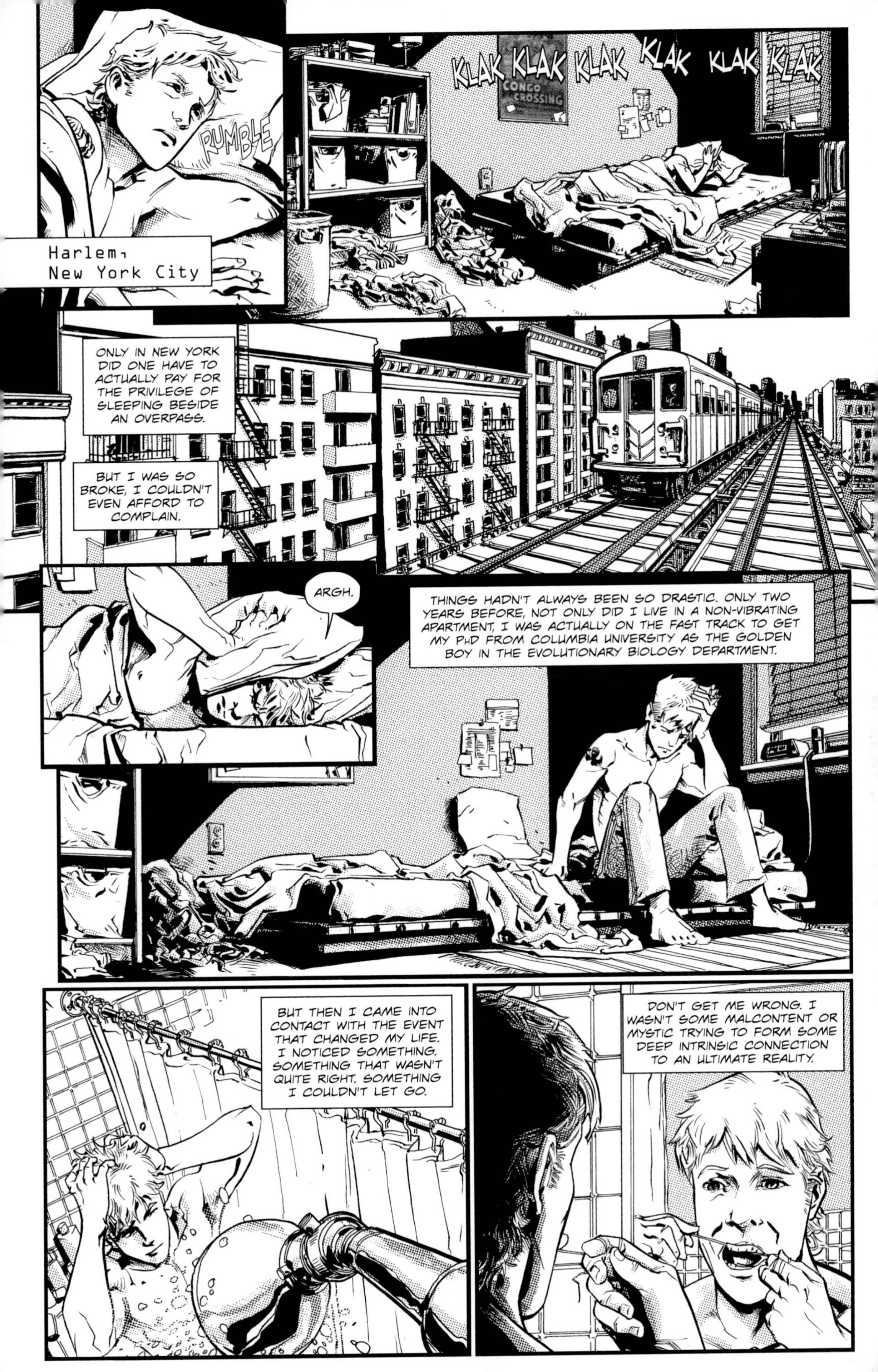
RUMBLE
Harlem,
New York City
KLAK KLAK KLAK KLAK KLAK KLAK
CONGO CROSSING
ONLY IN NEW YORK DID ONE HAVE TO ACTUALLY PAY FOR THE PRIVILEGE OF SLEEPING BESIDE AN OVERPASS.
BUT I WAS SO BROKE, I COULDN'T EVEN AFFORD TO COMPLAIN.
ARGH.
THINGS HADN'T ALWAYS BEEN SO DRASTIC. ONLY TWO YEARS BEFORE, NOT ONLY DID I LIVE IN A NON-VIBRATING APARTMENT, I WAS ACTUALLY ON THE FAST TRACK TO GET MY PhD FROM COLUMBIA UNIVERSITY AS THE GOLDEN BOY IN THE EVOLUTIONARY BIOLOGY DEPARTMENT.
BUT THEN I CAME INTO CONTACT WITH THE EVENT THAT CHANGED MY LIFE. I NOTICED SOMETHING. SOMETHING THAT WASN'T QUITE RIGHT. SOMETHING I COULDN'T LET GO.
DON'T GET ME WRONG. I WASN'T SOME MALCONTENT OR MYSTIC TRYING TO FORM SOME DEEP INTRINSIC CONNECTION TO AN ULTIMATE REALITY.

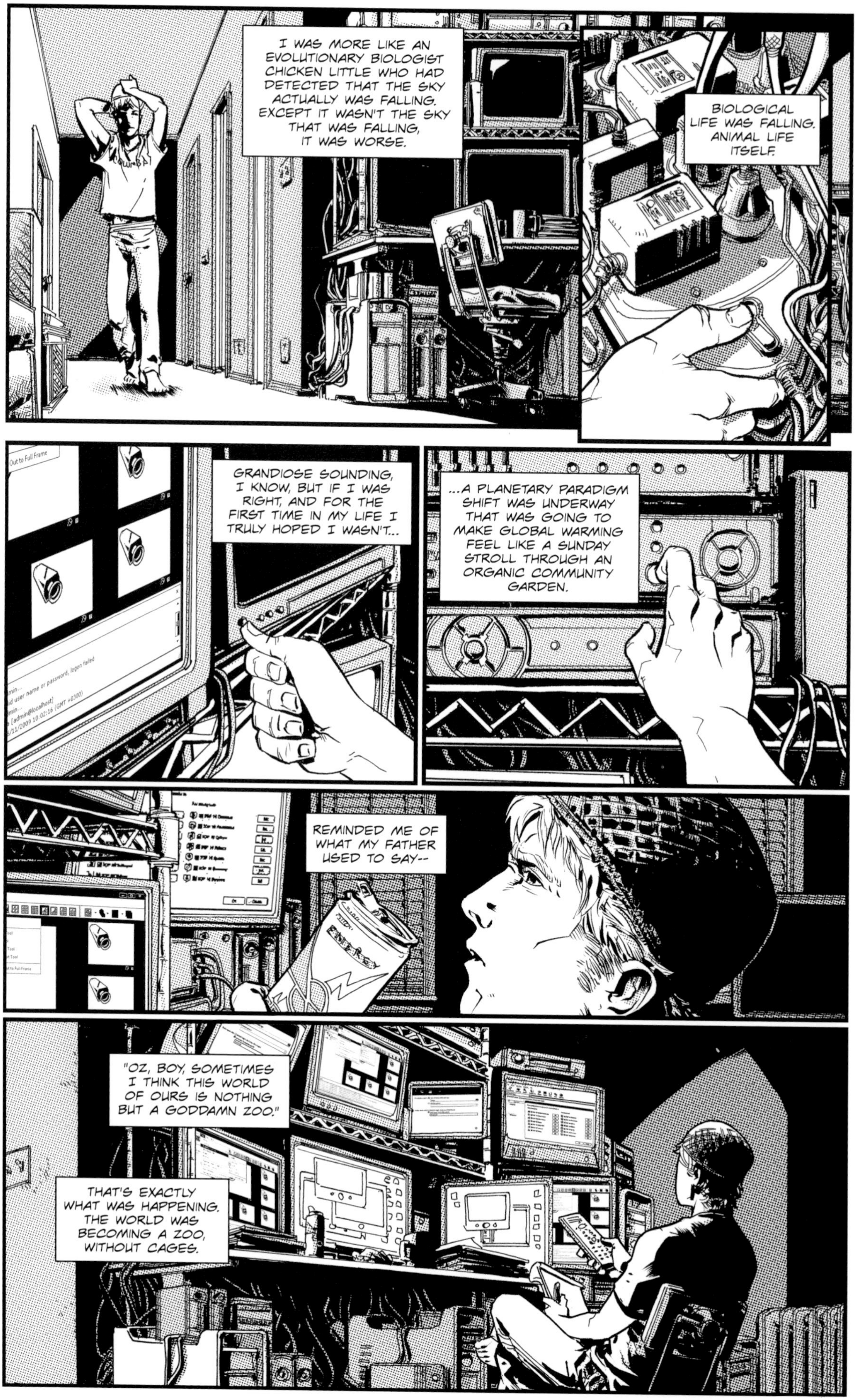

I WAS MORE LIKE AN EVOLUTIONARY BIOLOGIST CHICKEN LITTLE WHO HAD DETECTED THAT THE SKY ACTUALLY WAS FALLING. EXCEPT IT WASN'T THE SKY THAT WAS FALLING, IT WAS WORSE.
BIOLOGICAL LIFE WAS FALLING. ANIMAL LIFE ITSELF.
GRANDIOSE SOUNDING, I KNOW, BUT IF I WAS RIGHT, AND FOR THE FIRST TIME IN MY LIFE I TRULY HOPED I WASN'T...
...A PLANETARY PARADIGM SHIFT WAS UNDERWAY THAT WAS GOING TO MAKE GLOBAL WARMING FEEL LIKE A SUNDAY STROLL THROUGH AN ORGANIC COMMUNITY GARDEN.
REMINDED ME OF WHAT MY FATHER USED TO SAY--
"OZ, BOY, SOMETIMES I THINK THIS WORLD OF OURS IS NOTHING BUT A GODDAMN ZOO."
THAT'S EXACTLY WHAT WAS HAPPENING. THE WORLD WAS BECOMING A ZOO, WITHOUT CAGES.

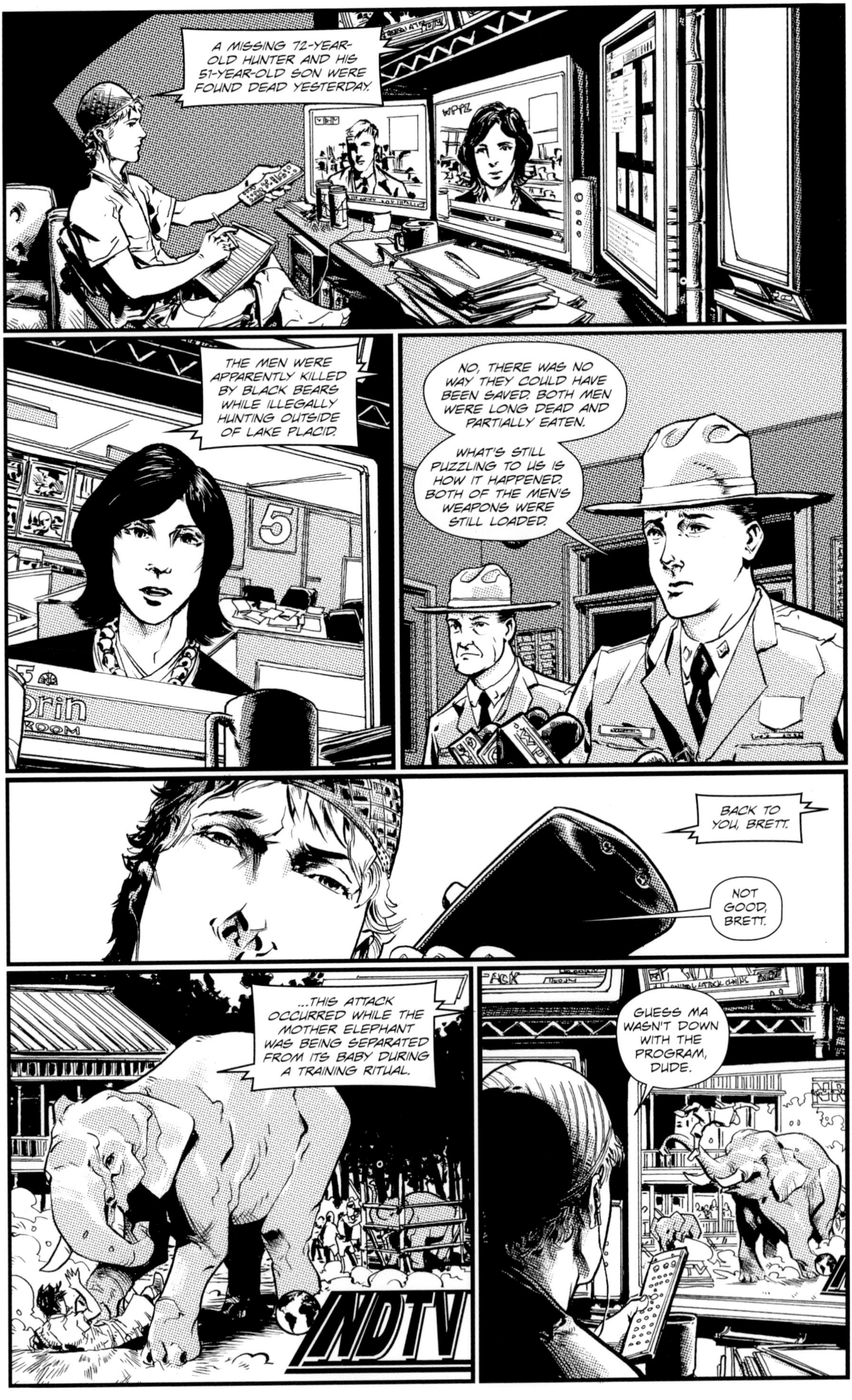
A MISSING 72-YEAR-OLD HUNTER AND HIS 51-YEAR-OLD SON WERE FOUND DEAD YESTERDAY.
THE MEN WERE APPARENTLY KILLED BY BLACK BEARS WHILE ILLEGALLY HUNTING OUTSIDE OF LAKE PLACID.
NO, THERE WAS NO WAY THEY COULD HAVE BEEN SAVED. BOTH MEN WERE LONG DEAD AND PARTIALLY EATEN.
WHAT'S STILL PUZZLING TO US IS HOW IT HAPPENED. BOTH OF THE MEN'S WEAPONS WERE STILL LOADED.
BACK TO YOU, BRETT.
NOT GOOD, BRETT.
...THIS ATTACK OCCURRED WHILE THE MOTHER ELEPHANT WAS BEING SEPARATED FROM ITS BABY DURING A TRAINING RITUAL.
GUESS MA WASN'T DOWN WITH THE PROGRAM, DUDE.
NDTV

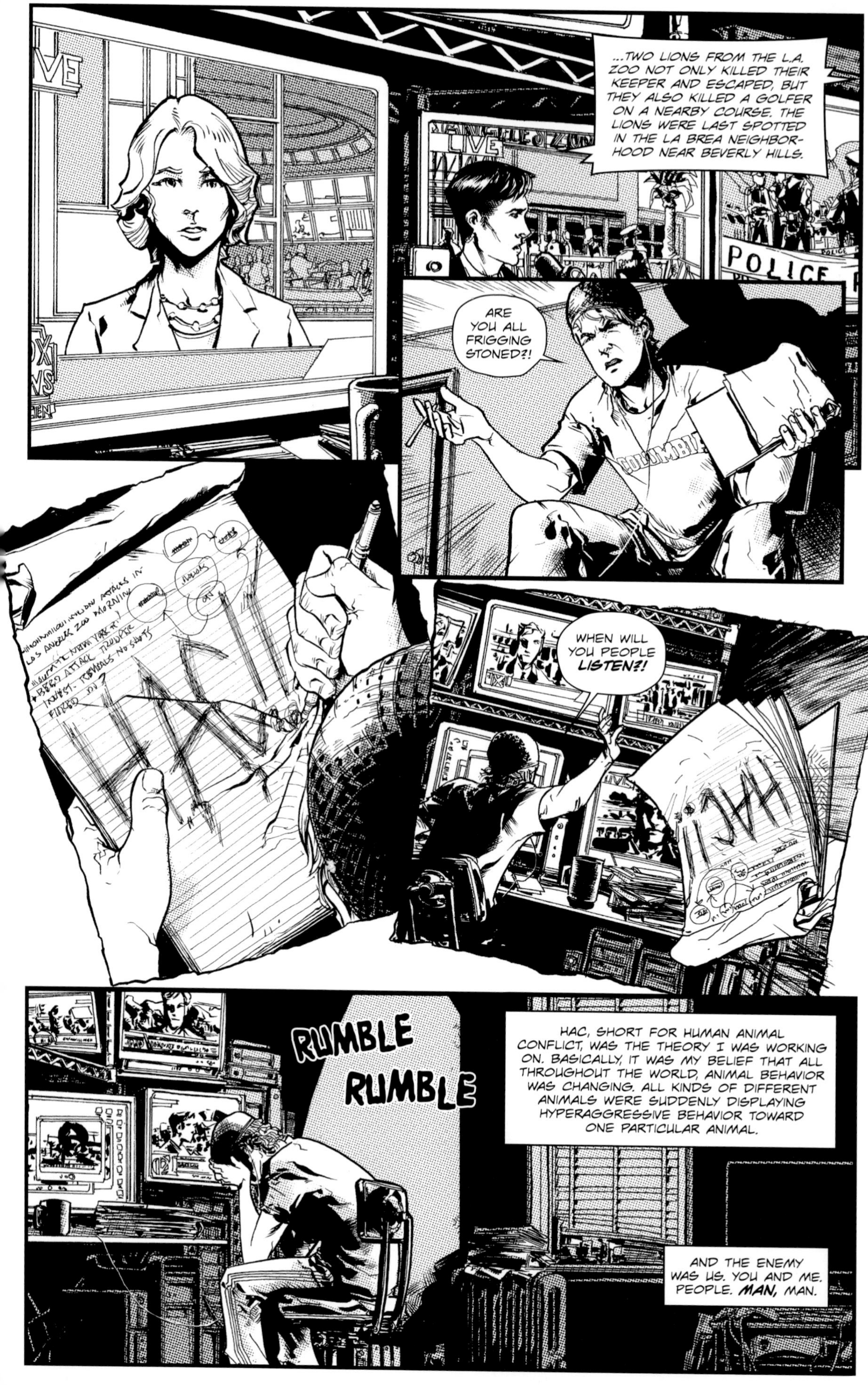

...TWO LIONS FROM THE L.A. ZOO NOT ONLY KILLED THEIR KEEPER AND ESCAPED, BUT THEY ALSO KILLED A GOLFER ON A NEARBY COURSE. THE LIONS WERE LAST SPOTTED IN THE LA BREA NEIGHBORHOOD NEAR BEVERLY HILLS.
POLICE
ARE YOU ALL FRIGGING STONED?!
COLUMBIA
HAC
WHEN WILL YOU PEOPLE LISTEN?!
HAC!
RUMBLE
RUMBLE
HAC, SHORT FOR HUMAN ANIMAL CONFLICT, WAS THE THEORY I WAS WORKING ON. BASICALLY, IT WAS MY BELIEF THAT ALL THROUGHOUT THE WORLD, ANIMAL BEHAVIOR WAS CHANGING. ALL KINDS OF DIFFERENT ANIMALS WERE SUDDENLY DISPLAYING HYPERAGGRESSIVE BEHAVIOR TOWARD ONE PARTICULAR ANIMAL.
AND THE ENEMY WAS US. YOU AND ME. PEOPLE. MAN, MAN.

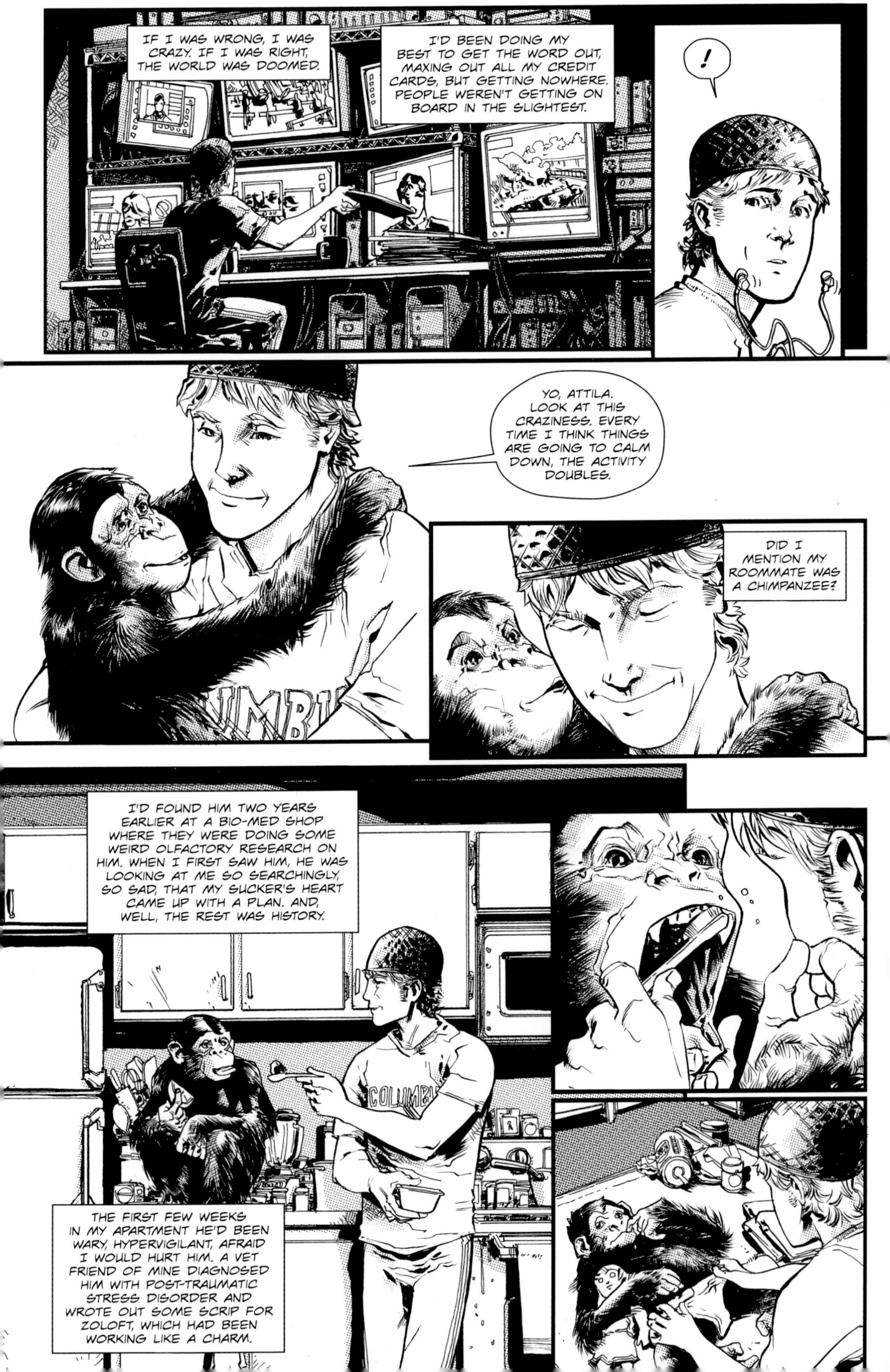
IF I WAS WRONG, I WAS CRAZY. IF I WAS RIGHT, THE WORLD WAS DOOMED.
I'D BEEN DOING MY BEST TO GET THE WORD OUT, MAXING OUT ALL MY CREDIT CARDS, BUT GETTING NOWHERE. PEOPLE WEREN'T GETTING ON BOARD IN THE SLIGHTEST.
!
YO, ATTILA. LOOK AT THIS CRAZINESS. EVERY TIME I THINK THINGS ARE GOING TO CALM DOWN, THE ACTIVITY DOUBLES.
DID I MENTION MY ROOMMATE WAS A CHIMPANZEE?
I'D FOUND HIM TWO YEARS EARLIER AT A BIO-MED SHOP WHERE THEY WERE DOING SOME WEIRD OLFACTORY RESEARCH ON HIM. WHEN I FIRST SAW HIM, HE WAS LOOKING AT ME SO SEARCHINGLY, SO SAD, THAT MY SUCKER'S HEART CAME UP WITH A PLAN. AND, WELL, THE REST WAS HISTORY.
THE FIRST FEW WEEKS IN MY APARTMENT HE'D BEEN WARY, HYPERVIGILANT, AFRAID I WOULD HURT HIM. A VET FRIEND OF MINE DIAGNOSED HIM WITH POST-TRAUMATIC STRESS DISORDER AND WROTE OUT SOME SCRIP FOR ZOLOFT, WHICH HAD BEEN WORKING LIKE A CHARM.

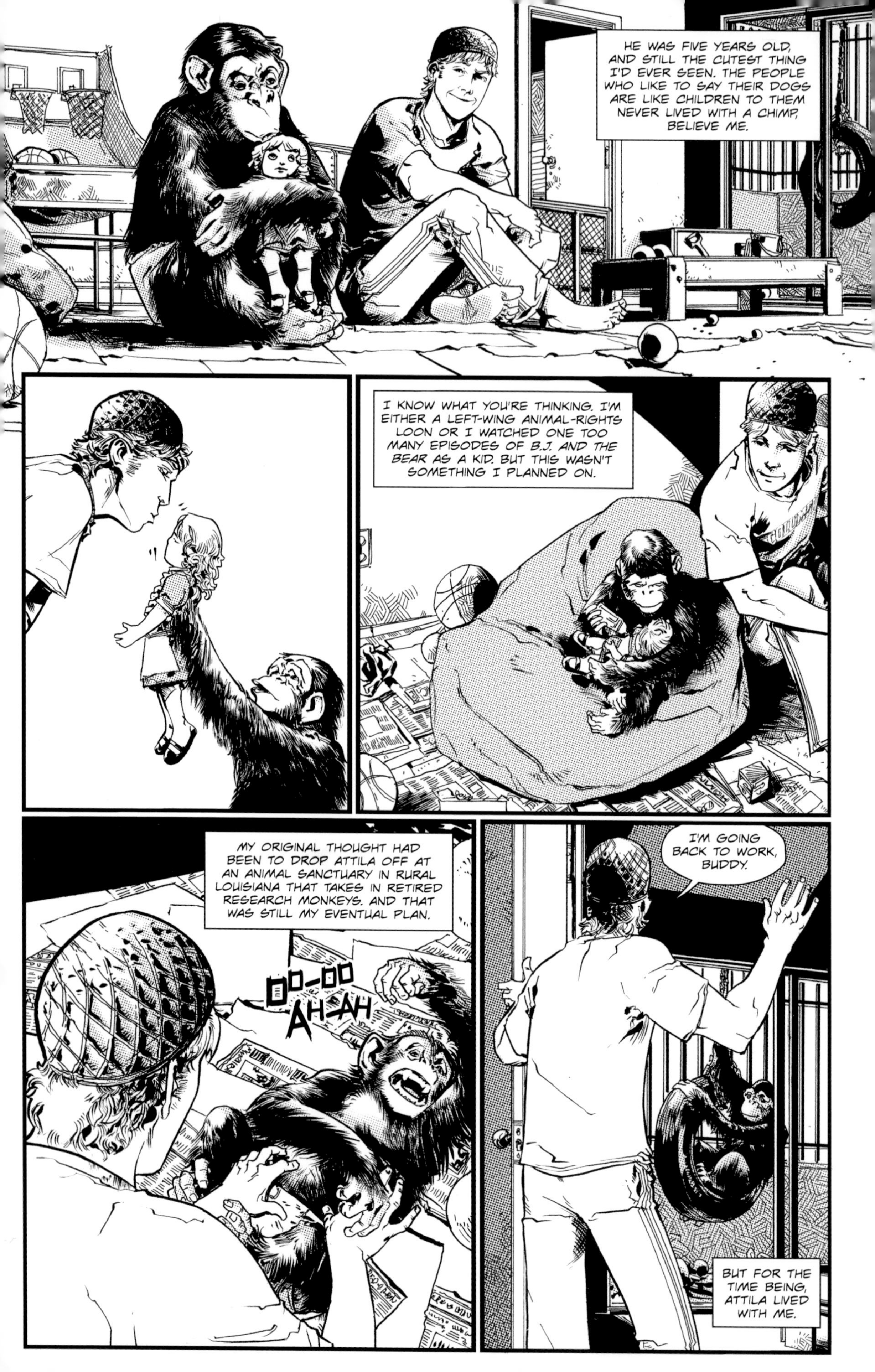
HE WAS FIVE YEARS OLD, AND STILL THE CUTEST THING I'D EVER SEEN. THE PEOPLE WHO LIKE TO SAY THEIR DOGS ARE LIKE CHILDREN TO THEM NEVER LIVED WITH A CHIMP, BELIEVE ME.
I KNOW WHAT YOU'RE THINKING. I'M EITHER A LEFT-WING ANIMAL-RIGHTS LOON OR I WATCHED ONE TOO MANY EPISODES OF B.J. AND THE BEAR AS A KID. BUT THIS WASN'T SOMETHING I PLANNED ON.
MY ORIGINAL THOUGHT HAD BEEN TO DROP ATTILA OFF AT AN ANIMAL SANCTUARY IN RURAL LOUISIANA THAT TAKES IN RETIRED RESEARCH MONKEYS. AND THAT WAS STILL MY EVENTUAL PLAN.
OO-OO AH-AH
I'M GOING BACK TO WORK, BUDDY.
BUT FOR THE TIME BEING, ATTILA LIVED WITH ME.

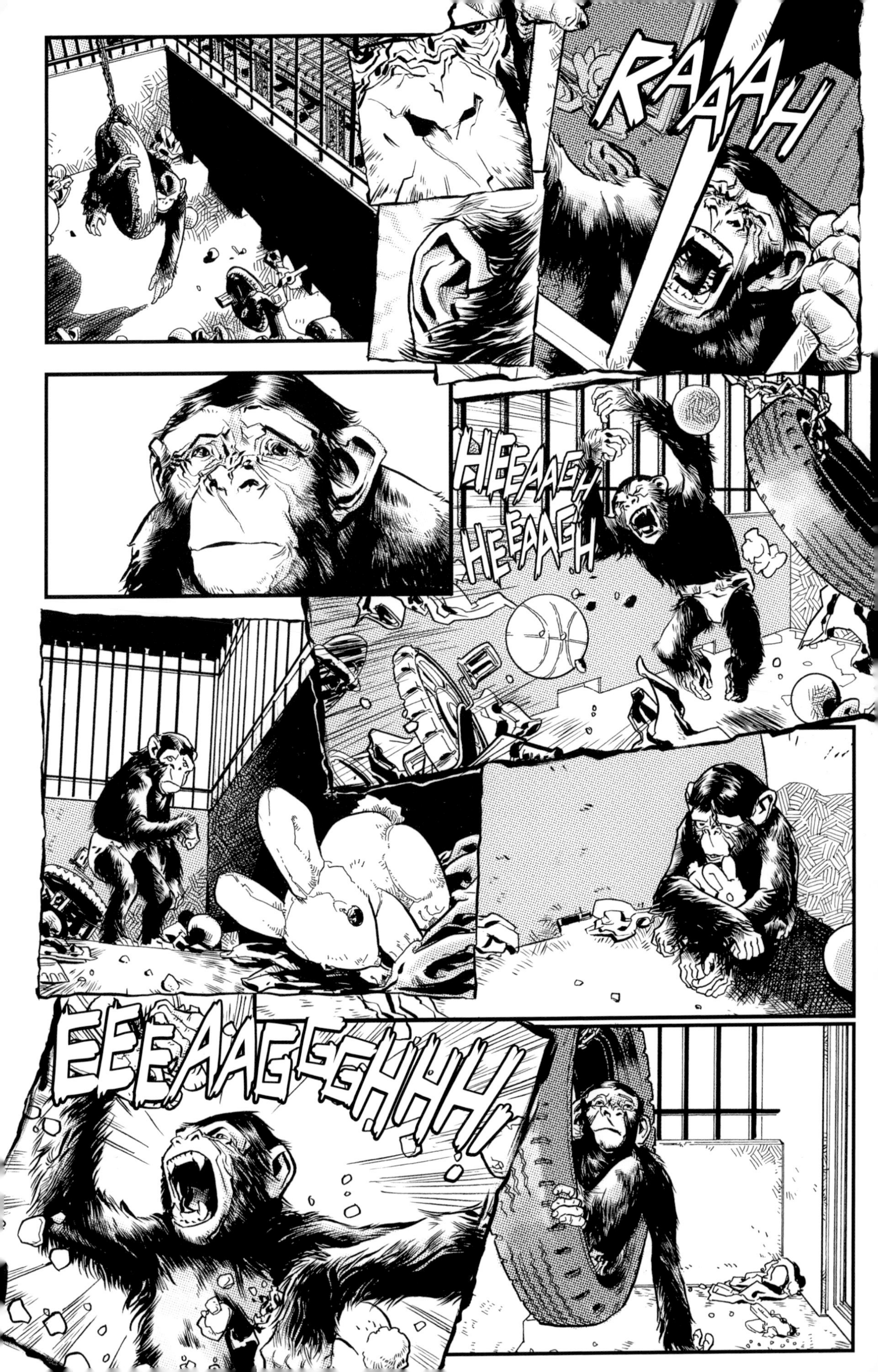
RAAAH
HEEAAGH
HEEAACH
EEEAAGGHHH!

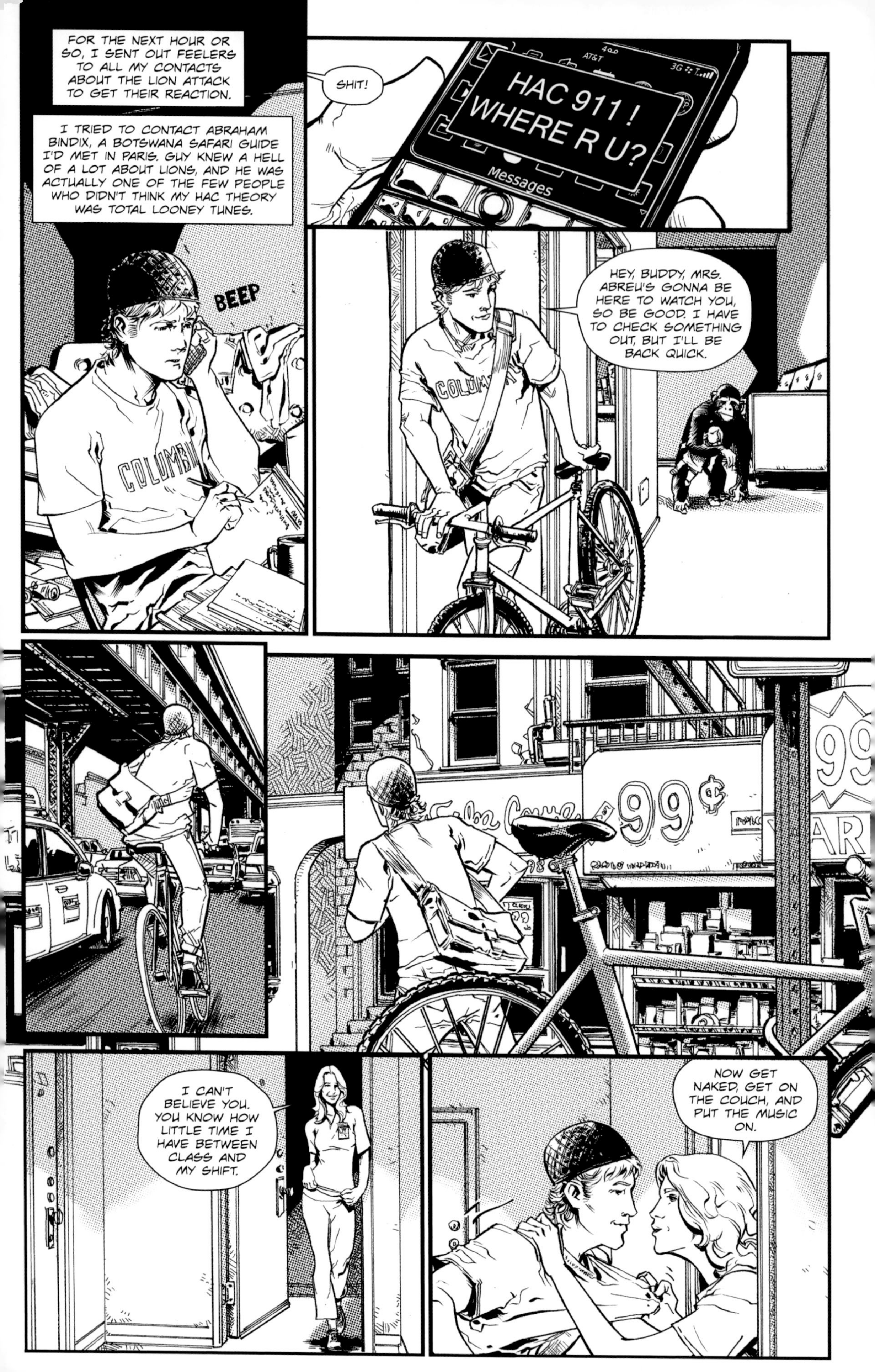

FOR THE NEXT HOUR OR SO, I SENT OUT FEELERS TO ALL MY CONTACTS ABOUT THE LION ATTACK TO GET THEIR REACTION.
I TRIED TO CONTACT ABRAHAM BINDIX, A BOTSWANA SAFARI GUIDE I'D MET IN PARIS. GUY KNEW A HELL OF A LOT ABOUT LIONS, AND HE WAS ACTUALLY ONE OF THE FEW PEOPLE WHO DIDN'T THINK MY HAC THEORY WAS TOTAL LOONEY TUNES.
BEEP
SHIT!
AT&T
3G
HAC 911 ! WHERE R U?
Messages
HEY, BUDDY, MRS. ABREU'S GONNA BE HERE TO WATCH YOU, SO BE GOOD. I HAVE TO CHECK SOMETHING OUT, BUT I'LL BE BACK QUICK.
COLUMBIA
99¢
I CAN'T BELIEVE YOU. YOU KNOW HOW LITTLE TIME I HAVE BETWEEN CLASS AND MY SHIFT.
NOW GET NAKED, GET ON THE COUCH, AND PUT THE MUSIC ON.

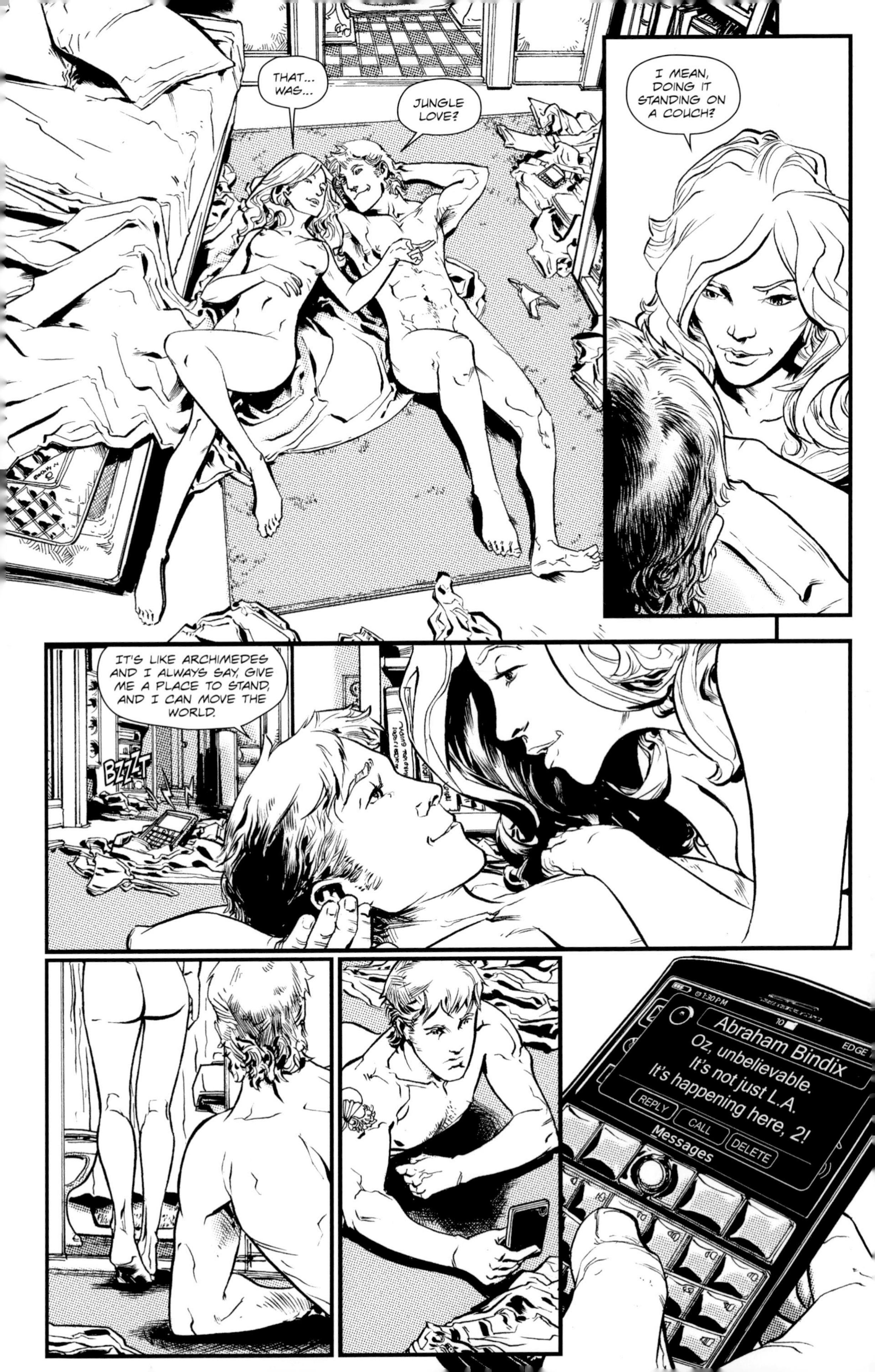
THAT... WAS...
JUNGLE LOVE?
I MEAN, DOING IT STANDING ON A COUCH?
IT'S LIKE ARCHIMEDES AND I ALWAYS SAY, GIVE ME A PLACE TO STAND, AND I CAN MOVE THE WORLD.
BZZZT
Abraham Bindix
Oz, unbelievable. It's not just L.A. It's happening here, 2!
REPLY
CALL
DELETE
Messages

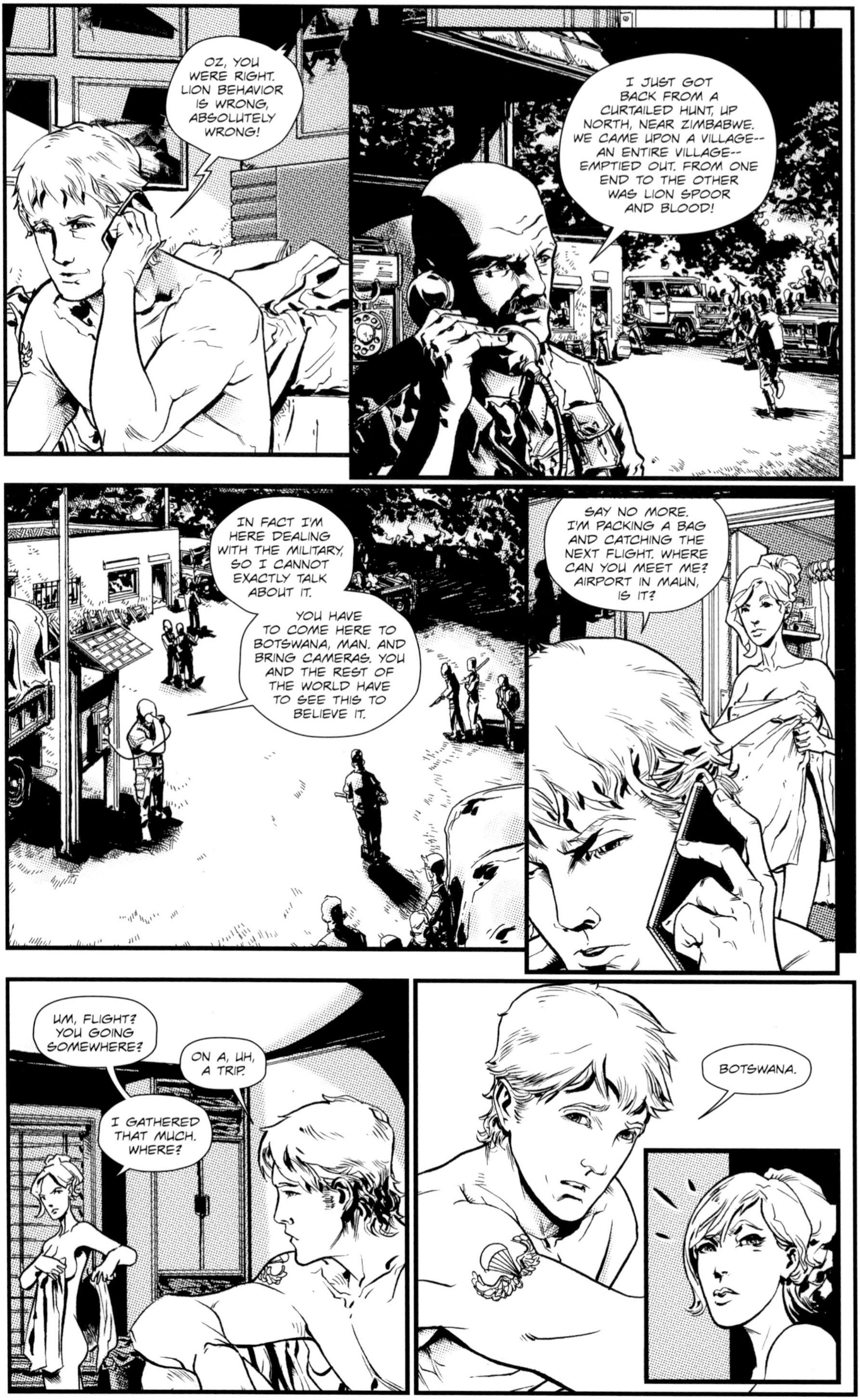

OZ, YOU WERE RIGHT. LION BEHAVIOR IS WRONG, ABSOLUTELY WRONG!
I JUST GOT BACK FROM A CURTAILED HUNT, UP NORTH, NEAR ZIMBABWE. WE CAME UPON A VILLAGE-- AN ENTIRE VILLAGE-- EMPTIED OUT. FROM ONE END TO THE OTHER WAS LION SPOOR AND BLOOD!
IN FACT I'M HERE DEALING WITH THE MILITARY, SO I CANNOT EXACTLY TALK ABOUT IT.
YOU HAVE TO COME HERE TO BOTSWANA, MAN. AND BRING CAMERAS. YOU AND THE REST OF THE WORLD HAVE TO SEE THIS TO BELIEVE IT.
SAY NO MORE. I'M PACKING A BAG AND CATCHING THE NEXT FLIGHT. WHERE CAN YOU MEET ME? AIRPORT IN MAUN, IS IT?
UM, FLIGHT? YOU GOING SOMEWHERE?
ON A, UH, A TRIP.
I GATHERED THAT MUCH. WHERE?
BOTSWANA.

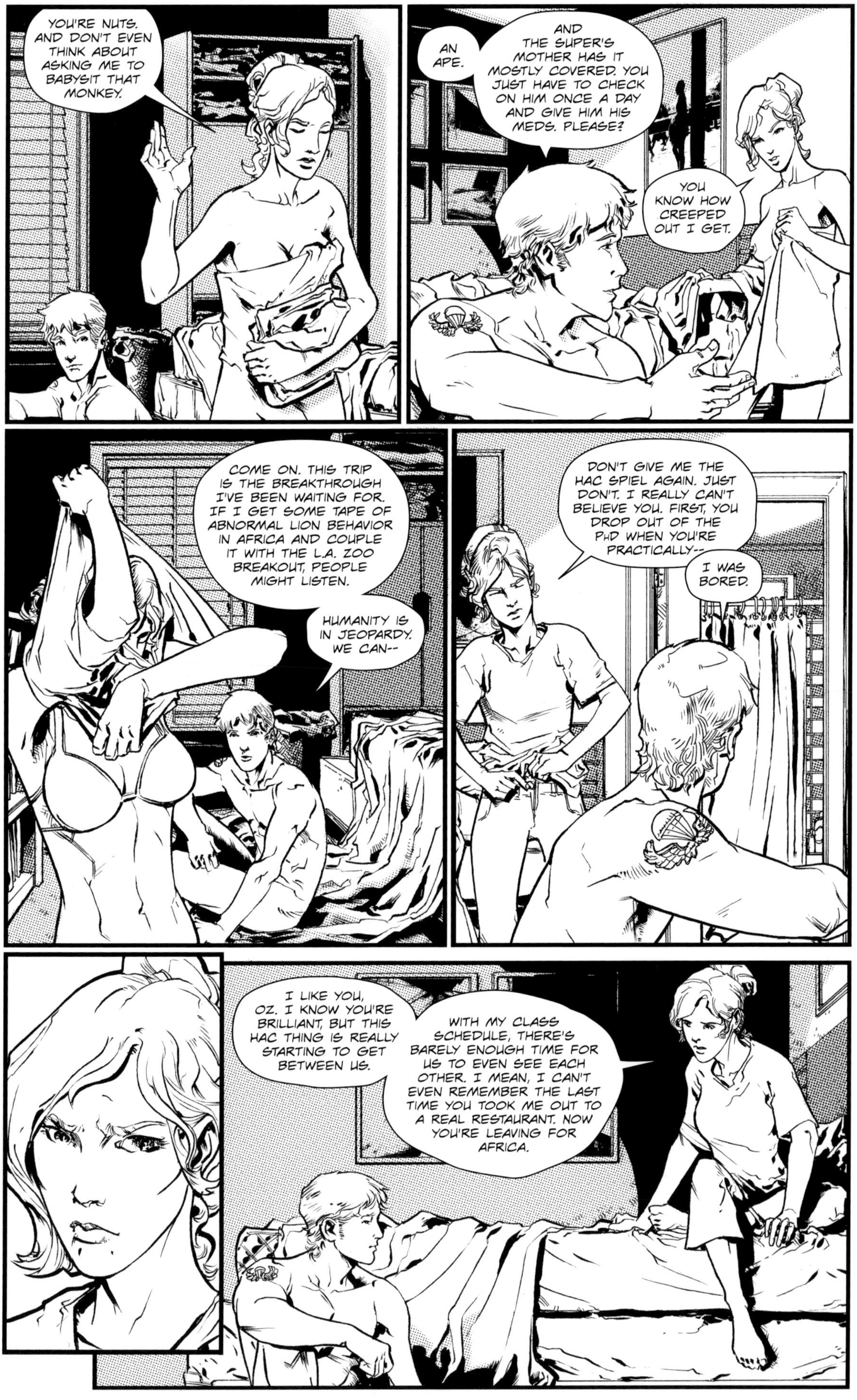
YOU'RE NUTS. AND DON'T EVEN THINK ABOUT ASKING ME TO BABYSIT THAT MONKEY.
AN APE.
AND THE SUPER'S MOTHER HAS IT MOSTLY COVERED. YOU JUST HAVE TO CHECK ON HIM ONCE A DAY AND GIVE HIM HIS MEDS. PLEASE?
YOU KNOW HOW CREEPED OUT I GET.
COME ON. THIS TRIP IS THE BREAKTHROUGH I'VE BEEN WAITING FOR. IF I GET SOME TAPE OF ABNORMAL LION BEHAVIOR IN AFRICA AND COUPLE IT WITH THE L.A. ZOO BREAKOUT, PEOPLE MIGHT LISTEN.
HUMANITY IS IN JEOPARDY. WE CAN--
DON'T GIVE ME THE HAC SPIEL AGAIN. JUST DON'T. I REALLY CAN'T BELIEVE YOU. FIRST, YOU DROP OUT OF THE PhD WHEN YOU'RE PRACTICALLY--
I WAS BORED.
I LIKE YOU, OZ. I KNOW YOU'RE BRILLIANT, BUT THIS HAC THING IS REALLY STARTING TO GET BETWEEN US.
WITH MY CLASS SCHEDULE, THERE'S BARELY ENOUGH TIME FOR US TO EVEN SEE EACH OTHER. I MEAN, I CAN'T EVEN REMEMBER THE LAST TIME YOU TOOK ME OUT TO A REAL RESTAURANT. NOW YOU'RE LEAVING FOR AFRICA.

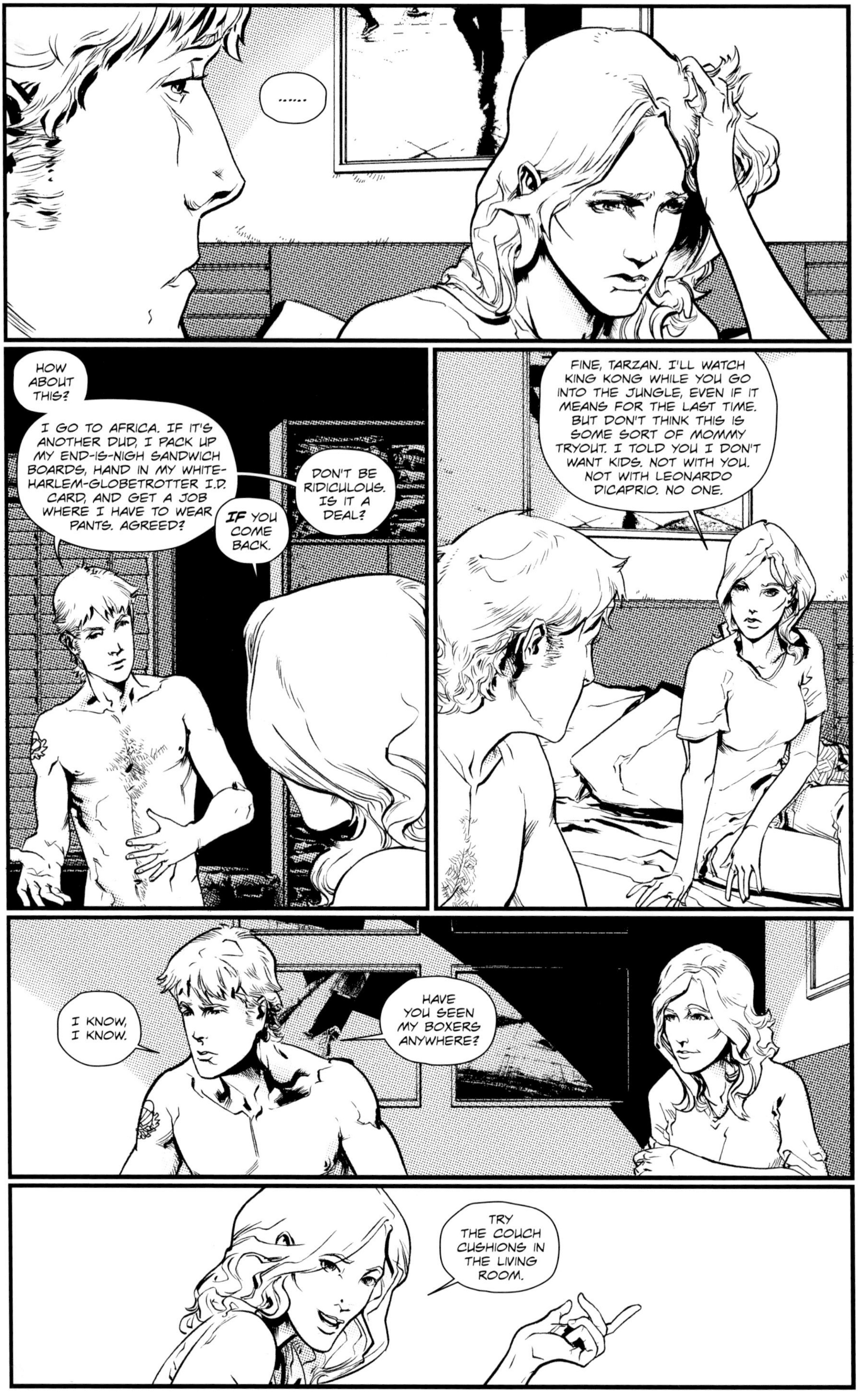
......
HOW ABOUT THIS?
I GO TO AFRICA. IF IT'S ANOTHER DUD, I PACK UP MY END-IS-NIGH SANDWICH BOARDS, HAND IN MY WHITE-HARLEM-GLOBETROTTER I.D. CARD, AND GET A JOB WHERE I HAVE TO WEAR PANTS. AGREED?
DON'T BE RIDICULOUS. IS IT A DEAL?
IF YOU COME BACK.
FINE, TARZAN. I'LL WATCH KING KONG WHILE YOU GO INTO THE JUNGLE, EVEN IF IT MEANS FOR THE LAST TIME. BUT DON'T THINK THIS IS SOME SORT OF MOMMY TRYOUT. I TOLD YOU I DON'T WANT KIDS. NOT WITH YOU. NOT WITH LEONARDO DICAPRIO. NO ONE.
I KNOW, I KNOW.
HAVE YOU SEEN MY BOXERS ANYWHERE?
TRY THE COUCH CUSHIONS IN THE LIVING ROOM.

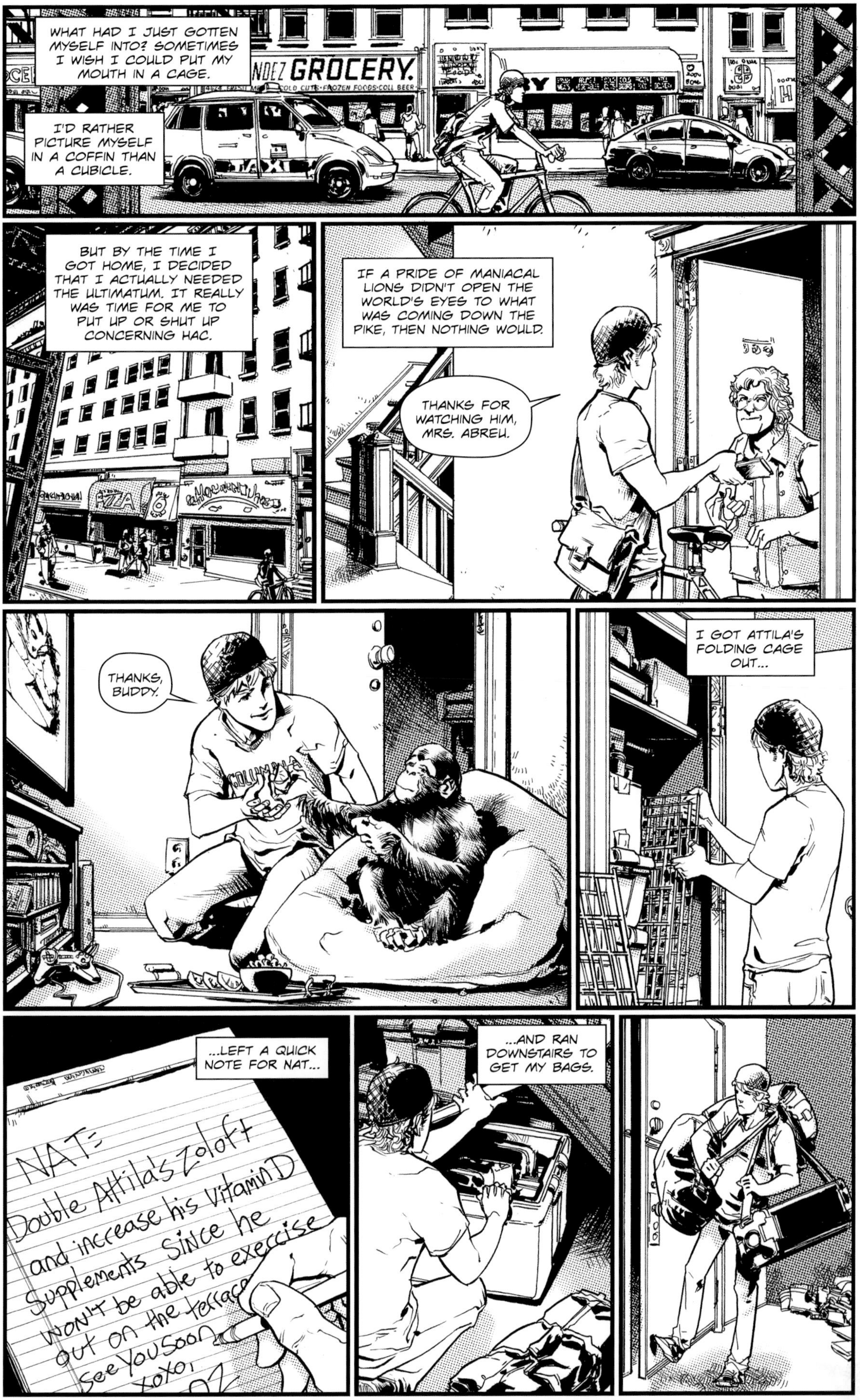
WHAT HAD I JUST GOTTEN MYSELF INTO? SOMETIMES I WISH I COULD PUT MY MOUTH IN A CAGE.
I'D RATHER PICTURE MYSELF IN A COFFIN THAN A CUBICLE.
GROCERY.
COLD CUTS · FROZEN FOODS · COLD BEER
TAXI
BUT BY THE TIME I GOT HOME, I DECIDED THAT I ACTUALLY NEEDED THE ULTIMATUM. IT REALLY WAS TIME FOR ME TO PUT UP OR SHUT UP CONCERNING HAC.
PIZZA
IF A PRIDE OF MANIACAL LIONS DIDN'T OPEN THE WORLD'S EYES TO WHAT WAS COMING DOWN THE PIKE, THEN NOTHING WOULD.
THANKS FOR WATCHING HIM, MRS. ABREU.
THANKS, BUDDY.
COLUMBIA
I GOT ATTILA'S FOLDING CAGE OUT...
...LEFT A QUICK NOTE FOR NAT...
NAT:
Double Attila's Zoloft
and increase his vitamin D
Supplements. Since he
won't be able to exercise
out on the terrace.
See you soon
xoxo,
OZ
...AND RAN DOWNSTAIRS TO GET MY BAGS.

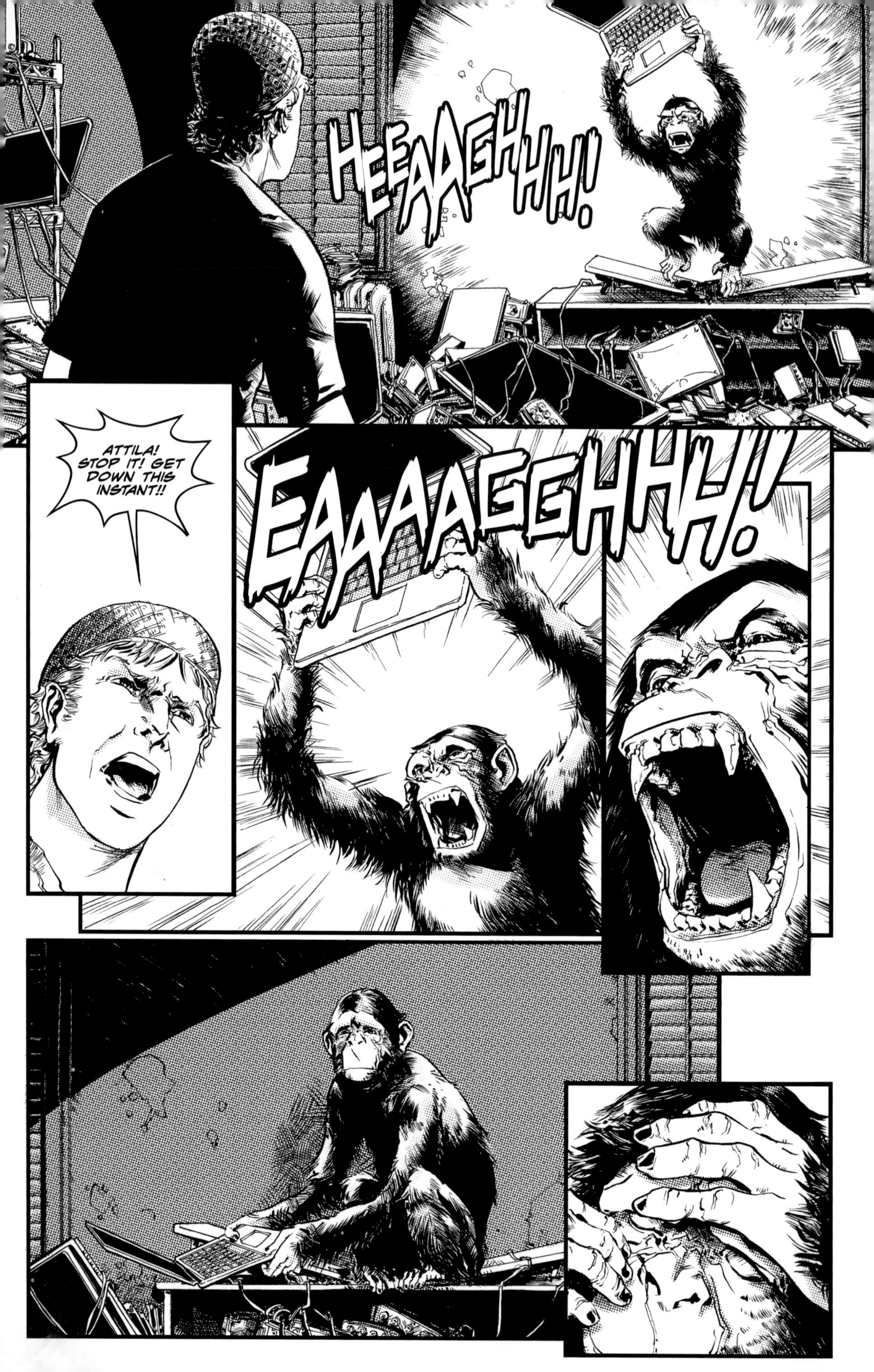
HEEAAGHHH!
ATTILA! STOP IT! GET DOWN THIS INSTANT!!
EAAAAGGHHH!

MARCH, MISTER.

BAD ATTILA. BAD BOY.

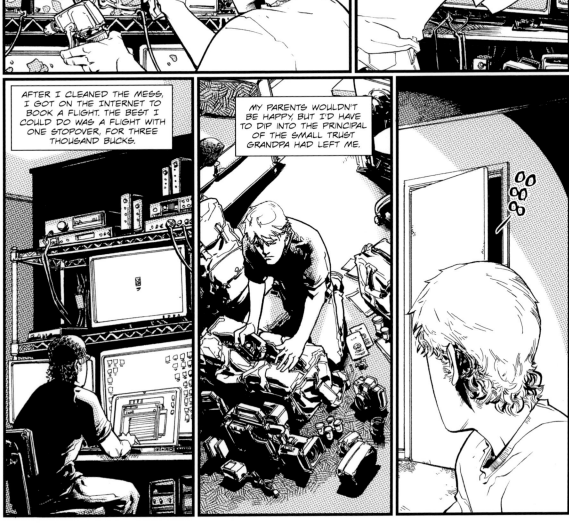

AFTER I CLEANED THE MESS, I GOT ON THE INTERNET TO BOOK A FLIGHT. THE BEST I COULD DO WAS A FLIGHT WITH ONE STOPOVER, FOR THREE THOUSAND BUCKS.

MY PARENTS WOULDN'T BE HAPPY, BUT I'D HAVE TO DIP INTO THE PRINCIPAL OF THE SMALL TRUST GRANDPA HAD LEFT ME.

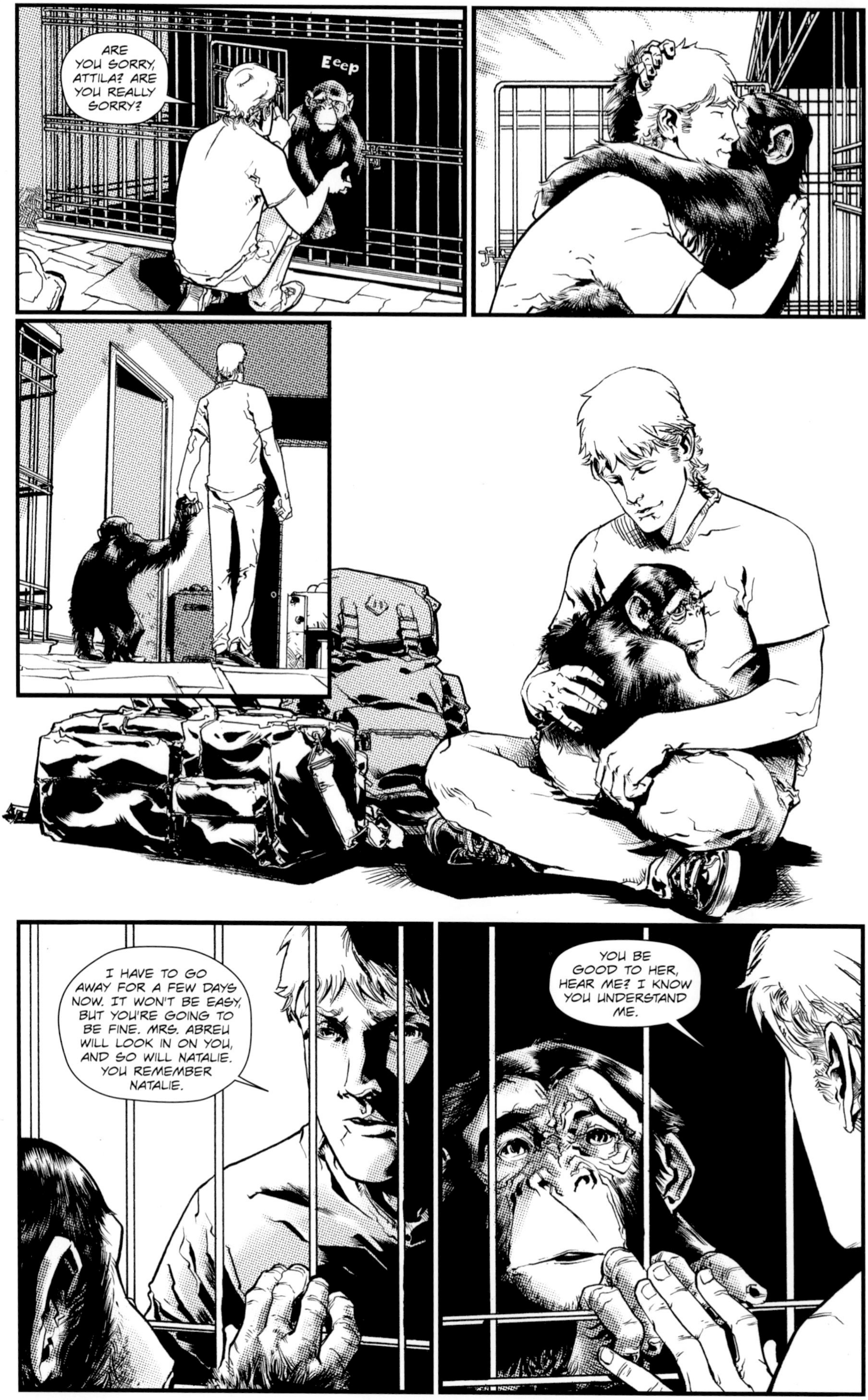
ARE YOU SORRY, ATTILA? ARE YOU REALLY SORRY?
Eeep
I HAVE TO GO AWAY FOR A FEW DAYS NOW. IT WON'T BE EASY, BUT YOU'RE GOING TO BE FINE. MRS. ABREU WILL LOOK IN ON YOU, AND SO WILL NATALIE. YOU REMEMBER NATALIE.
YOU BE GOOD TO HER, HEAR ME? I KNOW YOU UNDERSTAND ME.

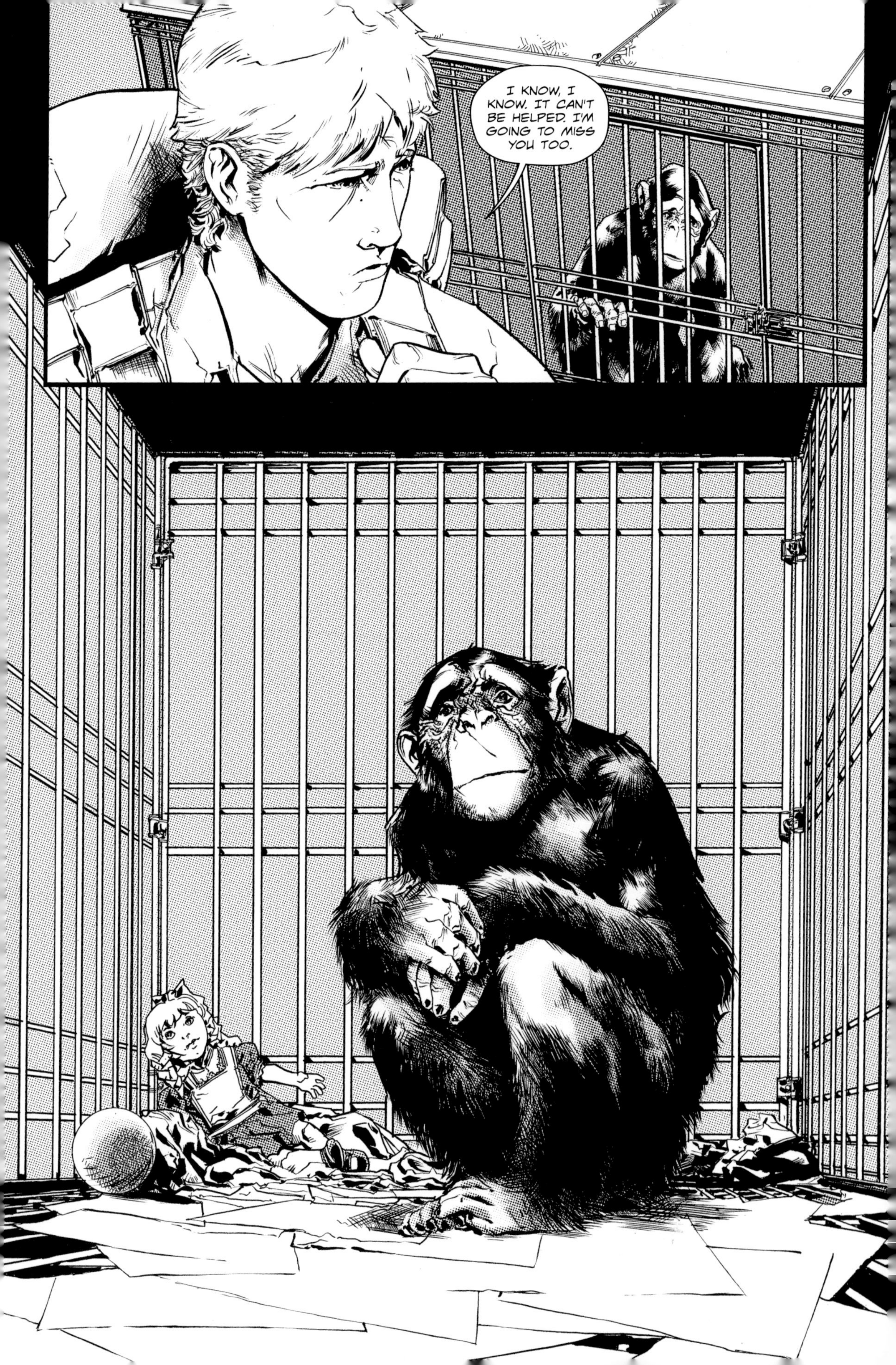
I KNOW, I KNOW. IT CAN'T BE HELPED. I'M GOING TO MISS YOU TOO.

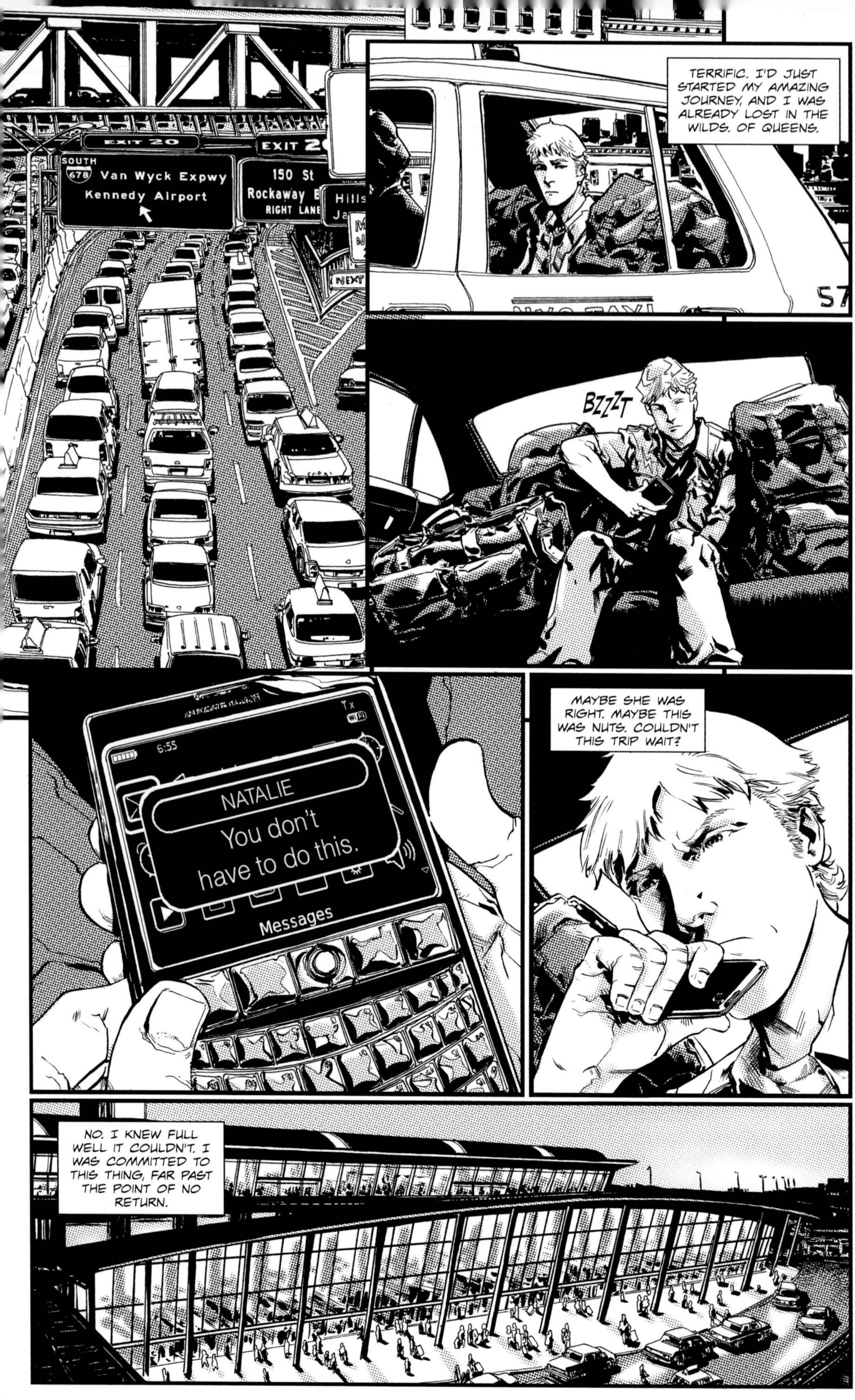
EXIT 20
SOUTH 678 Van Wyck Expwy
Kennedy Airport
150 St
Rockaway B
RIGHT LANE
TERRIFIC. I'D JUST STARTED MY AMAZING JOURNEY, AND I WAS ALREADY LOST IN THE WILDS. OF QUEENS.
BZZZT
6:55
NATALIE
You don't have to do this.
Messages
MAYBE SHE WAS RIGHT. MAYBE THIS WAS NUTS. COULDN'T THIS TRIP WAIT?
NO. I KNEW FULL WELL IT COULDN'T. I WAS COMMITTED TO THIS THING, FAR PAST THE POINT OF NO RETURN.

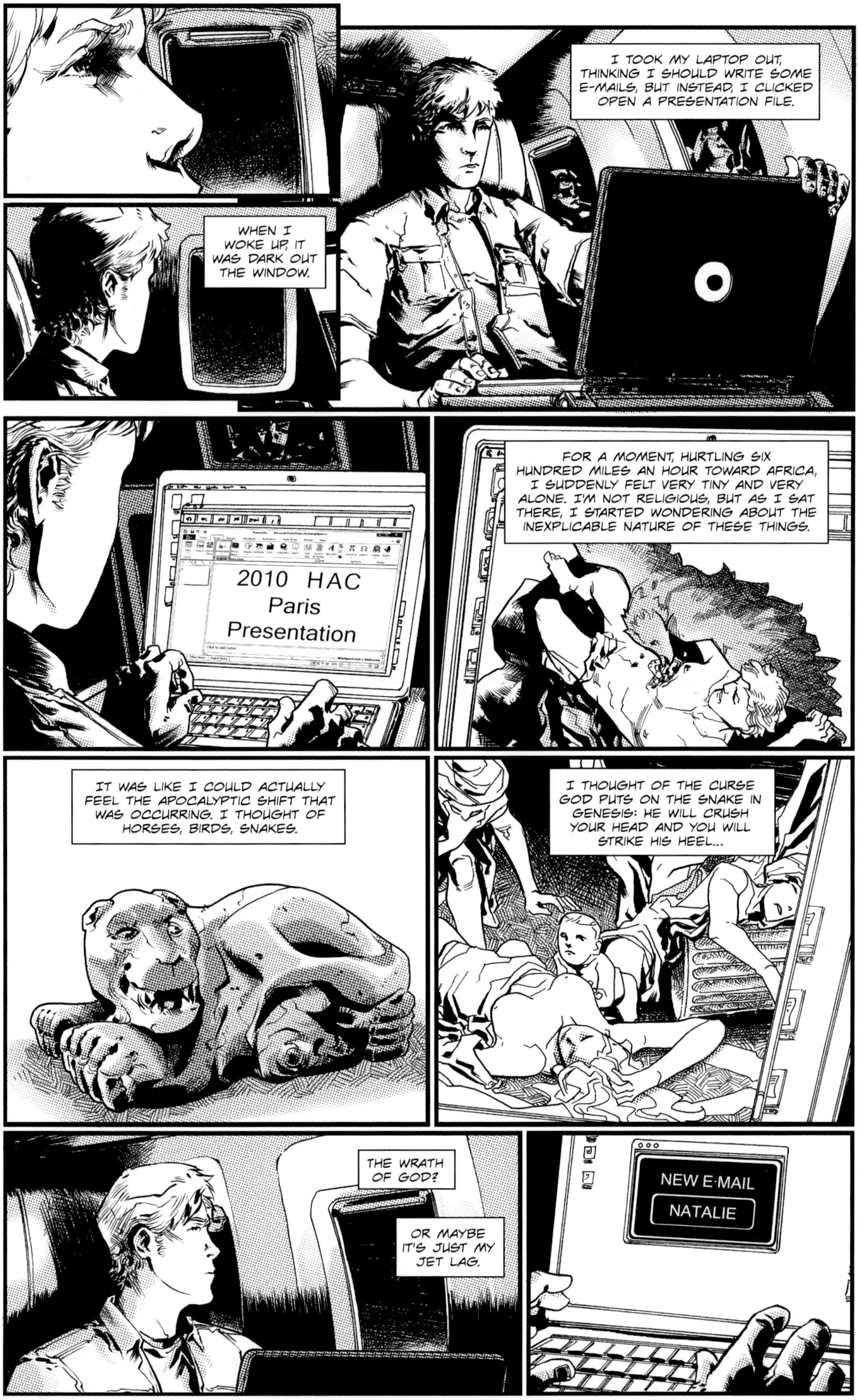
WHEN I WOKE UP, IT WAS DARK OUT THE WINDOW.
I TOOK MY LAPTOP OUT, THINKING I SHOULD WRITE SOME E-MAILS, BUT INSTEAD, I CLICKED OPEN A PRESENTATION FILE.
2010 HAC
Paris
Presentation
FOR A MOMENT, HURTLING SIX HUNDRED MILES AN HOUR TOWARD AFRICA, I SUDDENLY FELT VERY TINY AND VERY ALONE. I'M NOT RELIGIOUS, BUT AS I SAT THERE, I STARTED WONDERING ABOUT THE INEXPLICABLE NATURE OF THESE THINGS.
IT WAS LIKE I COULD ACTUALLY FEEL THE APOCALYPTIC SHIFT THAT WAS OCCURRING. I THOUGHT OF HORSES, BIRDS, SNAKES.
I THOUGHT OF THE CURSE GOD PUTS ON THE SNAKE IN GENESIS: HE WILL CRUSH YOUR HEAD AND YOU WILL STRIKE HIS HEEL...
THE WRATH OF GOD?
OR MAYBE IT'S JUST MY JET LAG.
NEW E-MAIL
NATALIE

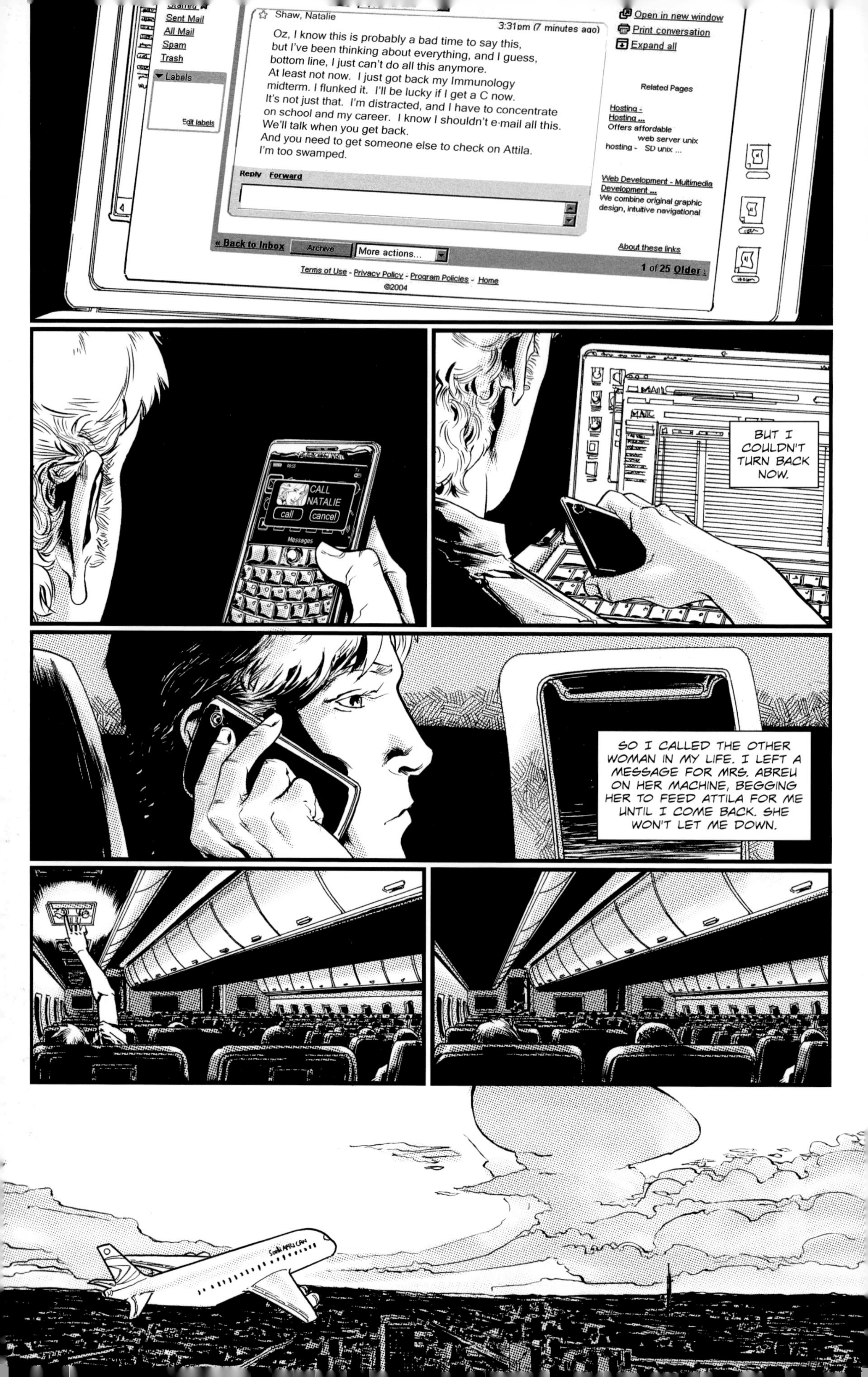

Sent Mail
All Mail
Spam
Trash
Labels
Edit labels
Shaw, Natalie
3:31pm (7 minutes ago)
Oz, I know this is probably a bad time to say this, but I've been thinking about everything, and I guess, bottom line, I just can't do all this anymore.
At least not now. I just got back my Immunology midterm. I flunked it. I'll be lucky if I get a C now.
It's not just that. I'm distracted, and I have to concentrate on school and my career. I know I shouldn't e-mail all this.
We'll talk when you get back.
And you need to get someone else to check on Attila.
I'm too swamped.
Reply Forward
« Back to Inbox
Archive
More actions...
Open in new window
Print conversation
Expand all
Related Pages
Hosting - Hosting ...
Offers affordable web server unix hosting - SD unix ...
Web Development - Multimedia Development ...
We combine original graphic design, intuitive navigational
About these links
1 of 25 Older
Terms of Use - Privacy Policy - Program Policies - Home
©2004
CALL NATALIE
call
cancel
Messages
BUT I COULDN'T TURN BACK NOW.
SO I CALLED THE OTHER WOMAN IN MY LIFE. I LEFT A MESSAGE FOR MRS. ABREU ON HER MACHINE, BEGGING HER TO FEED ATTILA FOR ME UNTIL I COME BACK. SHE WON'T LET ME DOWN.

ZOO

THE GRAPHIC NOVEL

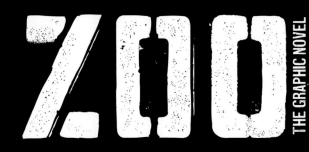

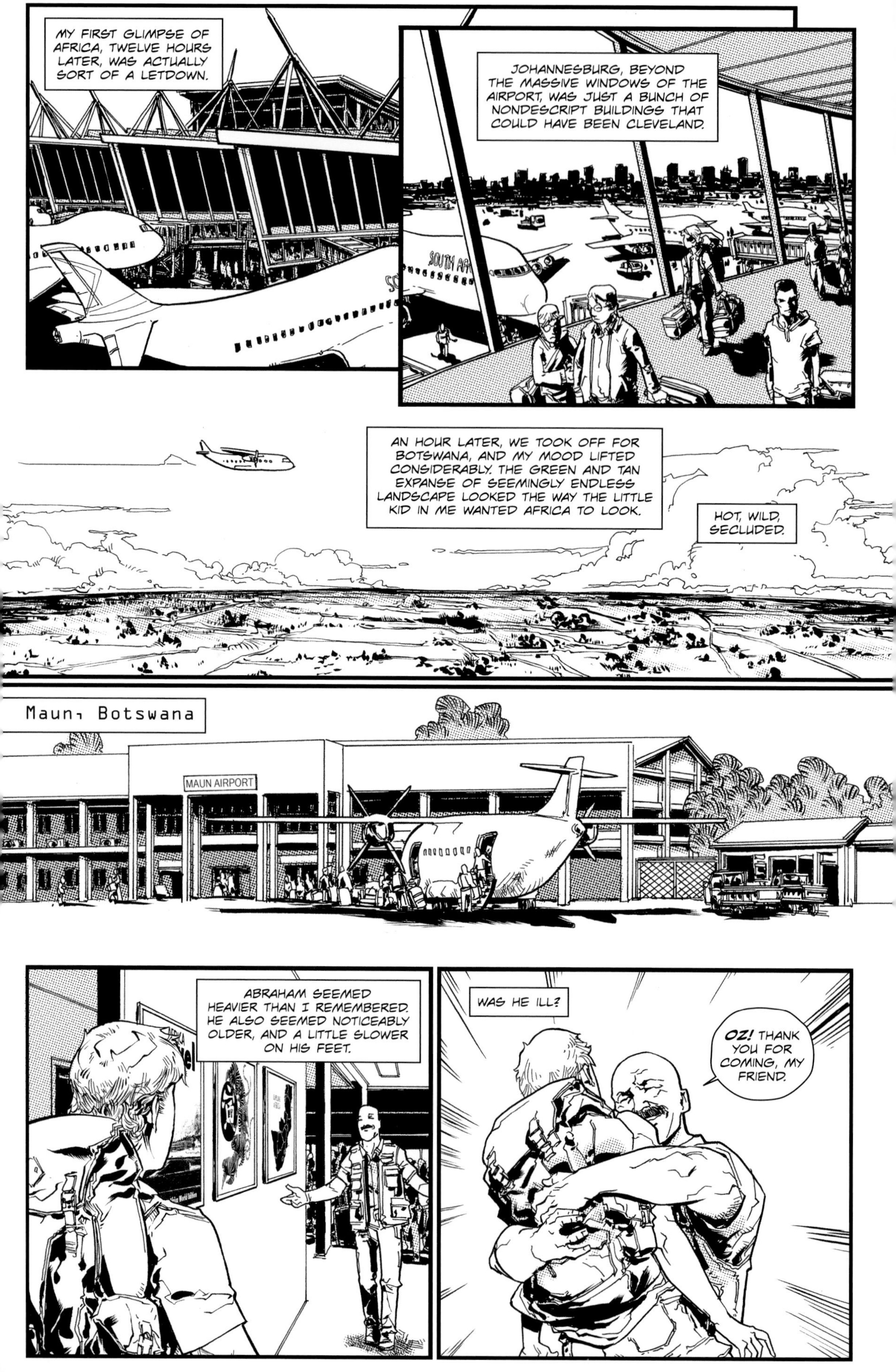

MY FIRST GLIMPSE OF AFRICA, TWELVE HOURS LATER, WAS ACTUALLY SORT OF A LETDOWN.
JOHANNESBURG, BEYOND THE MASSIVE WINDOWS OF THE AIRPORT, WAS JUST A BUNCH OF NONDESCRIPT BUILDINGS THAT COULD HAVE BEEN CLEVELAND.
AN HOUR LATER, WE TOOK OFF FOR BOTSWANA, AND MY MOOD LIFTED CONSIDERABLY. THE GREEN AND TAN EXPANSE OF SEEMINGLY ENDLESS LANDSCAPE LOOKED THE WAY THE LITTLE KID IN ME WANTED AFRICA TO LOOK.
HOT, WILD, SECLUDED.
Maun, Botswana
MAUN AIRPORT
ABRAHAM SEEMED HEAVIER THAN I REMEMBERED. HE ALSO SEEMED NOTICEABLY OLDER, AND A LITTLE SLOWER ON HIS FEET.
WAS HE ILL?
OZ! THANK YOU FOR COMING, MY FRIEND.

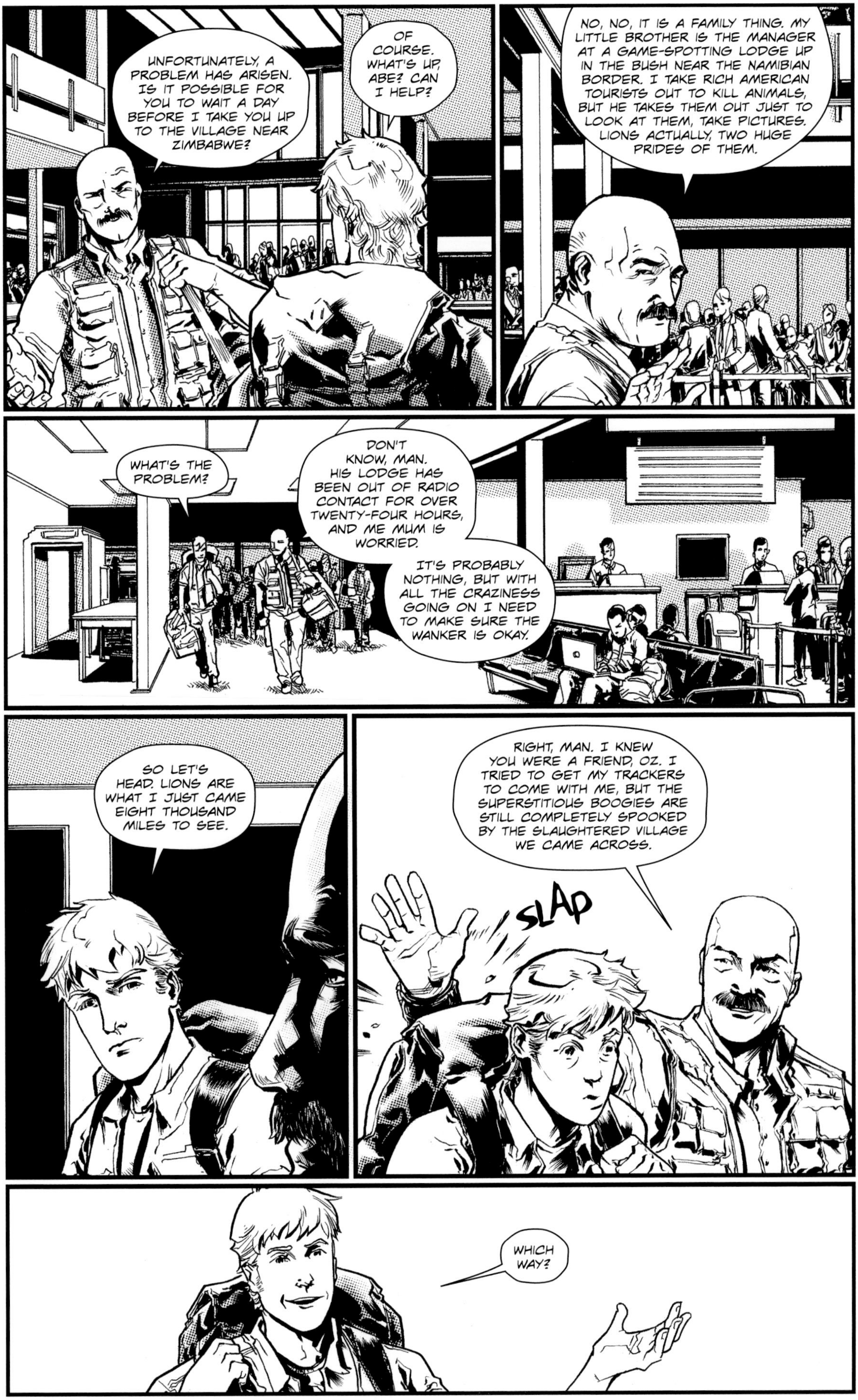
UNFORTUNATELY, A PROBLEM HAS ARISEN. IS IT POSSIBLE FOR YOU TO WAIT A DAY BEFORE I TAKE YOU UP TO THE VILLAGE NEAR ZIMBABWE?
OF COURSE. WHAT'S UP, ABE? CAN I HELP?
NO, NO, IT IS A FAMILY THING. MY LITTLE BROTHER IS THE MANAGER AT A GAME-SPOTTING LODGE UP IN THE BUSH NEAR THE NAMIBIAN BORDER. I TAKE RICH AMERICAN TOURISTS OUT TO KILL ANIMALS, BUT HE TAKES THEM OUT JUST TO LOOK AT THEM, TAKE PICTURES. LIONS ACTUALLY, TWO HUGE PRIDES OF THEM.
WHAT'S THE PROBLEM?
DON'T KNOW, MAN. HIS LODGE HAS BEEN OUT OF RADIO CONTACT FOR OVER TWENTY-FOUR HOURS, AND ME MUM IS WORRIED.
IT'S PROBABLY NOTHING, BUT WITH ALL THE CRAZINESS GOING ON I NEED TO MAKE SURE THE WANKER IS OKAY.
SO LET'S HEAD. LIONS ARE WHAT I JUST CAME EIGHT THOUSAND MILES TO SEE.
RIGHT, MAN. I KNEW YOU WERE A FRIEND, OZ. I TRIED TO GET MY TRACKERS TO COME WITH ME, BUT THE SUPERSTITIOUS BOOGIES ARE STILL COMPLETELY SPOOKED BY THE SLAUGHTERED VILLAGE WE CAME ACROSS.
SLAP
WHICH WAY?

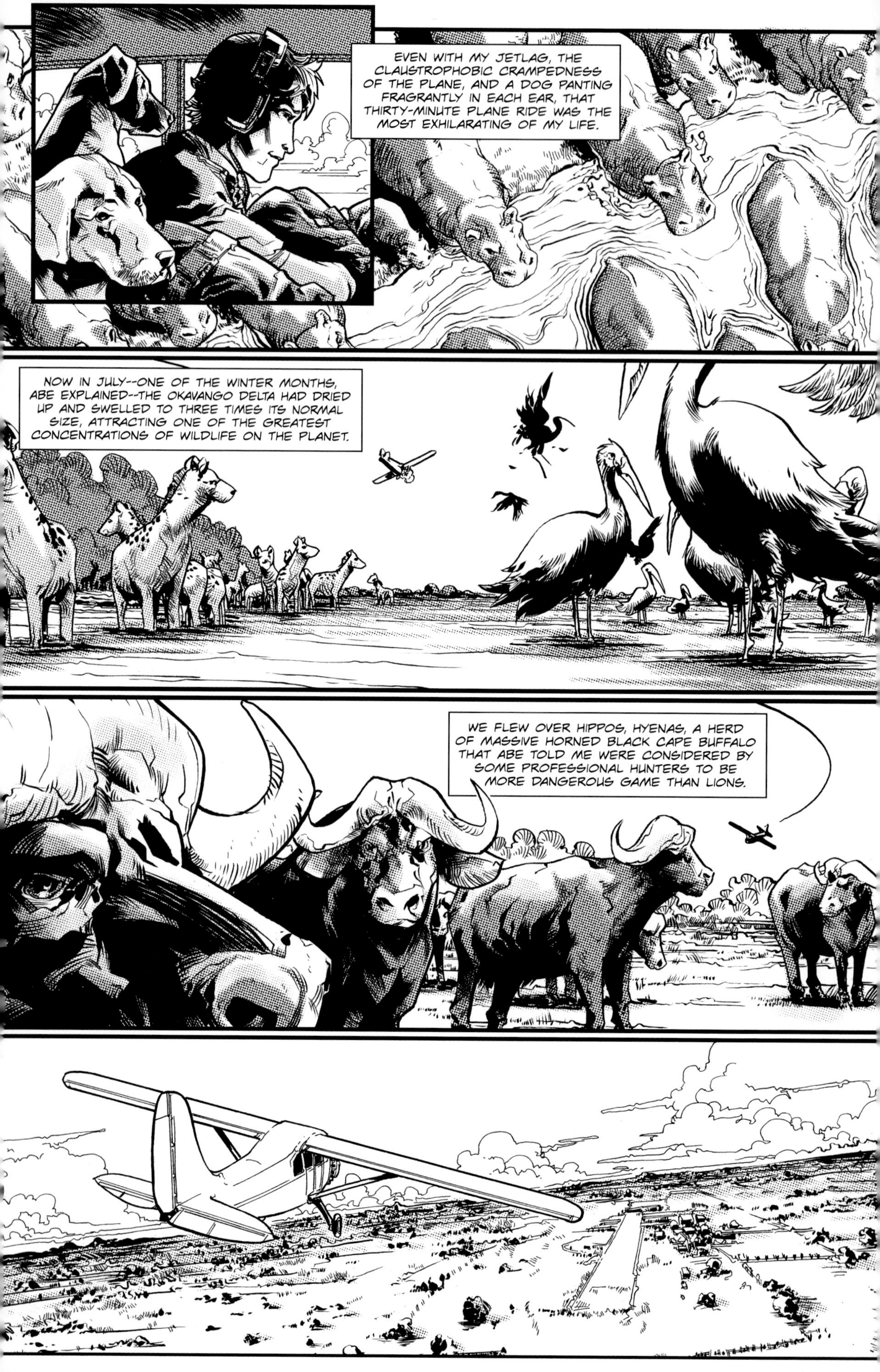
EVEN WITH MY JETLAG, THE CLAUSTROPHOBIC CRAMPEDNESS OF THE PLANE, AND A DOG PANTING FRAGRANTLY IN EACH EAR, THAT THIRTY-MINUTE PLANE RIDE WAS THE MOST EXHILARATING OF MY LIFE.
NOW IN JULY--ONE OF THE WINTER MONTHS, ABE EXPLAINED--THE OKAVANGO DELTA HAD DRIED UP AND SWELLED TO THREE TIMES ITS NORMAL SIZE, ATTRACTING ONE OF THE GREATEST CONCENTRATIONS OF WILDLIFE ON THE PLANET.
WE FLEW OVER HIPPOS, HYENAS, A HERD OF MASSIVE HORNED BLACK CAPE BUFFALO THAT ABE TOLD ME WERE CONSIDERED BY SOME PROFESSIONAL HUNTERS TO BE MORE DANGEROUS GAME THAN LIONS.

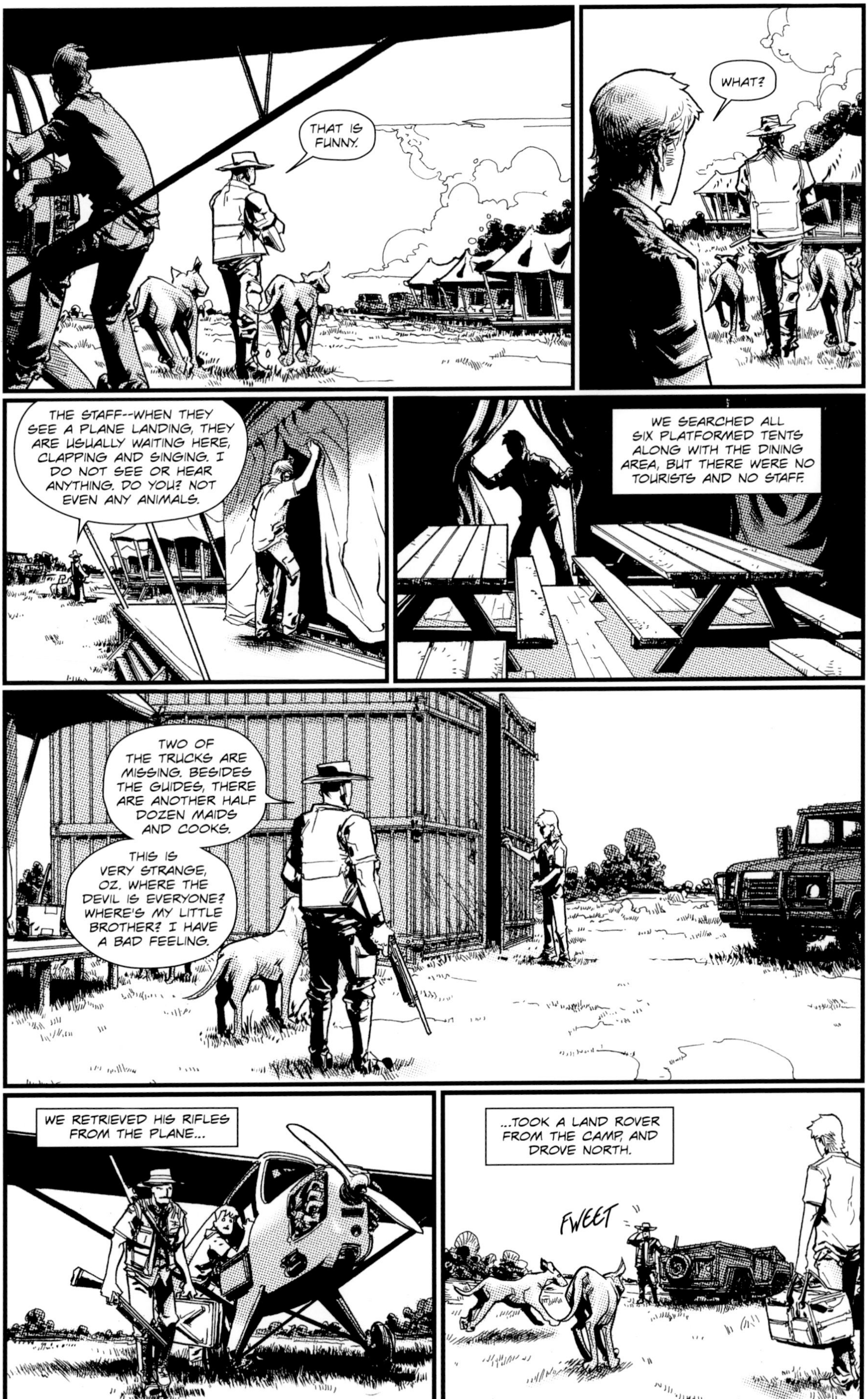
THAT IS FUNNY.
WHAT?
THE STAFF--WHEN THEY SEE A PLANE LANDING, THEY ARE USUALLY WAITING HERE, CLAPPING AND SINGING. I DO NOT SEE OR HEAR ANYTHING. DO YOU? NOT EVEN ANY ANIMALS.
WE SEARCHED ALL SIX PLATFORMED TENTS ALONG WITH THE DINING AREA, BUT THERE WERE NO TOURISTS AND NO STAFF.
TWO OF THE TRUCKS ARE MISSING. BESIDES THE GUIDES, THERE ARE ANOTHER HALF DOZEN MAIDS AND COOKS.
THIS IS VERY STRANGE, OZ. WHERE THE DEVIL IS EVERYONE? WHERE'S MY LITTLE BROTHER? I HAVE A BAD FEELING.
WE RETRIEVED HIS RIFLES FROM THE PLANE...
...TOOK A LAND ROVER FROM THE CAMP, AND DROVE NORTH.
FWEET

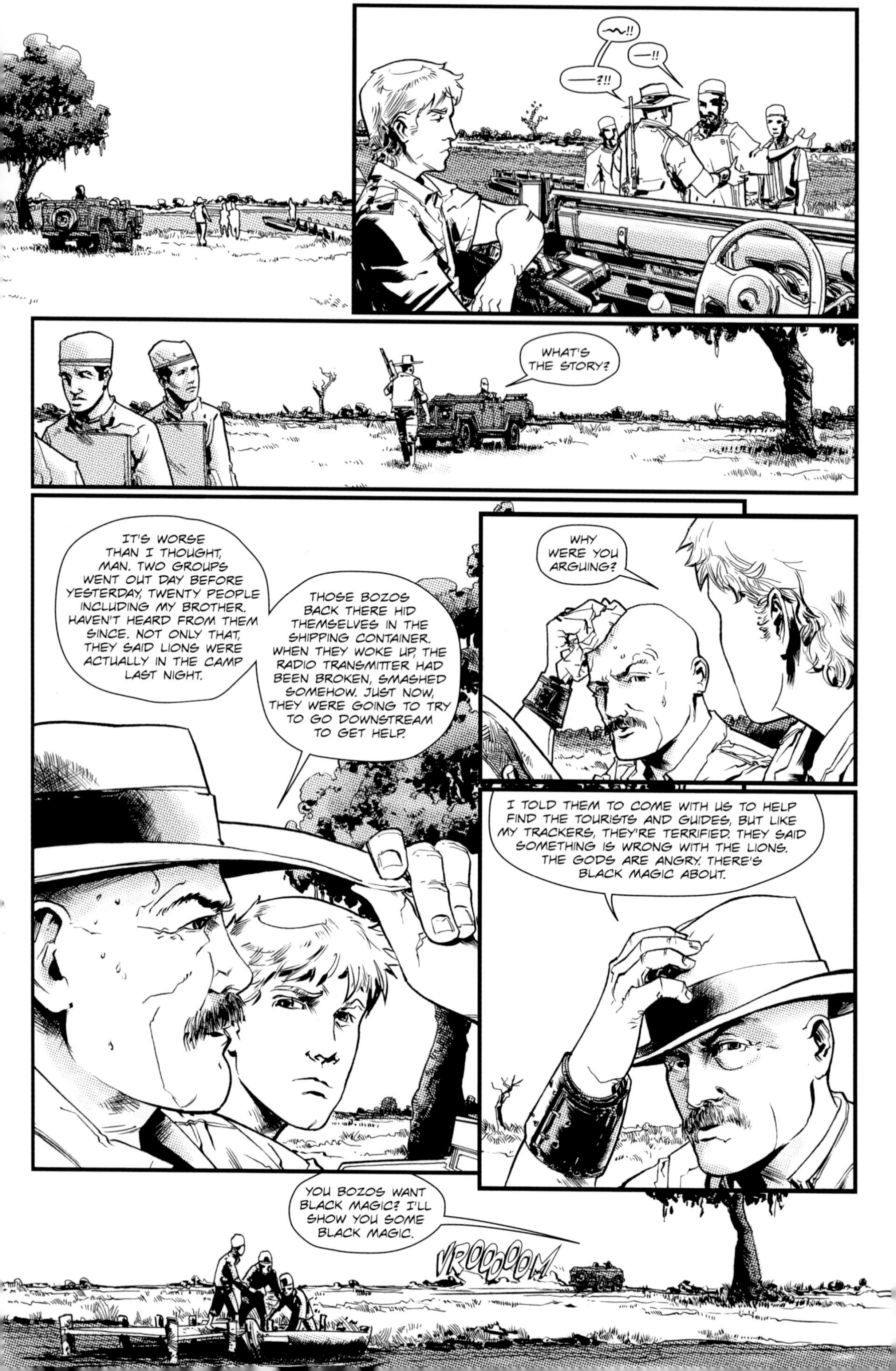
~~!!
—!!
——?!!
WHAT'S THE STORY?
IT'S WORSE THAN I THOUGHT, MAN. TWO GROUPS WENT OUT DAY BEFORE YESTERDAY, TWENTY PEOPLE INCLUDING MY BROTHER. HAVEN'T HEARD FROM THEM SINCE. NOT ONLY THAT, THEY SAID LIONS WERE ACTUALLY IN THE CAMP LAST NIGHT.
THOSE BOZOS BACK THERE HID THEMSELVES IN THE SHIPPING CONTAINER. WHEN THEY WOKE UP, THE RADIO TRANSMITTER HAD BEEN BROKEN, SMASHED SOMEHOW. JUST NOW, THEY WERE GOING TO TRY TO GO DOWNSTREAM TO GET HELP.
WHY WERE YOU ARGUING?
I TOLD THEM TO COME WITH US TO HELP FIND THE TOURISTS AND GUIDES, BUT LIKE MY TRACKERS, THEY'RE TERRIFIED. THEY SAID SOMETHING IS WRONG WITH THE LIONS. THE GODS ARE ANGRY. THERE'S BLACK MAGIC ABOUT.
YOU BOZOS WANT BLACK MAGIC? I'LL SHOW YOU SOME BLACK MAGIC.
VROOOOOM

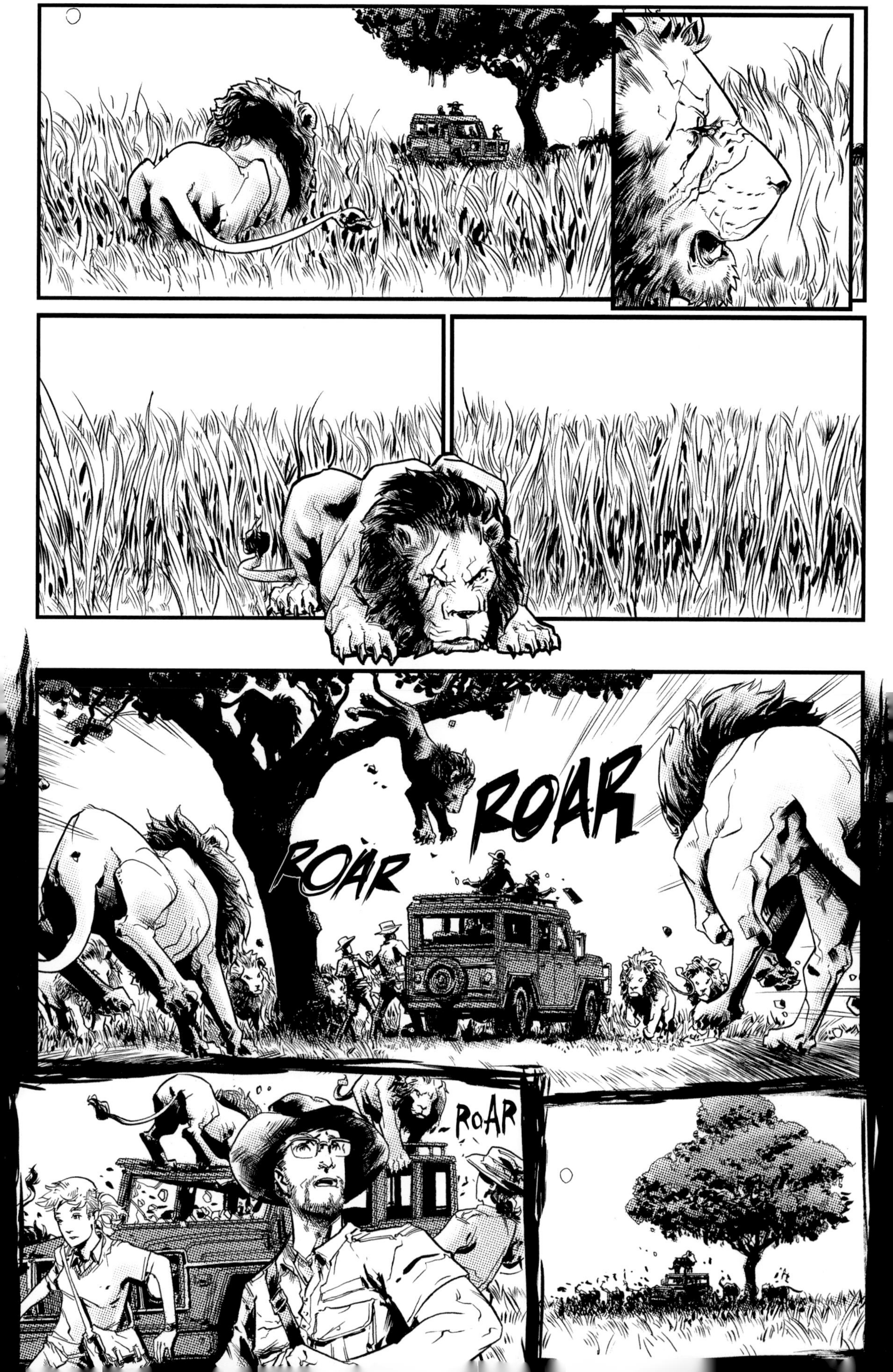
ROAR
ROAR
ROAR

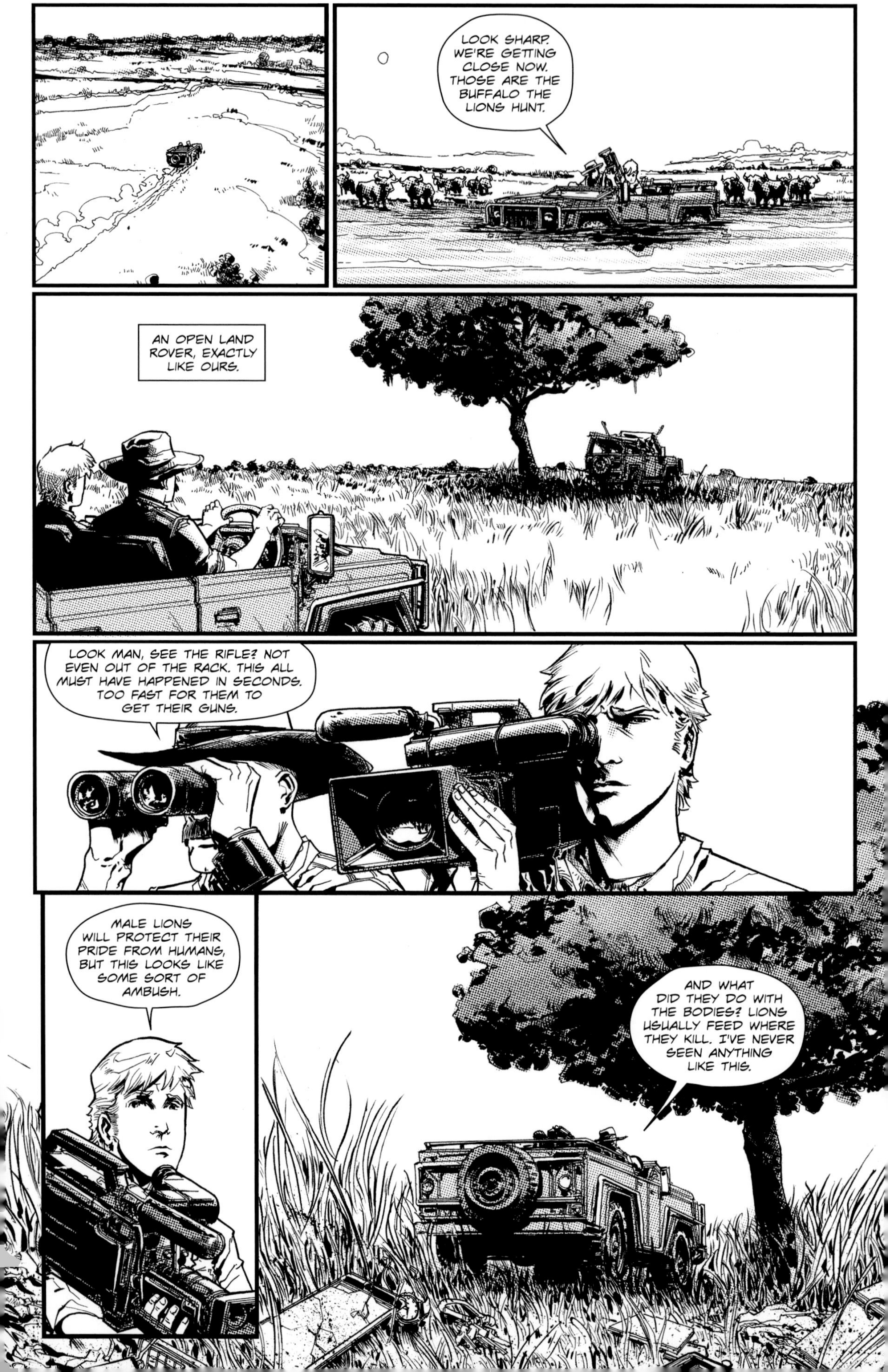

LOOK SHARP. WE'RE GETTING CLOSE NOW. THOSE ARE THE BUFFALO THE LIONS HUNT.
AN OPEN LAND ROVER, EXACTLY LIKE OURS.
LOOK MAN, SEE THE RIFLE? NOT EVEN OUT OF THE RACK. THIS ALL MUST HAVE HAPPENED IN SECONDS. TOO FAST FOR THEM TO GET THEIR GUNS.
MALE LIONS WILL PROTECT THEIR PRIDE FROM HUMANS, BUT THIS LOOKS LIKE SOME SORT OF AMBUSH.
AND WHAT DID THEY DO WITH THE BODIES? LIONS USUALLY FEED WHERE THEY KILL. I'VE NEVER SEEN ANYTHING LIKE THIS.

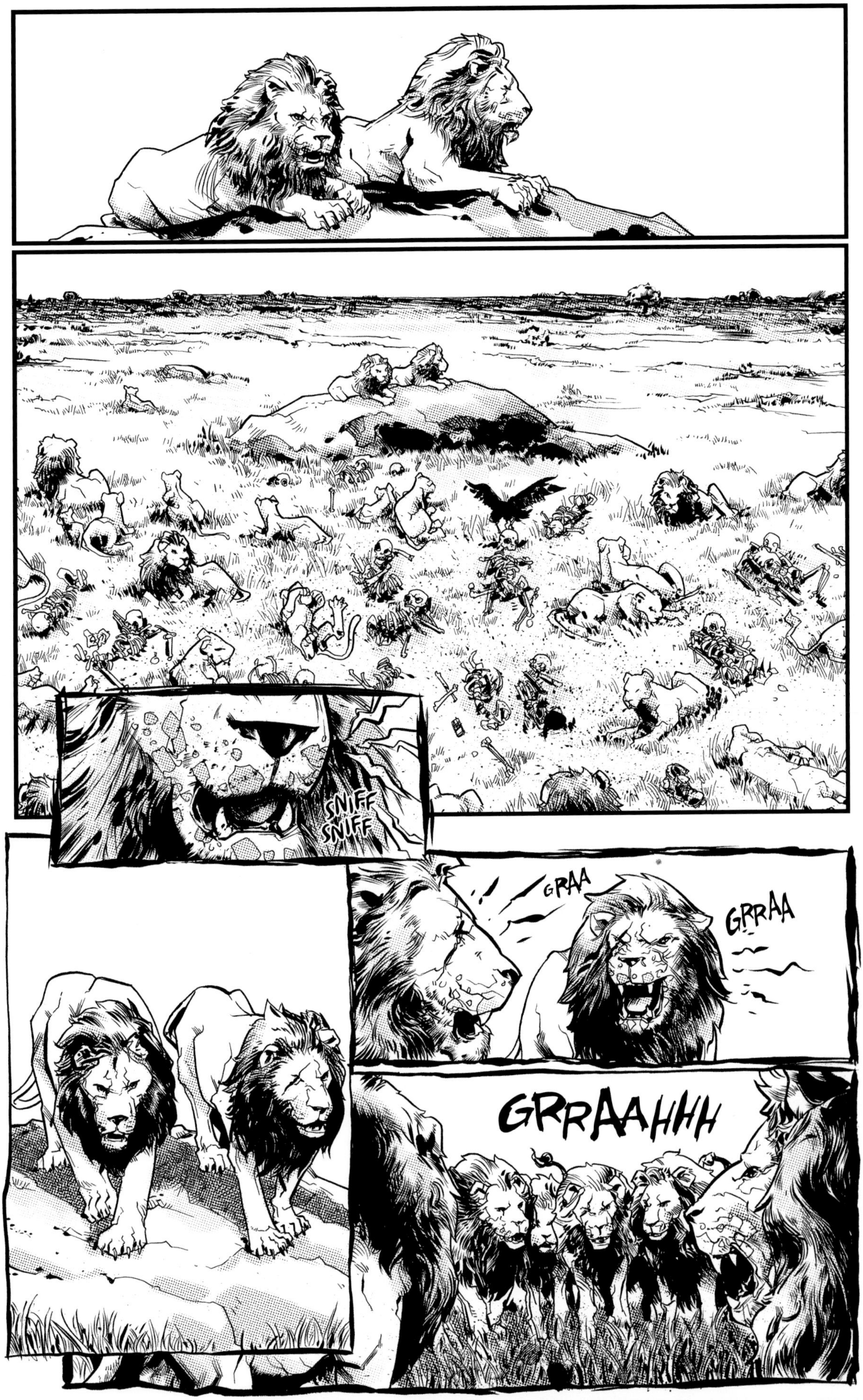
SNIFF
SNIFF
GRAA
GRRAA
GRRAAHHH

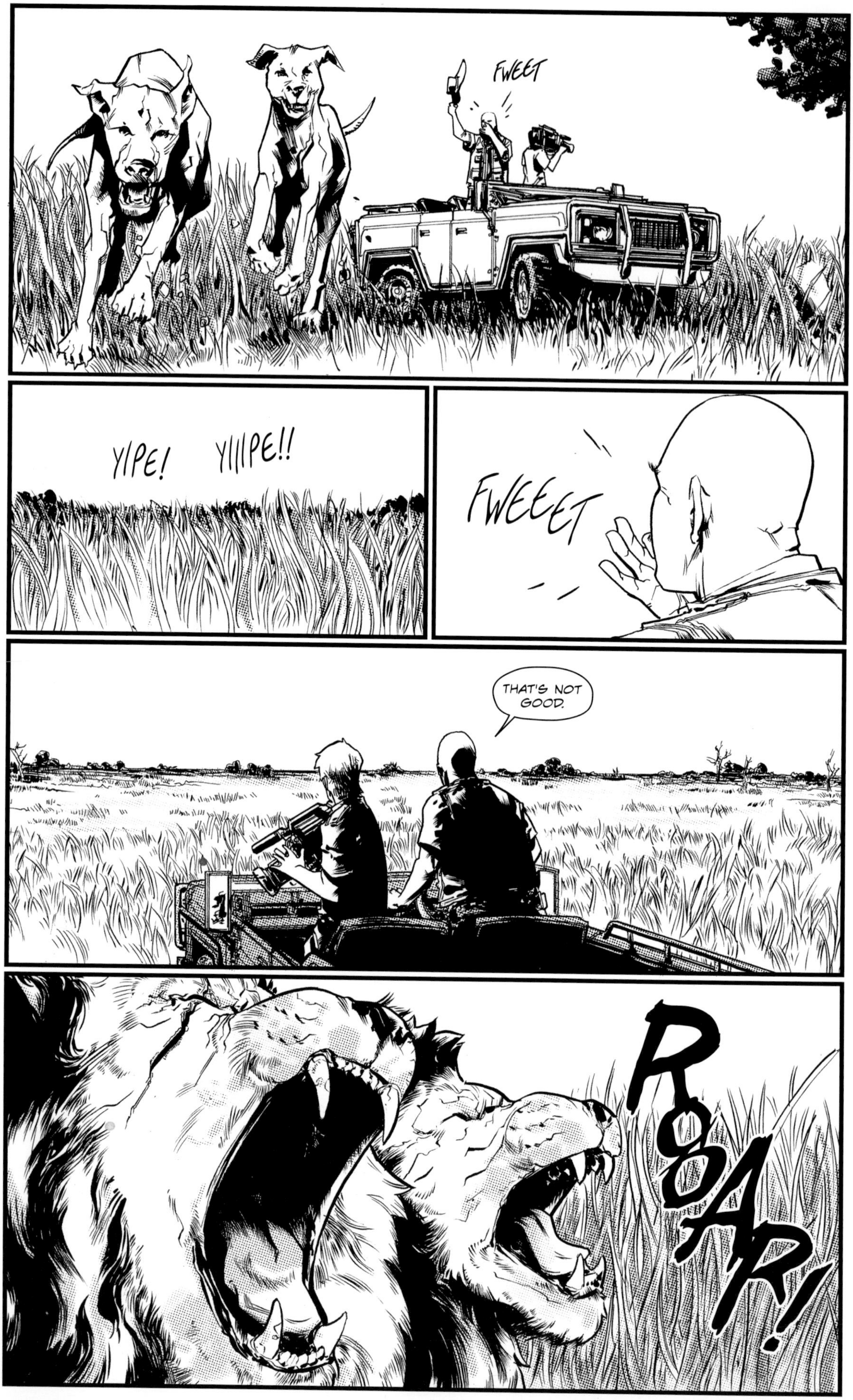
FWEET
YIPE!
YIIIPE!!
FWEEET
THAT'S NOT GOOD.
ROAR!

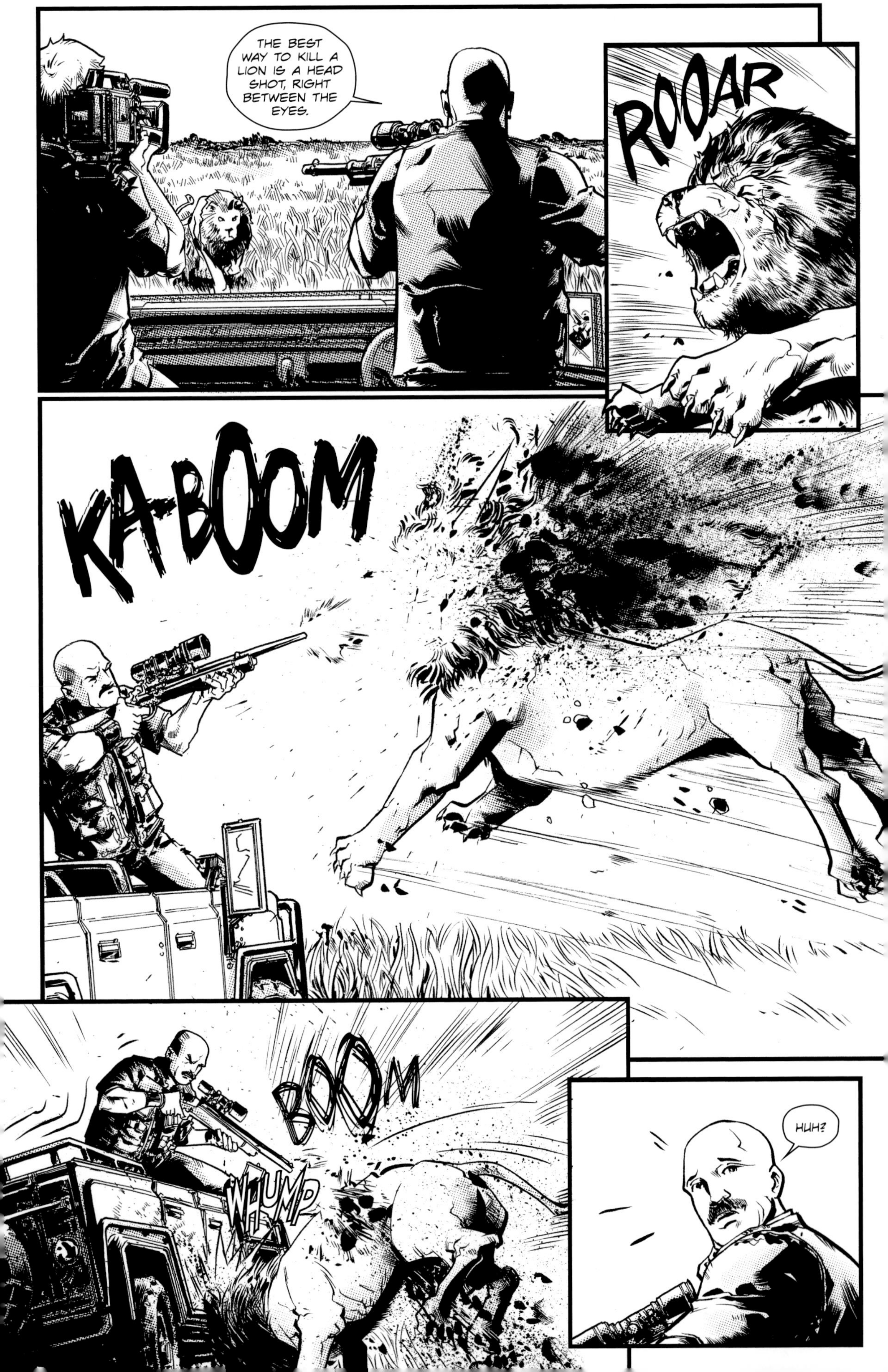
THE BEST WAY TO KILL A LION IS A HEAD SHOT, RIGHT BETWEEN THE EYES.
ROOAR
KA-BOOM
BOOM
WHUMP
HUH?

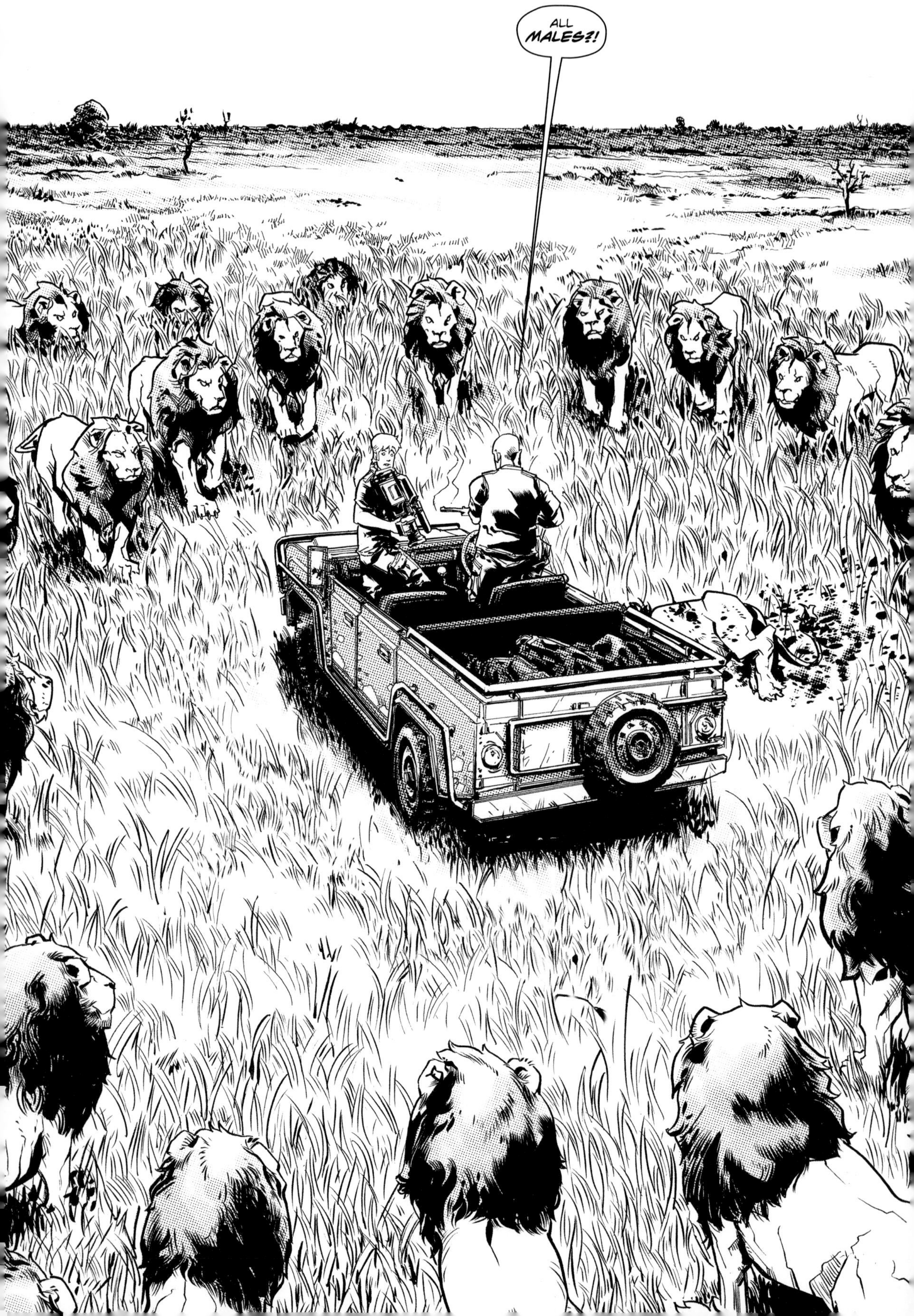
ALL MALES?!

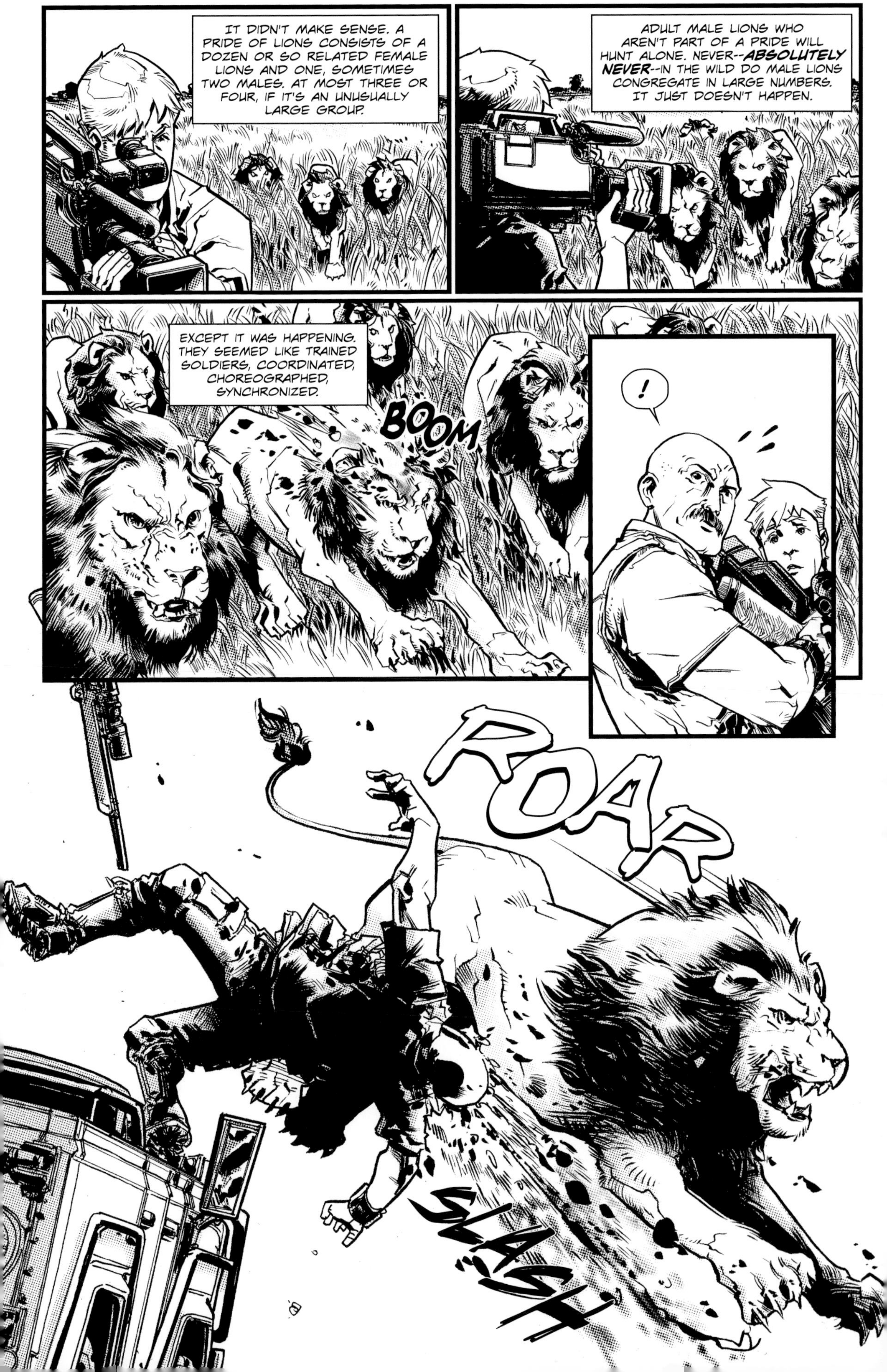
IT DIDN'T MAKE SENSE. A PRIDE OF LIONS CONSISTS OF A DOZEN OR SO RELATED FEMALE LIONS AND ONE, SOMETIMES TWO MALES. AT MOST THREE OR FOUR, IF IT'S AN UNUSUALLY LARGE GROUP.
ADULT MALE LIONS WHO AREN'T PART OF A PRIDE WILL HUNT ALONE. NEVER--ABSOLUTELY NEVER--IN THE WILD DO MALE LIONS CONGREGATE IN LARGE NUMBERS. IT JUST DOESN'T HAPPEN.
EXCEPT IT WAS HAPPENING. THEY SEEMED LIKE TRAINED SOLDIERS, COORDINATED, CHOREOGRAPHED, SYNCHRONIZED.
BOOM
!
ROAR
SLASH

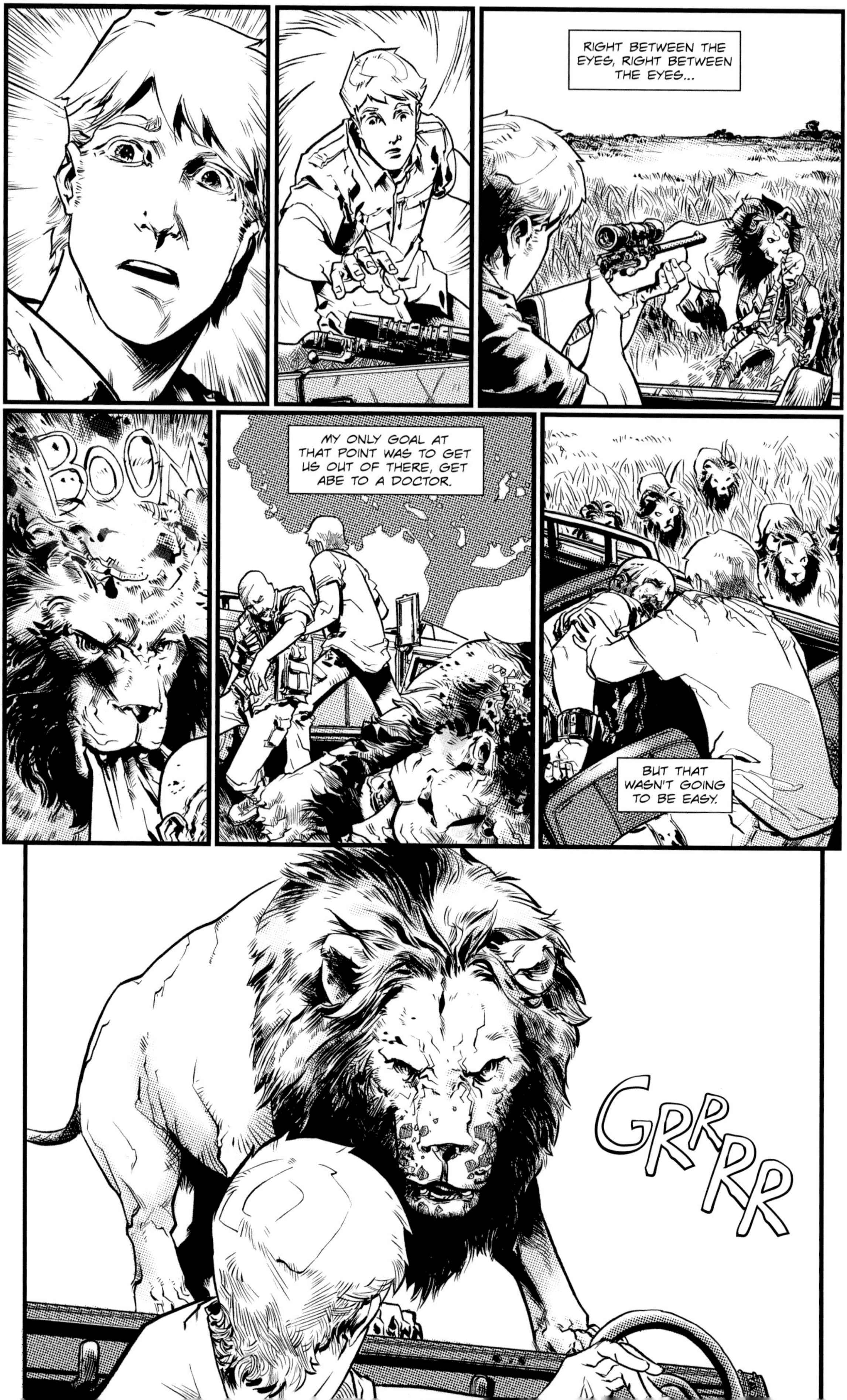
RIGHT BETWEEN THE EYES, RIGHT BETWEEN THE EYES...
BOOM
MY ONLY GOAL AT THAT POINT WAS TO GET US OUT OF THERE, GET ABE TO A DOCTOR.
BUT THAT WASN'T GOING TO BE EASY.
GRRRR

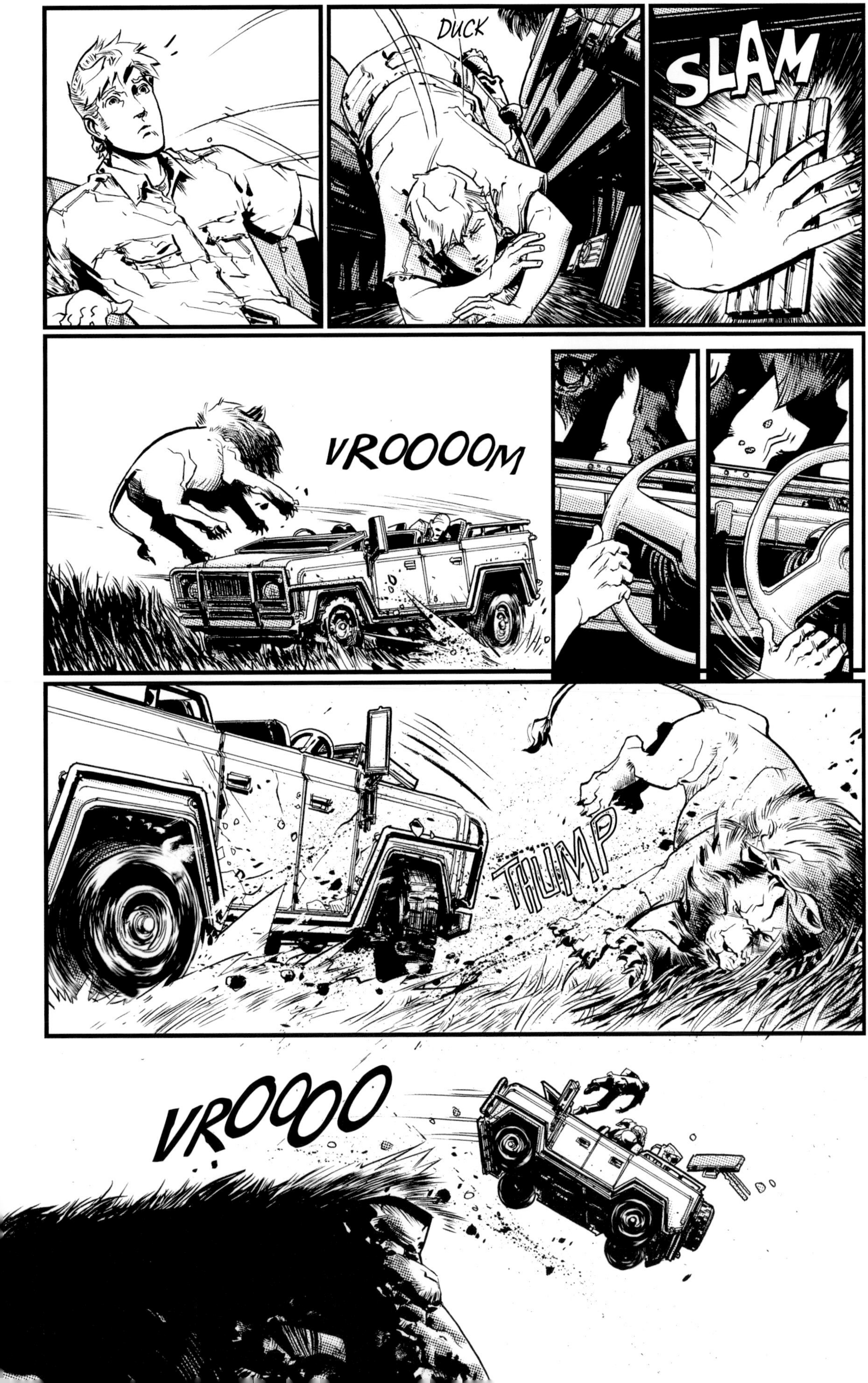
DUCK
SLAM
VROOOOM
THUMP
VROOOO

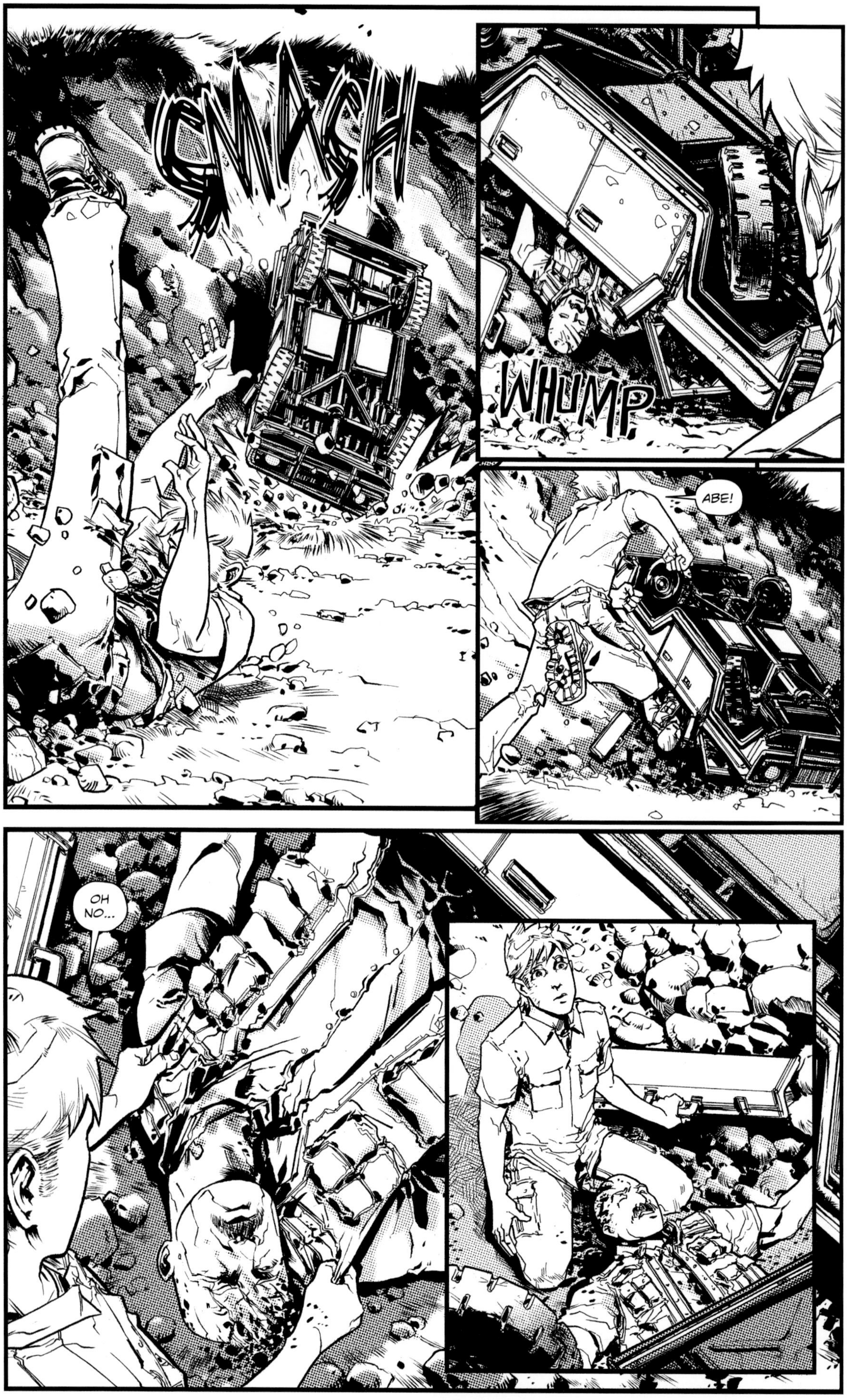

SMASH
WHUMP
ABE!
OH NO...

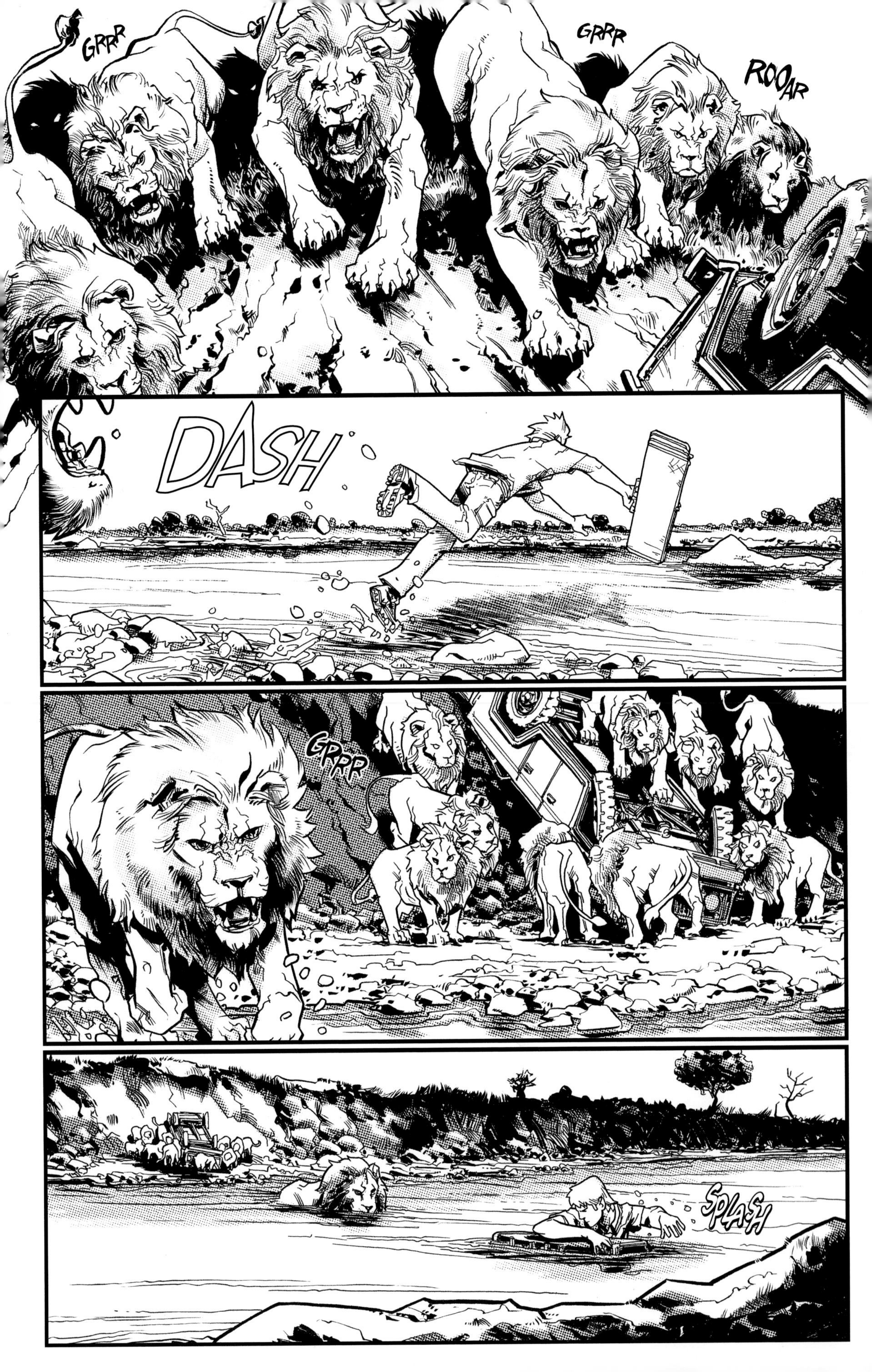
GRRR
GRRR
ROOAR
DASH
GRRR
SPLASH

CLICK

BRAKAKAKAKA KAKAKAKA

WHUMP.

SHUCK

NO! LEAVE HIM ALONE!

BUT THEY WERE GONE.

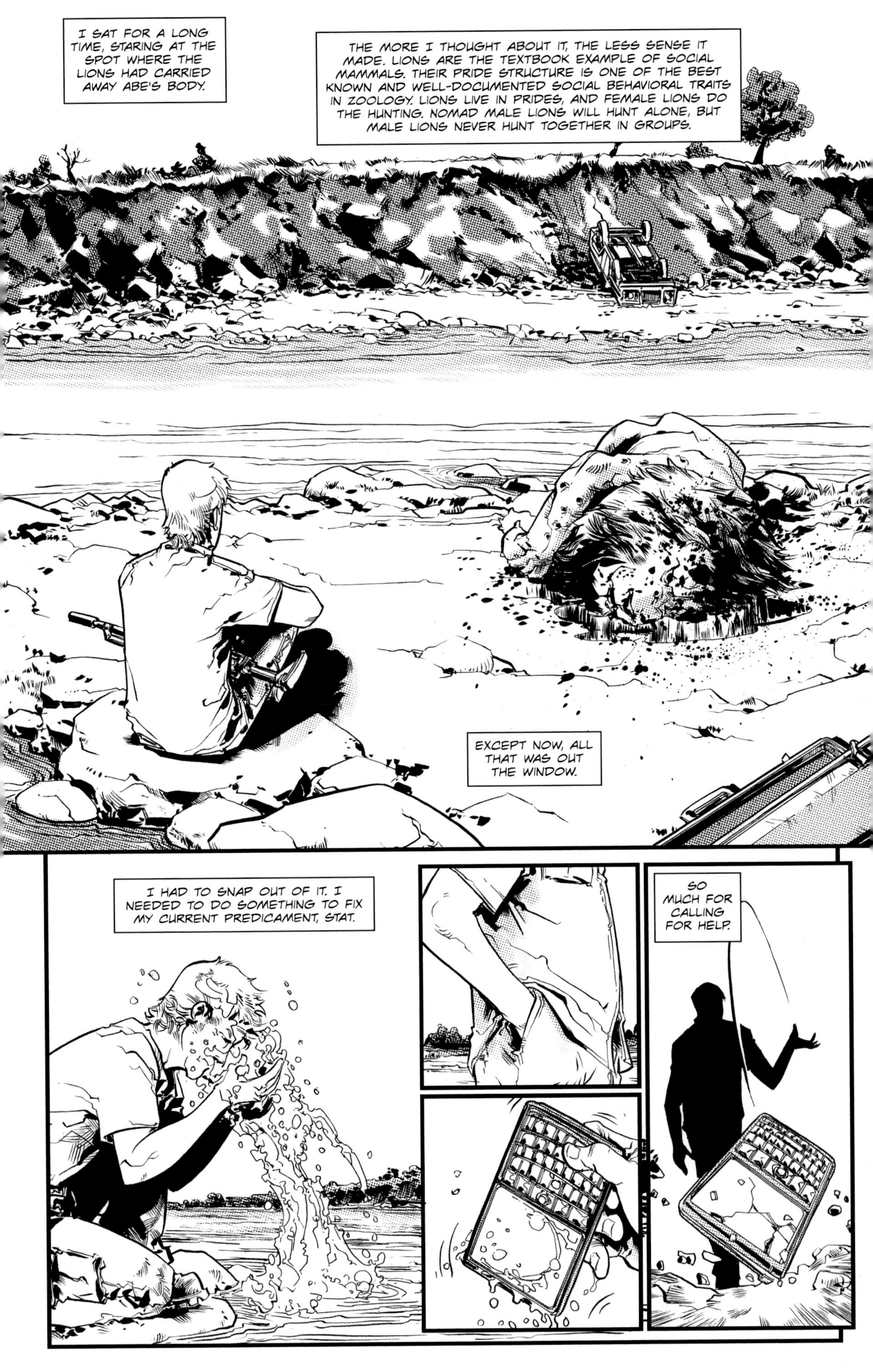
I SAT FOR A LONG TIME, STARING AT THE SPOT WHERE THE LIONS HAD CARRIED AWAY ABE'S BODY.
THE MORE I THOUGHT ABOUT IT, THE LESS SENSE IT MADE. LIONS ARE THE TEXTBOOK EXAMPLE OF SOCIAL MAMMALS. THEIR PRIDE STRUCTURE IS ONE OF THE BEST KNOWN AND WELL-DOCUMENTED SOCIAL BEHAVIORAL TRAITS IN ZOOLOGY. LIONS LIVE IN PRIDES, AND FEMALE LIONS DO THE HUNTING. NOMAD MALE LIONS WILL HUNT ALONE, BUT MALE LIONS NEVER HUNT TOGETHER IN GROUPS.
EXCEPT NOW, ALL THAT WAS OUT THE WINDOW.
I HAD TO SNAP OUT OF IT. I NEEDED TO DO SOMETHING TO FIX MY CURRENT PREDICAMENT, STAT.
SO MUCH FOR CALLING FOR HELP.

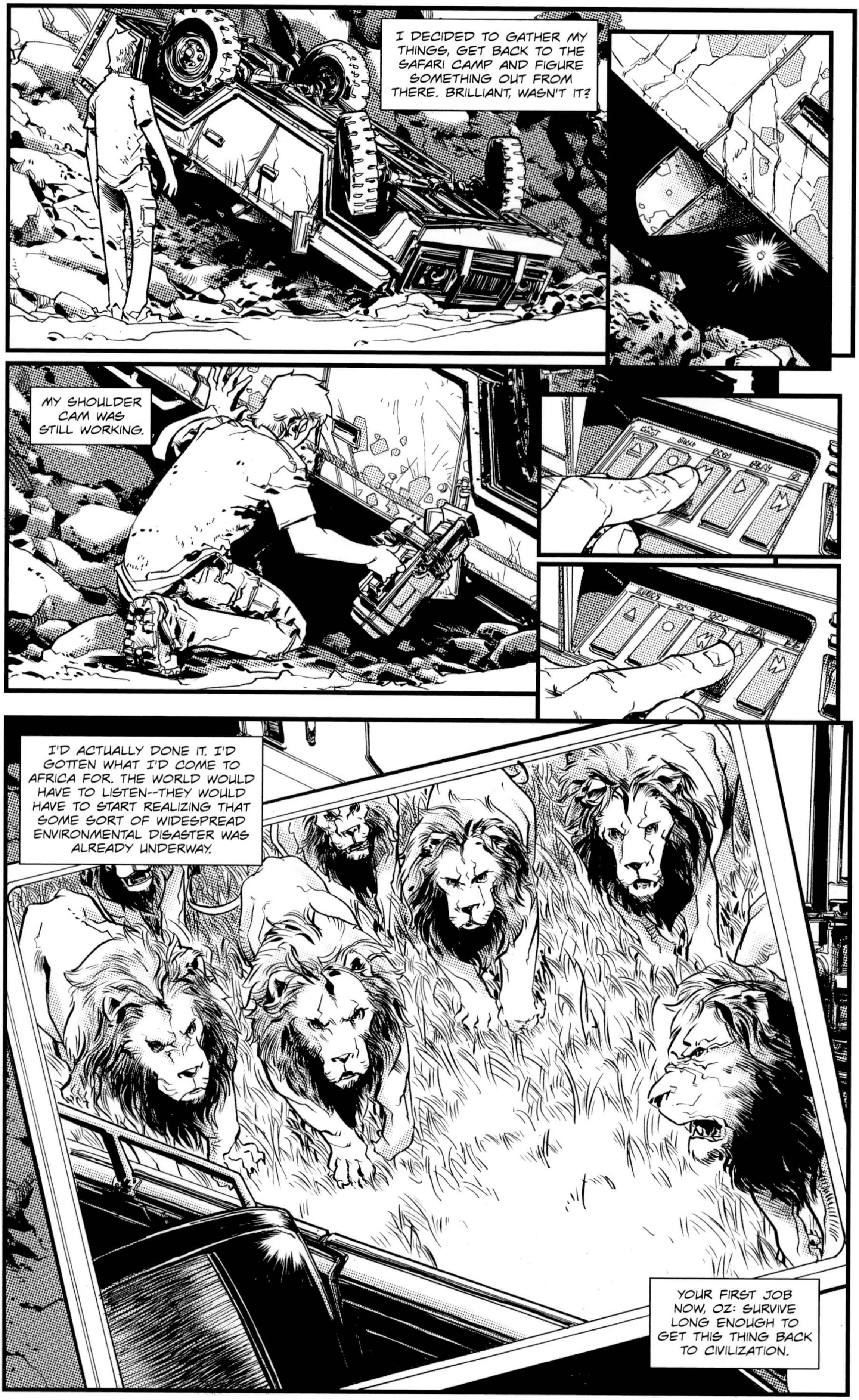
I DECIDED TO GATHER MY THINGS, GET BACK TO THE SAFARI CAMP AND FIGURE SOMETHING OUT FROM THERE. BRILLIANT, WASN'T IT?
MY SHOULDER CAM WAS STILL WORKING.
I'D ACTUALLY DONE IT. I'D GOTTEN WHAT I'D COME TO AFRICA FOR. THE WORLD WOULD HAVE TO LISTEN--THEY WOULD HAVE TO START REALIZING THAT SOME SORT OF WIDESPREAD ENVIRONMENTAL DISASTER WAS ALREADY UNDERWAY.
YOUR FIRST JOB NOW, OZ: SURVIVE LONG ENOUGH TO GET THIS THING BACK TO CIVILIZATION.

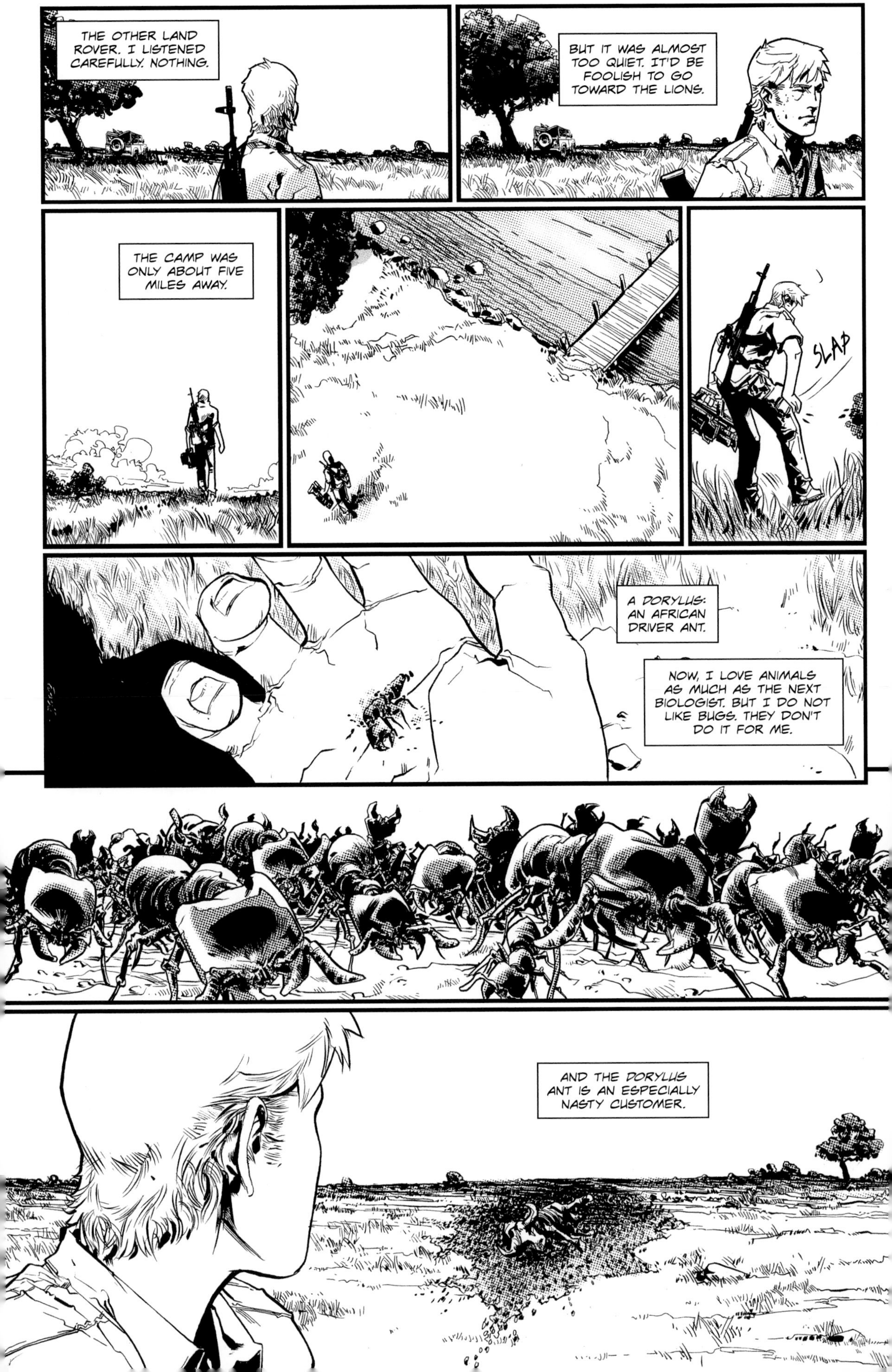
THE OTHER LAND ROVER. I LISTENED CAREFULLY. NOTHING.
BUT IT WAS ALMOST TOO QUIET. IT'D BE FOOLISH TO GO TOWARD THE LIONS.
THE CAMP WAS ONLY ABOUT FIVE MILES AWAY.
SLAP
A DORYLUS: AN AFRICAN DRIVER ANT.
NOW, I LOVE ANIMALS AS MUCH AS THE NEXT BIOLOGIST. BUT I DO NOT LIKE BUGS. THEY DON'T DO IT FOR ME.
AND THE DORYLUS ANT IS AN ESPECIALLY NASTY CUSTOMER.

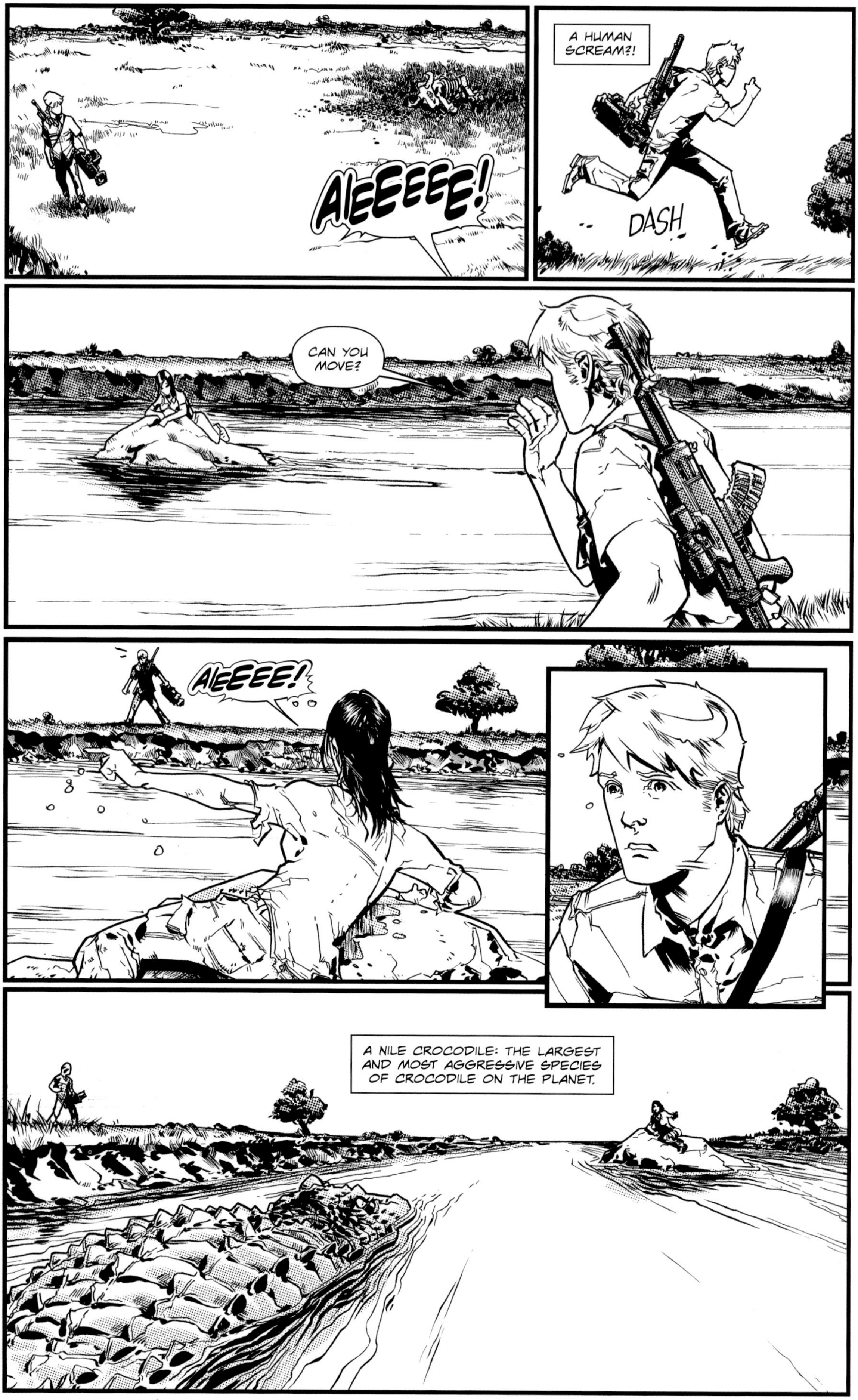
AIEEEEEE!
A HUMAN SCREAM?!
DASH
CAN YOU MOVE?
AIEEEE!
A NILE CROCODILE: THE LARGEST AND MOST AGGRESSIVE SPECIES OF CROCODILE ON THE PLANET.

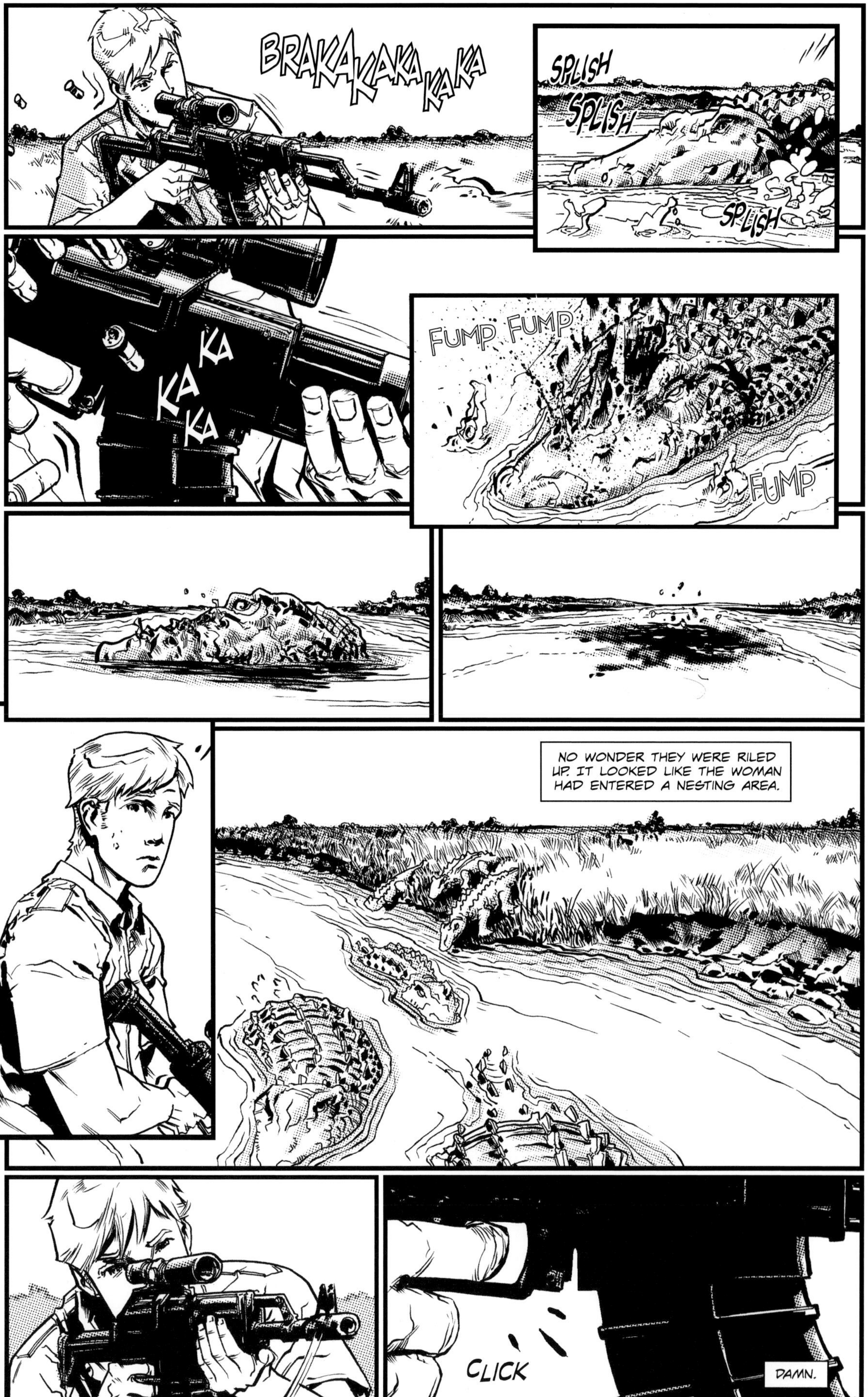
BRAKAKAKAKAKAKA
SPLISH
SPLISH
SPLISH
KA
KA
KA
FUMP FUMP
FUMP
NO WONDER THEY WERE RILED UP. IT LOOKED LIKE THE WOMAN HAD ENTERED A NESTING AREA.
CLICK
DAMN.

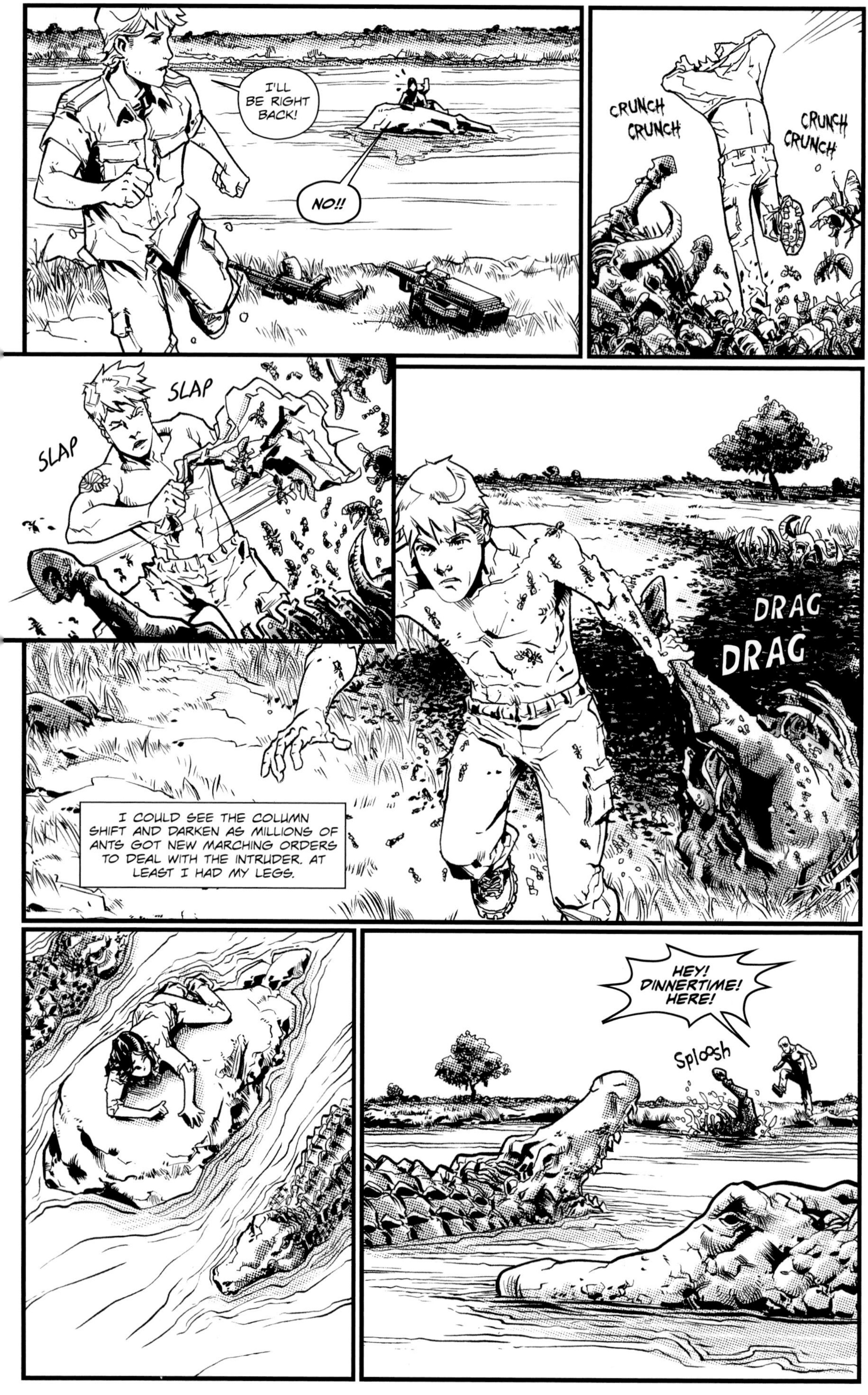
I'LL BE RIGHT BACK!
NO!!
CRUNCH CRUNCH
CRUNCH CRUNCH
SLAP
SLAP
DRAG
DRAG
I COULD SEE THE COLUMN SHIFT AND DARKEN AS MILLIONS OF ANTS GOT NEW MARCHING ORDERS TO DEAL WITH THE INTRUDER. AT LEAST I HAD MY LEGS.
HEY! DINNERTIME! HERE!
Sploosh

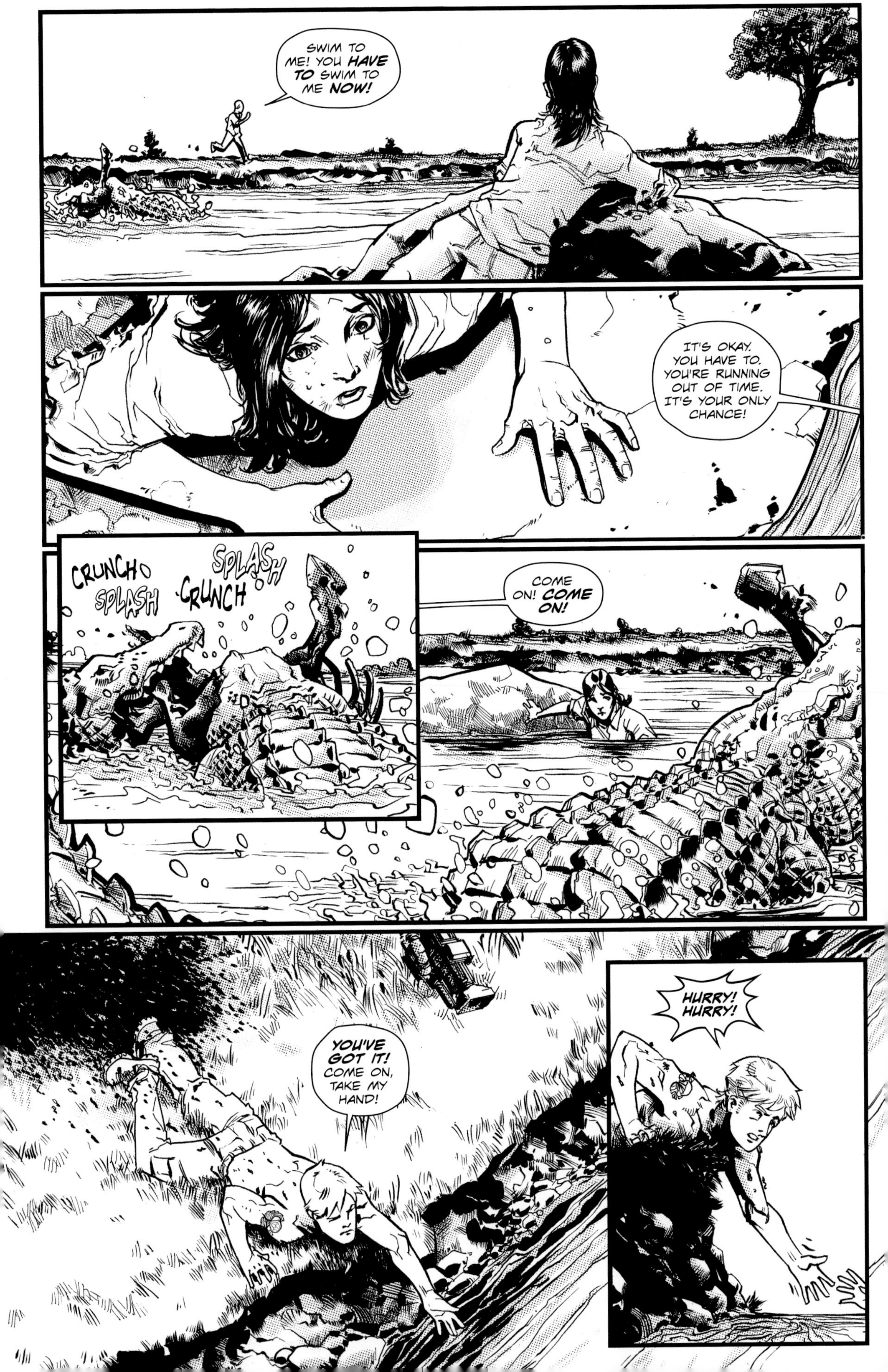
SWIM TO ME! YOU HAVE TO SWIM TO ME NOW!
IT'S OKAY. YOU HAVE TO. YOU'RE RUNNING OUT OF TIME. IT'S YOUR ONLY CHANCE!
CRUNCH
SPLASH
SPLASH
CRUNCH
COME ON! COME ON!
YOU'VE GOT IT! COME ON, TAKE MY HAND!
HURRY! HURRY!

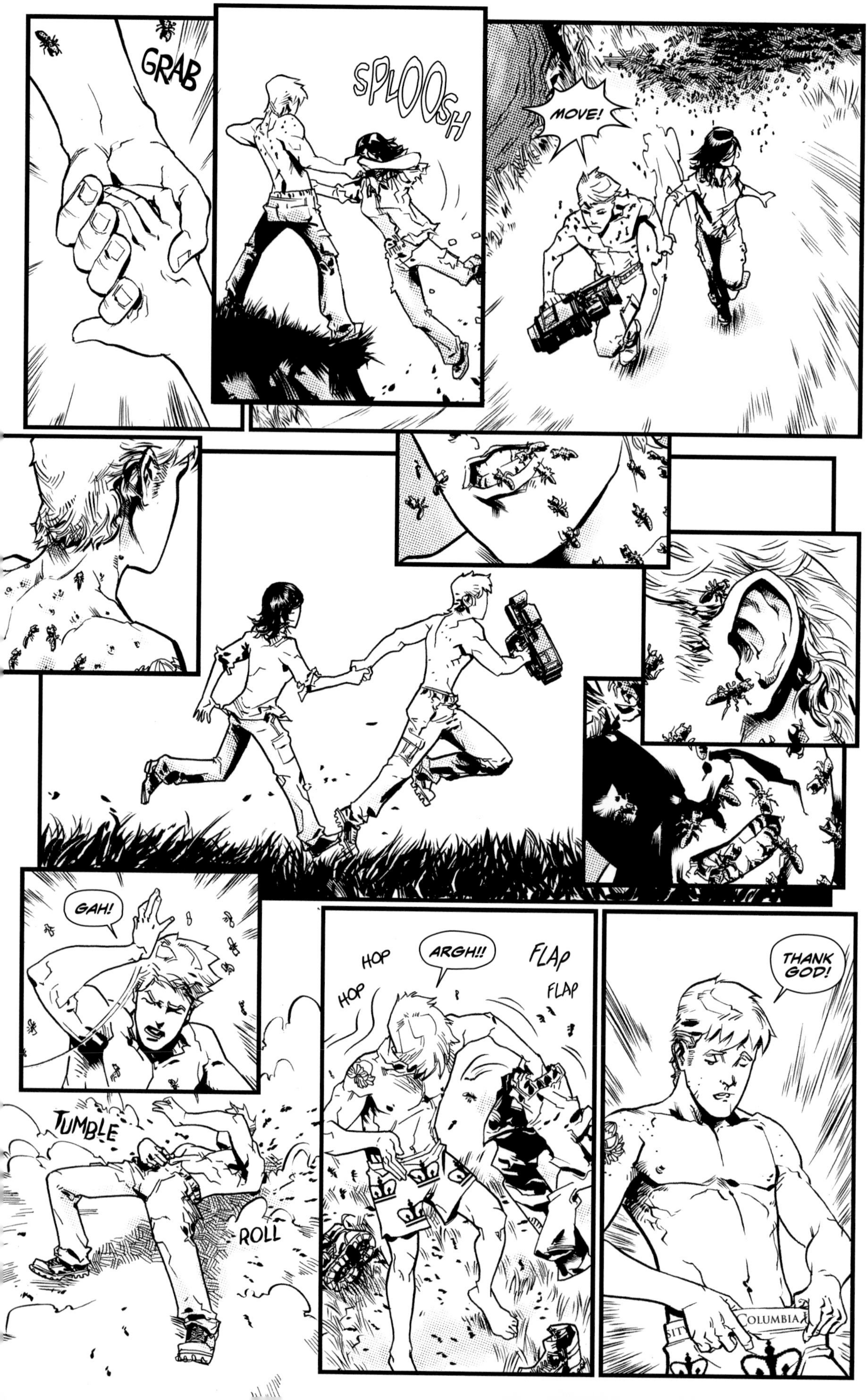
GRAB
SPLOOSH
MOVE!
GAH!
TUMBLE
ROLL
HOP
HOP
ARGH!!
FLAP
FLAP
THANK GOD!
COLUMBIA

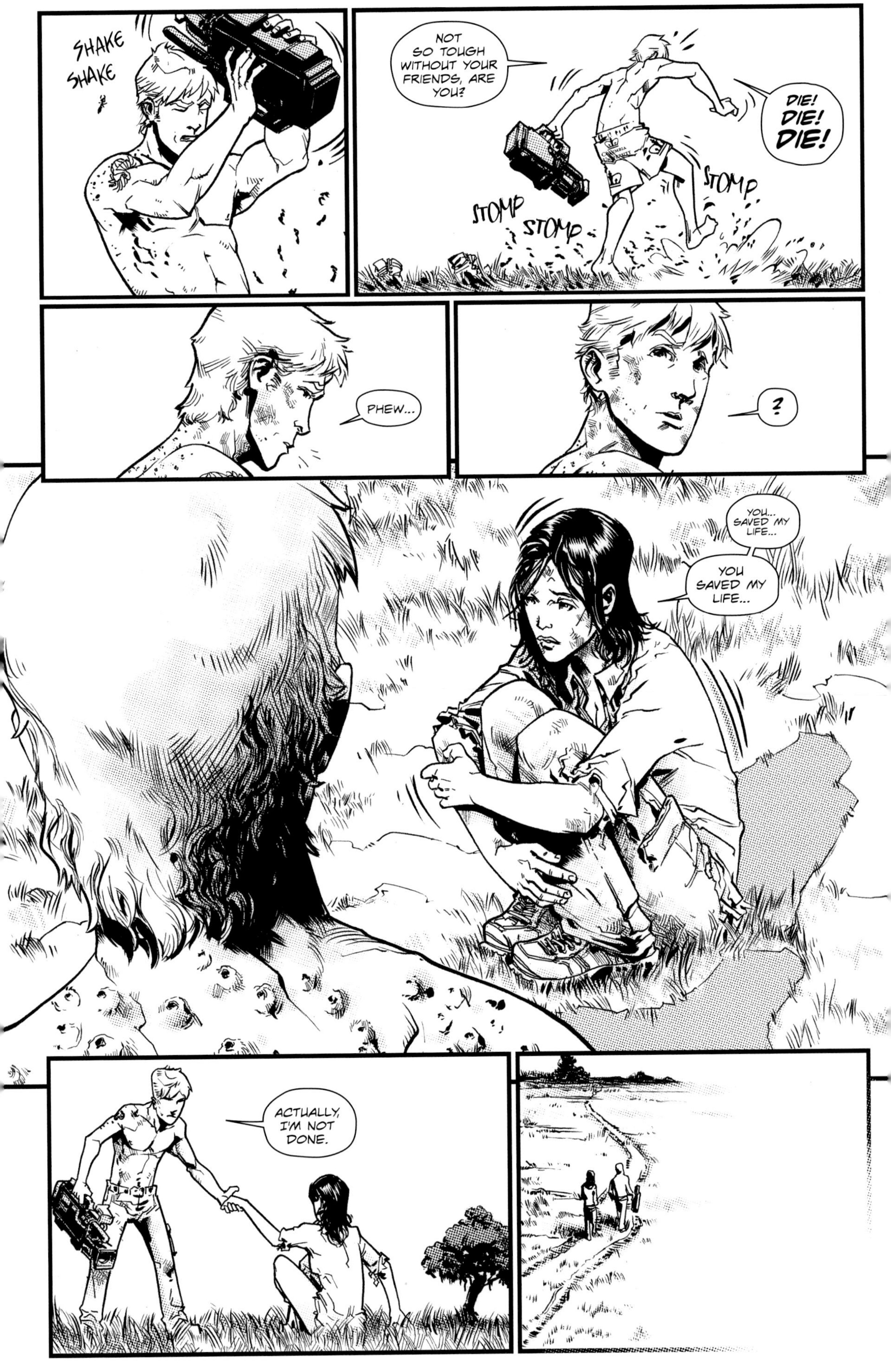
SHAKE
SHAKE
NOT SO TOUGH WITHOUT YOUR FRIENDS, ARE YOU?
DIE! DIE! DIE!
STOMP
STOMP
STOMP
PHEW...
?
YOU... SAVED MY LIFE...
YOU SAVED MY LIFE...
ACTUALLY, I'M NOT DONE.

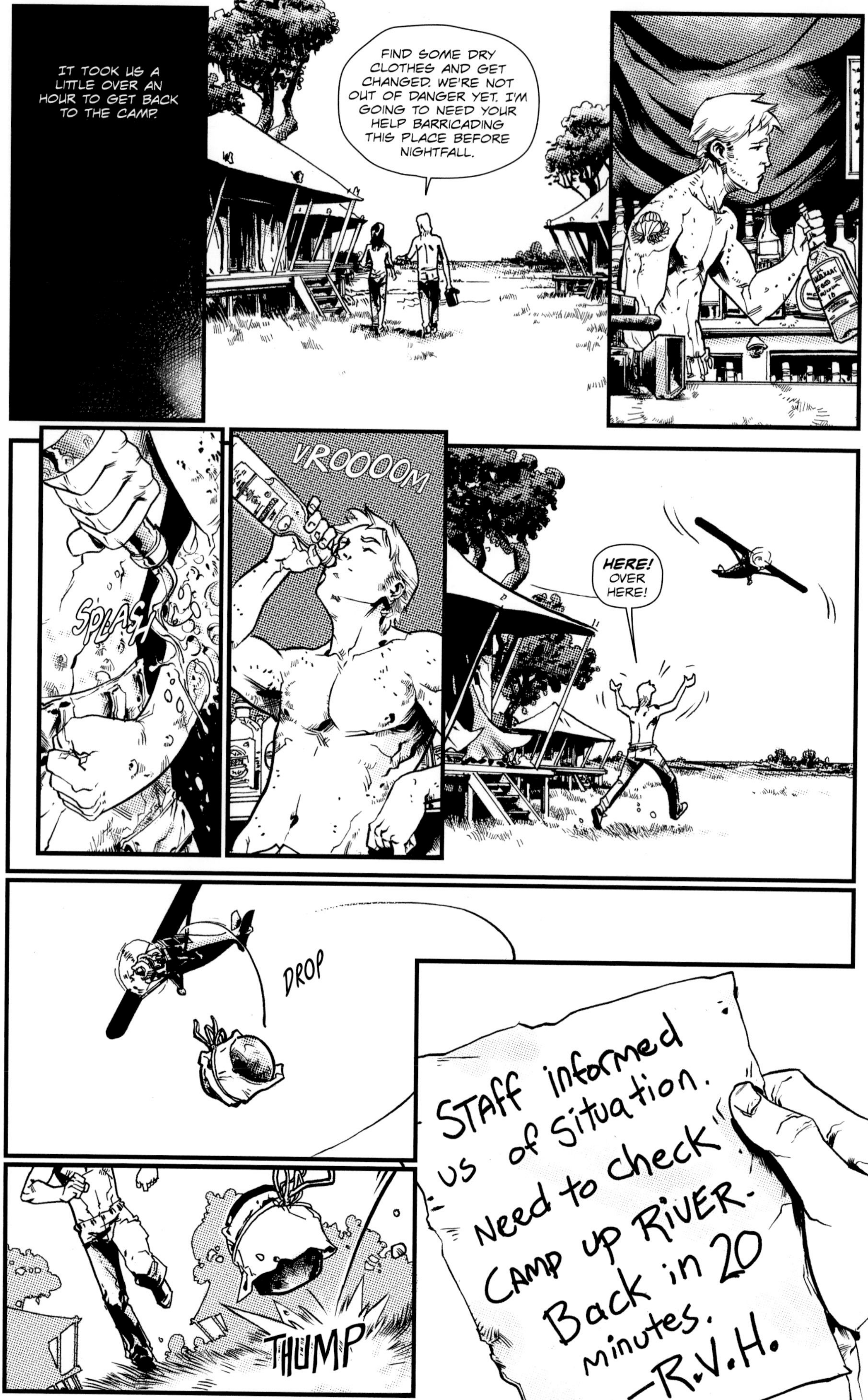
IT TOOK US A LITTLE OVER AN HOUR TO GET BACK TO THE CAMP.
FIND SOME DRY CLOTHES AND GET CHANGED. WE'RE NOT OUT OF DANGER YET. I'M GOING TO NEED YOUR HELP BARRICADING THIS PLACE BEFORE NIGHTFALL.
SPLASH
VROOOOM
HERE! OVER HERE!
DROP
THUMP
STAFF informed us of Situation. Need to check CAMP up RIVER. Back in 20 minutes. -R.V.H.

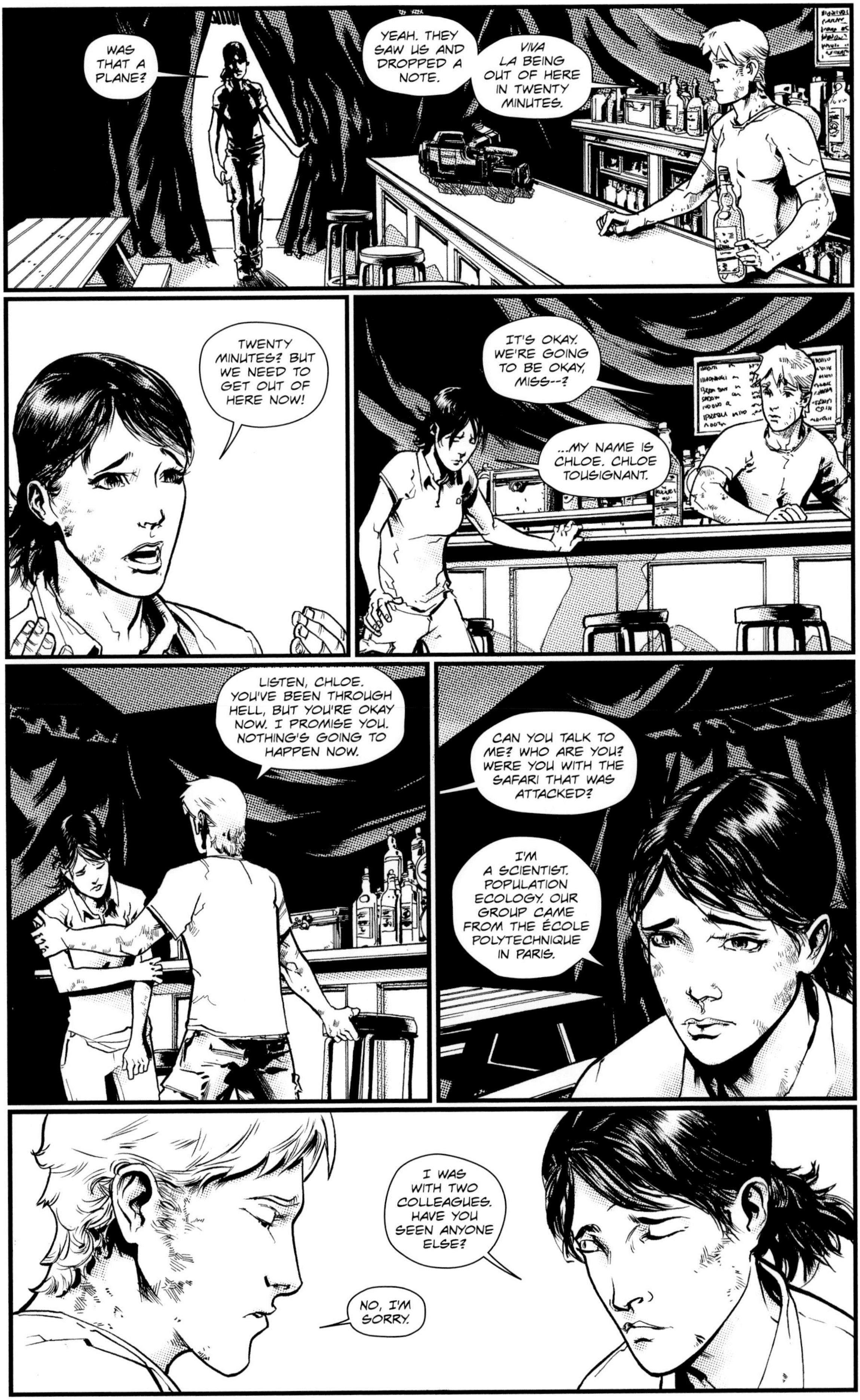
WAS THAT A PLANE?
YEAH. THEY SAW US AND DROPPED A NOTE.
VIVA LA BEING OUT OF HERE IN TWENTY MINUTES.
TWENTY MINUTES? BUT WE NEED TO GET OUT OF HERE NOW!
IT'S OKAY. WE'RE GOING TO BE OKAY, MISS--?
...MY NAME IS CHLOE. CHLOE TOUSIGNANT.
LISTEN, CHLOE. YOU'VE BEEN THROUGH HELL, BUT YOU'RE OKAY NOW. I PROMISE YOU. NOTHING'S GOING TO HAPPEN NOW.
CAN YOU TALK TO ME? WHO ARE YOU? WERE YOU WITH THE SAFARI THAT WAS ATTACKED?
I'M A SCIENTIST. POPULATION ECOLOGY. OUR GROUP CAME FROM THE ÉCOLE POLYTECHNIQUE IN PARIS.
I WAS WITH TWO COLLEAGUES. HAVE YOU SEEN ANYONE ELSE?
NO, I'M SORRY.

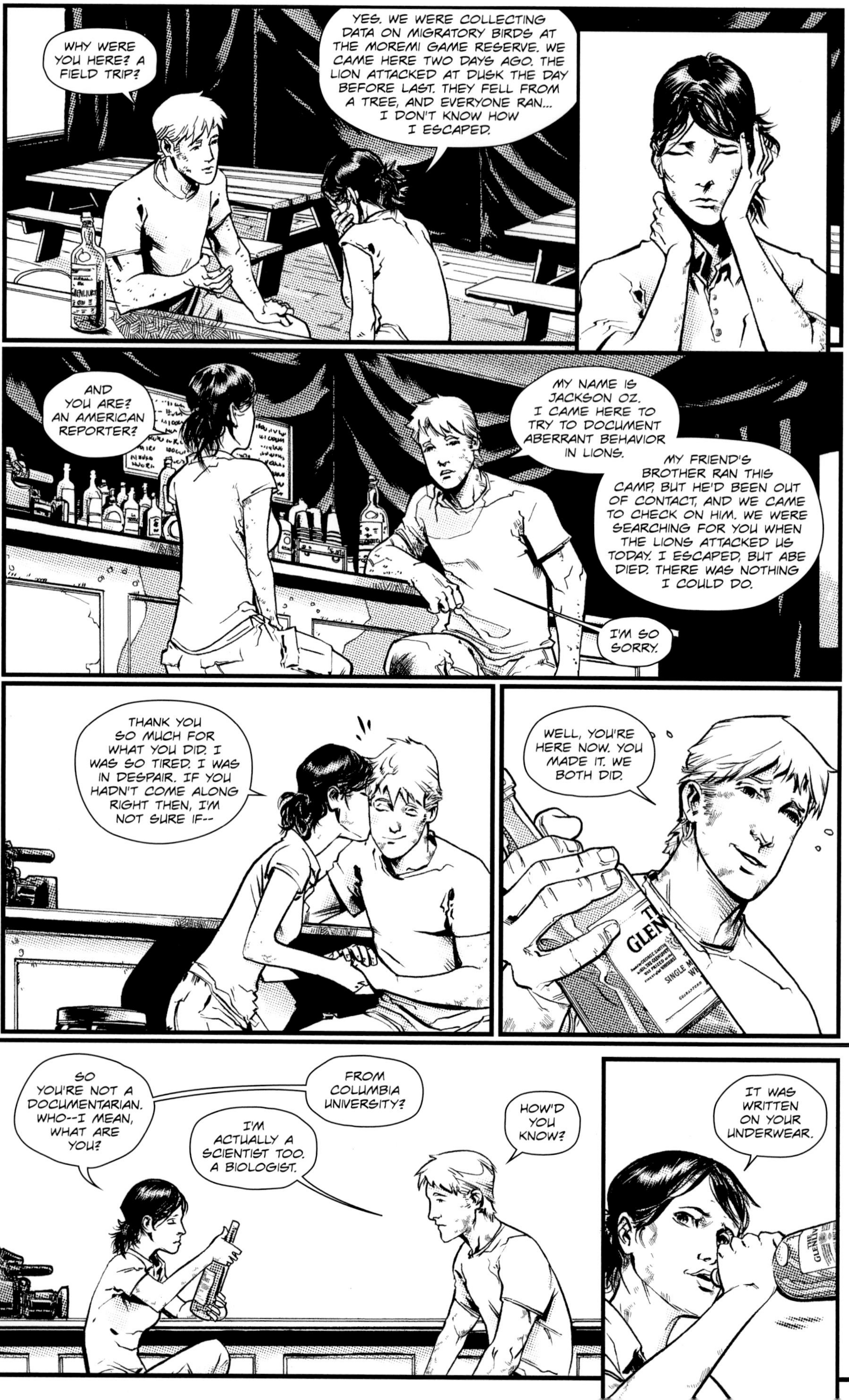
WHY WERE YOU HERE? A FIELD TRIP?
YES. WE WERE COLLECTING DATA ON MIGRATORY BIRDS AT THE MOREMI GAME RESERVE. WE CAME HERE TWO DAYS AGO. THE LION ATTACKED AT DUSK THE DAY BEFORE LAST. THEY FELL FROM A TREE, AND EVERYONE RAN... I DON'T KNOW HOW I ESCAPED.
AND YOU ARE? AN AMERICAN REPORTER?
MY NAME IS JACKSON OZ. I CAME HERE TO TRY TO DOCUMENT ABERRANT BEHAVIOR IN LIONS.
MY FRIEND'S BROTHER RAN THIS CAMP, BUT HE'D BEEN OUT OF CONTACT, AND WE CAME TO CHECK ON HIM. WE WERE SEARCHING FOR YOU WHEN THE LIONS ATTACKED US TODAY. I ESCAPED, BUT ABE DIED. THERE WAS NOTHING I COULD DO.
I'M SO SORRY.
THANK YOU SO MUCH FOR WHAT YOU DID. I WAS SO TIRED. I WAS IN DESPAIR. IF YOU HADN'T COME ALONG RIGHT THEN, I'M NOT SURE IF--
WELL, YOU'RE HERE NOW. YOU MADE IT. WE BOTH DID.
SO YOU'RE NOT A DOCUMENTARIAN. WHO--I MEAN, WHAT ARE YOU?
I'M ACTUALLY A SCIENTIST TOO. A BIOLOGIST.
FROM COLUMBIA UNIVERSITY?
HOW'D YOU KNOW?
IT WAS WRITTEN ON YOUR UNDERWEAR.

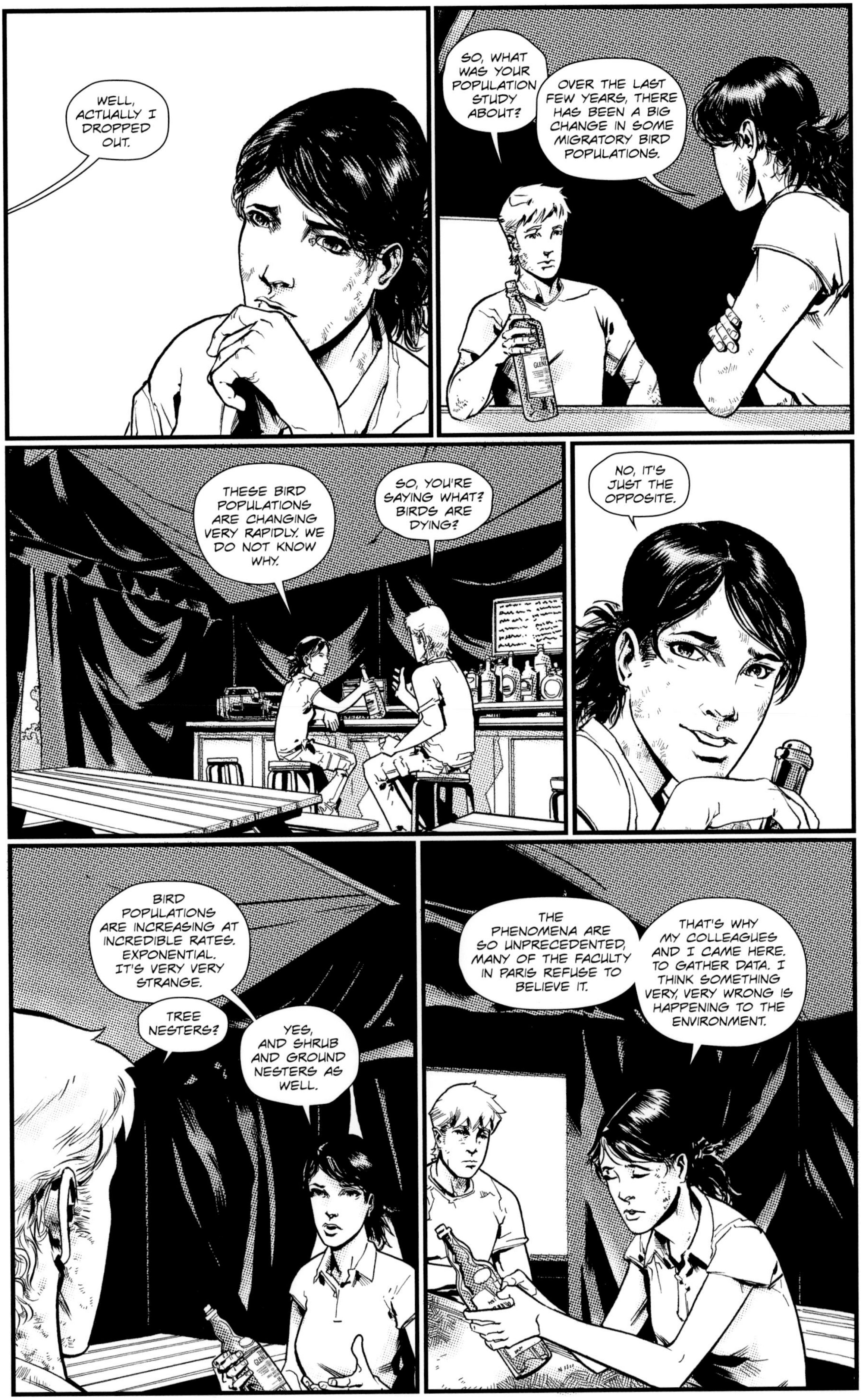
WELL, ACTUALLY I DROPPED OUT.
SO, WHAT WAS YOUR POPULATION STUDY ABOUT?
OVER THE LAST FEW YEARS, THERE HAS BEEN A BIG CHANGE IN SOME MIGRATORY BIRD POPULATIONS.
THESE BIRD POPULATIONS ARE CHANGING VERY RAPIDLY. WE DO NOT KNOW WHY.
SO, YOU'RE SAYING WHAT? BIRDS ARE DYING?
NO, IT'S JUST THE OPPOSITE.
BIRD POPULATIONS ARE INCREASING AT INCREDIBLE RATES. EXPONENTIAL. IT'S VERY VERY STRANGE.
TREE NESTERS?
YES, AND SHRUB AND GROUND NESTERS AS WELL.
THE PHENOMENA ARE SO UNPRECEDENTED, MANY OF THE FACULTY IN PARIS REFUSE TO BELIEVE IT.
THAT'S WHY MY COLLEAGUES AND I CAME HERE. TO GATHER DATA. I THINK SOMETHING VERY, VERY WRONG IS HAPPENING TO THE ENVIRONMENT.

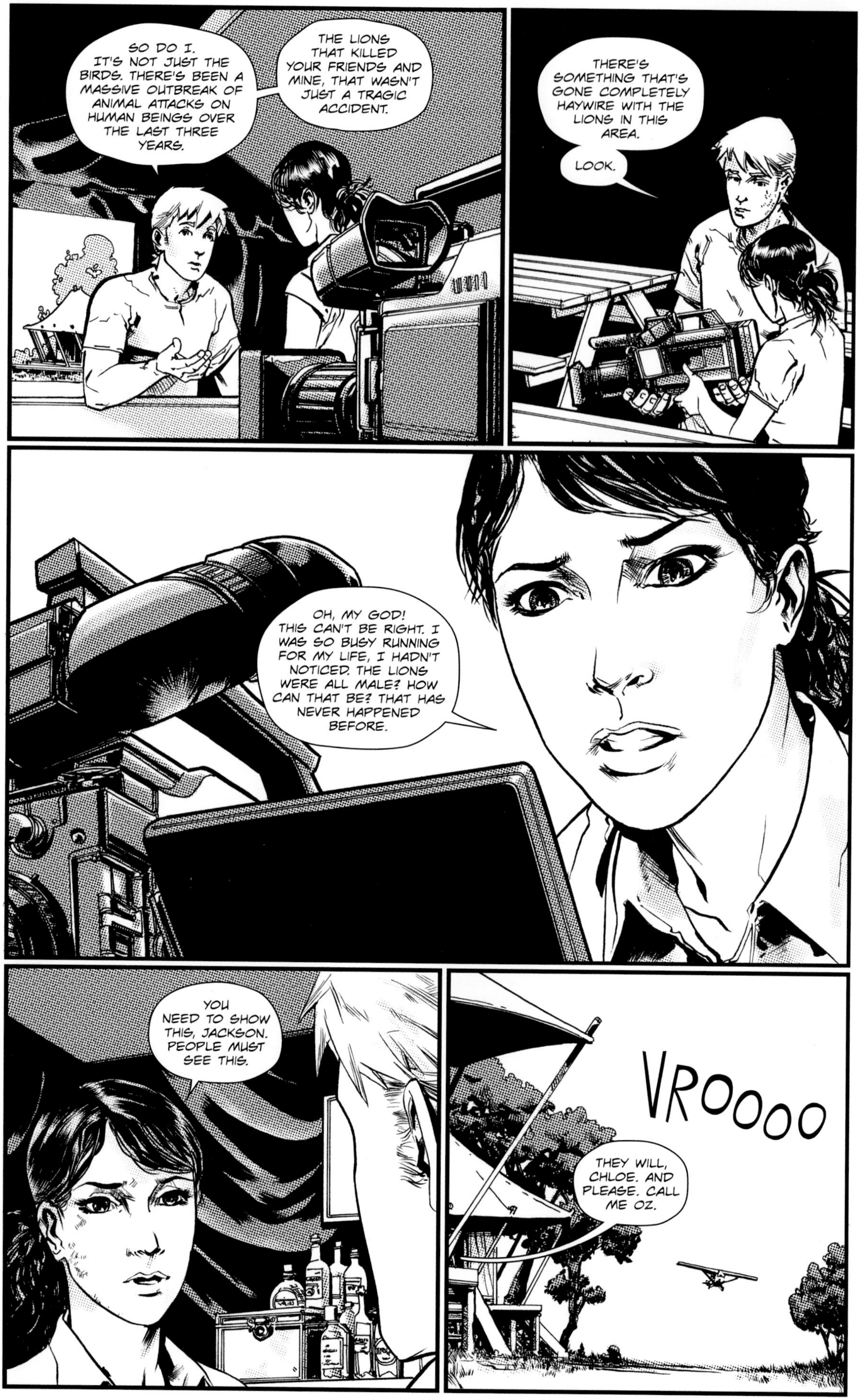
SO DO I. IT'S NOT JUST THE BIRDS. THERE'S BEEN A MASSIVE OUTBREAK OF ANIMAL ATTACKS ON HUMAN BEINGS OVER THE LAST THREE YEARS.
THE LIONS THAT KILLED YOUR FRIENDS AND MINE, THAT WASN'T JUST A TRAGIC ACCIDENT.
THERE'S SOMETHING THAT'S GONE COMPLETELY HAYWIRE WITH THE LIONS IN THIS AREA.
LOOK.
OH, MY GOD! THIS CAN'T BE RIGHT. I WAS SO BUSY RUNNING FOR MY LIFE, I HADN'T NOTICED. THE LIONS WERE ALL MALE? HOW CAN THAT BE? THAT HAS NEVER HAPPENED BEFORE.
YOU NEED TO SHOW THIS, JACKSON. PEOPLE MUST SEE THIS.
VROOOO
THEY WILL, CHLOE. AND PLEASE. CALL ME OZ.

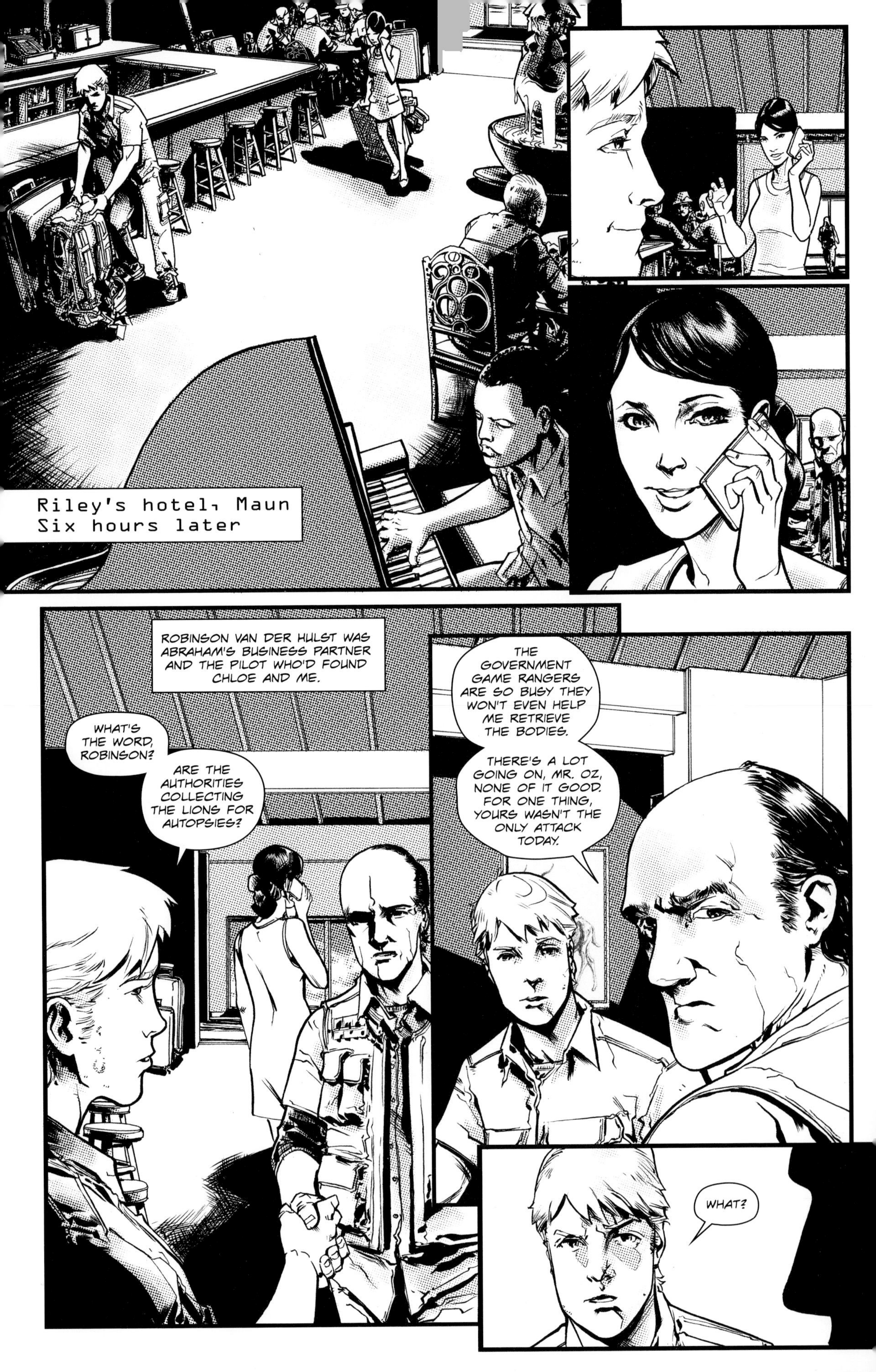
Riley's hotel, Maun
Six hours later
ROBINSON VAN DER HULST WAS ABRAHAM'S BUSINESS PARTNER AND THE PILOT WHO'D FOUND CHLOE AND ME.
WHAT'S THE WORD, ROBINSON?
ARE THE AUTHORITIES COLLECTING THE LIONS FOR AUTOPSIES?
THE GOVERNMENT GAME RANGERS ARE SO BUSY THEY WON'T EVEN HELP ME RETRIEVE THE BODIES.
THERE'S A LOT GOING ON, MR. OZ, NONE OF IT GOOD. FOR ONE THING, YOURS WASN'T THE ONLY ATTACK TODAY.
WHAT?

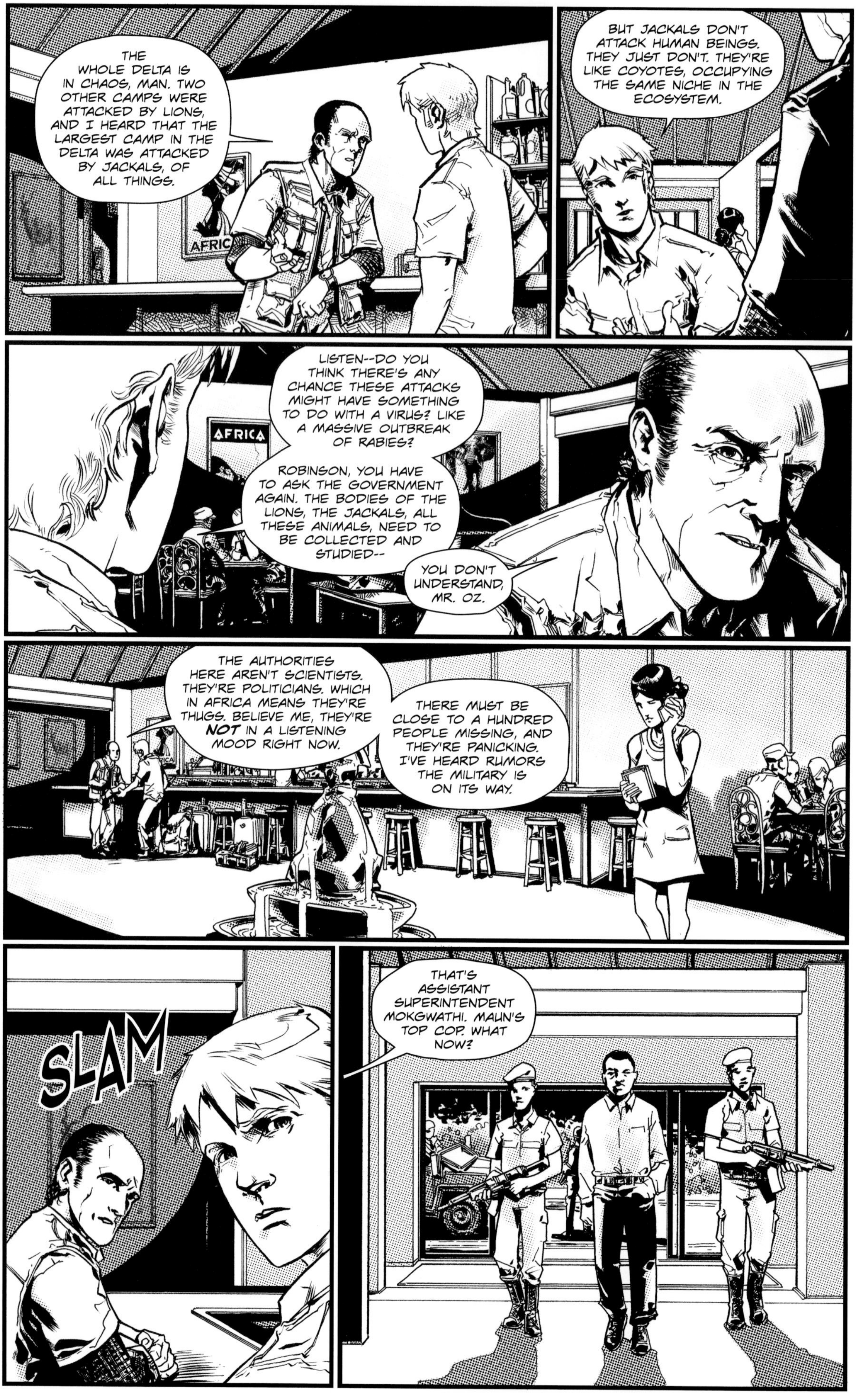
THE WHOLE DELTA IS IN CHAOS, MAN. TWO OTHER CAMPS WERE ATTACKED BY LIONS, AND I HEARD THAT THE LARGEST CAMP IN THE DELTA WAS ATTACKED BY JACKALS, OF ALL THINGS.
AFRICA
BUT JACKALS DON'T ATTACK HUMAN BEINGS. THEY JUST DON'T. THEY'RE LIKE COYOTES, OCCUPYING THE SAME NICHE IN THE ECOSYSTEM.
LISTEN--DO YOU THINK THERE'S ANY CHANCE THESE ATTACKS MIGHT HAVE SOMETHING TO DO WITH A VIRUS? LIKE A MASSIVE OUTBREAK OF RABIES?
ROBINSON, YOU HAVE TO ASK THE GOVERNMENT AGAIN. THE BODIES OF THE LIONS, THE JACKALS, ALL THESE ANIMALS, NEED TO BE COLLECTED AND STUDIED--
AFRICA
YOU DON'T UNDERSTAND, MR. OZ.
THE AUTHORITIES HERE AREN'T SCIENTISTS. THEY'RE POLITICIANS. WHICH IN AFRICA MEANS THEY'RE THUGS. BELIEVE ME, THEY'RE NOT IN A LISTENING MOOD RIGHT NOW.
THERE MUST BE CLOSE TO A HUNDRED PEOPLE MISSING, AND THEY'RE PANICKING. I'VE HEARD RUMORS THE MILITARY IS ON ITS WAY.
SLAM
THAT'S ASSISTANT SUPERINTENDENT MOKGWATHI. MAUN'S TOP COP. WHAT NOW?

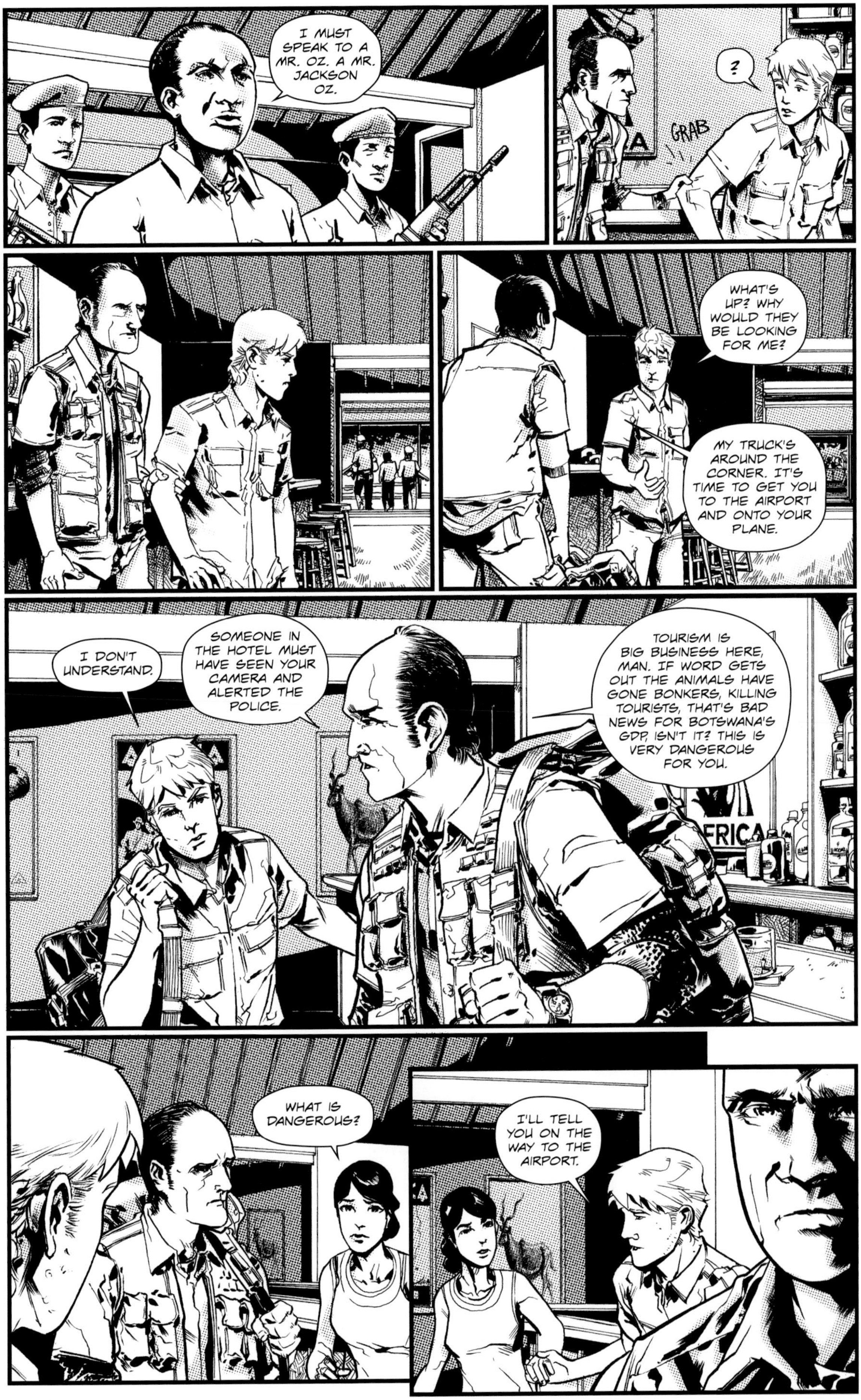
I MUST SPEAK TO A MR. OZ. A MR. JACKSON OZ.
?
GRAB
WHAT'S UP? WHY WOULD THEY BE LOOKING FOR ME?
MY TRUCK'S AROUND THE CORNER. IT'S TIME TO GET YOU TO THE AIRPORT AND ONTO YOUR PLANE.
I DON'T UNDERSTAND.
SOMEONE IN THE HOTEL MUST HAVE SEEN YOUR CAMERA AND ALERTED THE POLICE.
TOURISM IS BIG BUSINESS HERE, MAN. IF WORD GETS OUT THE ANIMALS HAVE GONE BONKERS, KILLING TOURISTS, THAT'S BAD NEWS FOR BOTSWANA'S GDP, ISN'T IT? THIS IS VERY DANGEROUS FOR YOU.
AFRICA
WHAT IS DANGEROUS?
I'LL TELL YOU ON THE WAY TO THE AIRPORT.

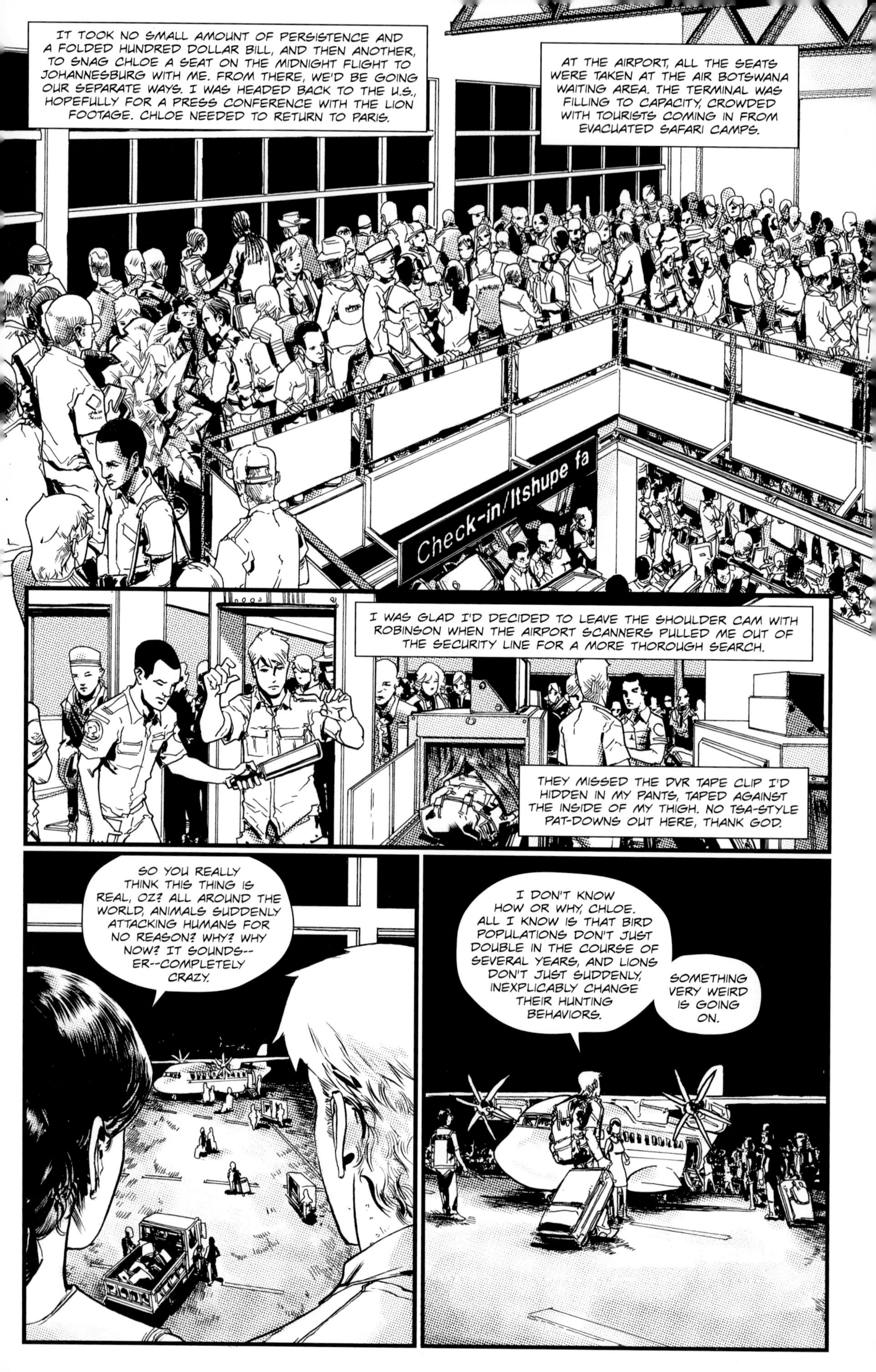
IT TOOK NO SMALL AMOUNT OF PERSISTENCE AND A FOLDED HUNDRED DOLLAR BILL, AND THEN ANOTHER, TO SNAG CHLOE A SEAT ON THE MIDNIGHT FLIGHT TO JOHANNESBURG WITH ME. FROM THERE, WE'D BE GOING OUR SEPARATE WAYS. I WAS HEADED BACK TO THE U.S., HOPEFULLY FOR A PRESS CONFERENCE WITH THE LION FOOTAGE. CHLOE NEEDED TO RETURN TO PARIS.
AT THE AIRPORT, ALL THE SEATS WERE TAKEN AT THE AIR BOTSWANA WAITING AREA. THE TERMINAL WAS FILLING TO CAPACITY, CROWDED WITH TOURISTS COMING IN FROM EVACUATED SAFARI CAMPS.
Check-in/Itshupe fa
I WAS GLAD I'D DECIDED TO LEAVE THE SHOULDER CAM WITH ROBINSON WHEN THE AIRPORT SCANNERS PULLED ME OUT OF THE SECURITY LINE FOR A MORE THOROUGH SEARCH.
THEY MISSED THE DVR TAPE CLIP I'D HIDDEN IN MY PANTS, TAPED AGAINST THE INSIDE OF MY THIGH. NO TSA-STYLE PAT-DOWNS OUT HERE, THANK GOD.
SO YOU REALLY THINK THIS THING IS REAL, OZ? ALL AROUND THE WORLD, ANIMALS SUDDENLY ATTACKING HUMANS FOR NO REASON? WHY? WHY NOW? IT SOUNDS-- ER--COMPLETELY CRAZY.
I DON'T KNOW HOW OR WHY, CHLOE. ALL I KNOW IS THAT BIRD POPULATIONS DON'T JUST DOUBLE IN THE COURSE OF SEVERAL YEARS, AND LIONS DON'T JUST SUDDENLY, INEXPLICABLY CHANGE THEIR HUNTING BEHAVIORS.
SOMETHING VERY WEIRD IS GOING ON.

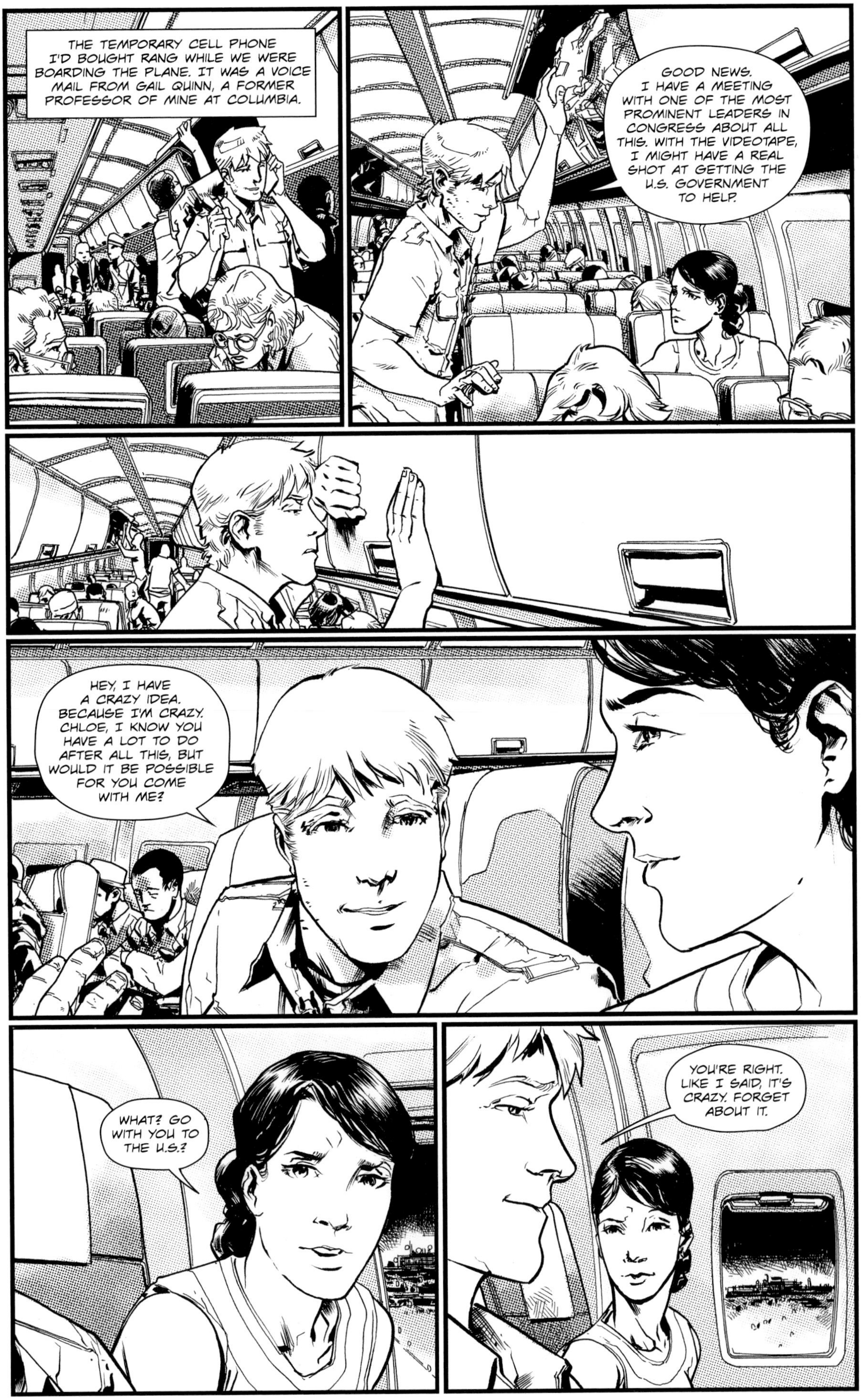
THE TEMPORARY CELL PHONE I'D BOUGHT RANG WHILE WE WERE BOARDING THE PLANE. IT WAS A VOICE MAIL FROM GAIL QUINN, A FORMER PROFESSOR OF MINE AT COLUMBIA.
GOOD NEWS. I HAVE A MEETING WITH ONE OF THE MOST PROMINENT LEADERS IN CONGRESS ABOUT ALL THIS. WITH THE VIDEOTAPE, I MIGHT HAVE A REAL SHOT AT GETTING THE U.S. GOVERNMENT TO HELP.
HEY, I HAVE A CRAZY IDEA. BECAUSE I'M CRAZY. CHLOE, I KNOW YOU HAVE A LOT TO DO AFTER ALL THIS, BUT WOULD IT BE POSSIBLE FOR YOU COME WITH ME?
WHAT? GO WITH YOU TO THE U.S.?
YOU'RE RIGHT. LIKE I SAID, IT'S CRAZY. FORGET ABOUT IT.

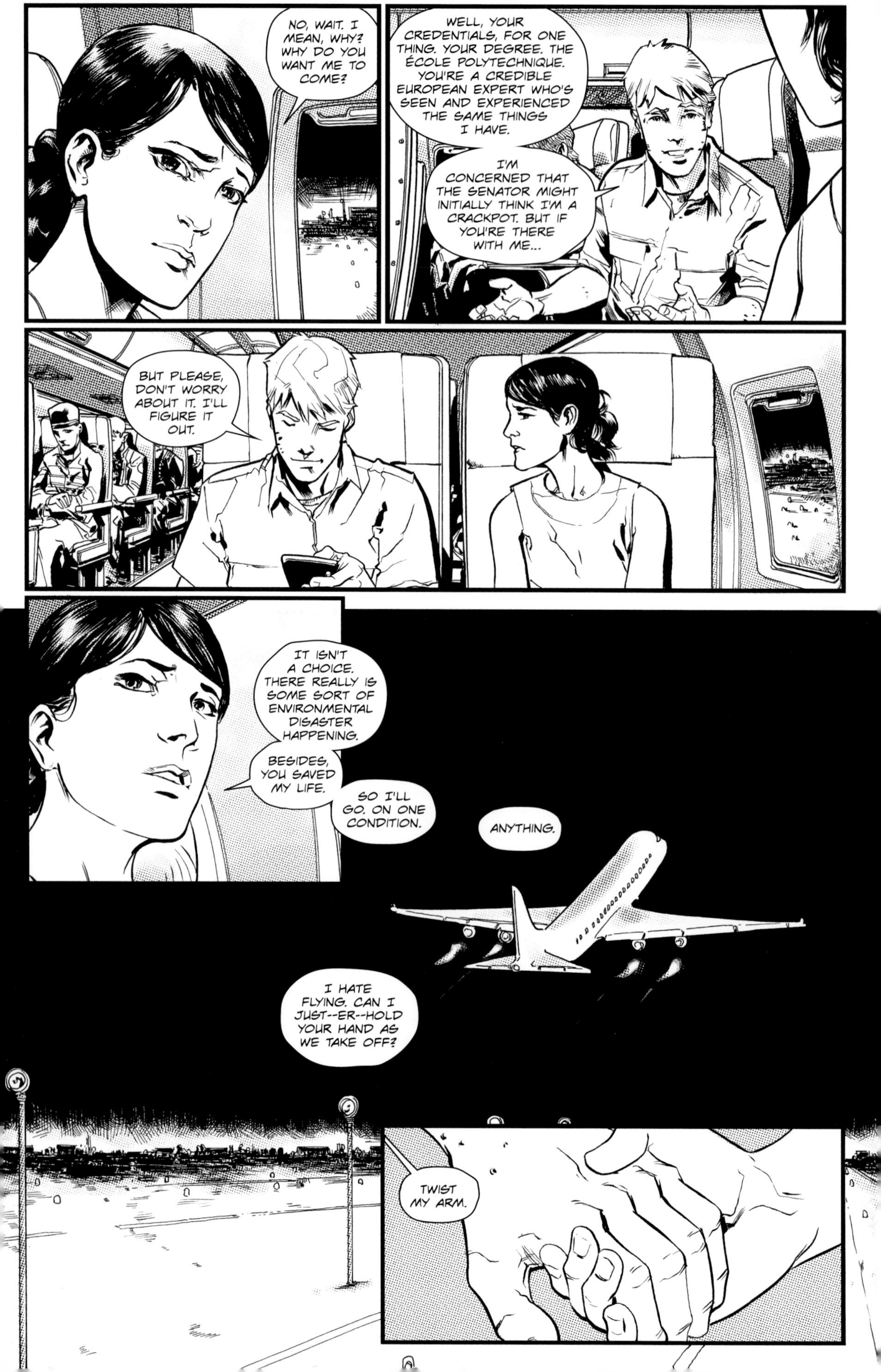
NO, WAIT. I MEAN, WHY? WHY DO YOU WANT ME TO COME?
WELL, YOUR CREDENTIALS, FOR ONE THING. YOUR DEGREE. THE ÉCOLE POLYTECHNIQUE. YOU'RE A CREDIBLE EUROPEAN EXPERT WHO'S SEEN AND EXPERIENCED THE SAME THINGS I HAVE.
I'M CONCERNED THAT THE SENATOR MIGHT INITIALLY THINK I'M A CRACKPOT. BUT IF YOU'RE THERE WITH ME...
BUT PLEASE, DON'T WORRY ABOUT IT. I'LL FIGURE IT OUT.
IT ISN'T A CHOICE. THERE REALLY IS SOME SORT OF ENVIRONMENTAL DISASTER HAPPENING.
BESIDES, YOU SAVED MY LIFE.
SO I'LL GO. ON ONE CONDITION.
ANYTHING.
I HATE FLYING. CAN I JUST--ER--HOLD YOUR HAND AS WE TAKE OFF?
TWIST MY ARM.

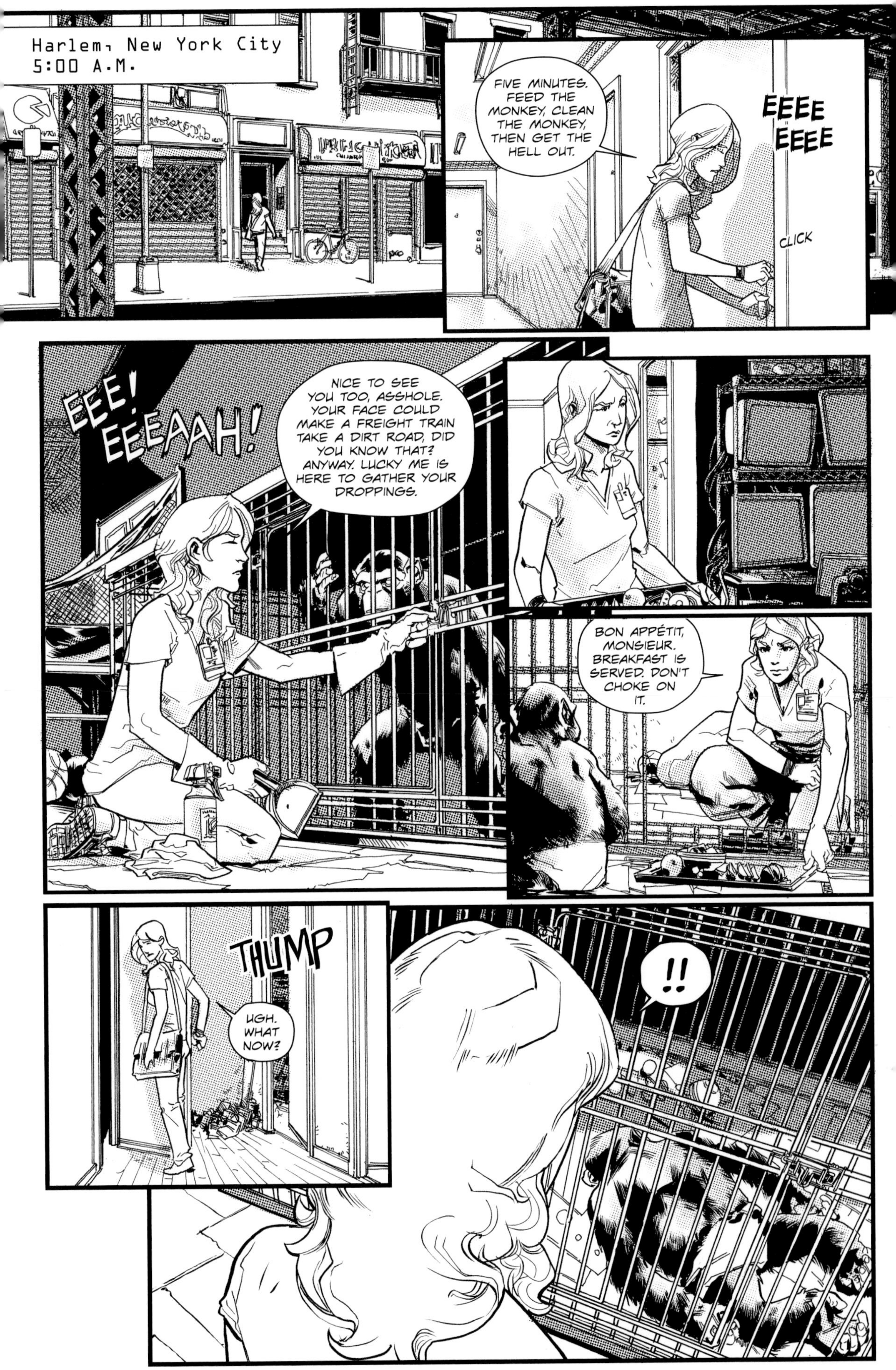
Harlem, New York City
5:00 A.M.
FIVE MINUTES. FEED THE MONKEY, CLEAN THE MONKEY, THEN GET THE HELL OUT.
EEEE EEEE
CLICK
EEE! EEEAAH!
NICE TO SEE YOU TOO, ASSHOLE. YOUR FACE COULD MAKE A FREIGHT TRAIN TAKE A DIRT ROAD, DID YOU KNOW THAT? ANYWAY. LUCKY ME IS HERE TO GATHER YOUR DROPPINGS.
BON APPÉTIT, MONSIEUR. BREAKFAST IS SERVED. DON'T CHOKE ON IT.
THUMP
UGH. WHAT NOW?
!!

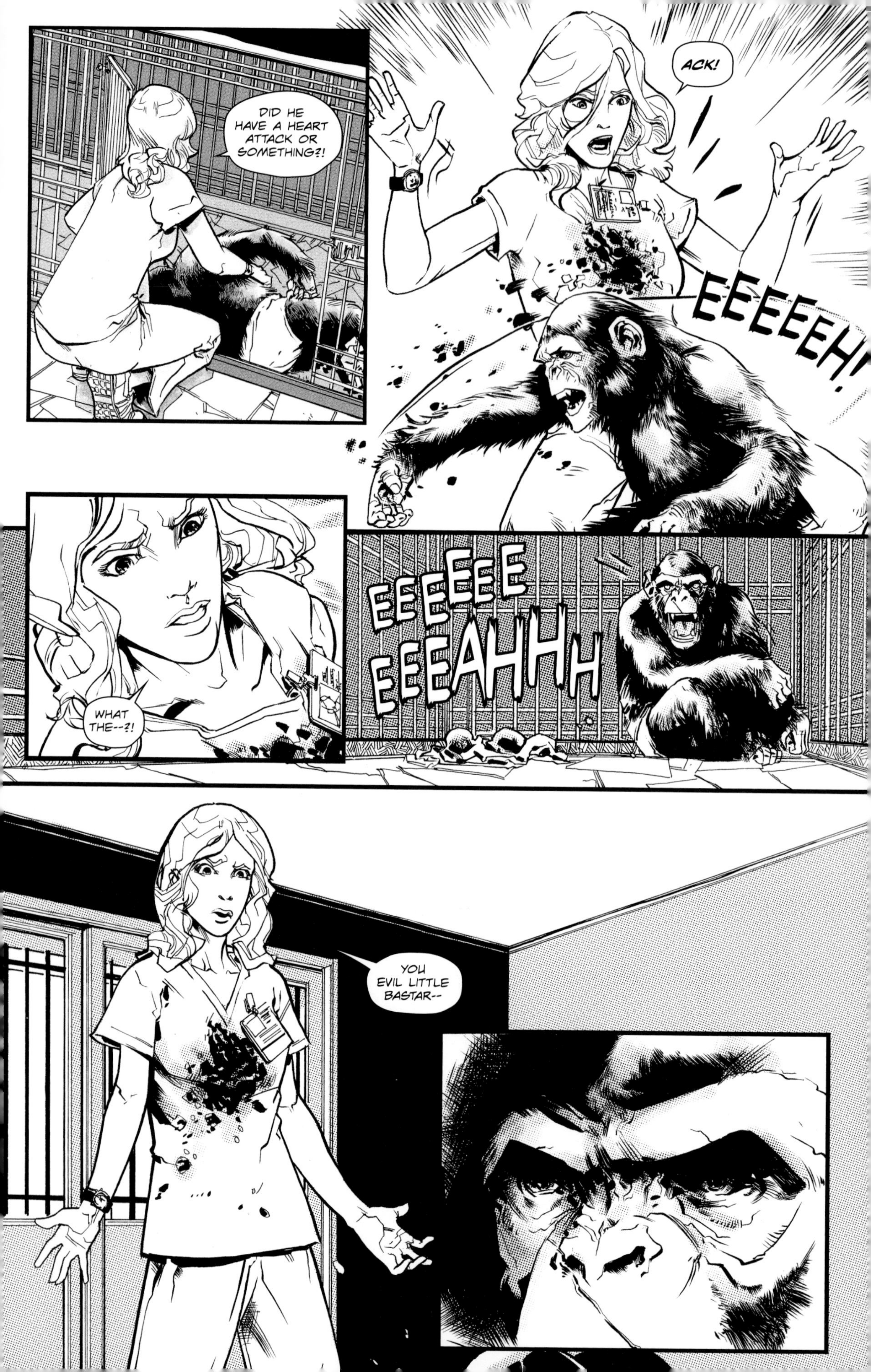
DID HE HAVE A HEART ATTACK OR SOMETHING?!
ACK!
EEEEEH!
WHAT THE--?!
EEEEEE EEEAHHH
YOU EVIL LITTLE BASTAR--

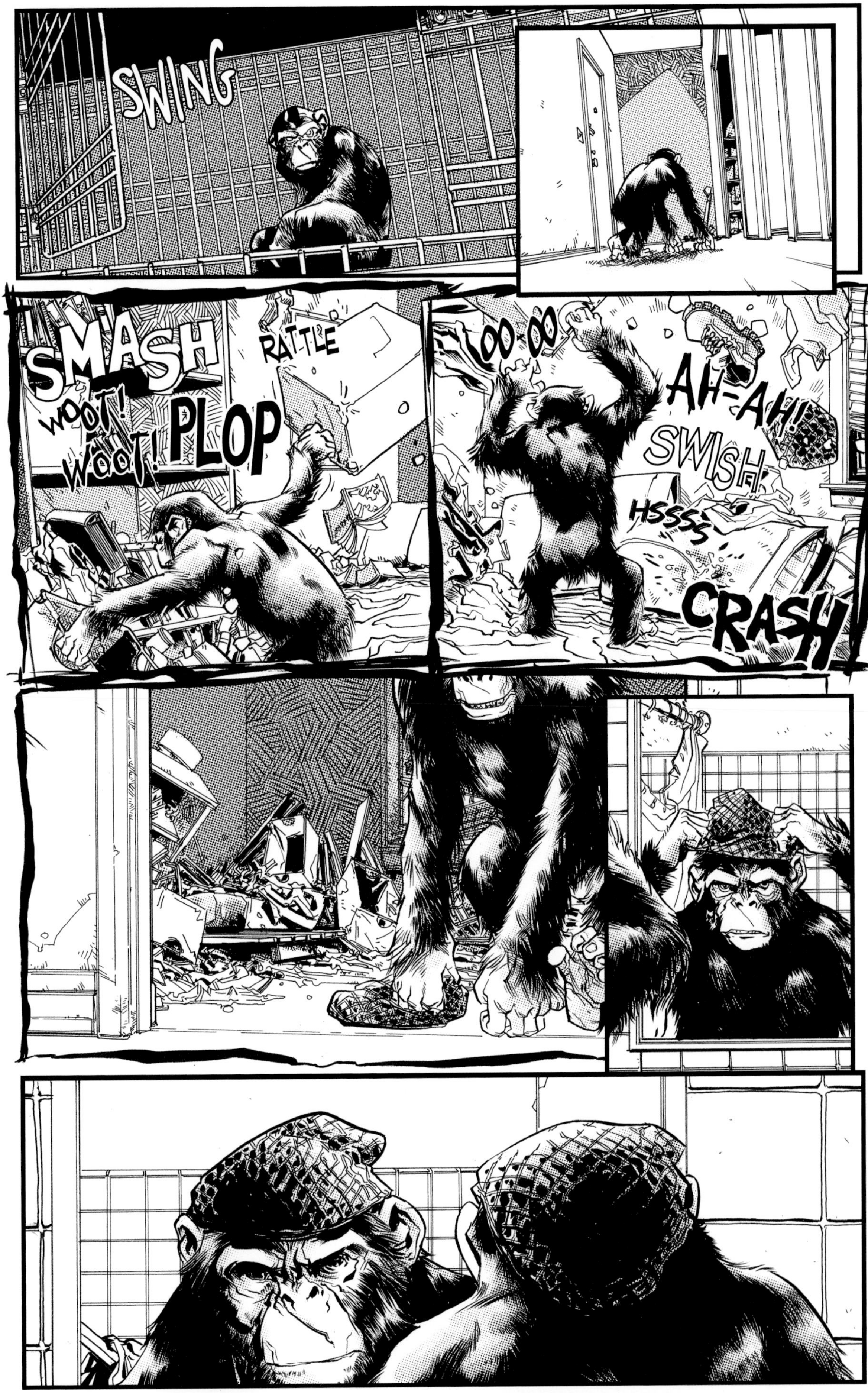
SWING
SMASH
RATTLE
WOOT! WOOT!
PLOP
OO-OO
AH-AH!
SWISH
HSSSS
CRASH

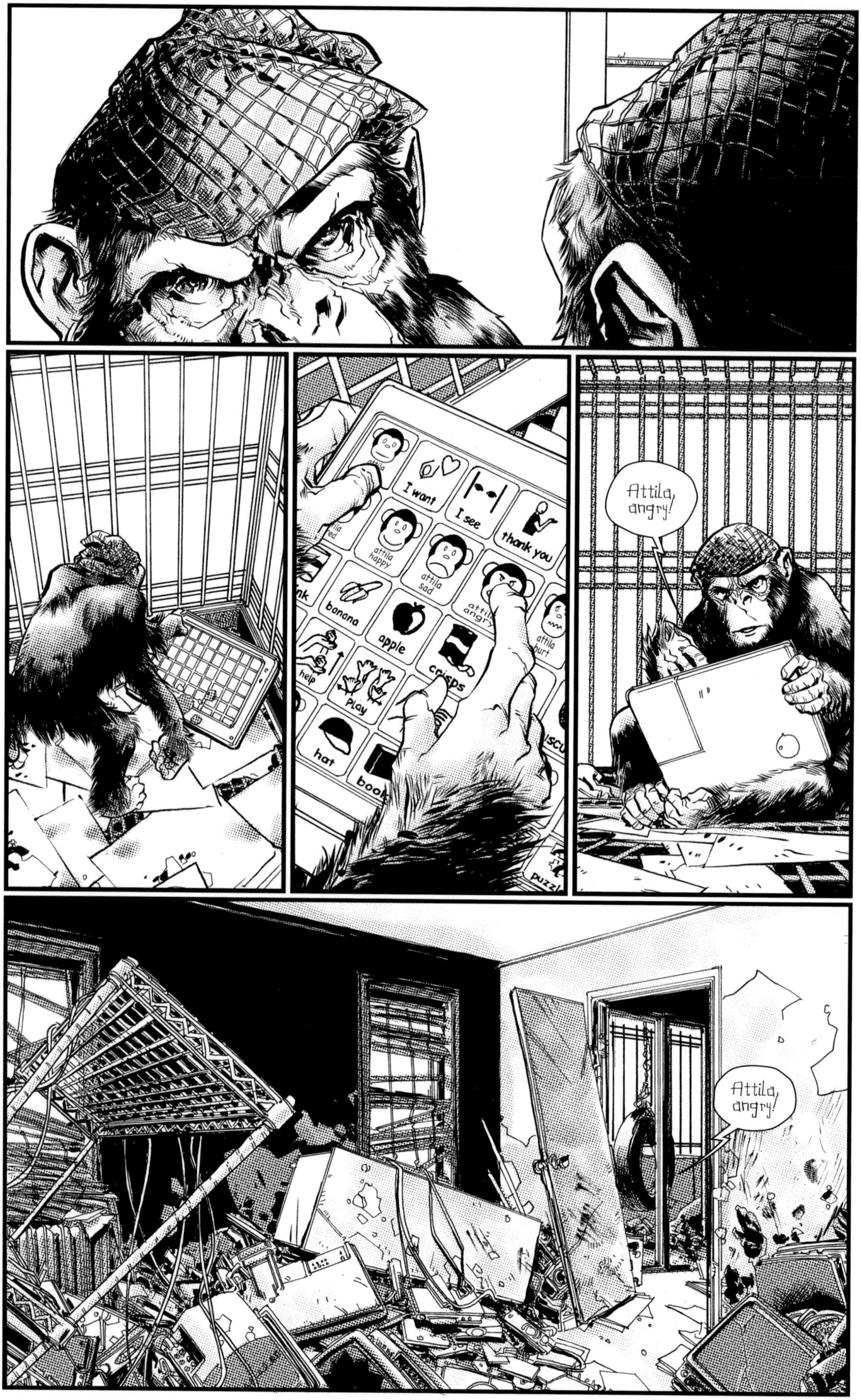
attila
I want
I see
thank you
attila happy
attila sad
banana
apple
attila angry
attila hurt
help
play
crisps
hat
book
Attila, angry!
Attila, angry!

ZOO

THE GRAPHIC NOVEL

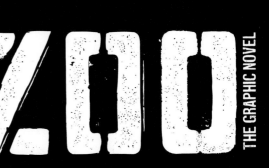

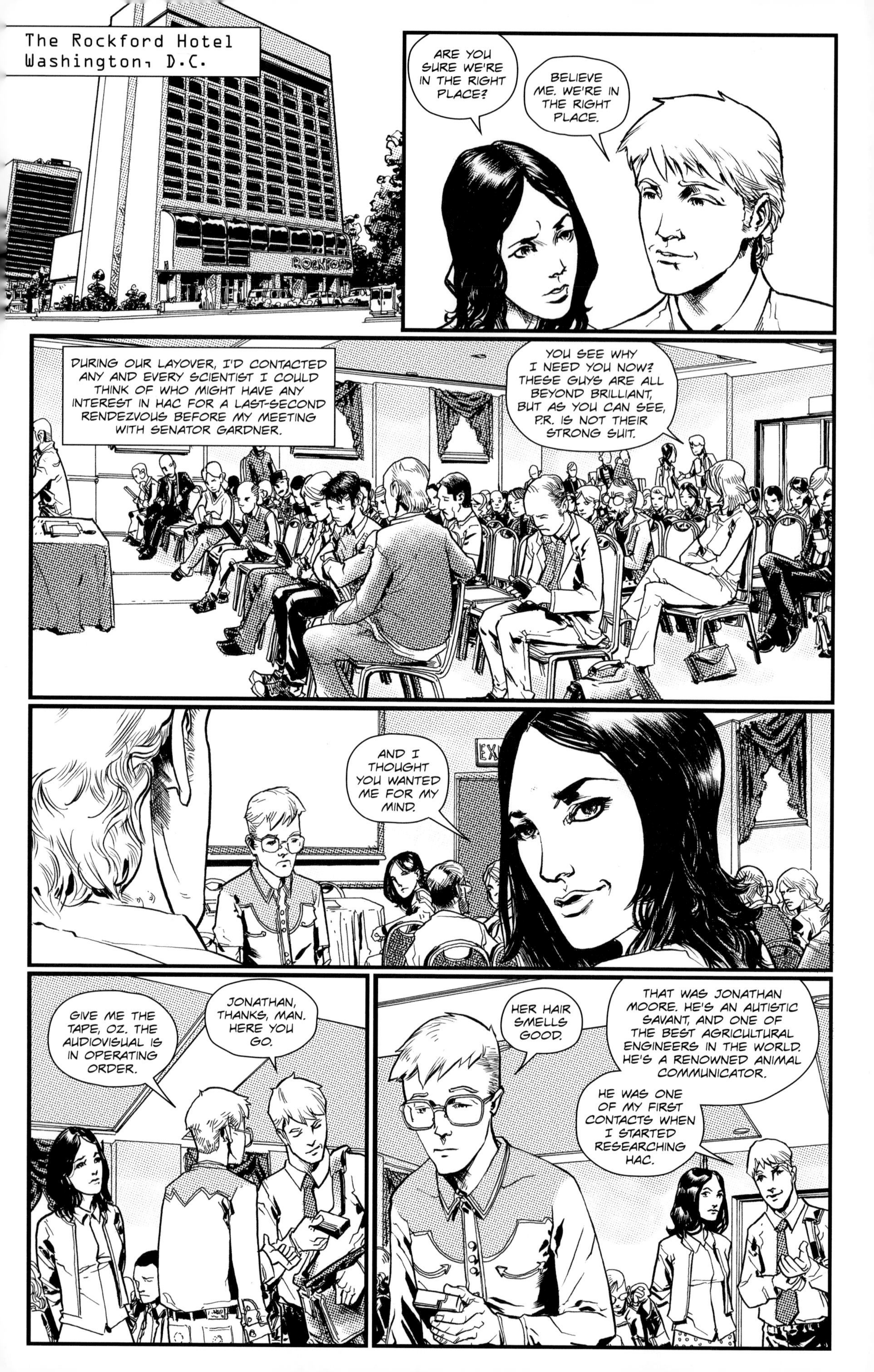
The Rockford Hotel
Washington, D.C.
ROCKFORD
ARE YOU SURE WE'RE IN THE RIGHT PLACE?
BELIEVE ME. WE'RE IN THE RIGHT PLACE.
DURING OUR LAYOVER, I'D CONTACTED ANY AND EVERY SCIENTIST I COULD THINK OF WHO MIGHT HAVE ANY INTEREST IN HAC FOR A LAST-SECOND RENDEZVOUS BEFORE MY MEETING WITH SENATOR GARDNER.
YOU SEE WHY I NEED YOU NOW? THESE GUYS ARE ALL BEYOND BRILLIANT, BUT AS YOU CAN SEE, P.R. IS NOT THEIR STRONG SUIT.
AND I THOUGHT YOU WANTED ME FOR MY MIND.
GIVE ME THE TAPE, OZ. THE AUDIOVISUAL IS IN OPERATING ORDER.
JONATHAN, THANKS, MAN. HERE YOU GO.
HER HAIR SMELLS GOOD.
THAT WAS JONATHAN MOORE. HE'S AN AUTISTIC SAVANT, AND ONE OF THE BEST AGRICULTURAL ENGINEERS IN THE WORLD. HE'S A RENOWNED ANIMAL COMMUNICATOR.
HE WAS ONE OF MY FIRST CONTACTS WHEN I STARTED RESEARCHING HAC.

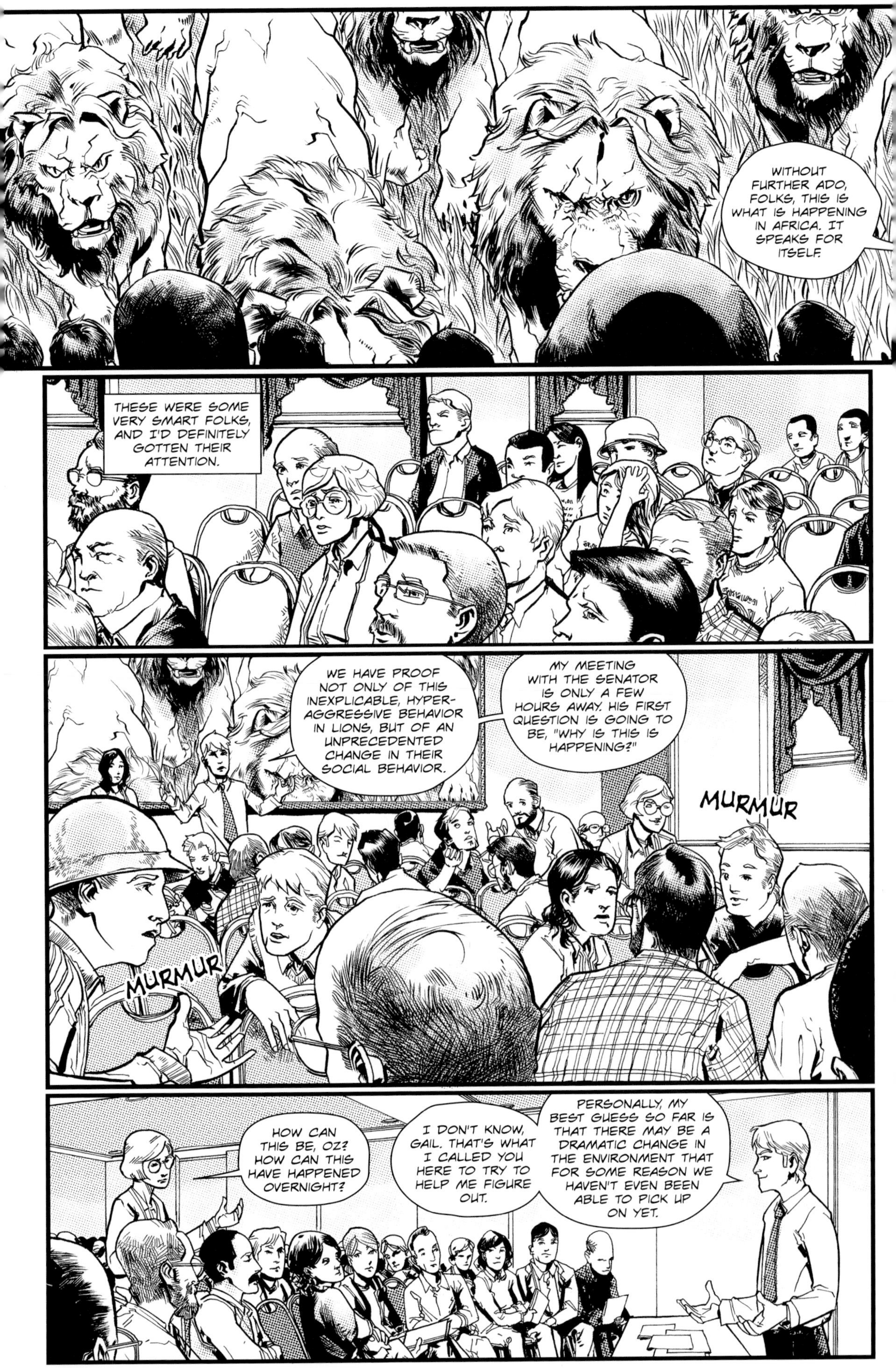
WITHOUT FURTHER ADO, FOLKS, THIS IS WHAT IS HAPPENING IN AFRICA. IT SPEAKS FOR ITSELF.
THESE WERE SOME VERY SMART FOLKS, AND I'D DEFINITELY GOTTEN THEIR ATTENTION.
WE HAVE PROOF NOT ONLY OF THIS INEXPLICABLE, HYPER-AGGRESSIVE BEHAVIOR IN LIONS, BUT OF AN UNPRECEDENTED CHANGE IN THEIR SOCIAL BEHAVIOR.
MY MEETING WITH THE SENATOR IS ONLY A FEW HOURS AWAY. HIS FIRST QUESTION IS GOING TO BE, "WHY IS THIS IS HAPPENING?"
MURMUR
MURMUR
HOW CAN THIS BE, OZ? HOW CAN THIS HAVE HAPPENED OVERNIGHT?
I DON'T KNOW, GAIL. THAT'S WHAT I CALLED YOU HERE TO TRY TO HELP ME FIGURE OUT.
PERSONALLY, MY BEST GUESS SO FAR IS THAT THERE MAY BE A DRAMATIC CHANGE IN THE ENVIRONMENT THAT FOR SOME REASON WE HAVEN'T EVEN BEEN ABLE TO PICK UP ON YET.

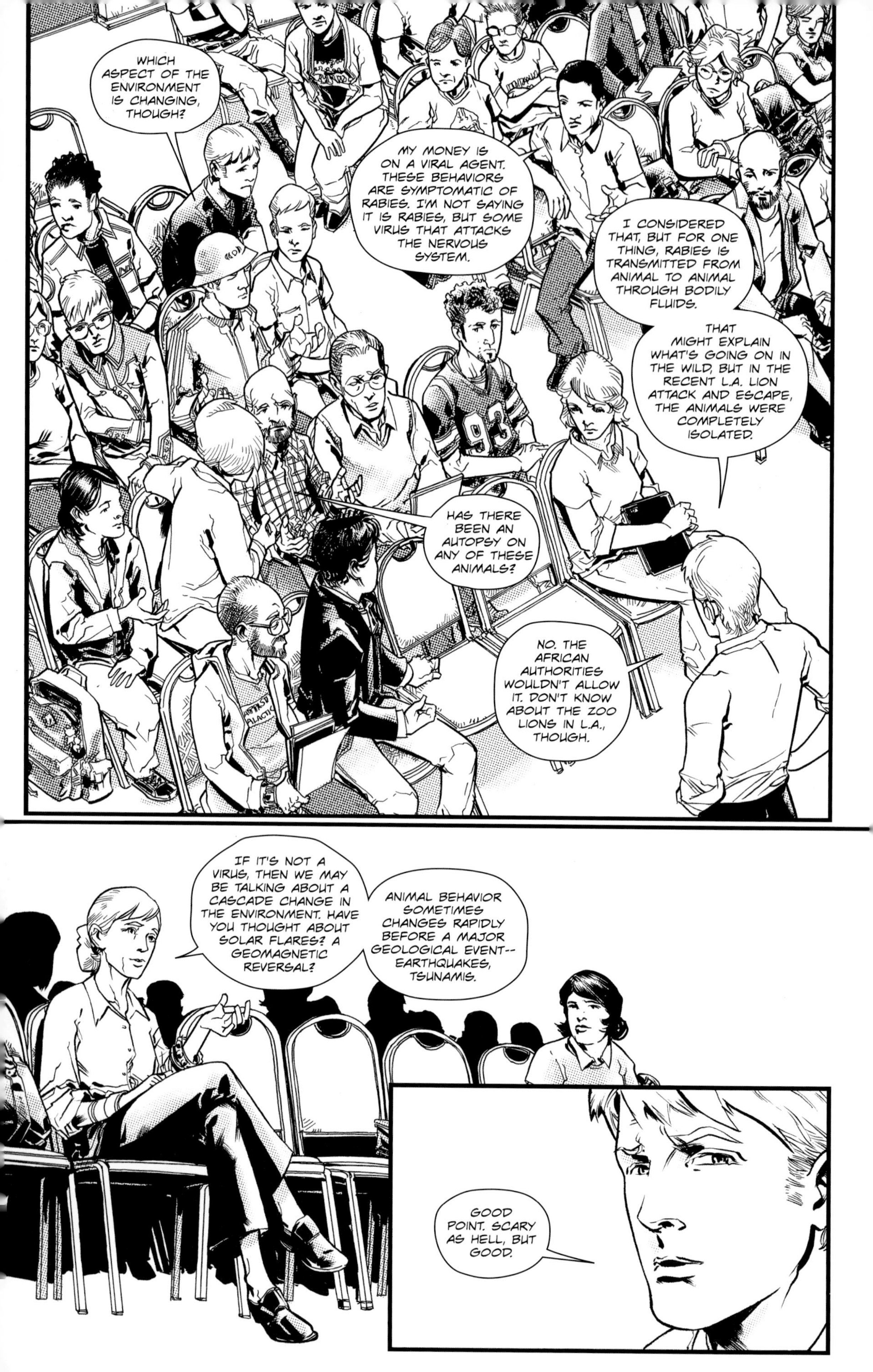
WHICH ASPECT OF THE ENVIRONMENT IS CHANGING, THOUGH?
MY MONEY IS ON A VIRAL AGENT. THESE BEHAVIORS ARE SYMPTOMATIC OF RABIES. I'M NOT SAYING IT IS RABIES, BUT SOME VIRUS THAT ATTACKS THE NERVOUS SYSTEM.
I CONSIDERED THAT, BUT FOR ONE THING, RABIES IS TRANSMITTED FROM ANIMAL TO ANIMAL THROUGH BODILY FLUIDS.
THAT MIGHT EXPLAIN WHAT'S GOING ON IN THE WILD, BUT IN THE RECENT L.A. LION ATTACK AND ESCAPE, THE ANIMALS WERE COMPLETELY ISOLATED.
HAS THERE BEEN AN AUTOPSY ON ANY OF THESE ANIMALS?
NO. THE AFRICAN AUTHORITIES WOULDN'T ALLOW IT. DON'T KNOW ABOUT THE ZOO LIONS IN L.A., THOUGH.
IF IT'S NOT A VIRUS, THEN WE MAY BE TALKING ABOUT A CASCADE CHANGE IN THE ENVIRONMENT. HAVE YOU THOUGHT ABOUT SOLAR FLARES? A GEOMAGNETIC REVERSAL?
ANIMAL BEHAVIOR SOMETIMES CHANGES RAPIDLY BEFORE A MAJOR GEOLOGICAL EVENT-- EARTHQUAKES, TSUNAMIS.
GOOD POINT. SCARY AS HELL, BUT GOOD.

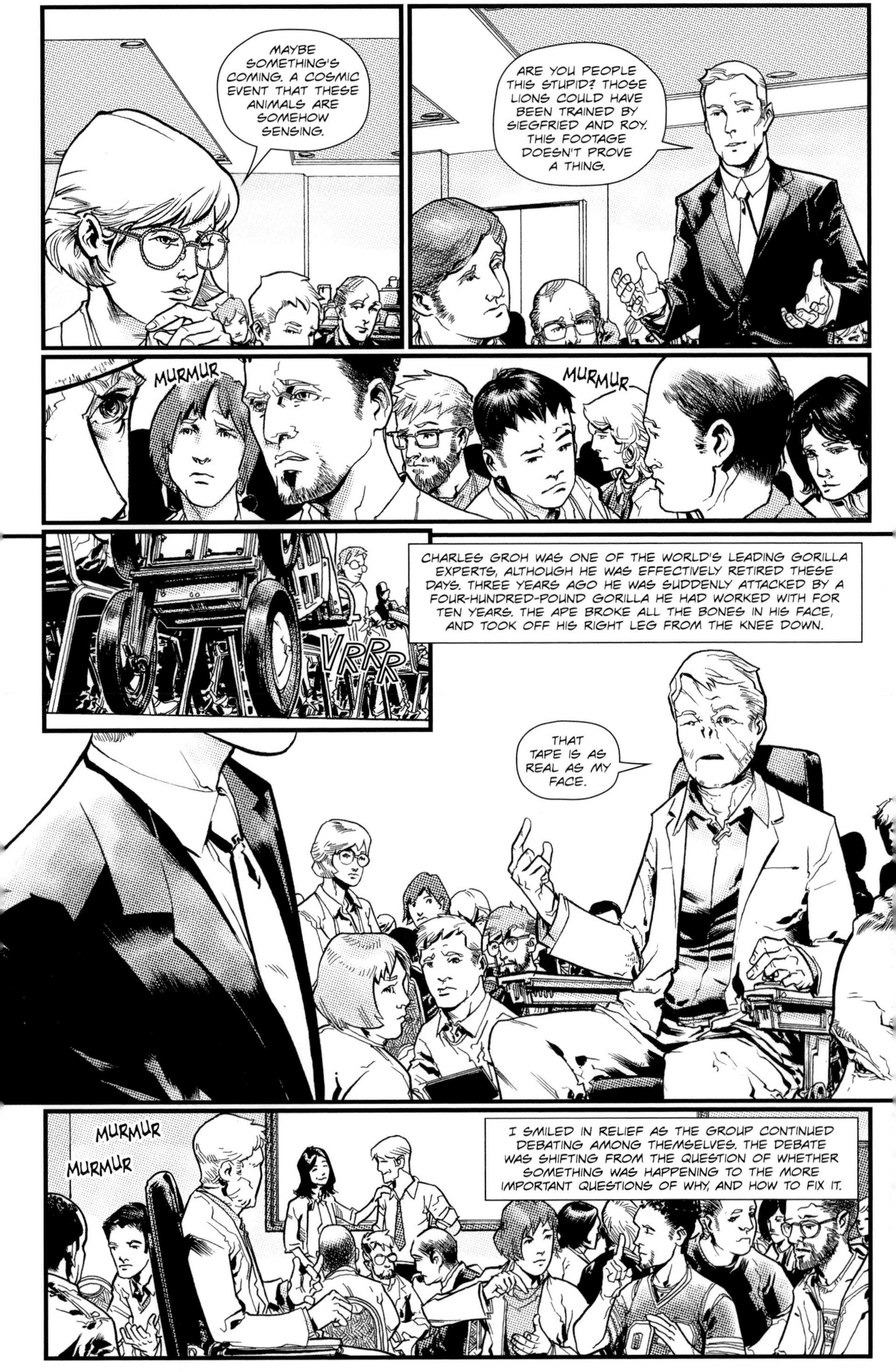
MAYBE SOMETHING'S COMING. A COSMIC EVENT THAT THESE ANIMALS ARE SOMEHOW SENSING.
ARE YOU PEOPLE THIS STUPID? THOSE LIONS COULD HAVE BEEN TRAINED BY SIEGFRIED AND ROY. THIS FOOTAGE DOESN'T PROVE A THING.
MURMUR
MURMUR
VRRR
CHARLES GROH WAS ONE OF THE WORLD'S LEADING GORILLA EXPERTS, ALTHOUGH HE WAS EFFECTIVELY RETIRED THESE DAYS. THREE YEARS AGO HE WAS SUDDENLY ATTACKED BY A FOUR-HUNDRED-POUND GORILLA HE HAD WORKED WITH FOR TEN YEARS. THE APE BROKE ALL THE BONES IN HIS FACE, AND TOOK OFF HIS RIGHT LEG FROM THE KNEE DOWN.
THAT TAPE IS AS REAL AS MY FACE.
MURMUR
MURMUR
I SMILED IN RELIEF AS THE GROUP CONTINUED DEBATING AMONG THEMSELVES. THE DEBATE WAS SHIFTING FROM THE QUESTION OF WHETHER SOMETHING WAS HAPPENING TO THE MORE IMPORTANT QUESTIONS OF WHY, AND HOW TO FIX IT.

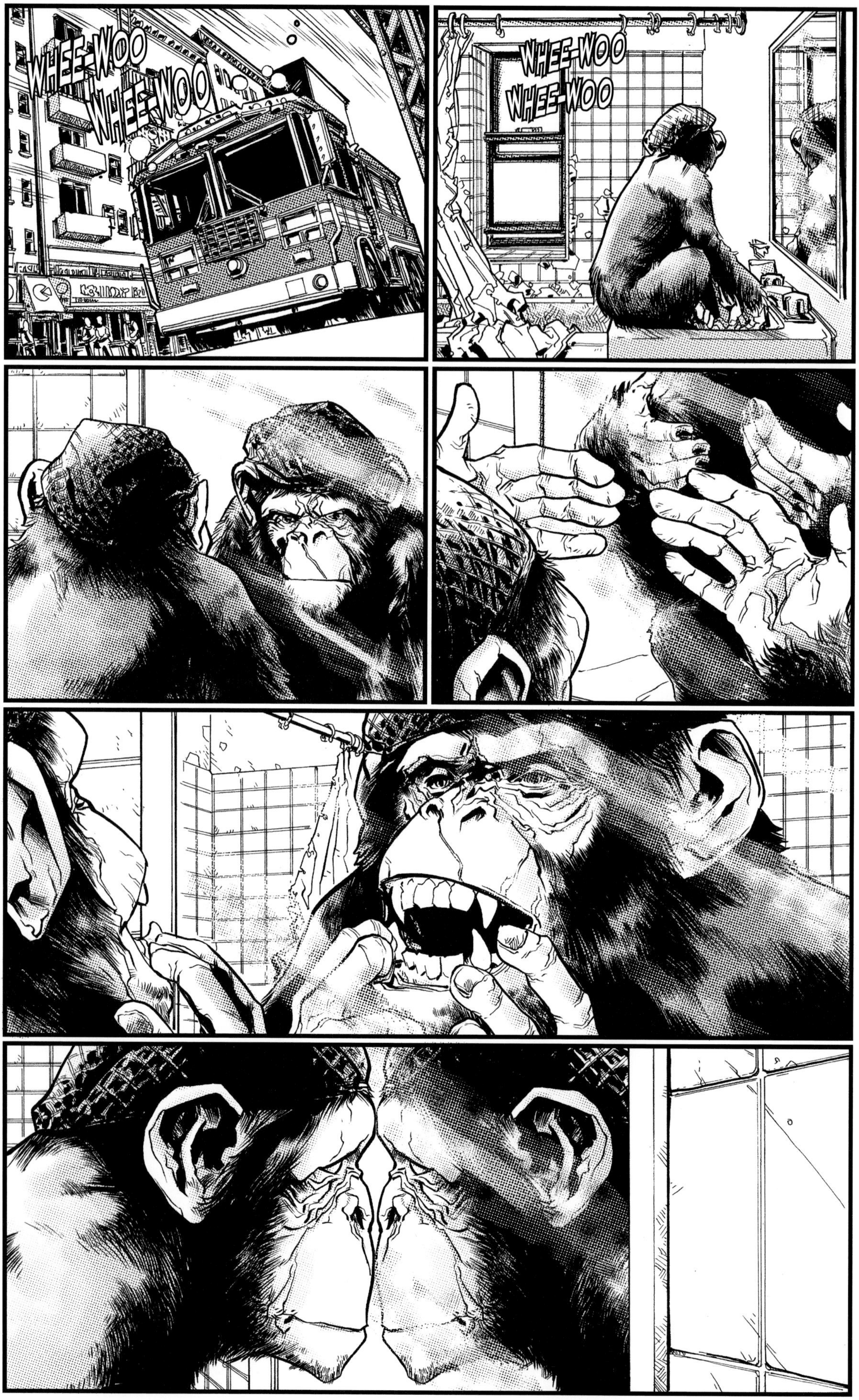
WHEE-WOO
WHEE-WOO
WHEE-WOO
WHEE-WOO

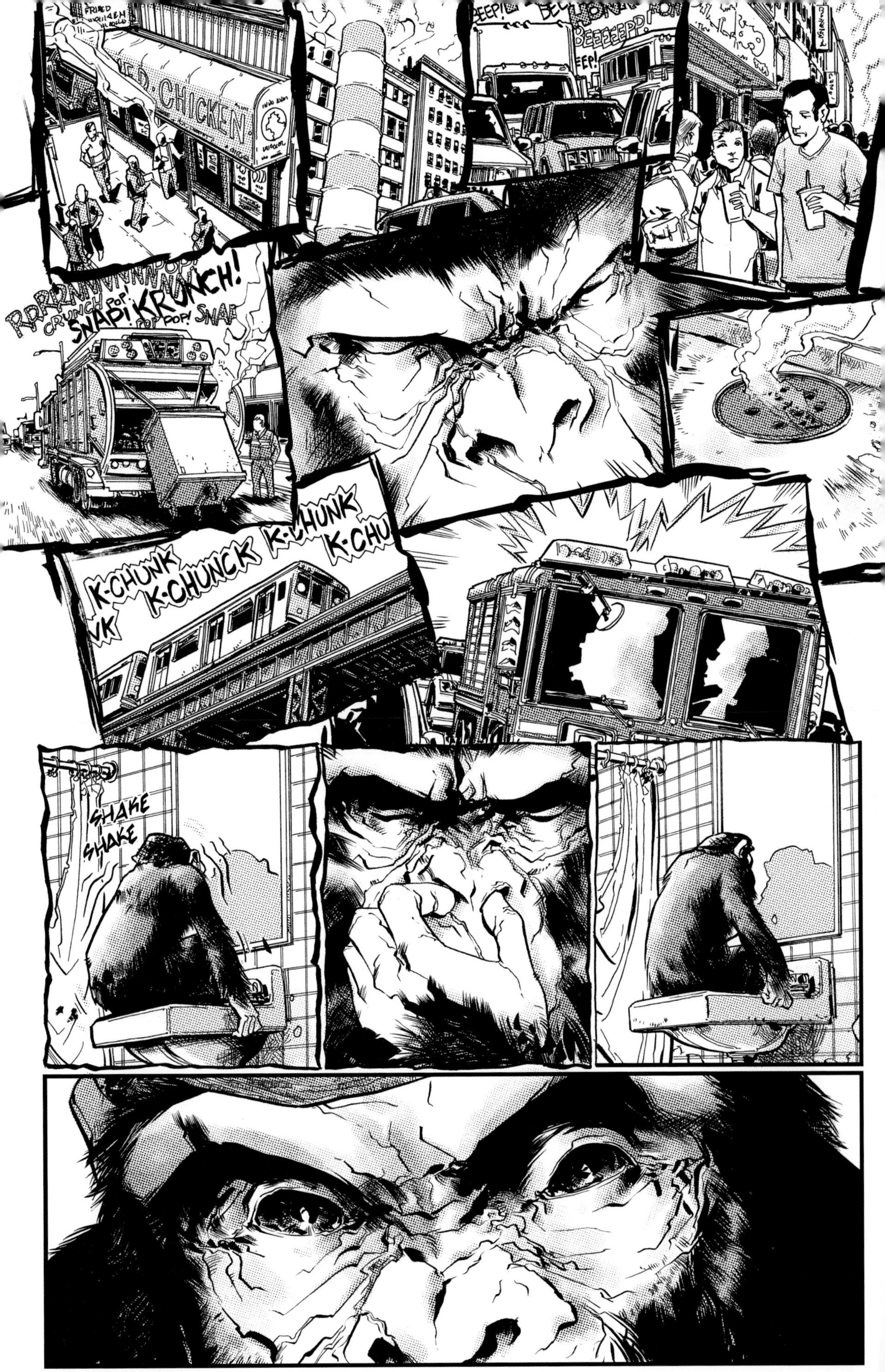
CHICKEN.
BEEP!
BEEEEEPP!
EEP!
RRRRNNNNNNNNPOP!
CRUNCH POP!
SNAP! KRUNCH!
POP POP! SNAP
K-CHUNK
K-CHUNCK
K-CHUNK
K-CHU
VK
SHAKE
SHAKE

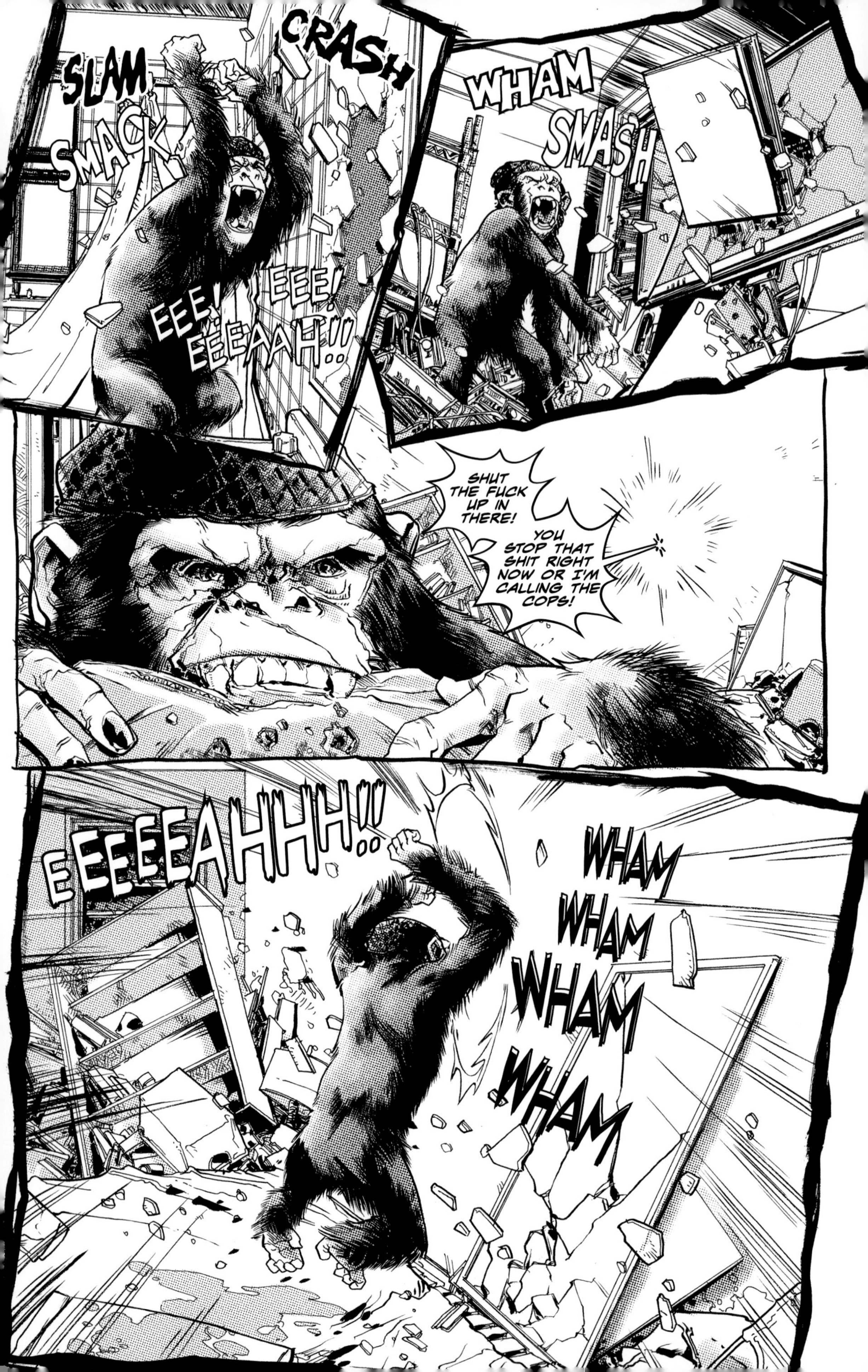
SLAM
CRASH
SMACK
EEE! EEE!
EEEAAH!!
WHAM
SMASH
SHUT THE FUCK UP IN THERE!
YOU STOP THAT SHIT RIGHT NOW OR I'M CALLING THE COPS!
EEEEEAHHH!!
WHAM
WHAM
WHAM
WHAM

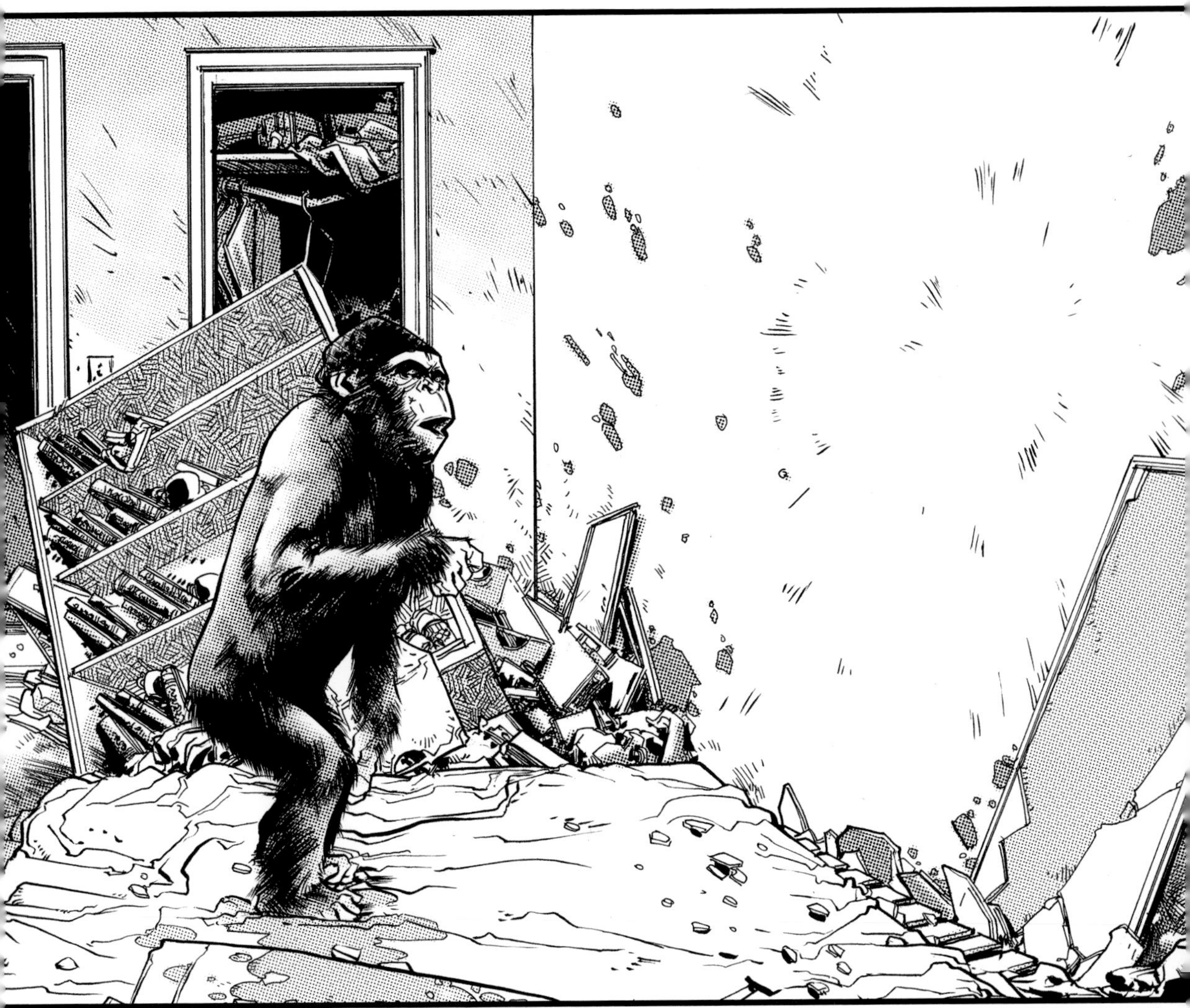

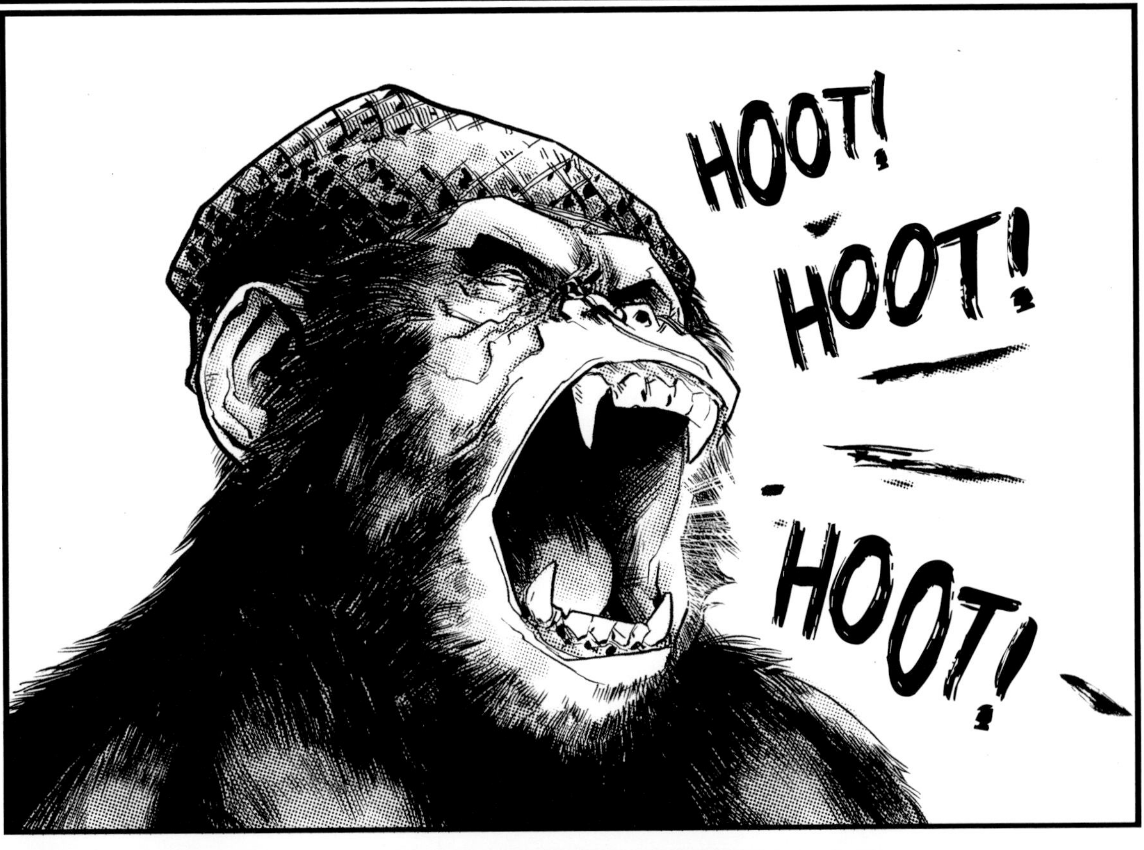
HOOT!
HOOT!
HOOT!

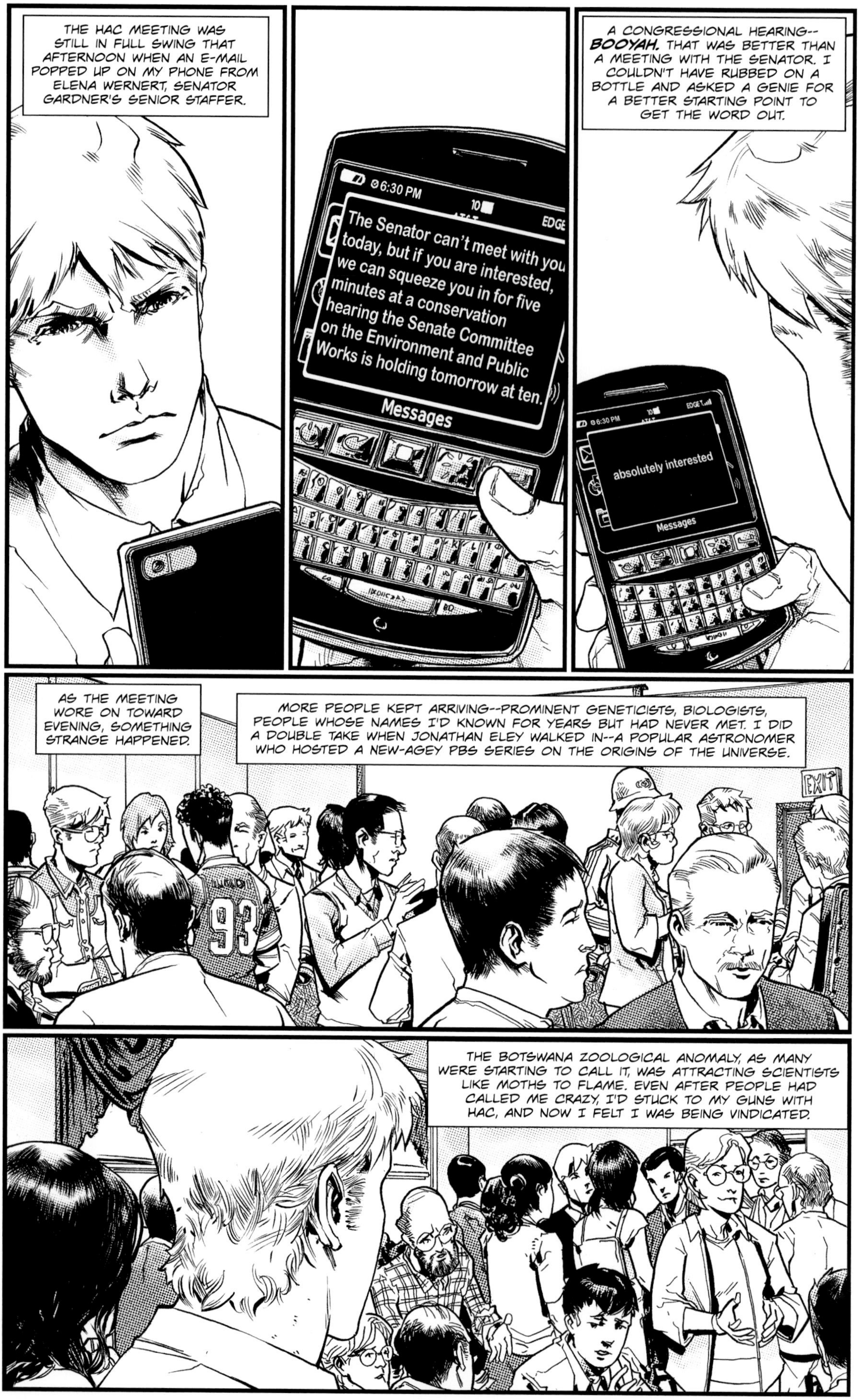
THE HAC MEETING WAS STILL IN FULL SWING THAT AFTERNOON WHEN AN E-MAIL POPPED UP ON MY PHONE FROM ELENA WERNERT, SENATOR GARDNER'S SENIOR STAFFER.
6:30 PM
EDGE
The Senator can't meet with you today, but if you are interested, we can squeeze you in for five minutes at a conservation hearing the Senate Committee on the Environment and Public Works is holding tomorrow at ten.
Messages
A CONGRESSIONAL HEARING-- **BOOYAH.** THAT WAS BETTER THAN A MEETING WITH THE SENATOR. I COULDN'T HAVE RUBBED ON A BOTTLE AND ASKED A GENIE FOR A BETTER STARTING POINT TO GET THE WORD OUT.
6:30 PM
EDGE
absolutely interested
Messages
AS THE MEETING WORE ON TOWARD EVENING, SOMETHING STRANGE HAPPENED.
MORE PEOPLE KEPT ARRIVING--PROMINENT GENETICISTS, BIOLOGISTS, PEOPLE WHOSE NAMES I'D KNOWN FOR YEARS BUT HAD NEVER MET. I DID A DOUBLE TAKE WHEN JONATHAN ELEY WALKED IN--A POPULAR ASTRONOMER WHO HOSTED A NEW-AGEY PBS SERIES ON THE ORIGINS OF THE UNIVERSE.
93
EXIT
THE BOTSWANA ZOOLOGICAL ANOMALY, AS MANY WERE STARTING TO CALL IT, WAS ATTRACTING SCIENTISTS LIKE MOTHS TO FLAME. EVEN AFTER PEOPLE HAD CALLED ME CRAZY, I'D STUCK TO MY GUNS WITH HAC, AND NOW I FELT I WAS BEING VINDICATED.

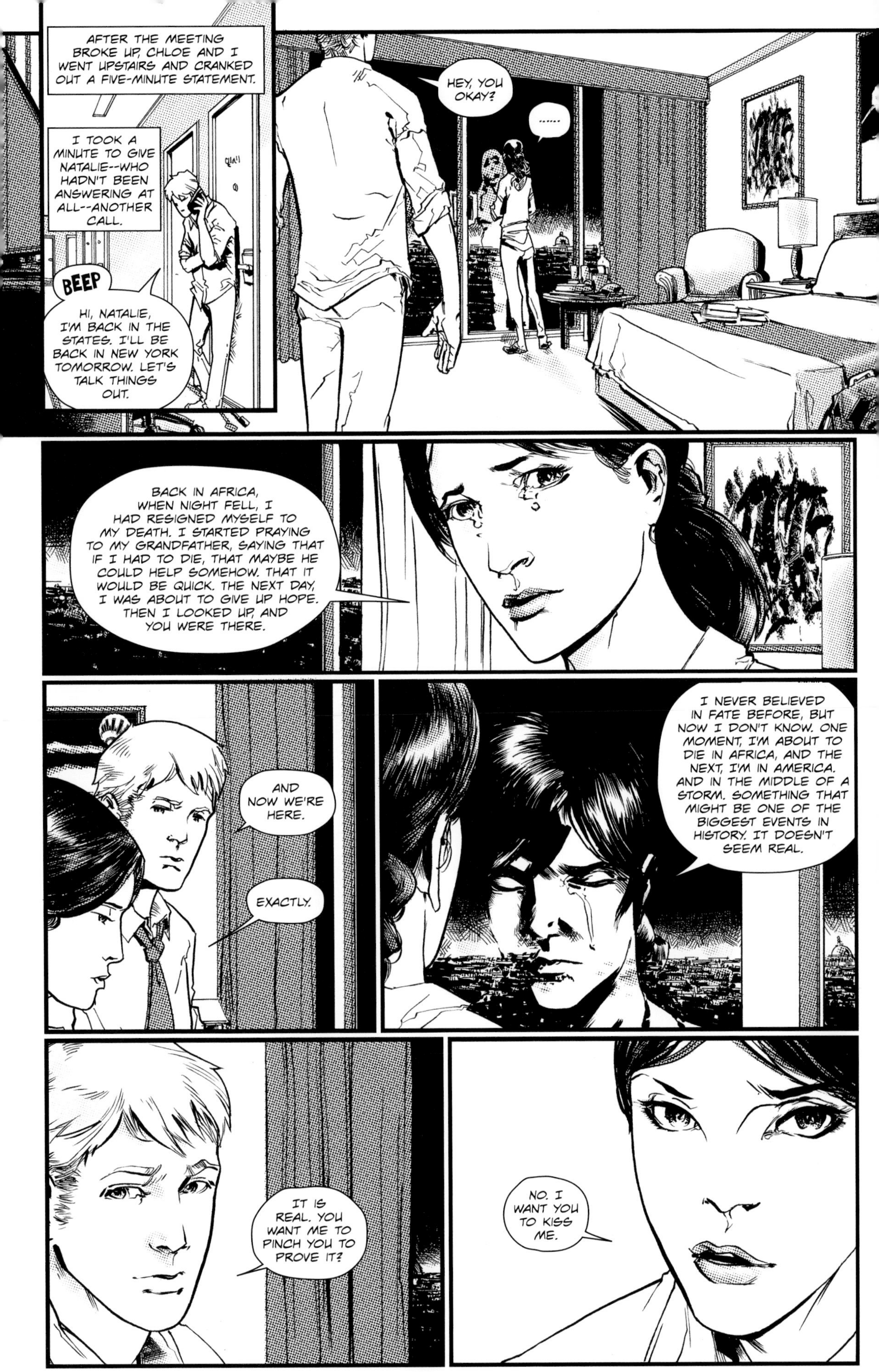
AFTER THE MEETING BROKE UP, CHLOE AND I WENT UPSTAIRS AND CRANKED OUT A FIVE-MINUTE STATEMENT.
I TOOK A MINUTE TO GIVE NATALIE--WHO HADN'T BEEN ANSWERING AT ALL--ANOTHER CALL.
BEEP
HI, NATALIE, I'M BACK IN THE STATES. I'LL BE BACK IN NEW YORK TOMORROW. LET'S TALK THINGS OUT.
HEY, YOU OKAY?
......
BACK IN AFRICA, WHEN NIGHT FELL, I HAD RESIGNED MYSELF TO MY DEATH. I STARTED PRAYING TO MY GRANDFATHER, SAYING THAT IF I HAD TO DIE, THAT MAYBE HE COULD HELP SOMEHOW. THAT IT WOULD BE QUICK. THE NEXT DAY, I WAS ABOUT TO GIVE UP HOPE. THEN I LOOKED UP, AND YOU WERE THERE.
AND NOW WE'RE HERE.
EXACTLY.
I NEVER BELIEVED IN FATE BEFORE, BUT NOW I DON'T KNOW. ONE MOMENT, I'M ABOUT TO DIE IN AFRICA, AND THE NEXT, I'M IN AMERICA. AND IN THE MIDDLE OF A STORM. SOMETHING THAT MIGHT BE ONE OF THE BIGGEST EVENTS IN HISTORY. IT DOESN'T SEEM REAL.
IT IS REAL. YOU WANT ME TO PINCH YOU TO PROVE IT?
NO. I WANT YOU TO KISS ME.

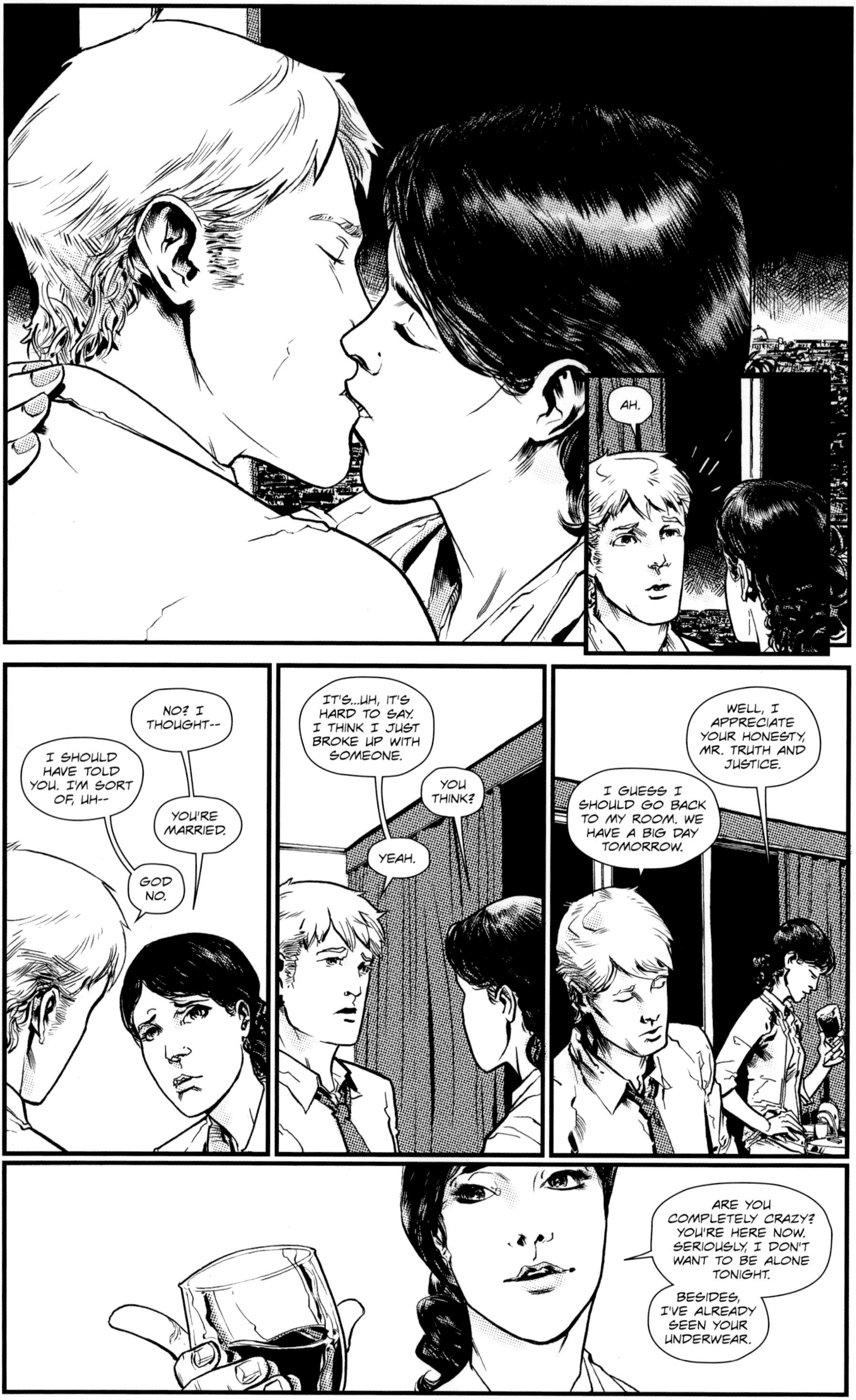
AH.
I SHOULD HAVE TOLD YOU. I'M SORT OF, UH--
NO? I THOUGHT--
YOU'RE MARRIED.
GOD NO.
IT'S...UH, IT'S HARD TO SAY. I THINK I JUST BROKE UP WITH SOMEONE.
YOU THINK?
YEAH.
I GUESS I SHOULD GO BACK TO MY ROOM. WE HAVE A BIG DAY TOMORROW.
WELL, I APPRECIATE YOUR HONESTY, MR. TRUTH AND JUSTICE.
ARE YOU COMPLETELY CRAZY? YOU'RE HERE NOW. SERIOUSLY, I DON'T WANT TO BE ALONE TONIGHT.
BESIDES, I'VE ALREADY SEEN YOUR UNDERWEAR.

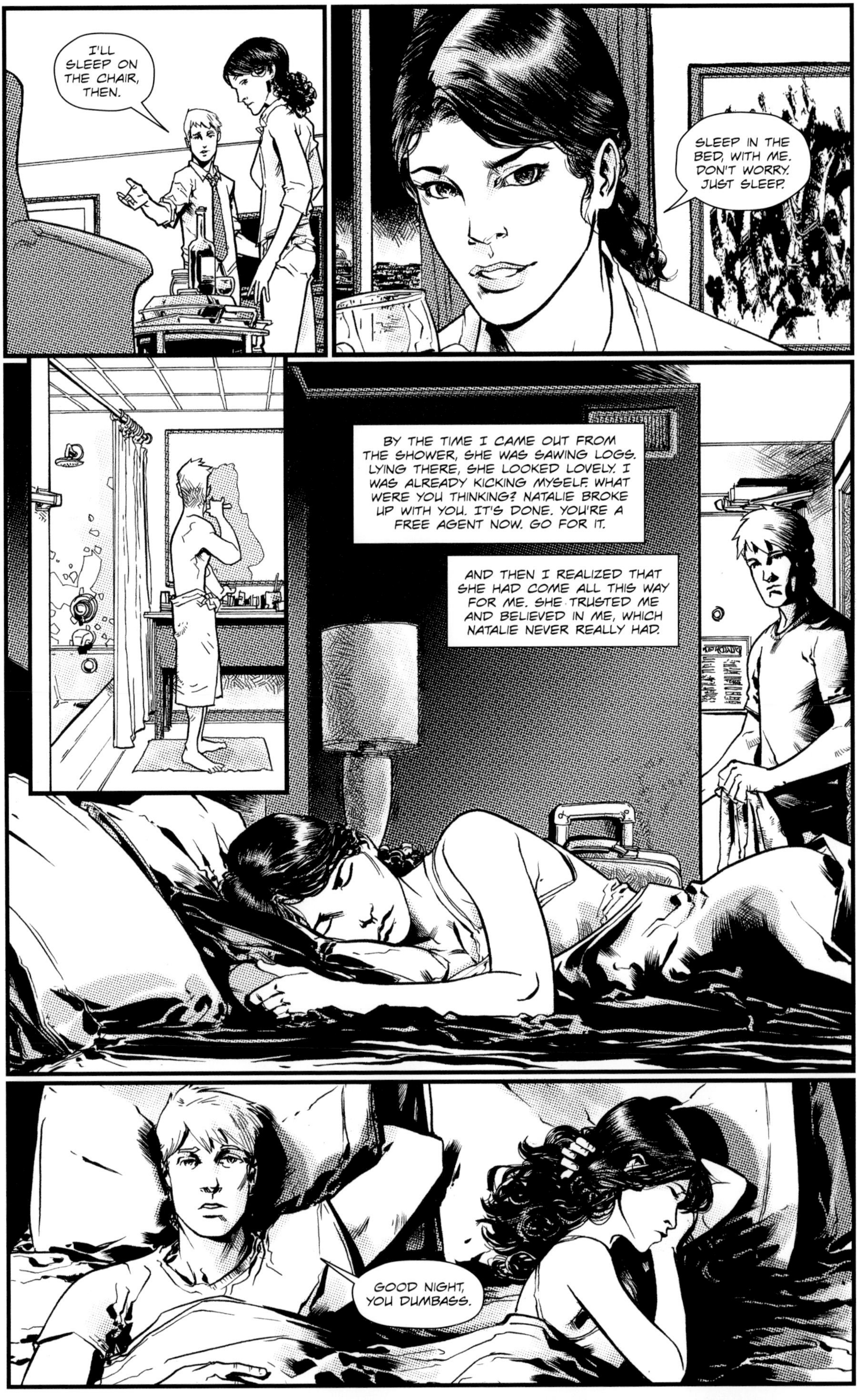
I'LL SLEEP ON THE CHAIR, THEN.
SLEEP IN THE BED, WITH ME. DON'T WORRY. JUST SLEEP.
BY THE TIME I CAME OUT FROM THE SHOWER, SHE WAS SAWING LOGS. LYING THERE, SHE LOOKED LOVELY. I WAS ALREADY KICKING MYSELF. WHAT WERE YOU THINKING? NATALIE BROKE UP WITH YOU. IT'S DONE. YOU'RE A FREE AGENT NOW. GO FOR IT.
AND THEN I REALIZED THAT SHE HAD COME ALL THIS WAY FOR ME. SHE TRUSTED ME AND BELIEVED IN ME, WHICH NATALIE NEVER REALLY HAD.
GOOD NIGHT, YOU DUMBASS.

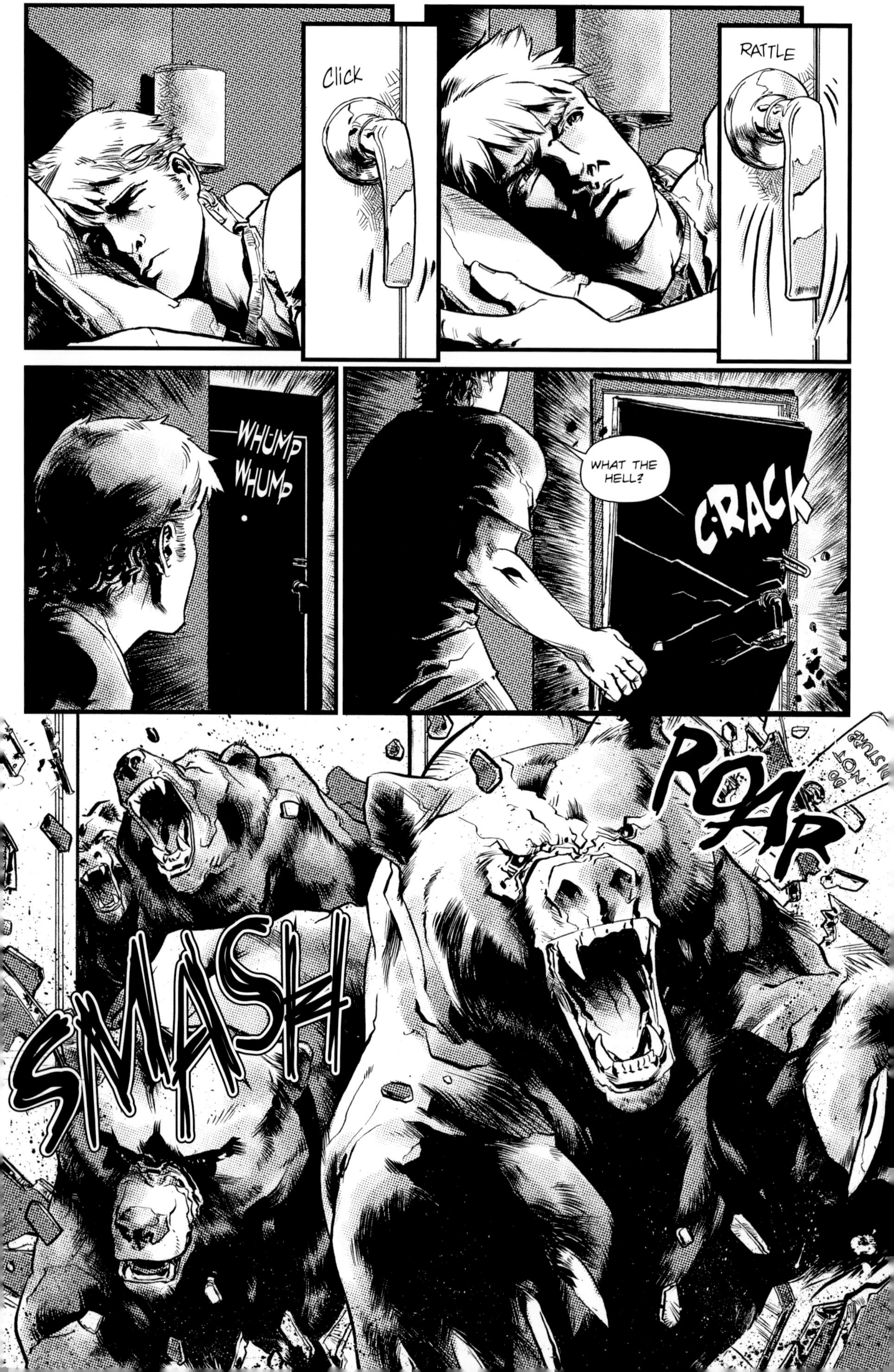
CLICK
RATTLE
WHUMP
WHUMP
WHAT THE HELL?
CRACK
ROAR
SMASH

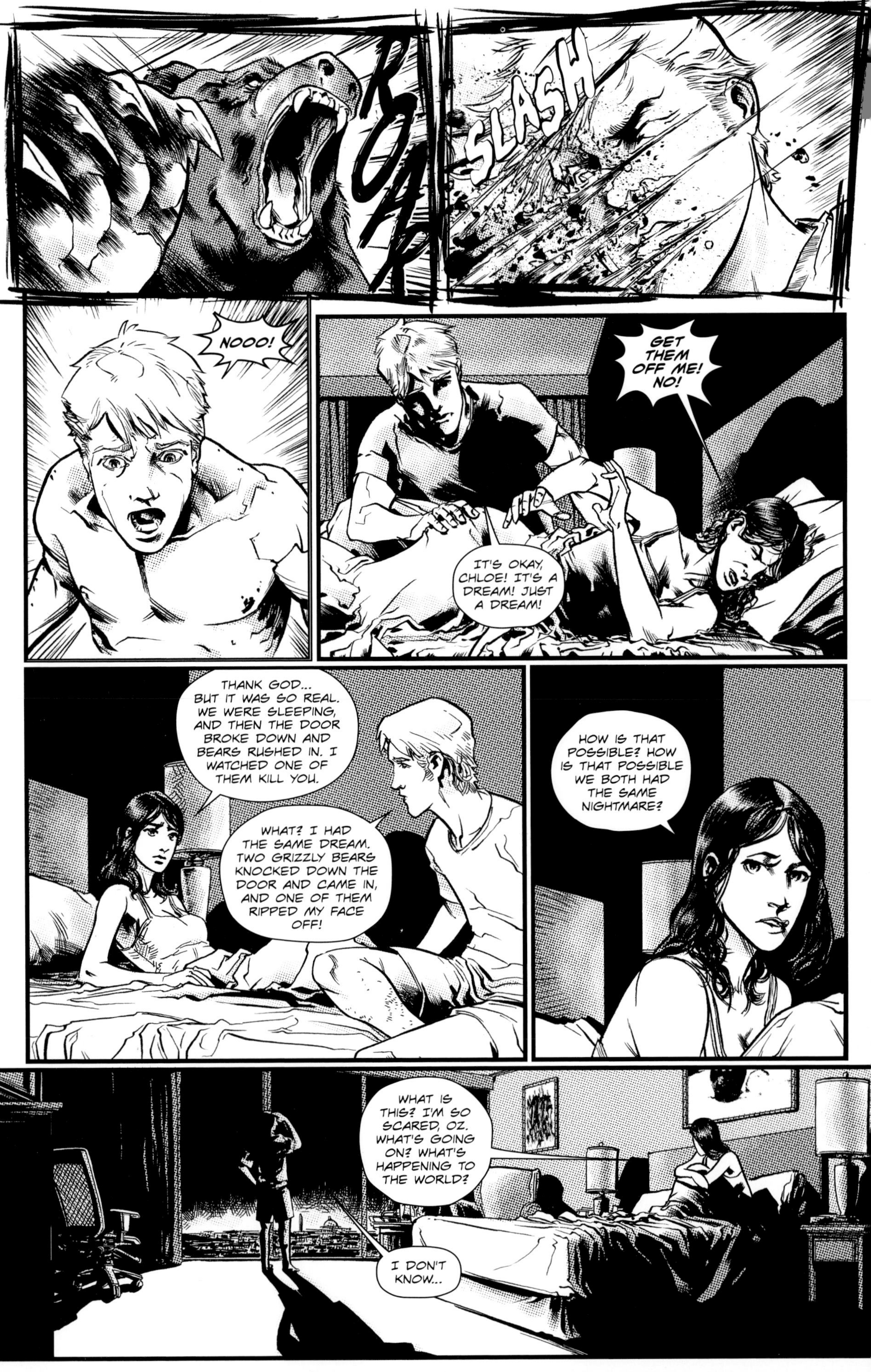
ROAR
SLASH
NOOO!
GET THEM OFF ME! NO!
IT'S OKAY, CHLOE! IT'S A DREAM! JUST A DREAM!
THANK GOD... BUT IT WAS SO REAL. WE WERE SLEEPING, AND THEN THE DOOR BROKE DOWN AND BEARS RUSHED IN. I WATCHED ONE OF THEM KILL YOU.
WHAT? I HAD THE SAME DREAM. TWO GRIZZLY BEARS KNOCKED DOWN THE DOOR AND CAME IN, AND ONE OF THEM RIPPED MY FACE OFF!
HOW IS THAT POSSIBLE? HOW IS THAT POSSIBLE WE BOTH HAD THE SAME NIGHTMARE?
WHAT IS THIS? I'M SO SCARED, OZ. WHAT'S GOING ON? WHAT'S HAPPENING TO THE WORLD?
I DON'T KNOW...

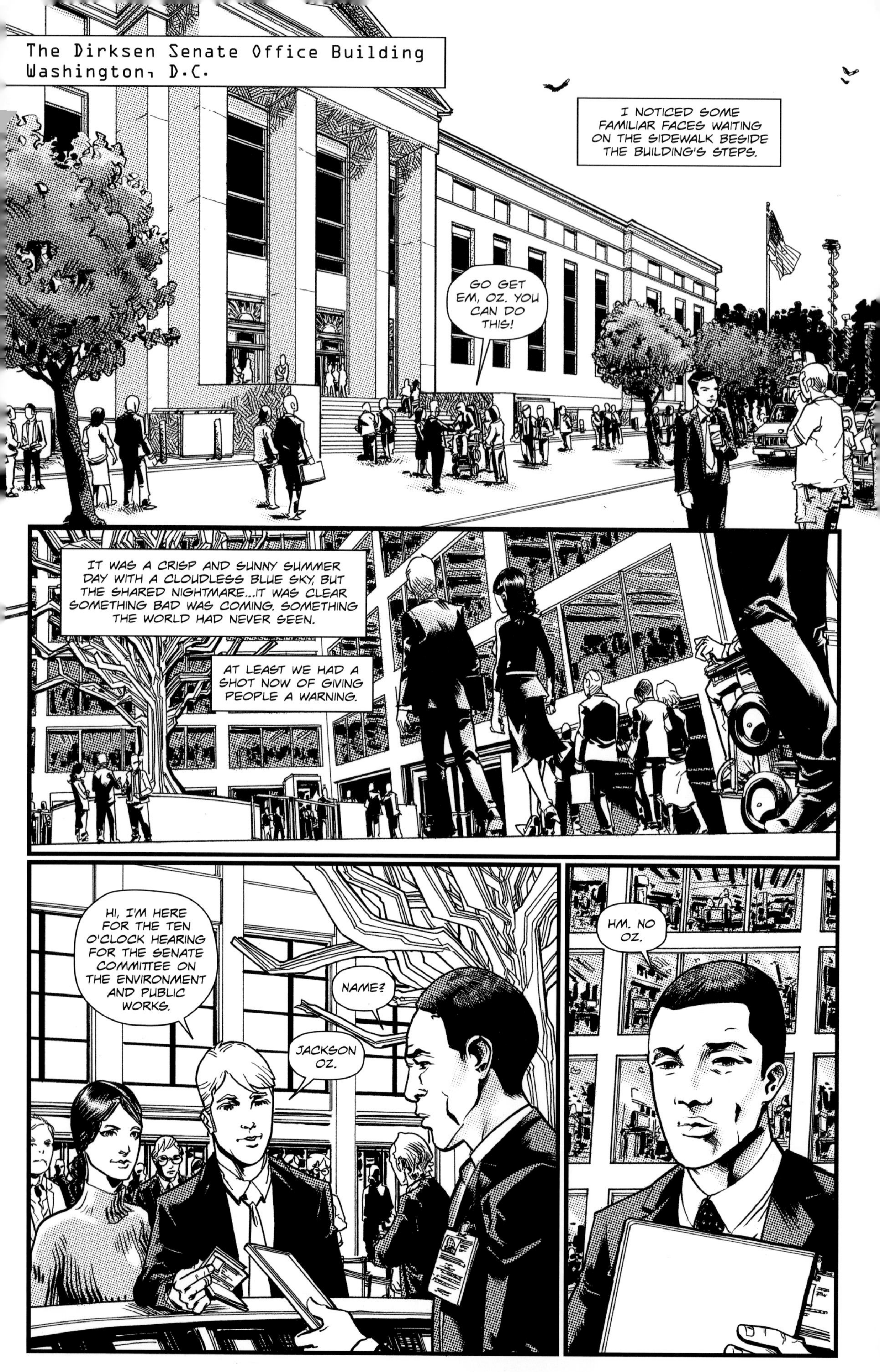
The Dirksen Senate Office Building
Washington, D.C.
I NOTICED SOME FAMILIAR FACES WAITING ON THE SIDEWALK BESIDE THE BUILDING'S STEPS.
GO GET EM, OZ. YOU CAN DO THIS!
IT WAS A CRISP AND SUNNY SUMMER DAY WITH A CLOUDLESS BLUE SKY, BUT THE SHARED NIGHTMARE...IT WAS CLEAR SOMETHING BAD WAS COMING. SOMETHING THE WORLD HAD NEVER SEEN.
AT LEAST WE HAD A SHOT NOW OF GIVING PEOPLE A WARNING.
HI, I'M HERE FOR THE TEN O'CLOCK HEARING FOR THE SENATE COMMITTEE ON THE ENVIRONMENT AND PUBLIC WORKS.
NAME?
JACKSON OZ.
HM. NO OZ.

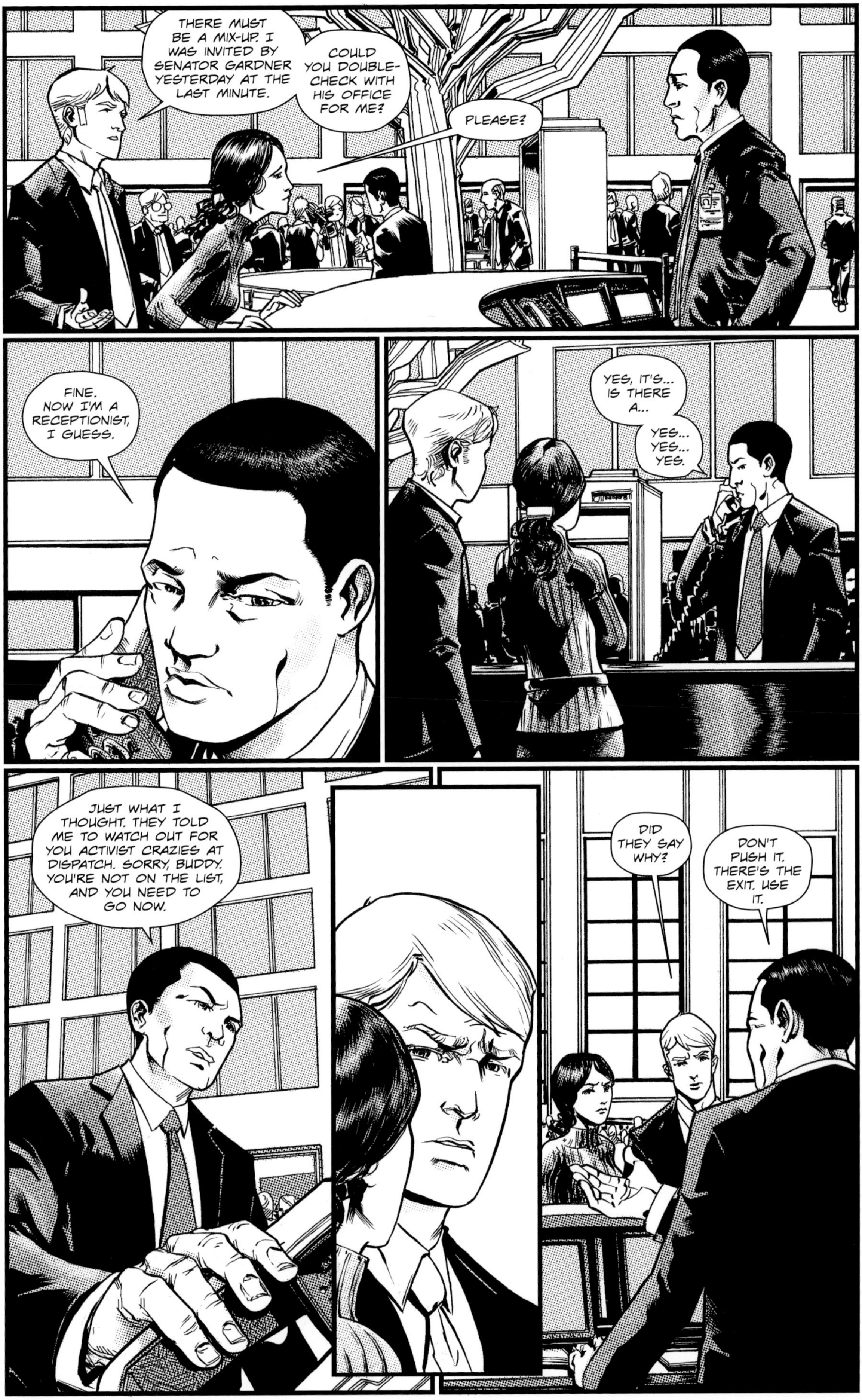
THERE MUST BE A MIX-UP. I WAS INVITED BY SENATOR GARDNER YESTERDAY AT THE LAST MINUTE.
COULD YOU DOUBLE-CHECK WITH HIS OFFICE FOR ME?
PLEASE?
FINE. NOW I'M A RECEPTIONIST, I GUESS.
YES, IT'S... IS THERE A...
YES... YES... YES.
JUST WHAT I THOUGHT. THEY TOLD ME TO WATCH OUT FOR YOU ACTIVIST CRAZIES AT DISPATCH. SORRY, BUDDY. YOU'RE NOT ON THE LIST, AND YOU NEED TO GO NOW.
DID THEY SAY WHY?
DON'T PUSH IT. THERE'S THE EXIT. USE IT.

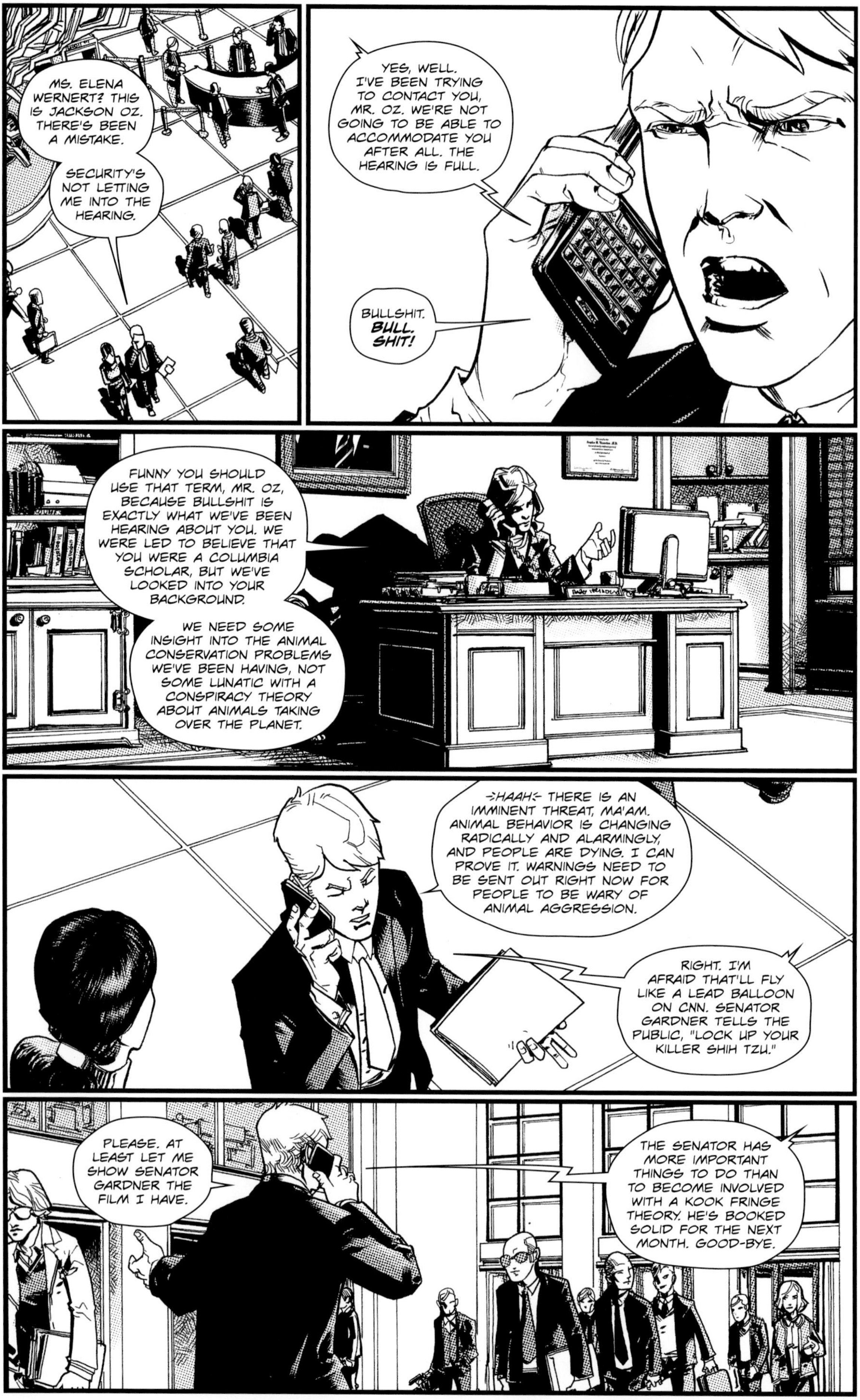
MS. ELENA WERNERT? THIS IS JACKSON OZ. THERE'S BEEN A MISTAKE.
SECURITY'S NOT LETTING ME INTO THE HEARING.
YES, WELL. I'VE BEEN TRYING TO CONTACT YOU, MR. OZ. WE'RE NOT GOING TO BE ABLE TO ACCOMMODATE YOU AFTER ALL. THE HEARING IS FULL.
BULLSHIT. BULL. SHIT!
FUNNY YOU SHOULD USE THAT TERM, MR. OZ, BECAUSE BULLSHIT IS EXACTLY WHAT WE'VE BEEN HEARING ABOUT YOU. WE WERE LED TO BELIEVE THAT YOU WERE A COLUMBIA SCHOLAR, BUT WE'VE LOOKED INTO YOUR BACKGROUND.
WE NEED SOME INSIGHT INTO THE ANIMAL CONSERVATION PROBLEMS WE'VE BEEN HAVING, NOT SOME LUNATIC WITH A CONSPIRACY THEORY ABOUT ANIMALS TAKING OVER THE PLANET.
-HAAH- THERE IS AN IMMINENT THREAT, MA'AM. ANIMAL BEHAVIOR IS CHANGING RADICALLY AND ALARMINGLY, AND PEOPLE ARE DYING. I CAN PROVE IT. WARNINGS NEED TO BE SENT OUT RIGHT NOW FOR PEOPLE TO BE WARY OF ANIMAL AGGRESSION.
RIGHT. I'M AFRAID THAT'LL FLY LIKE A LEAD BALLOON ON CNN. SENATOR GARDNER TELLS THE PUBLIC, "LOCK UP YOUR KILLER SHIH TZU."
PLEASE. AT LEAST LET ME SHOW SENATOR GARDNER THE FILM I HAVE.
THE SENATOR HAS MORE IMPORTANT THINGS TO DO THAN TO BECOME INVOLVED WITH A KOOK FRINGE THEORY. HE'S BOOKED SOLID FOR THE NEXT MONTH. GOOD-BYE.

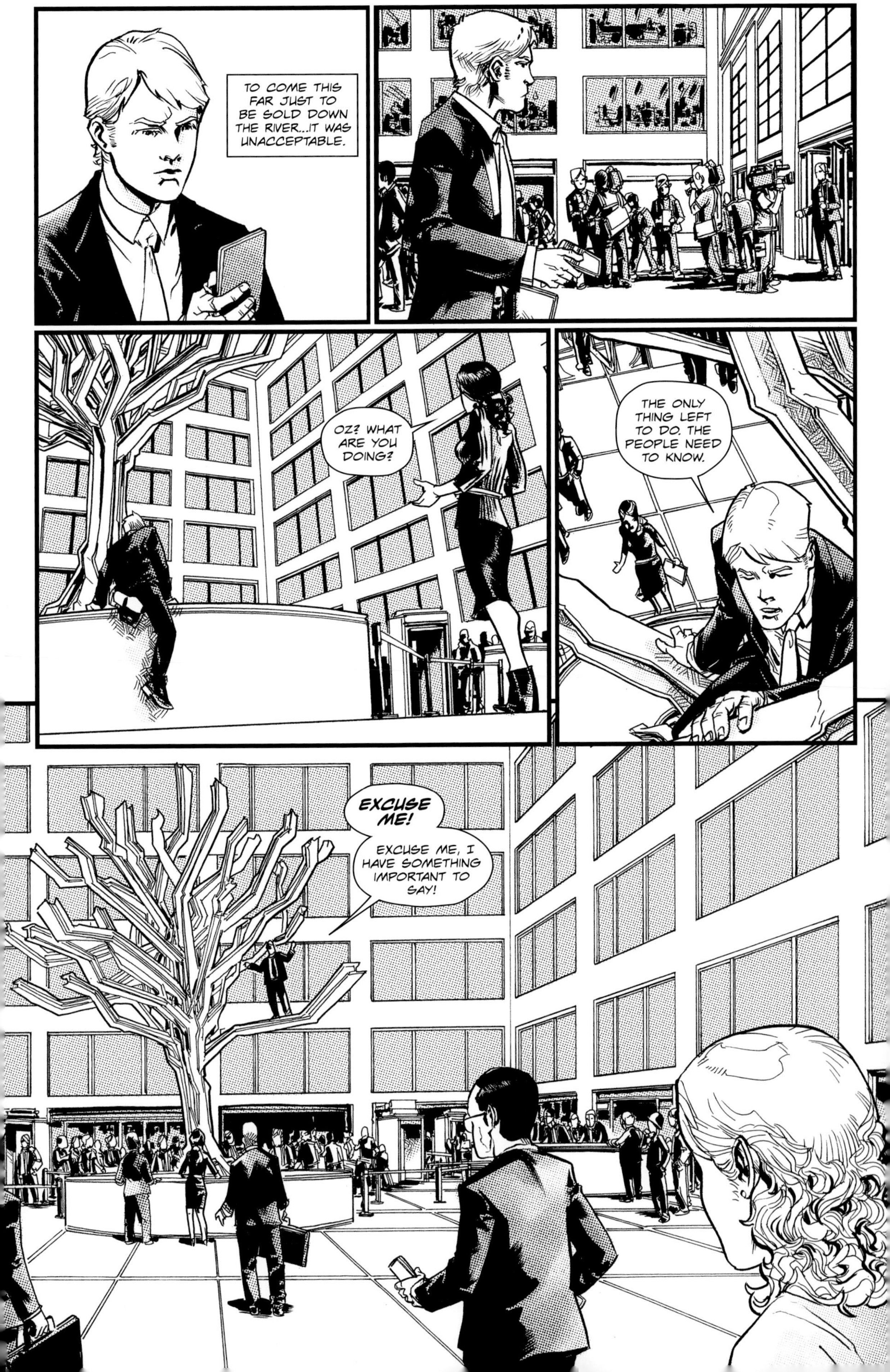

TO COME THIS FAR JUST TO BE SOLD DOWN THE RIVER...IT WAS UNACCEPTABLE.
OZ? WHAT ARE YOU DOING?
THE ONLY THING LEFT TO DO. THE PEOPLE NEED TO KNOW.
EXCUSE ME!
EXCUSE ME, I HAVE SOMETHING IMPORTANT TO SAY!

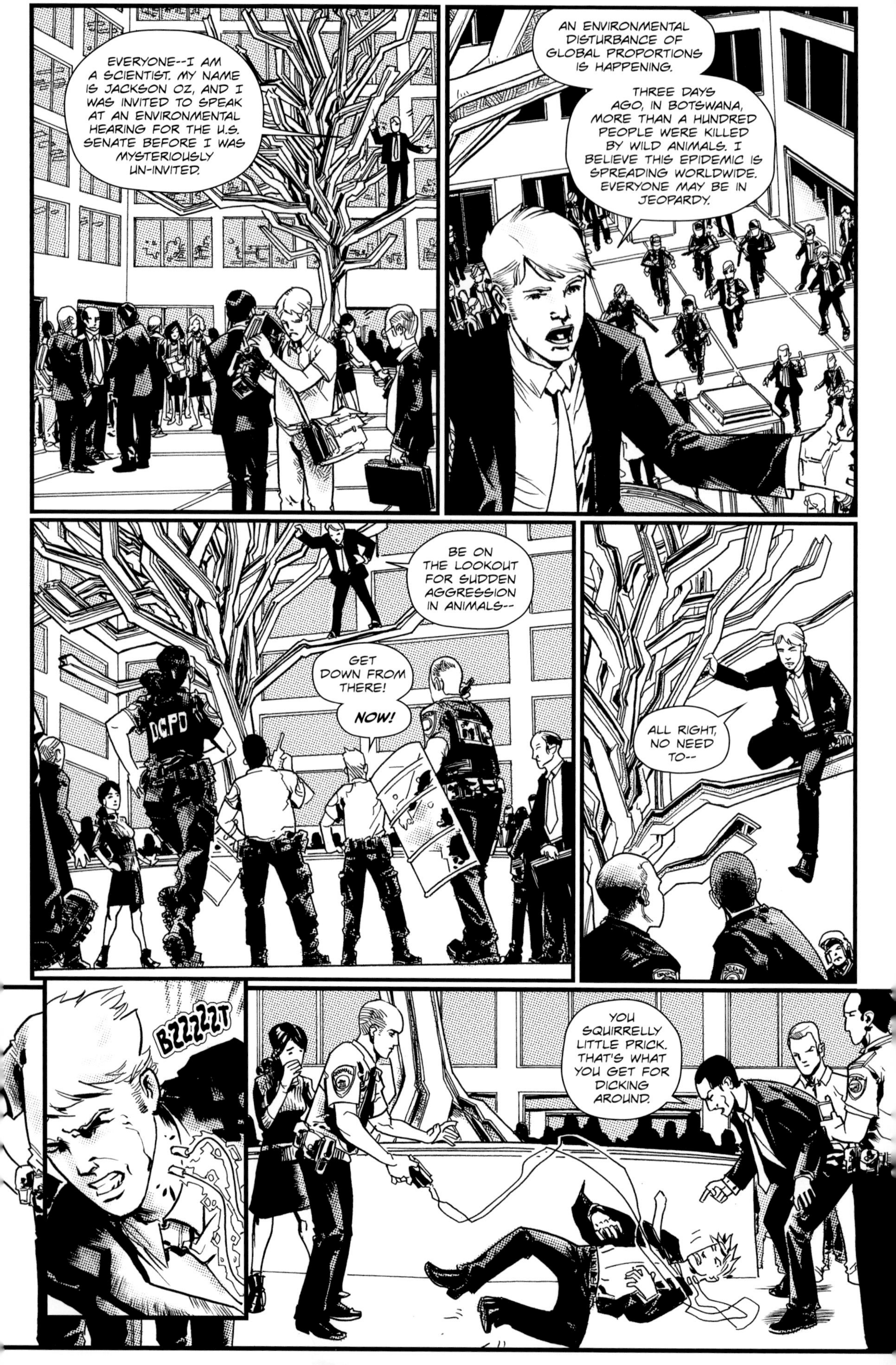
EVERYONE--I AM A SCIENTIST. MY NAME IS JACKSON OZ, AND I WAS INVITED TO SPEAK AT AN ENVIRONMENTAL HEARING FOR THE U.S. SENATE BEFORE I WAS MYSTERIOUSLY UN-INVITED.
AN ENVIRONMENTAL DISTURBANCE OF GLOBAL PROPORTIONS IS HAPPENING.
THREE DAYS AGO, IN BOTSWANA, MORE THAN A HUNDRED PEOPLE WERE KILLED BY WILD ANIMALS. I BELIEVE THIS EPIDEMIC IS SPREADING WORLDWIDE. EVERYONE MAY BE IN JEOPARDY.
BE ON THE LOOKOUT FOR SUDDEN AGGRESSION IN ANIMALS--
GET DOWN FROM THERE!
NOW!
DCPD
ALL RIGHT, NO NEED TO--
BZZZZZZT
YOU SQUIRRELLY LITTLE PRICK. THAT'S WHAT YOU GET FOR DICKING AROUND.

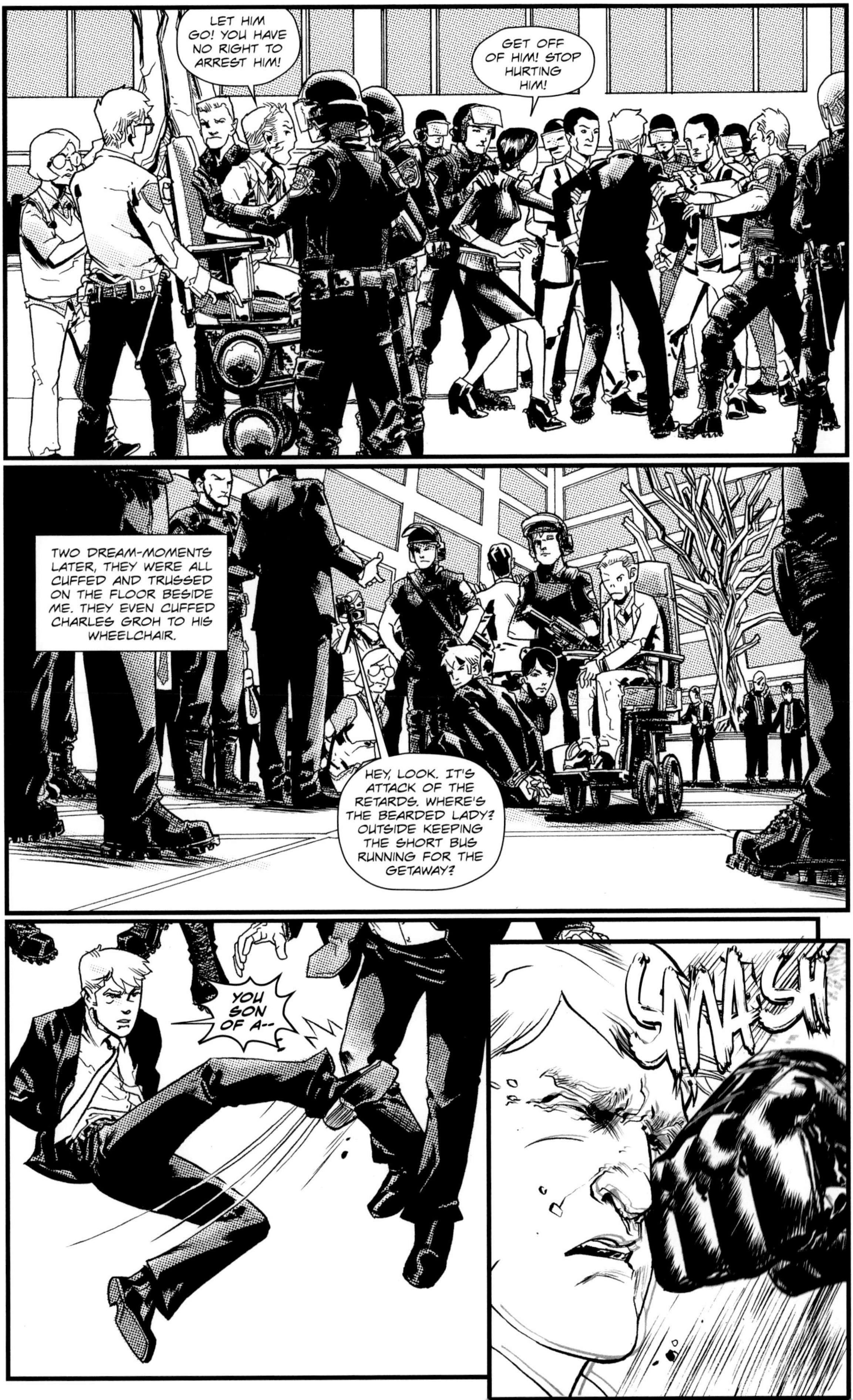

LET HIM GO! YOU HAVE NO RIGHT TO ARREST HIM!
GET OFF OF HIM! STOP HURTING HIM!
TWO DREAM-MOMENTS LATER, THEY WERE ALL CUFFED AND TRUSSED ON THE FLOOR BESIDE ME. THEY EVEN CUFFED CHARLES GROH TO HIS WHEELCHAIR.
HEY, LOOK. IT'S ATTACK OF THE RETARDS. WHERE'S THE BEARDED LADY? OUTSIDE KEEPING THE SHORT BUS RUNNING FOR THE GETAWAY?
YOU SON OF A--
SMASH

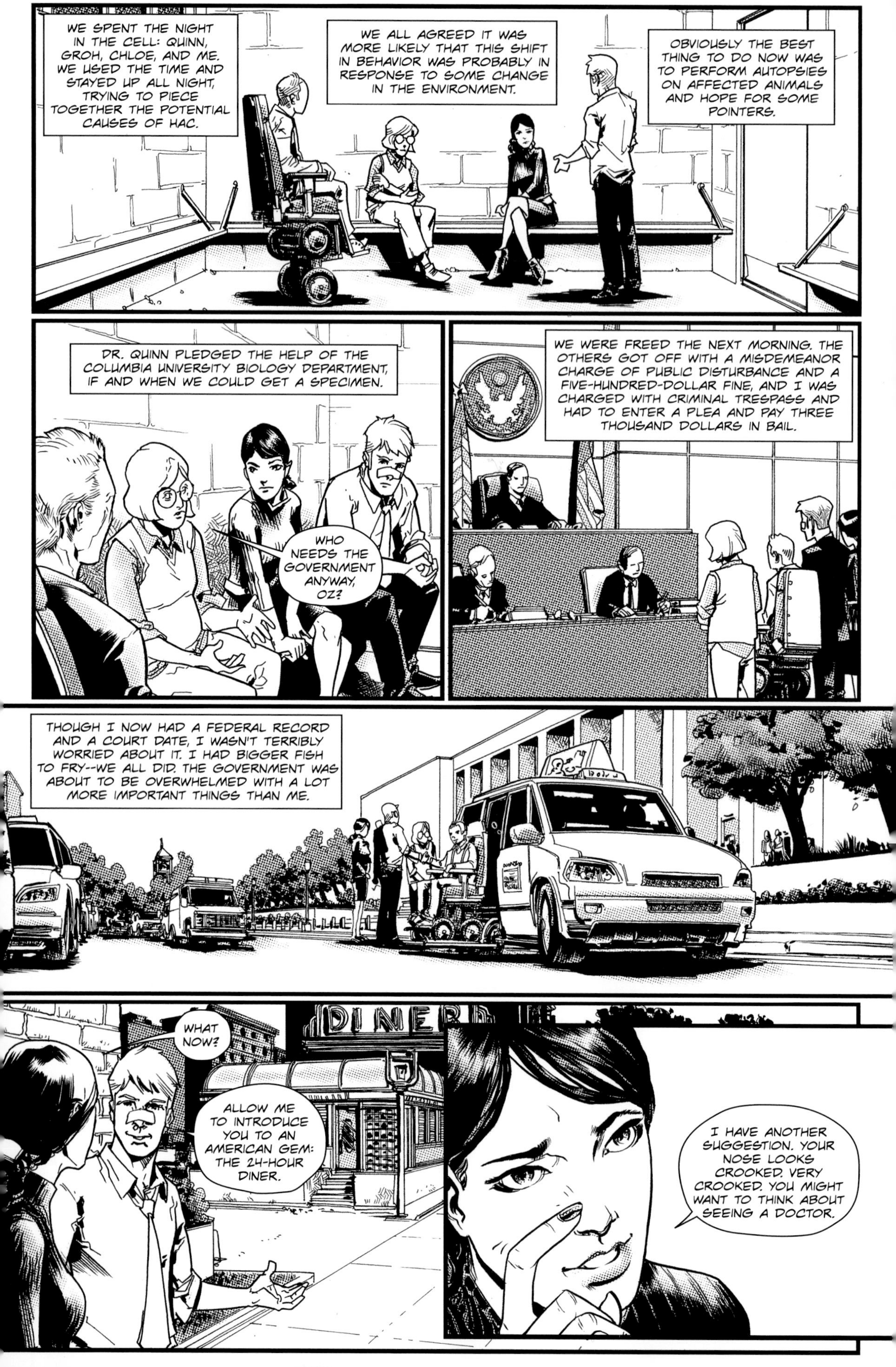
WE SPENT THE NIGHT IN THE CELL: QUINN, GROH, CHLOE, AND ME. WE USED THE TIME AND STAYED UP ALL NIGHT, TRYING TO PIECE TOGETHER THE POTENTIAL CAUSES OF HAC.
WE ALL AGREED IT WAS MORE LIKELY THAT THIS SHIFT IN BEHAVIOR WAS PROBABLY IN RESPONSE TO SOME CHANGE IN THE ENVIRONMENT.
OBVIOUSLY THE BEST THING TO DO NOW WAS TO PERFORM AUTOPSIES ON AFFECTED ANIMALS AND HOPE FOR SOME POINTERS.
DR. QUINN PLEDGED THE HELP OF THE COLUMBIA UNIVERSITY BIOLOGY DEPARTMENT, IF AND WHEN WE COULD GET A SPECIMEN.
WHO NEEDS THE GOVERNMENT ANYWAY, OZ?
WE WERE FREED THE NEXT MORNING. THE OTHERS GOT OFF WITH A MISDEMEANOR CHARGE OF PUBLIC DISTURBANCE AND A FIVE-HUNDRED-DOLLAR FINE, AND I WAS CHARGED WITH CRIMINAL TRESPASS AND HAD TO ENTER A PLEA AND PAY THREE THOUSAND DOLLARS IN BAIL.
THOUGH I NOW HAD A FEDERAL RECORD AND A COURT DATE, I WASN'T TERRIBLY WORRIED ABOUT IT. I HAD BIGGER FISH TO FRY--WE ALL DID. THE GOVERNMENT WAS ABOUT TO BE OVERWHELMED WITH A LOT MORE IMPORTANT THINGS THAN ME.
DINER
WHAT NOW?
ALLOW ME TO INTRODUCE YOU TO AN AMERICAN GEM: THE 24-HOUR DINER.
I HAVE ANOTHER SUGGESTION. YOUR NOSE LOOKS CROOKED. VERY CROOKED. YOU MIGHT WANT TO THINK ABOUT SEEING A DOCTOR.

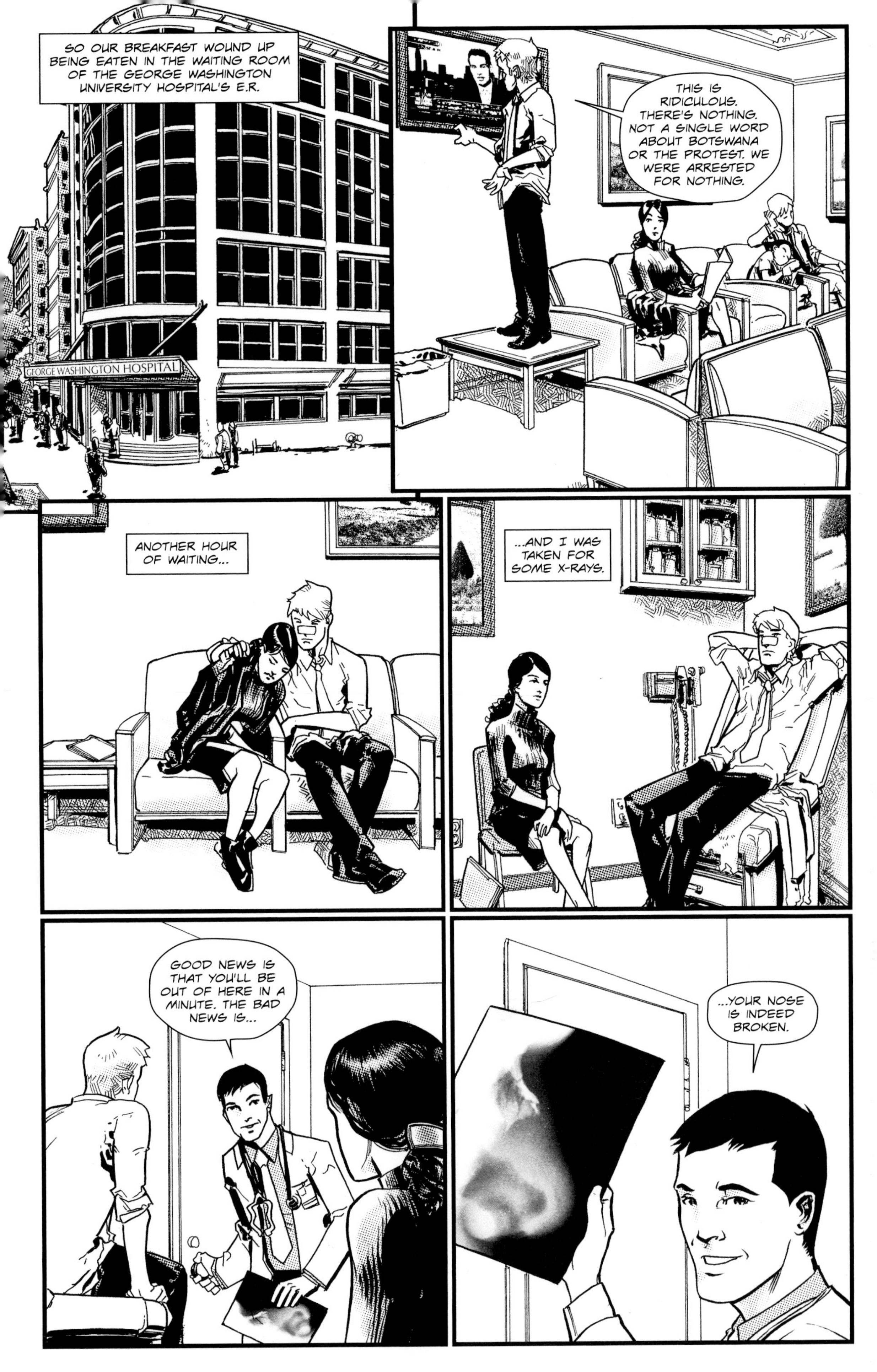
SO OUR BREAKFAST WOUND UP BEING EATEN IN THE WAITING ROOM OF THE GEORGE WASHINGTON UNIVERSITY HOSPITAL'S E.R.
GEORGE WASHINGTON HOSPITAL
THIS IS RIDICULOUS. THERE'S NOTHING. NOT A SINGLE WORD ABOUT BOTSWANA OR THE PROTEST. WE WERE ARRESTED FOR NOTHING.
ANOTHER HOUR OF WAITING...
...AND I WAS TAKEN FOR SOME X-RAYS.
GOOD NEWS IS THAT YOU'LL BE OUT OF HERE IN A MINUTE. THE BAD NEWS IS...
...YOUR NOSE IS INDEED BROKEN.

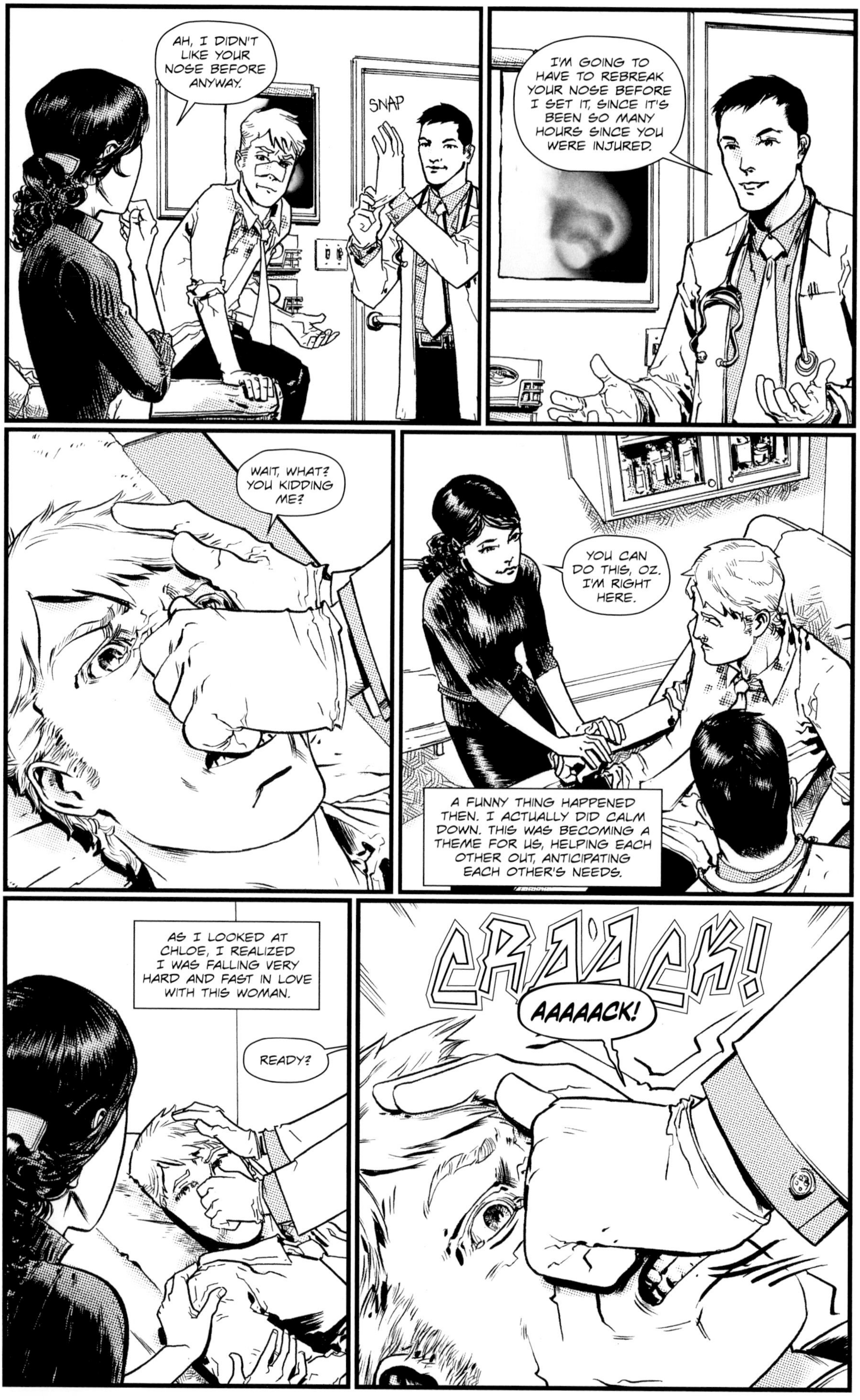
AH, I DIDN'T LIKE YOUR NOSE BEFORE ANYWAY.
SNAP
I'M GOING TO HAVE TO REBREAK YOUR NOSE BEFORE I SET IT, SINCE IT'S BEEN SO MANY HOURS SINCE YOU WERE INJURED.
WAIT, WHAT? YOU KIDDING ME?
YOU CAN DO THIS, OZ. I'M RIGHT HERE.
A FUNNY THING HAPPENED THEN. I ACTUALLY DID CALM DOWN. THIS WAS BECOMING A THEME FOR US, HELPING EACH OTHER OUT, ANTICIPATING EACH OTHER'S NEEDS.
AS I LOOKED AT CHLOE, I REALIZED I WAS FALLING VERY HARD AND FAST IN LOVE WITH THIS WOMAN.
READY?
CRAACK!
AAAAACK!

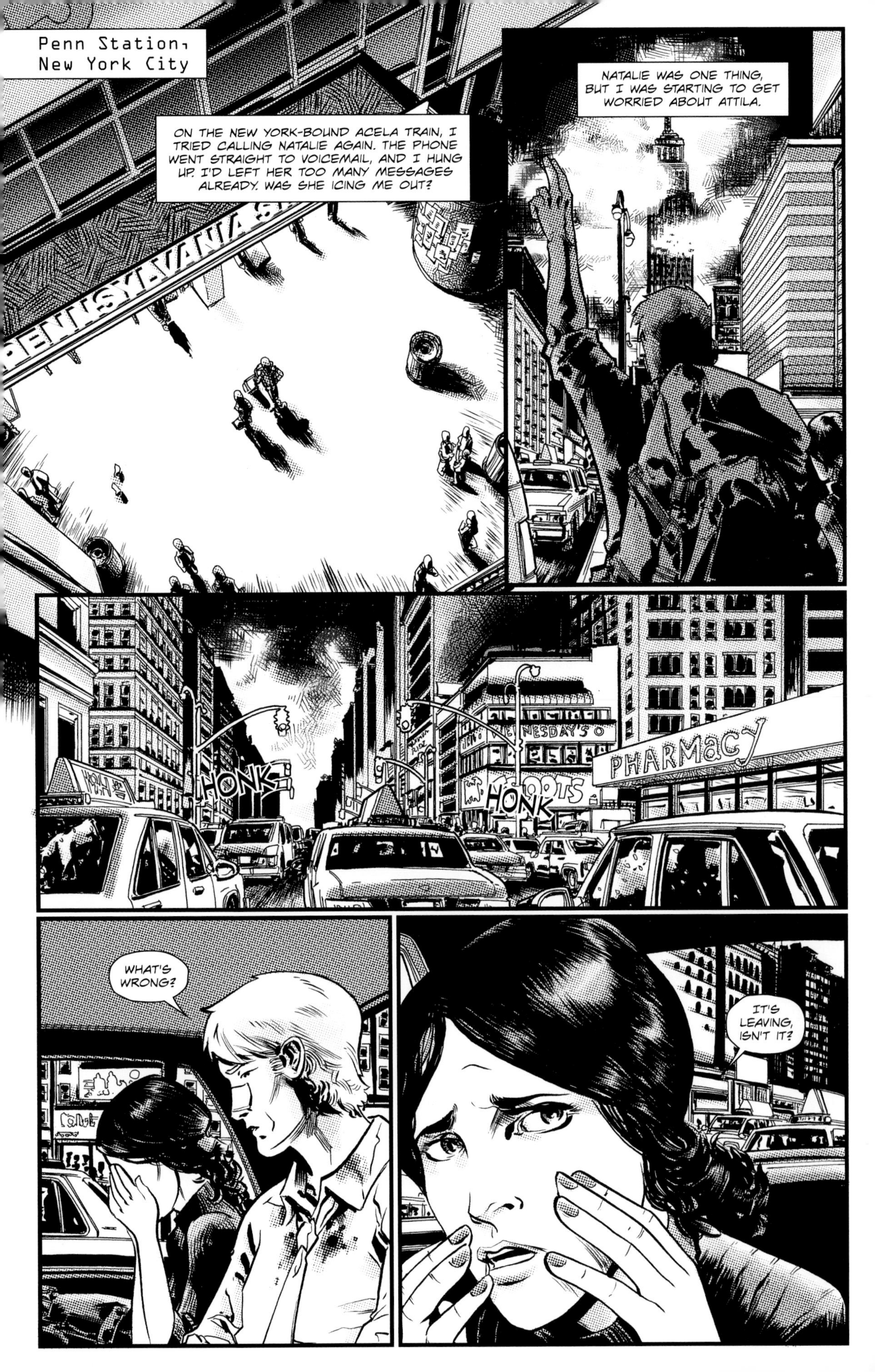
Penn Station, New York City
ON THE NEW YORK-BOUND ACELA TRAIN, I TRIED CALLING NATALIE AGAIN. THE PHONE WENT STRAIGHT TO VOICEMAIL, AND I HUNG UP. I'D LEFT HER TOO MANY MESSAGES ALREADY. WAS SHE ICING ME OUT?
NATALIE WAS ONE THING, BUT I WAS STARTING TO GET WORRIED ABOUT ATTILA.
HONK
HONK
PHARMACY
WHAT'S WRONG?
IT'S LEAVING, ISN'T IT?

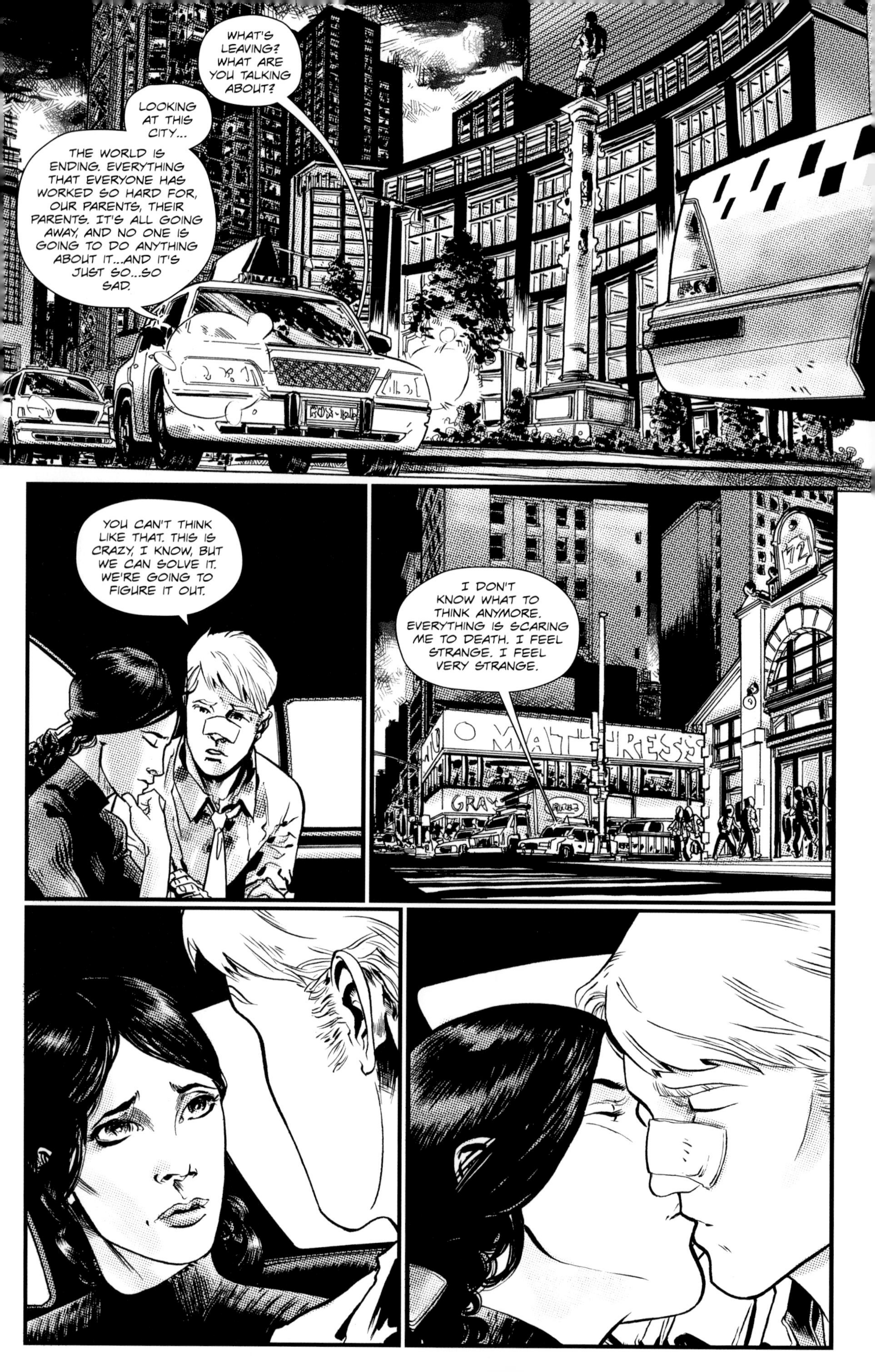
WHAT'S LEAVING? WHAT ARE YOU TALKING ABOUT?
LOOKING AT THIS CITY...
THE WORLD IS ENDING. EVERYTHING THAT EVERYONE HAS WORKED SO HARD FOR, OUR PARENTS, THEIR PARENTS. IT'S ALL GOING AWAY, AND NO ONE IS GOING TO DO ANYTHING ABOUT IT...AND IT'S JUST SO...SO SAD.
YOU CAN'T THINK LIKE THAT. THIS IS CRAZY, I KNOW, BUT WE CAN SOLVE IT. WE'RE GOING TO FIGURE IT OUT.
I DON'T KNOW WHAT TO THINK ANYMORE. EVERYTHING IS SCARING ME TO DEATH. I FEEL STRANGE. I FEEL VERY STRANGE.

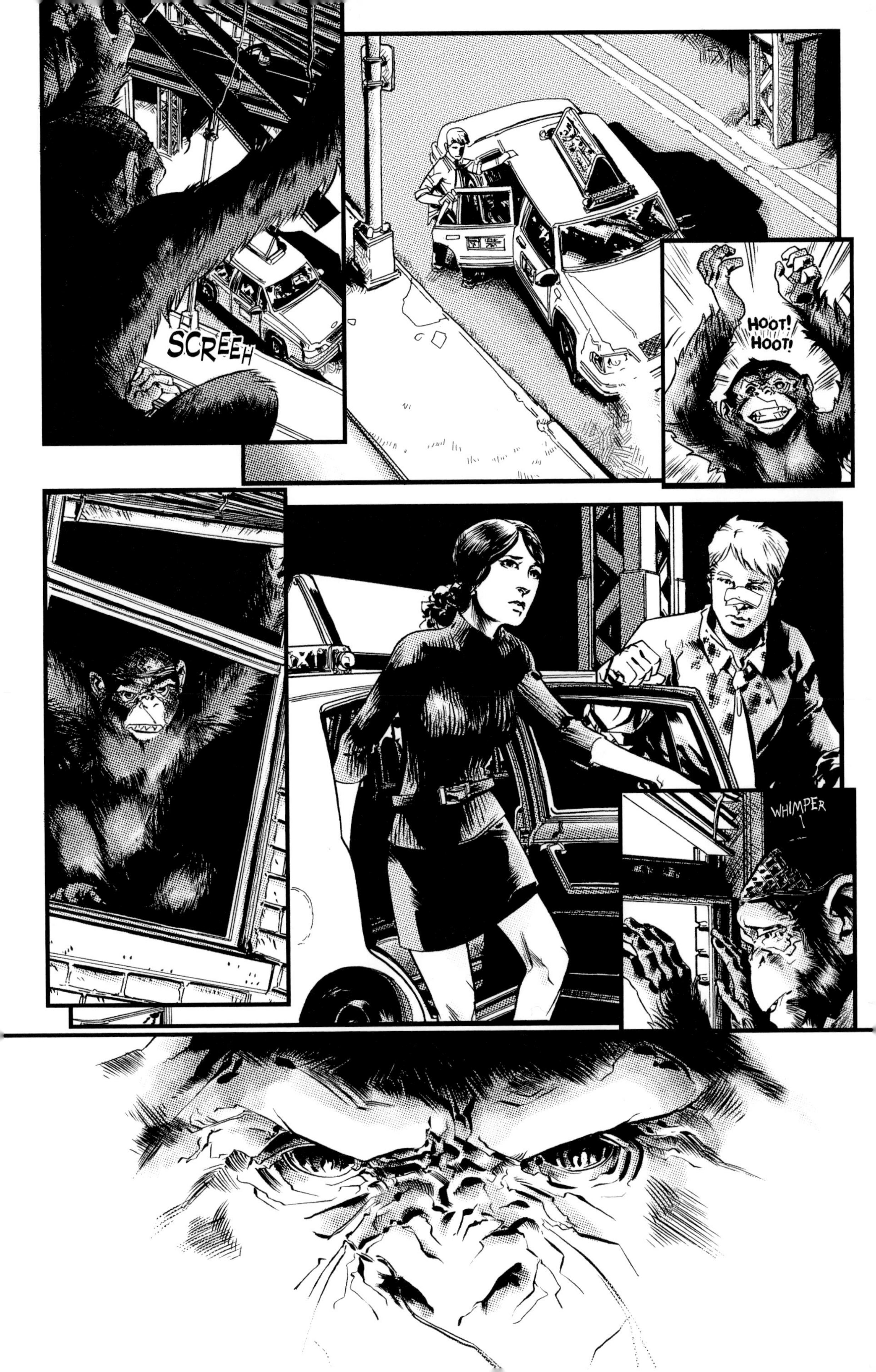
SCREEH
HOOT! HOOT!
WHIMPER

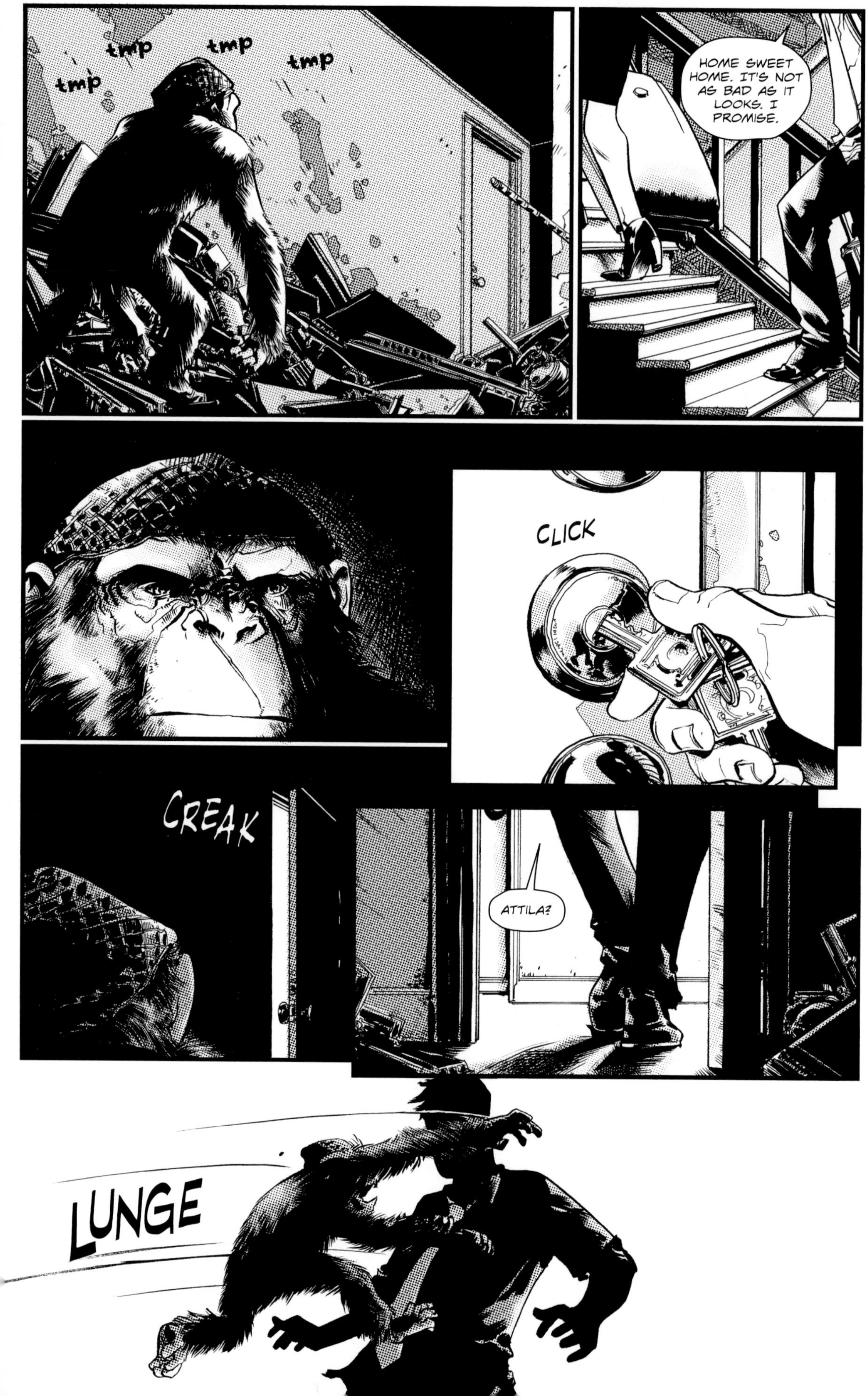
tmp
tmp
tmp
tmp
HOME SWEET HOME. IT'S NOT AS BAD AS IT LOOKS. I PROMISE.
CLICK
CREAK
ATTILA?
LUNGE

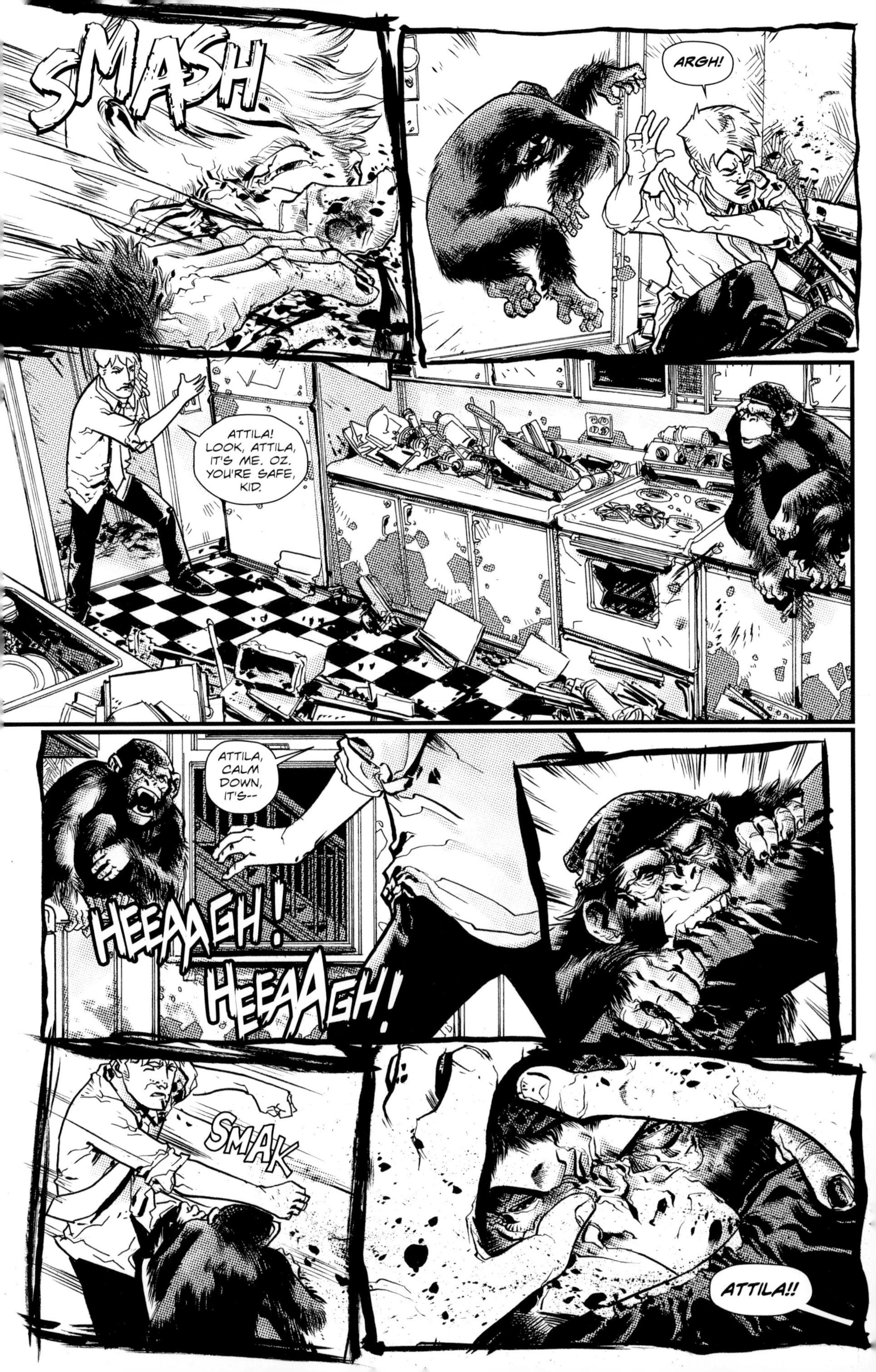
SMASH
ARGH!
ATTILA! LOOK, ATTILA, IT'S ME. OZ. YOU'RE SAFE, KID.
ATTILA, CALM DOWN, IT'S--
HEEAAGH!
HEEAAGH!
SMAK
ATTILA!!

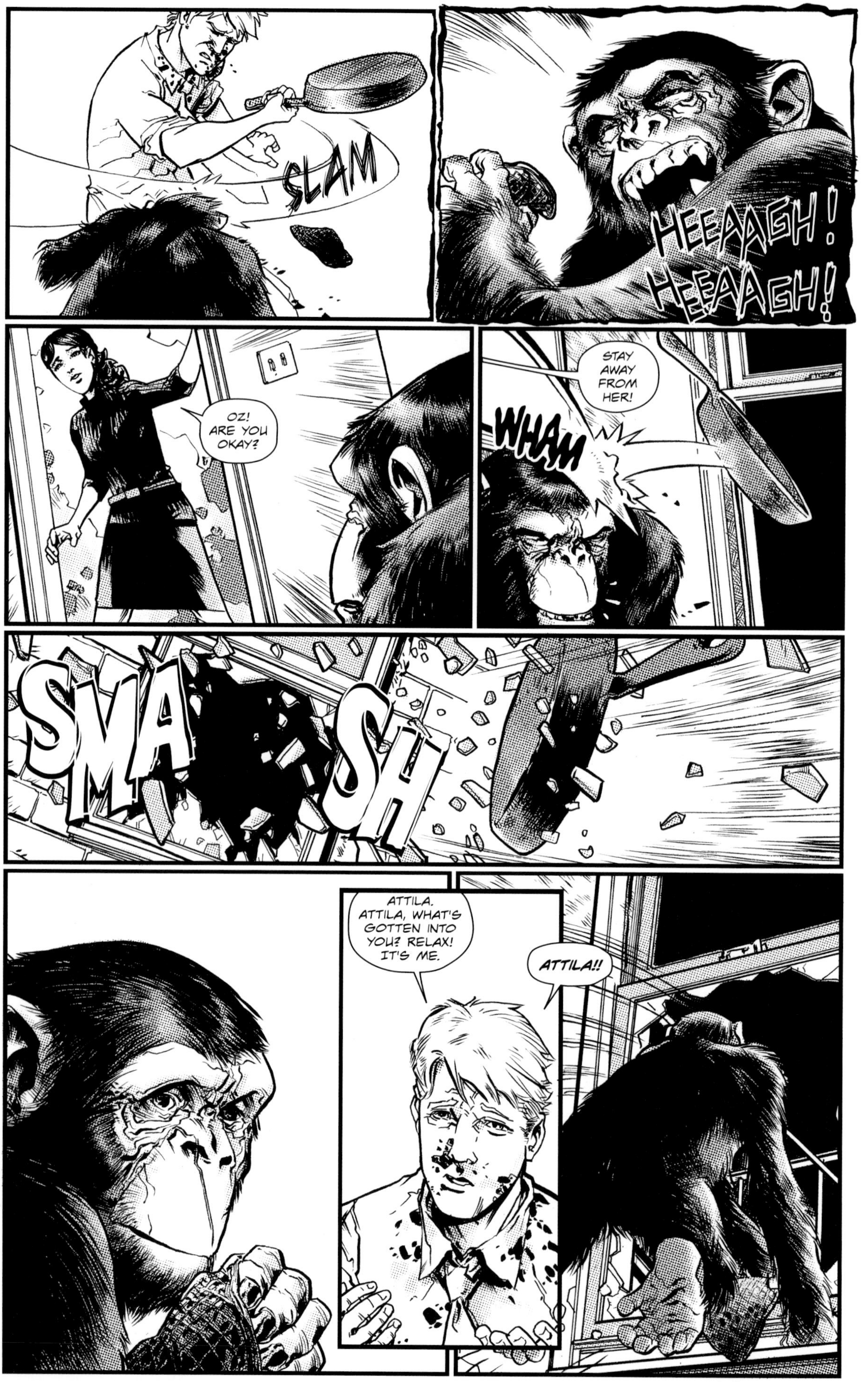
SLAM
HEEAAGH! HEEAAGH!
OZ! ARE YOU OKAY?
STAY AWAY FROM HER!
WHAM
SMASH
ATTILA. ATTILA, WHAT'S GOTTEN INTO YOU? RELAX! IT'S ME.
ATTILA!!

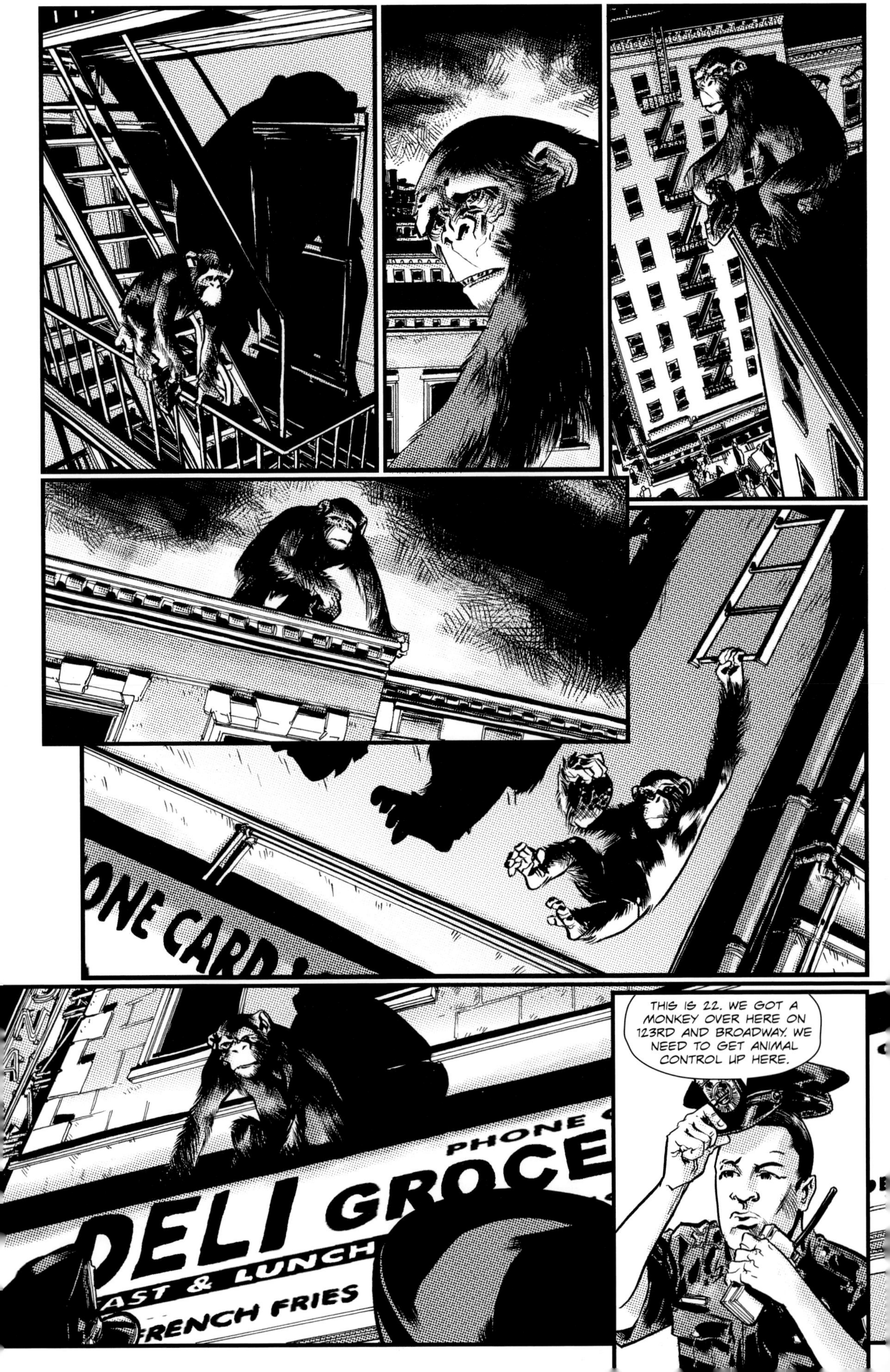
ONE CARD
PHONE
DELI GROCE
AST & LUNCH
FRENCH FRIES
THIS IS 22. WE GOT A MONKEY OVER HERE ON 123RD AND BROADWAY. WE NEED TO GET ANIMAL CONTROL UP HERE.

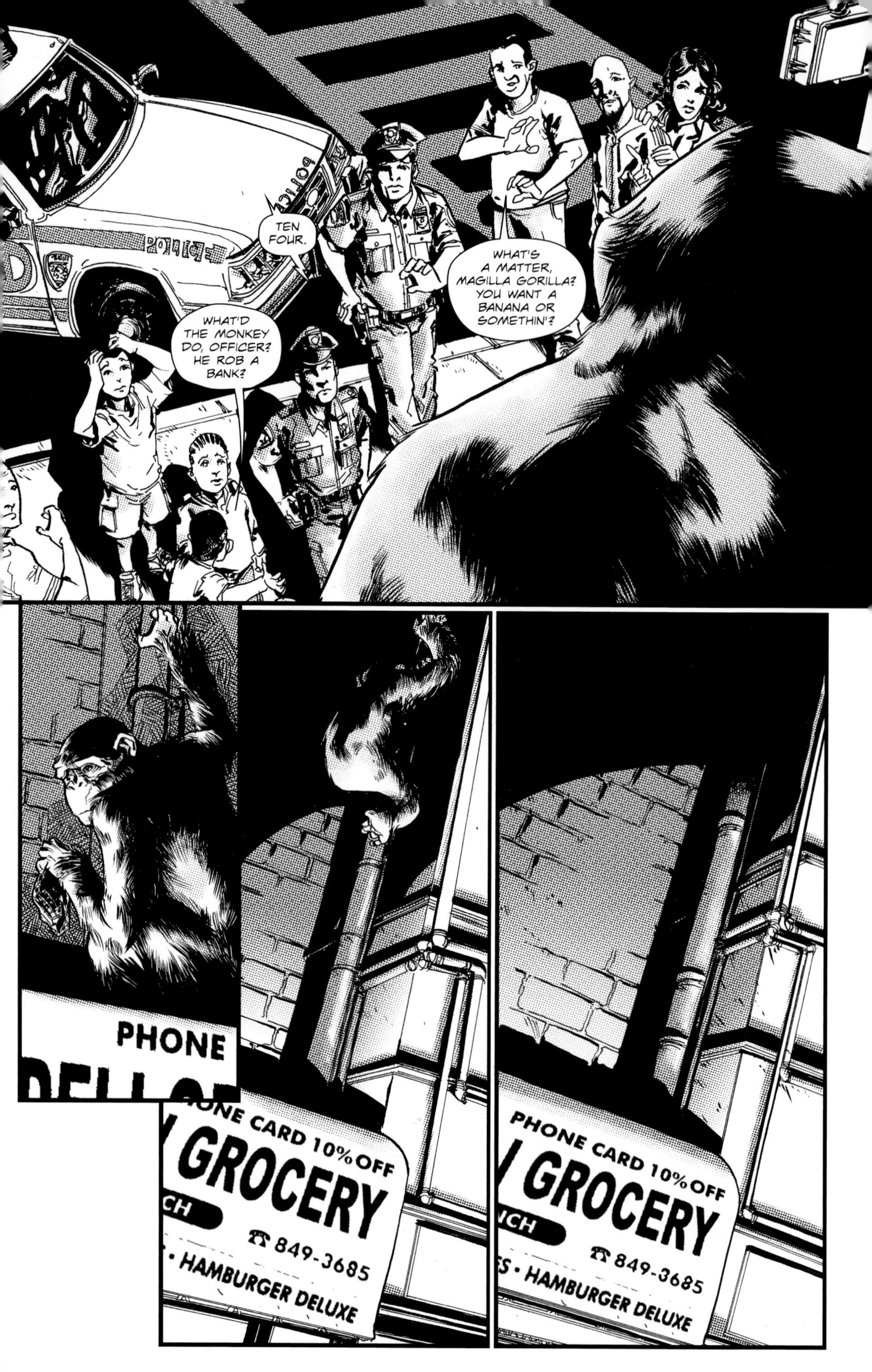
TEN FOUR.
WHAT'S A MATTER, MAGILLA GORILLA? YOU WANT A BANANA OR SOMETHIN'?
WHAT'D THE MONKEY DO, OFFICER? HE ROB A BANK?
POLICE
PHONE
PHONE CARD 10% OFF
GROCERY
849-3685
HAMBURGER DELUXE
PHONE CARD 10% OFF
GROCERY
849-3685
HAMBURGER DELUXE

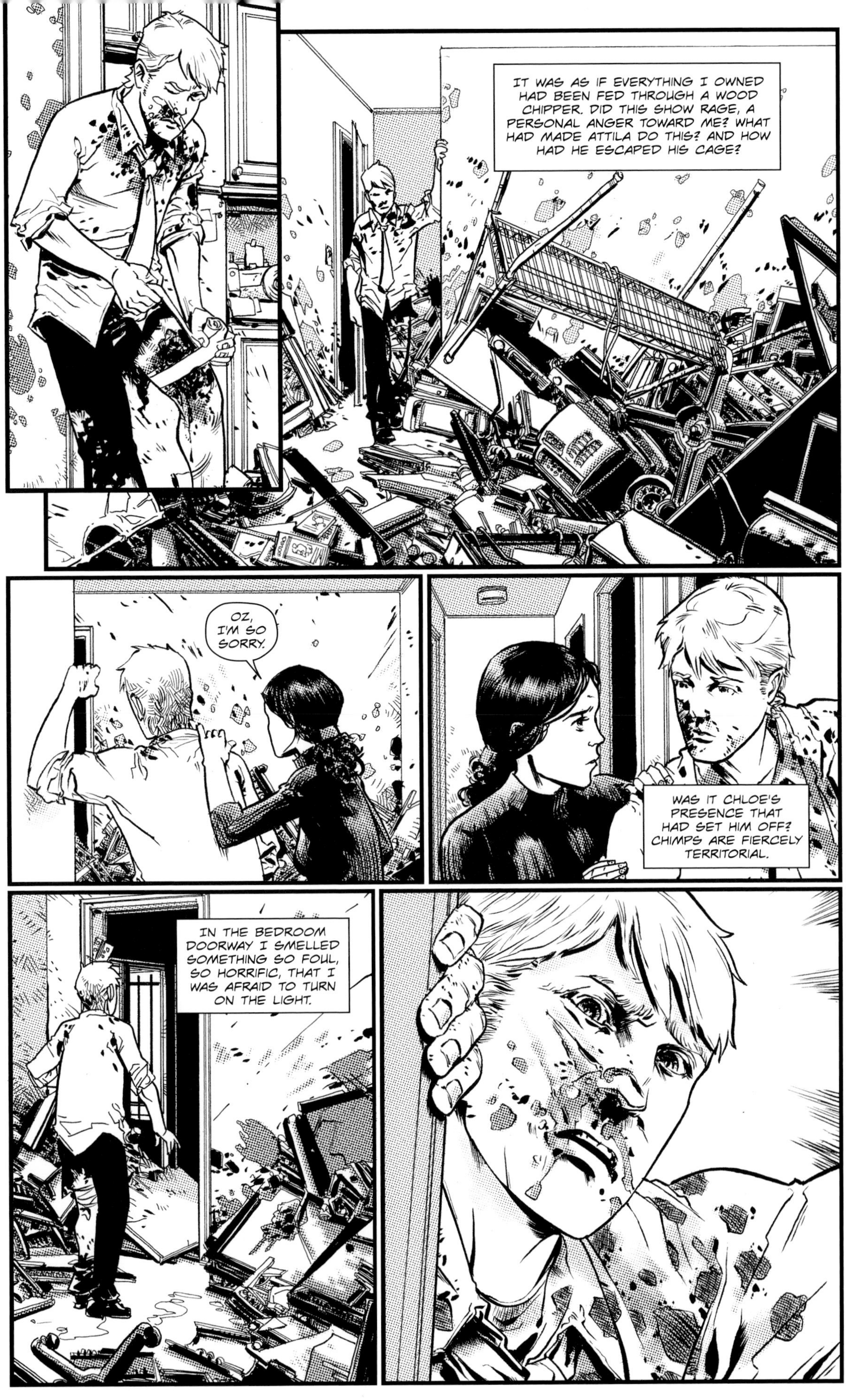
IT WAS AS IF EVERYTHING I OWNED HAD BEEN FED THROUGH A WOOD CHIPPER. DID THIS SHOW RAGE, A PERSONAL ANGER TOWARD ME? WHAT HAD MADE ATTILA DO THIS? AND HOW HAD HE ESCAPED HIS CAGE?
OZ, I'M SO SORRY.
WAS IT CHLOE'S PRESENCE THAT HAD SET HIM OFF? CHIMPS ARE FIERCELY TERRITORIAL.
IN THE BEDROOM DOORWAY I SMELLED SOMETHING SO FOUL, SO HORRIFIC, THAT I WAS AFRAID TO TURN ON THE LIGHT.

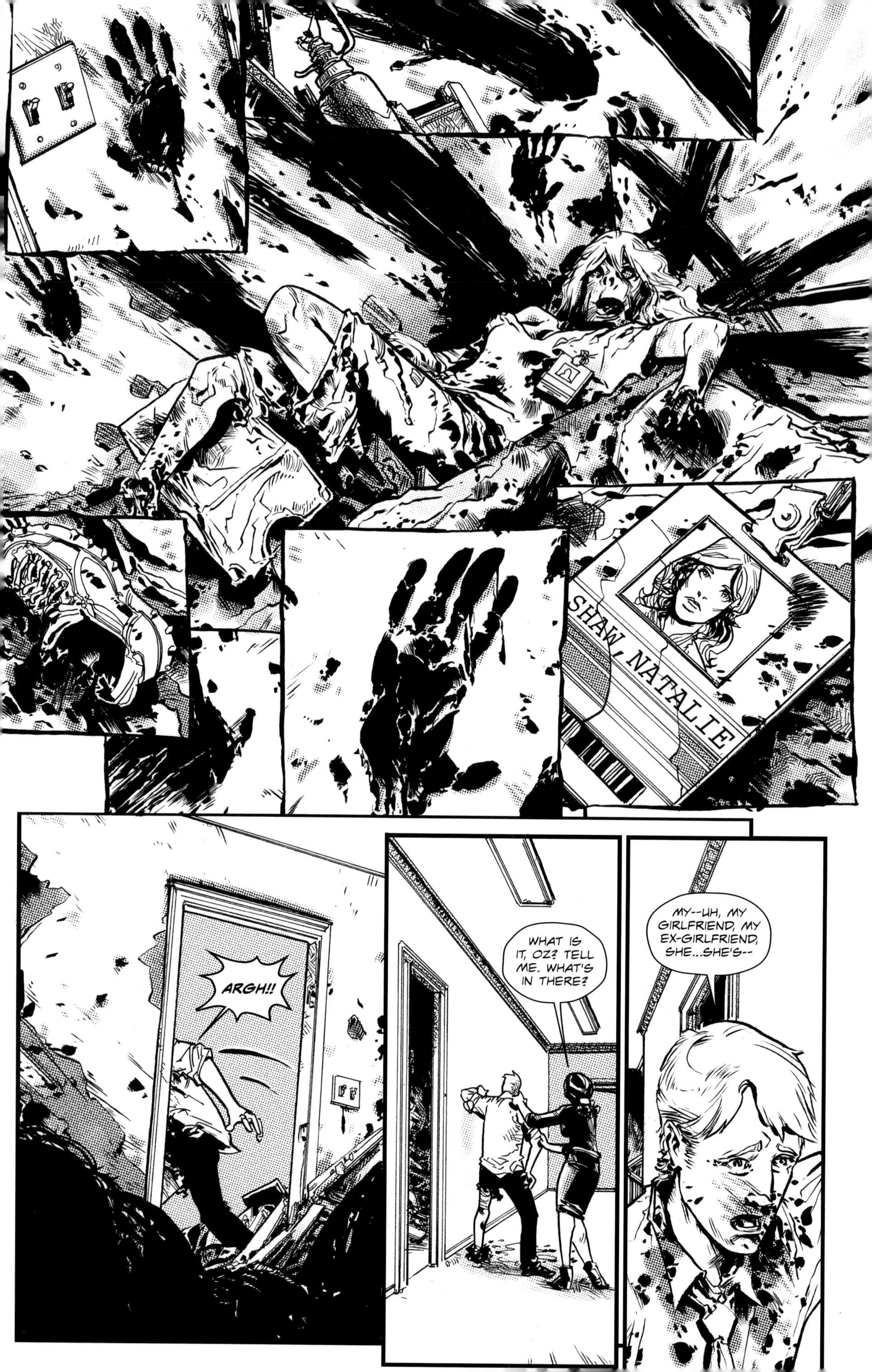
SHAW, NATALIE
ARGH!!
WHAT IS IT, OZ? TELL ME. WHAT'S IN THERE?
MY--UH, MY GIRLFRIEND, MY EX-GIRLFRIEND, SHE...SHE'S--

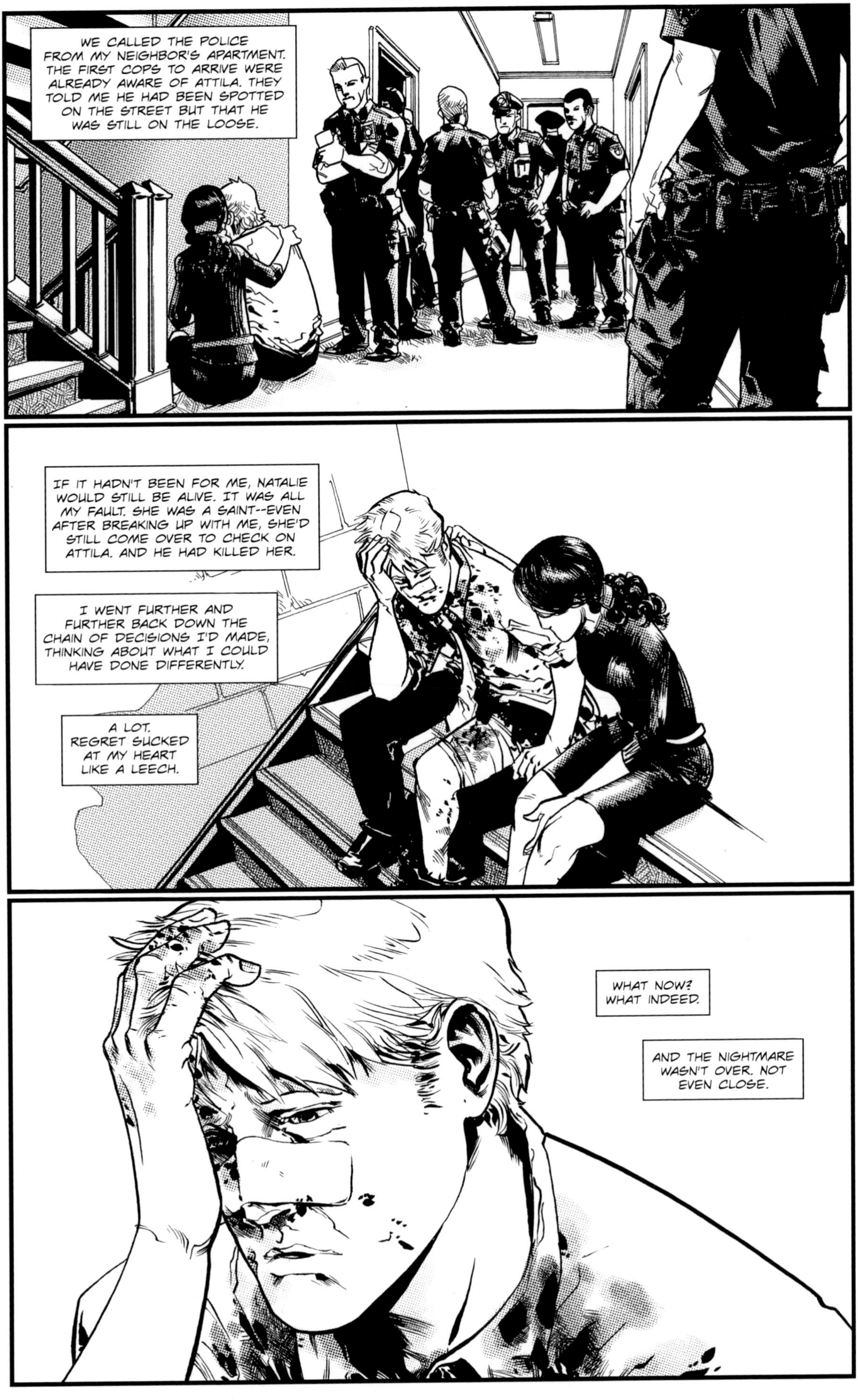
WE CALLED THE POLICE FROM MY NEIGHBOR'S APARTMENT. THE FIRST COPS TO ARRIVE WERE ALREADY AWARE OF ATTILA. THEY TOLD ME HE HAD BEEN SPOTTED ON THE STREET BUT THAT HE WAS STILL ON THE LOOSE.
IF IT HADN'T BEEN FOR ME, NATALIE WOULD STILL BE ALIVE. IT WAS ALL MY FAULT. SHE WAS A SAINT--EVEN AFTER BREAKING UP WITH ME, SHE'D STILL COME OVER TO CHECK ON ATTILA. AND HE HAD KILLED HER.
I WENT FURTHER AND FURTHER BACK DOWN THE CHAIN OF DECISIONS I'D MADE, THINKING ABOUT WHAT I COULD HAVE DONE DIFFERENTLY.
A LOT. REGRET SUCKED AT MY HEART LIKE A LEECH.
WHAT NOW? WHAT INDEED.
AND THE NIGHTMARE WASN'T OVER. NOT EVEN CLOSE.

ZOO

THE GRAPHIC NOVEL

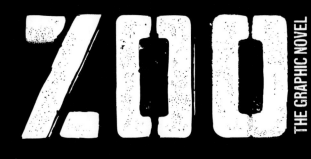

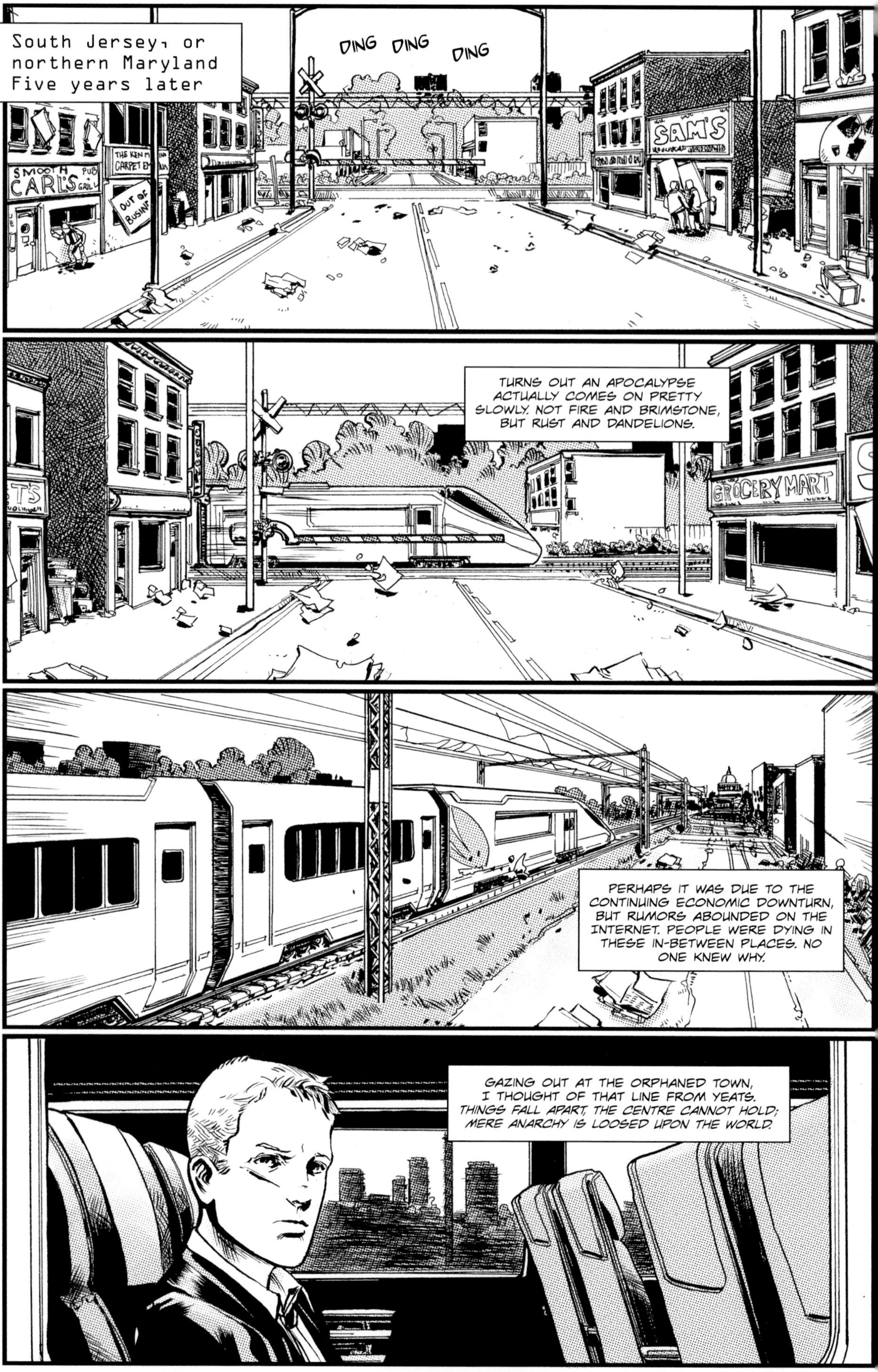
South Jersey, or
northern Maryland
Five years later
DING DING DING
SMOOTH CARL'S PUB + GRILL
SAM'S
TURNS OUT AN APOCALYPSE ACTUALLY COMES ON PRETTY SLOWLY. NOT FIRE AND BRIMSTONE, BUT RUST AND DANDELIONS.
GROCERY MART
PERHAPS IT WAS DUE TO THE CONTINUING ECONOMIC DOWNTURN, BUT RUMORS ABOUNDED ON THE INTERNET. PEOPLE WERE DYING IN THESE IN-BETWEEN PLACES. NO ONE KNEW WHY.
GAZING OUT AT THE ORPHANED TOWN, I THOUGHT OF THAT LINE FROM YEATS. THINGS FALL APART, THE CENTRE CANNOT HOLD; MERE ANARCHY IS LOOSED UPON THE WORLD.

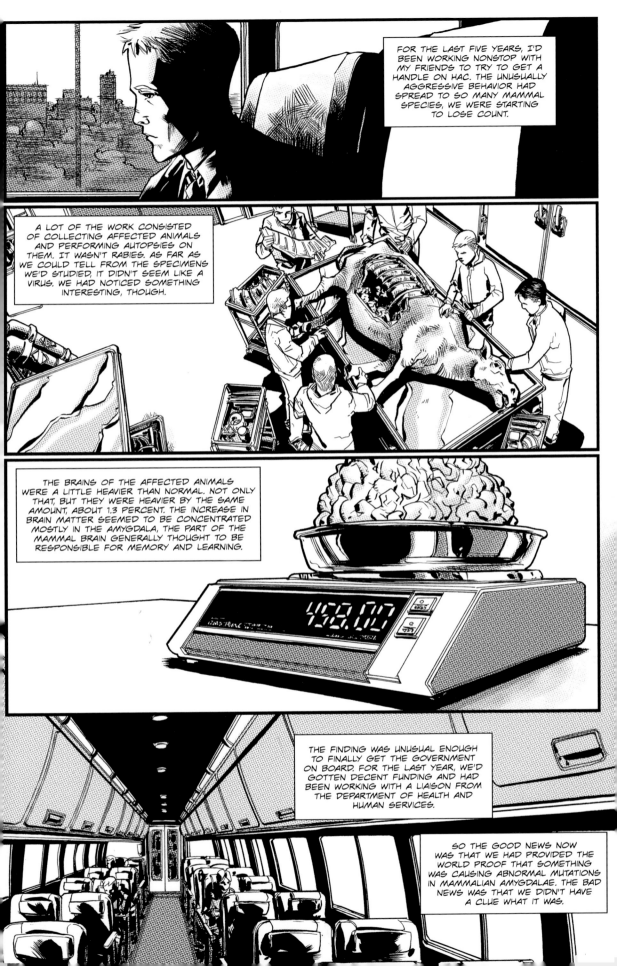

FOR THE LAST FIVE YEARS, I'D BEEN WORKING NONSTOP WITH MY FRIENDS TO TRY TO GET A HANDLE ON HAC. THE UNUSUALLY AGGRESSIVE BEHAVIOR HAD SPREAD TO SO MANY MAMMAL SPECIES, WE WERE STARTING TO LOSE COUNT.

A LOT OF THE WORK CONSISTED OF COLLECTING AFFECTED ANIMALS AND PERFORMING AUTOPSIES ON THEM. IT WASN'T RABIES. AS FAR AS WE COULD TELL FROM THE SPECIMENS WE'D STUDIED, IT DIDN'T SEEM LIKE A VIRUS. WE HAD NOTICED SOMETHING INTERESTING, THOUGH.

THE BRAINS OF THE AFFECTED ANIMALS WERE A LITTLE HEAVIER THAN NORMAL. NOT ONLY THAT, BUT THEY WERE HEAVIER BY THE SAME AMOUNT, ABOUT 1.3 PERCENT. THE INCREASE IN BRAIN MATTER SEEMED TO BE CONCENTRATED MOSTLY IN THE AMYGDALA, THE PART OF THE MAMMAL BRAIN GENERALLY THOUGHT TO BE RESPONSIBLE FOR MEMORY AND LEARNING.

THE FINDING WAS UNUSUAL ENOUGH TO FINALLY GET THE GOVERNMENT ON BOARD. FOR THE LAST YEAR, WE'D GOTTEN DECENT FUNDING AND HAD BEEN WORKING WITH A LIAISON FROM THE DEPARTMENT OF HEALTH AND HUMAN SERVICES.

SO THE GOOD NEWS NOW WAS THAT WE HAD PROVIDED THE WORLD PROOF THAT SOMETHING WAS CAUSING ABNORMAL MUTATIONS IN MAMMALIAN AMYGDALAE. THE BAD NEWS WAS THAT WE DIDN'T HAVE A CLUE WHAT IT WAS.

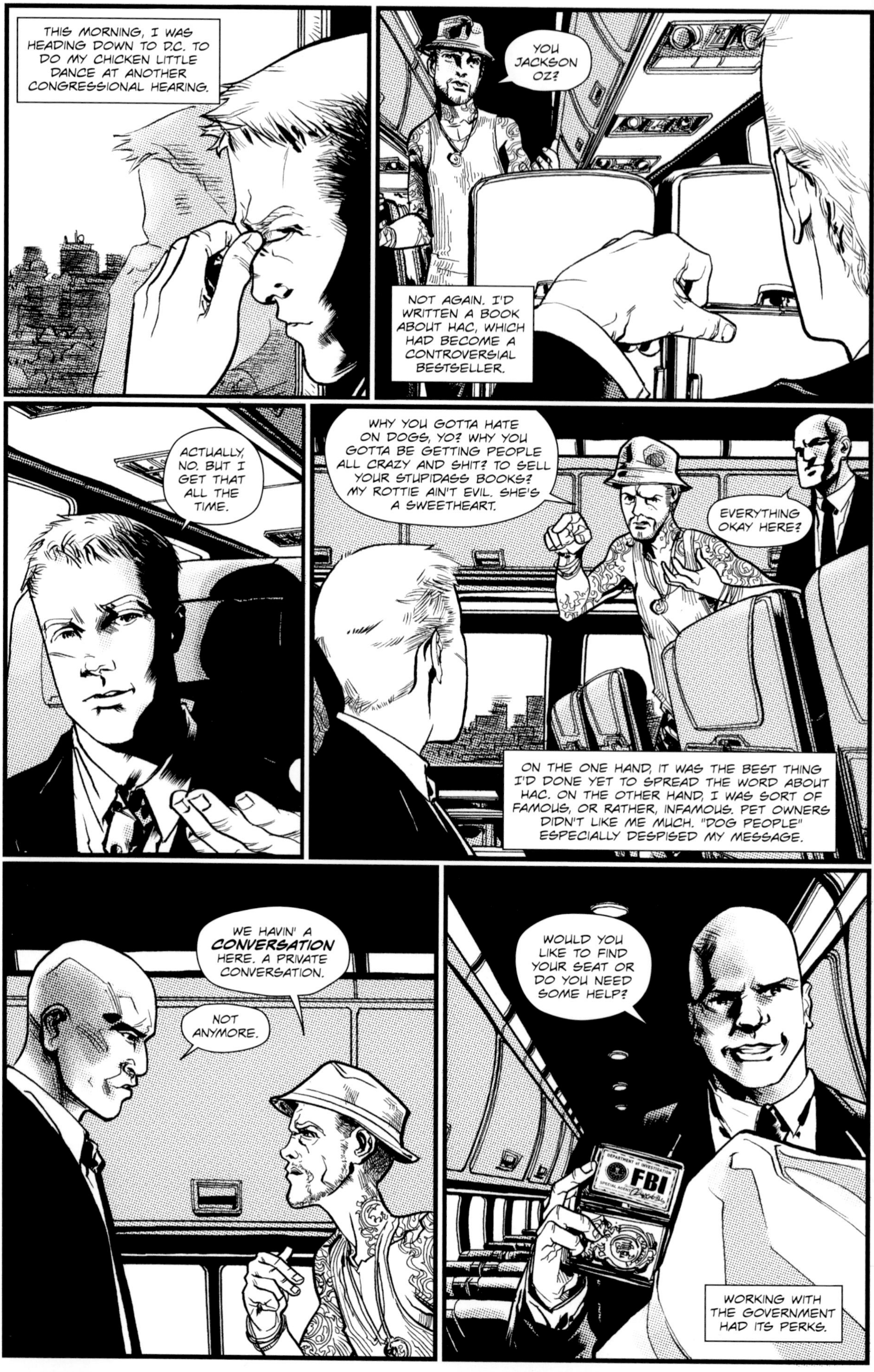

THIS MORNING, I WAS HEADING DOWN TO D.C. TO DO MY CHICKEN LITTLE DANCE AT ANOTHER CONGRESSIONAL HEARING.
YOU JACKSON OZ?
NOT AGAIN. I'D WRITTEN A BOOK ABOUT HAC, WHICH HAD BECOME A CONTROVERSIAL BESTSELLER.
ACTUALLY, NO. BUT I GET THAT ALL THE TIME.
WHY YOU GOTTA HATE ON DOGS, YO? WHY YOU GOTTA BE GETTING PEOPLE ALL CRAZY AND SHIT? TO SELL YOUR STUPIDASS BOOKS? MY ROTTIE AIN'T EVIL. SHE'S A SWEETHEART.
EVERYTHING OKAY HERE?
ON THE ONE HAND, IT WAS THE BEST THING I'D DONE YET TO SPREAD THE WORD ABOUT HAC. ON THE OTHER HAND, I WAS SORT OF FAMOUS, OR RATHER, INFAMOUS. PET OWNERS DIDN'T LIKE ME MUCH. "DOG PEOPLE" ESPECIALLY DESPISED MY MESSAGE.
WE HAVIN' A CONVERSATION HERE. A PRIVATE CONVERSATION.
NOT ANYMORE.
WOULD YOU LIKE TO FIND YOUR SEAT OR DO YOU NEED SOME HELP?
FBI
WORKING WITH THE GOVERNMENT HAD ITS PERKS.

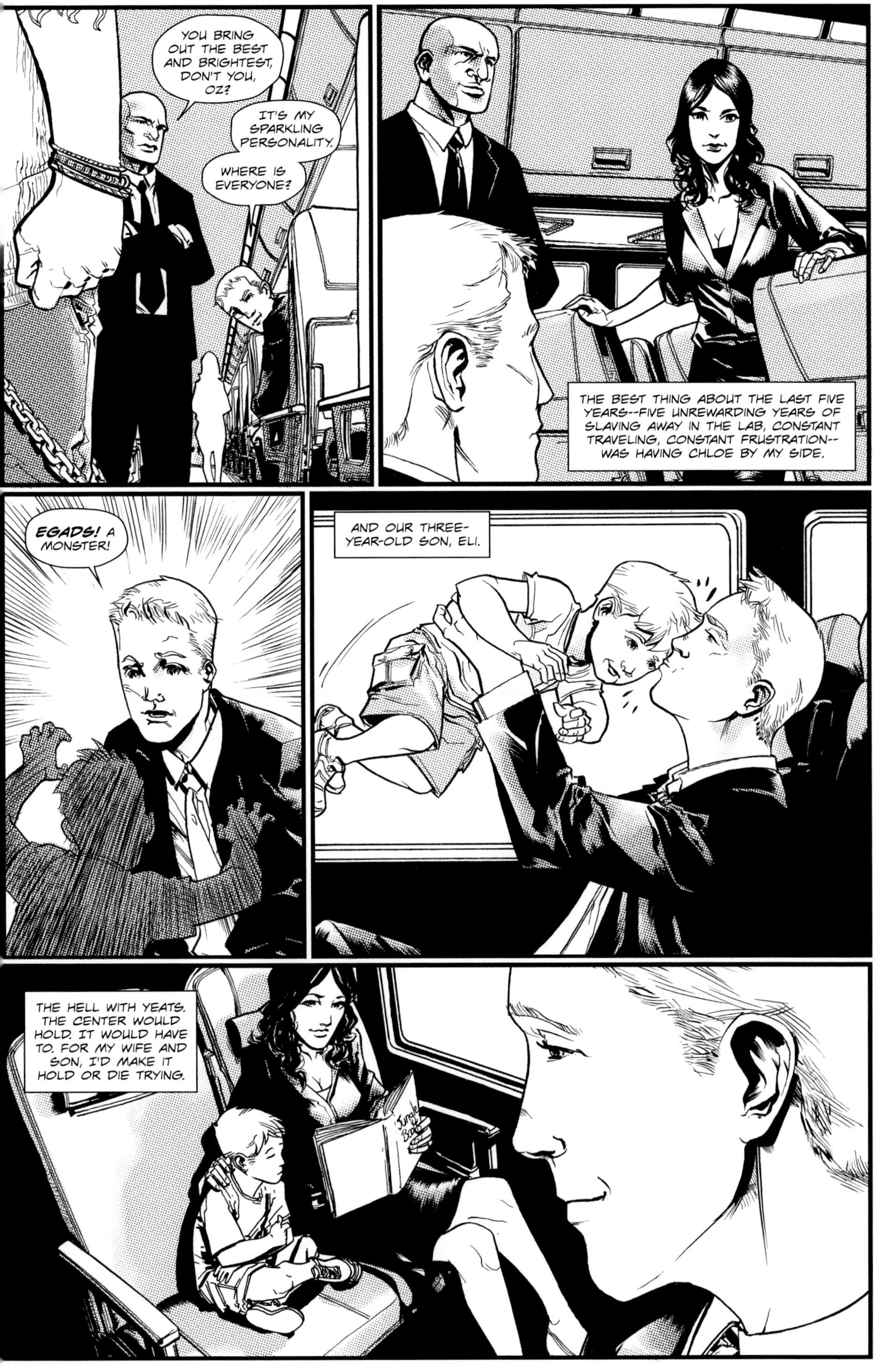
YOU BRING OUT THE BEST AND BRIGHTEST, DON'T YOU, OZ?
IT'S MY SPARKLING PERSONALITY.
WHERE IS EVERYONE?
THE BEST THING ABOUT THE LAST FIVE YEARS--FIVE UNREWARDING YEARS OF SLAVING AWAY IN THE LAB, CONSTANT TRAVELING, CONSTANT FRUSTRATION--WAS HAVING CHLOE BY MY SIDE.
EGADS! A MONSTER!
AND OUR THREE-YEAR-OLD SON, ELI.
THE HELL WITH YEATS. THE CENTER WOULD HOLD. IT WOULD HAVE TO. FOR MY WIFE AND SON, I'D MAKE IT HOLD OR DIE TRYING.

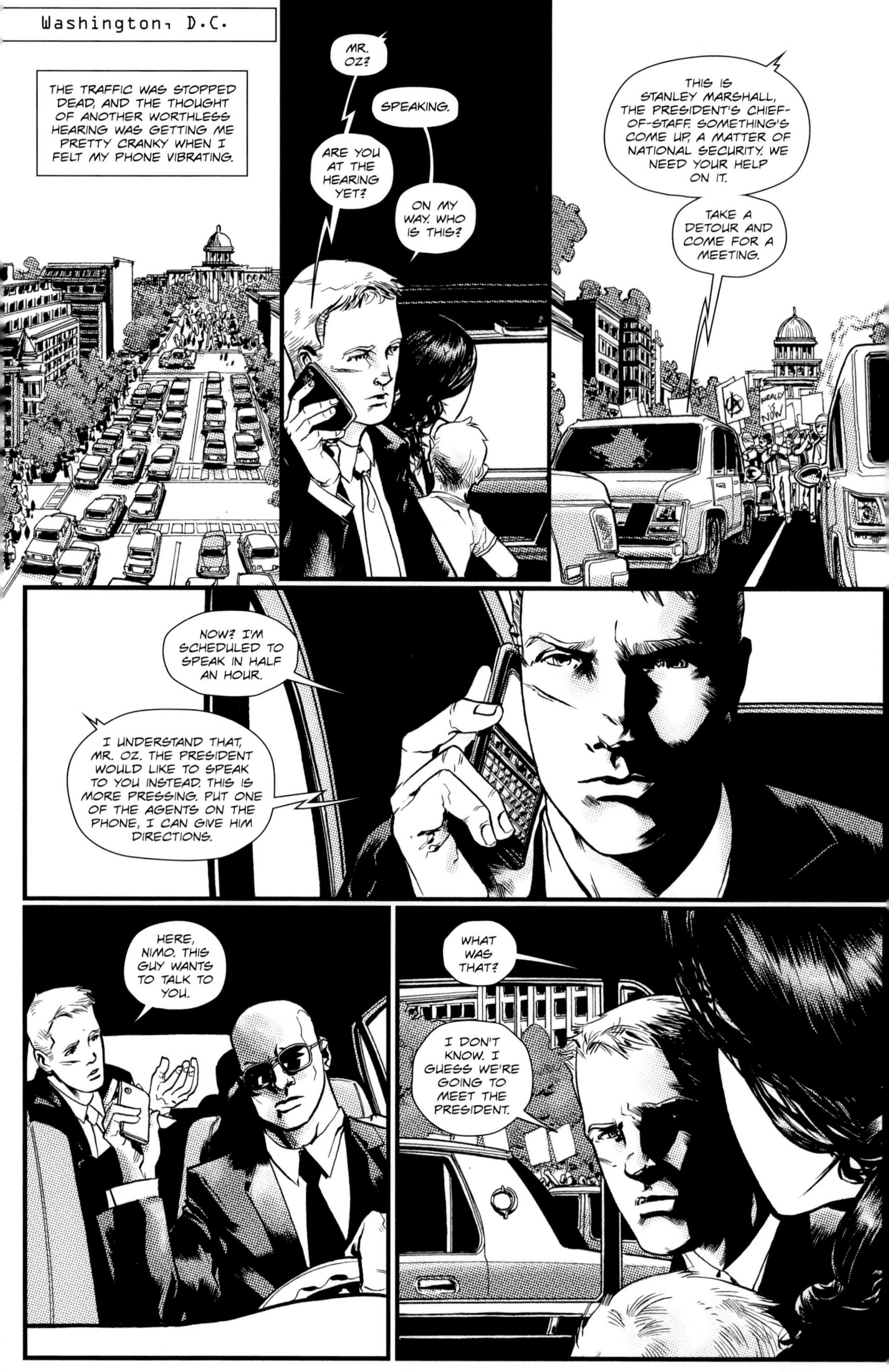
Washington, D.C.
THE TRAFFIC WAS STOPPED DEAD, AND THE THOUGHT OF ANOTHER WORTHLESS HEARING WAS GETTING ME PRETTY CRANKY WHEN I FELT MY PHONE VIBRATING.
MR. OZ?
SPEAKING.
ARE YOU AT THE HEARING YET?
ON MY WAY. WHO IS THIS?
THIS IS STANLEY MARSHALL, THE PRESIDENT'S CHIEF-OF-STAFF. SOMETHING'S COME UP, A MATTER OF NATIONAL SECURITY. WE NEED YOUR HELP ON IT.
TAKE A DETOUR AND COME FOR A MEETING.
NOW? I'M SCHEDULED TO SPEAK IN HALF AN HOUR.
I UNDERSTAND THAT, MR. OZ. THE PRESIDENT WOULD LIKE TO SPEAK TO YOU INSTEAD. THIS IS MORE PRESSING. PUT ONE OF THE AGENTS ON THE PHONE, I CAN GIVE HIM DIRECTIONS.
HERE, NIMO. THIS GUY WANTS TO TALK TO YOU.
WHAT WAS THAT?
I DON'T KNOW. I GUESS WE'RE GOING TO MEET THE PRESIDENT.

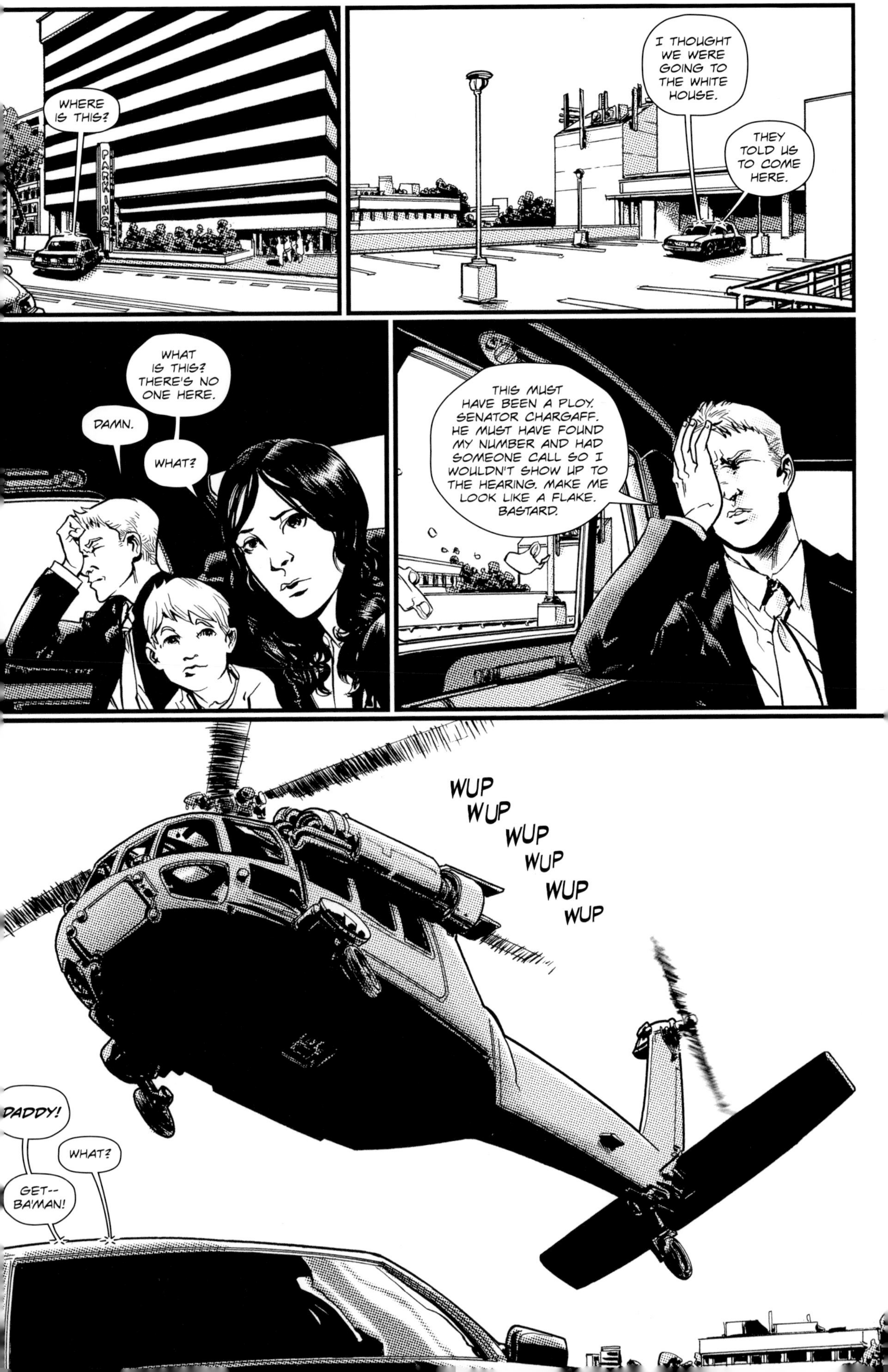
WHERE IS THIS?
PARKING
I THOUGHT WE WERE GOING TO THE WHITE HOUSE.
THEY TOLD US TO COME HERE.
WHAT IS THIS? THERE'S NO ONE HERE.
DAMN.
WHAT?
THIS MUST HAVE BEEN A PLOY. SENATOR CHARGAFF. HE MUST HAVE FOUND MY NUMBER AND HAD SOMEONE CALL SO I WOULDN'T SHOW UP TO THE HEARING. MAKE ME LOOK LIKE A FLAKE. BASTARD.
WUP WUP WUP WUP WUP WUP
DADDY!
WHAT?
GET-- BA'MAN!

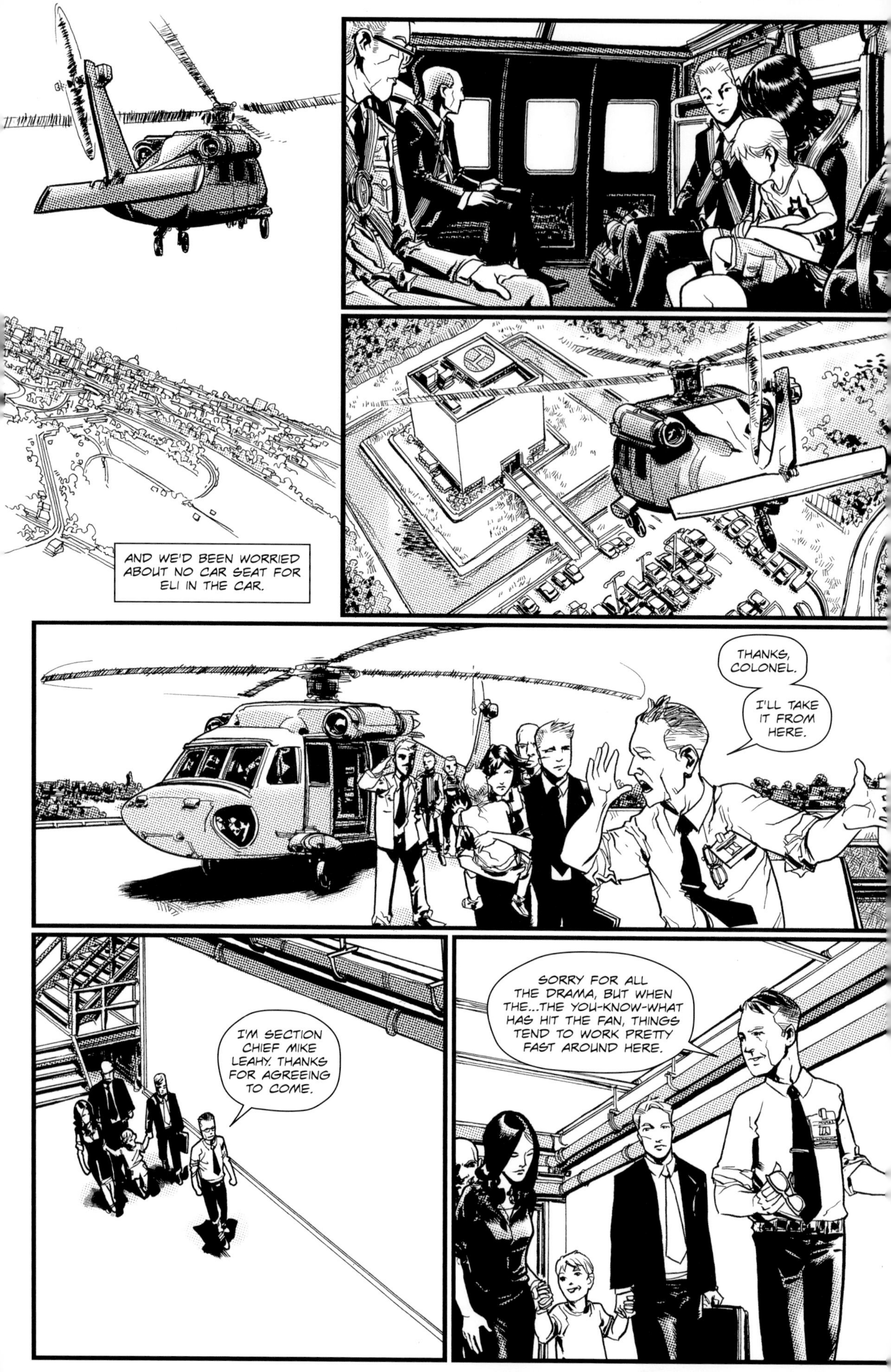
AND WE'D BEEN WORRIED ABOUT NO CAR SEAT FOR ELI IN THE CAR.
THANKS, COLONEL.
I'LL TAKE IT FROM HERE.
I'M SECTION CHIEF MIKE LEAHY. THANKS FOR AGREEING TO COME.
SORRY FOR ALL THE DRAMA, BUT WHEN THE...THE YOU-KNOW-WHAT HAS HIT THE FAN, THINGS TEND TO WORK PRETTY FAST AROUND HERE.

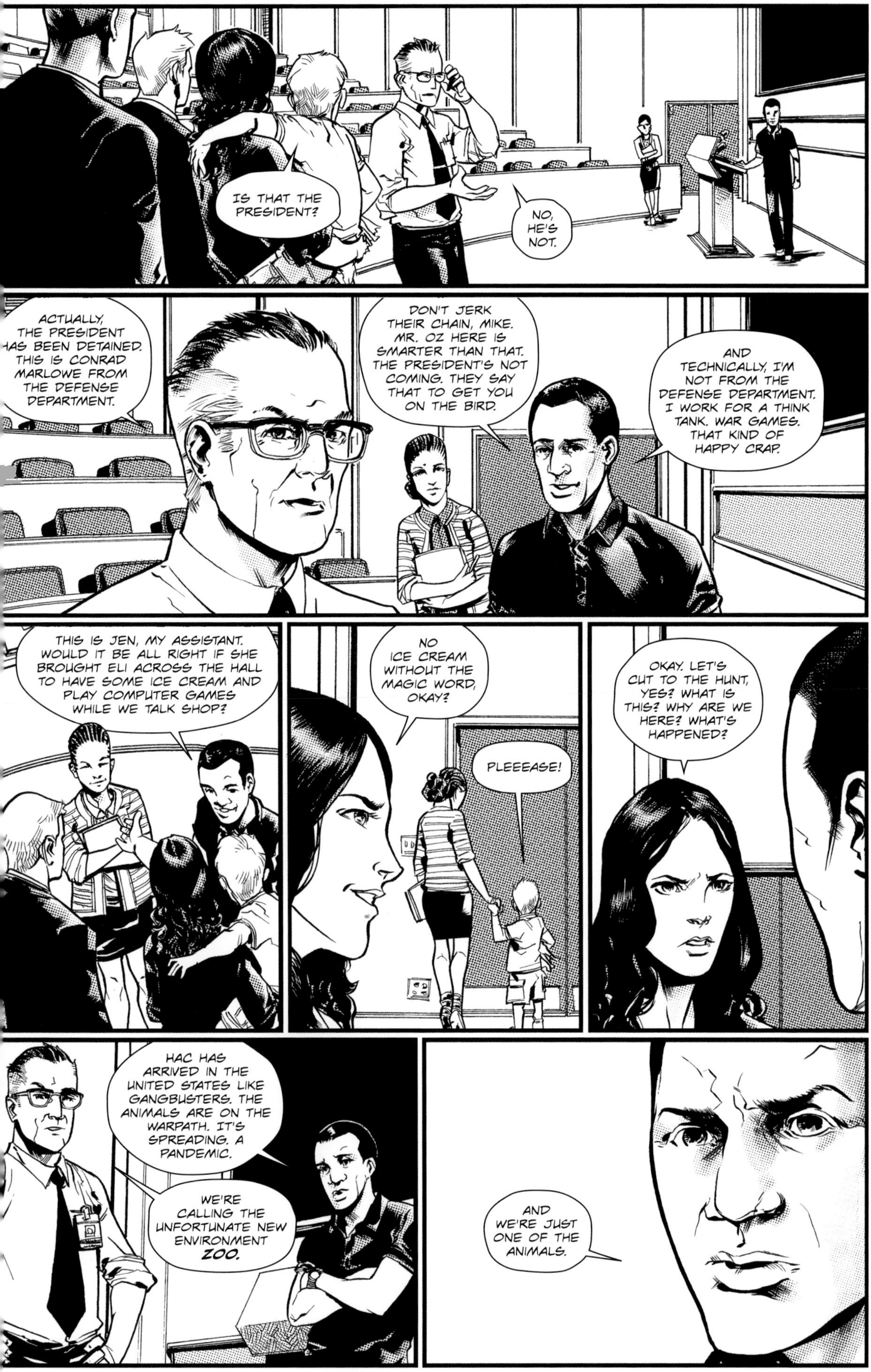
IS THAT THE PRESIDENT?
NO, HE'S NOT.
ACTUALLY, THE PRESIDENT HAS BEEN DETAINED. THIS IS CONRAD MARLOWE FROM THE DEFENSE DEPARTMENT.
DON'T JERK THEIR CHAIN, MIKE. MR. OZ HERE IS SMARTER THAN THAT. THE PRESIDENT'S NOT COMING. THEY SAY THAT TO GET YOU ON THE BIRD.
AND TECHNICALLY, I'M NOT FROM THE DEFENSE DEPARTMENT. I WORK FOR A THINK TANK. WAR GAMES. THAT KIND OF HAPPY CRAP.
THIS IS JEN, MY ASSISTANT. WOULD IT BE ALL RIGHT IF SHE BROUGHT ELI ACROSS THE HALL TO HAVE SOME ICE CREAM AND PLAY COMPUTER GAMES WHILE WE TALK SHOP?
NO ICE CREAM WITHOUT THE MAGIC WORD, OKAY?
PLEEEASE!
OKAY. LET'S CUT TO THE HUNT, YES? WHAT IS THIS? WHY ARE WE HERE? WHAT'S HAPPENED?
HAC HAS ARRIVED IN THE UNITED STATES LIKE GANGBUSTERS. THE ANIMALS ARE ON THE WARPATH. IT'S SPREADING. A PANDEMIC.
WE'RE CALLING THE UNFORTUNATE NEW ENVIRONMENT ZOO.
AND WE'RE JUST ONE OF THE ANIMALS.

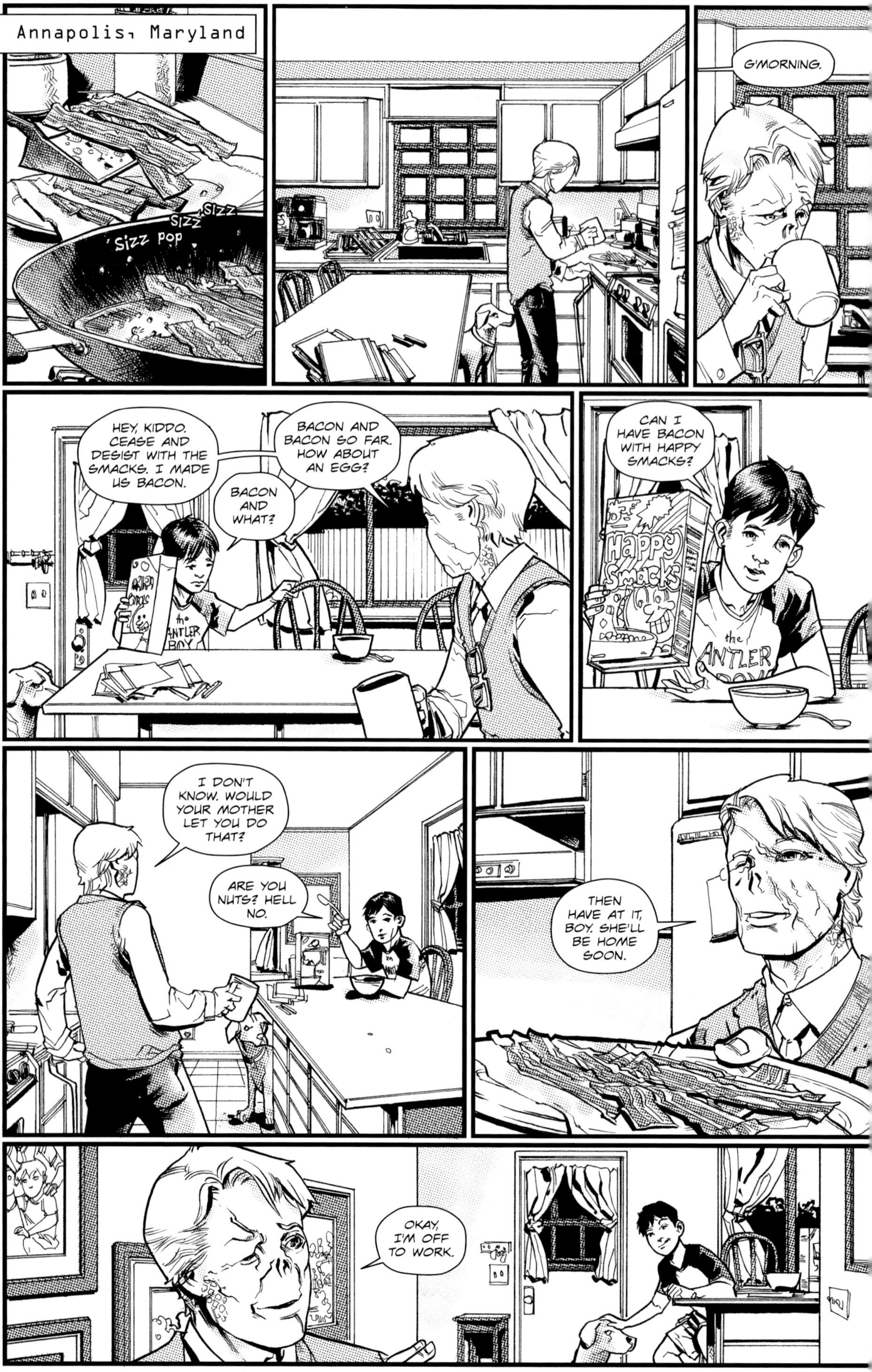
Annapolis, Maryland
Sizz pop
SIZZ
SIZZ
G'MORNING.
HEY, KIDDO. CEASE AND DESIST WITH THE SMACKS. I MADE US BACON.
BACON AND WHAT?
BACON AND BACON SO FAR. HOW ABOUT AN EGG?
CAN I HAVE BACON WITH HAPPY SMACKS?
Happy Smacks
the ANTLER BOY
I DON'T KNOW. WOULD YOUR MOTHER LET YOU DO THAT?
ARE YOU NUTS? HELL NO.
THEN HAVE AT IT, BOY. SHE'LL BE HOME SOON.
OKAY, I'M OFF TO WORK.

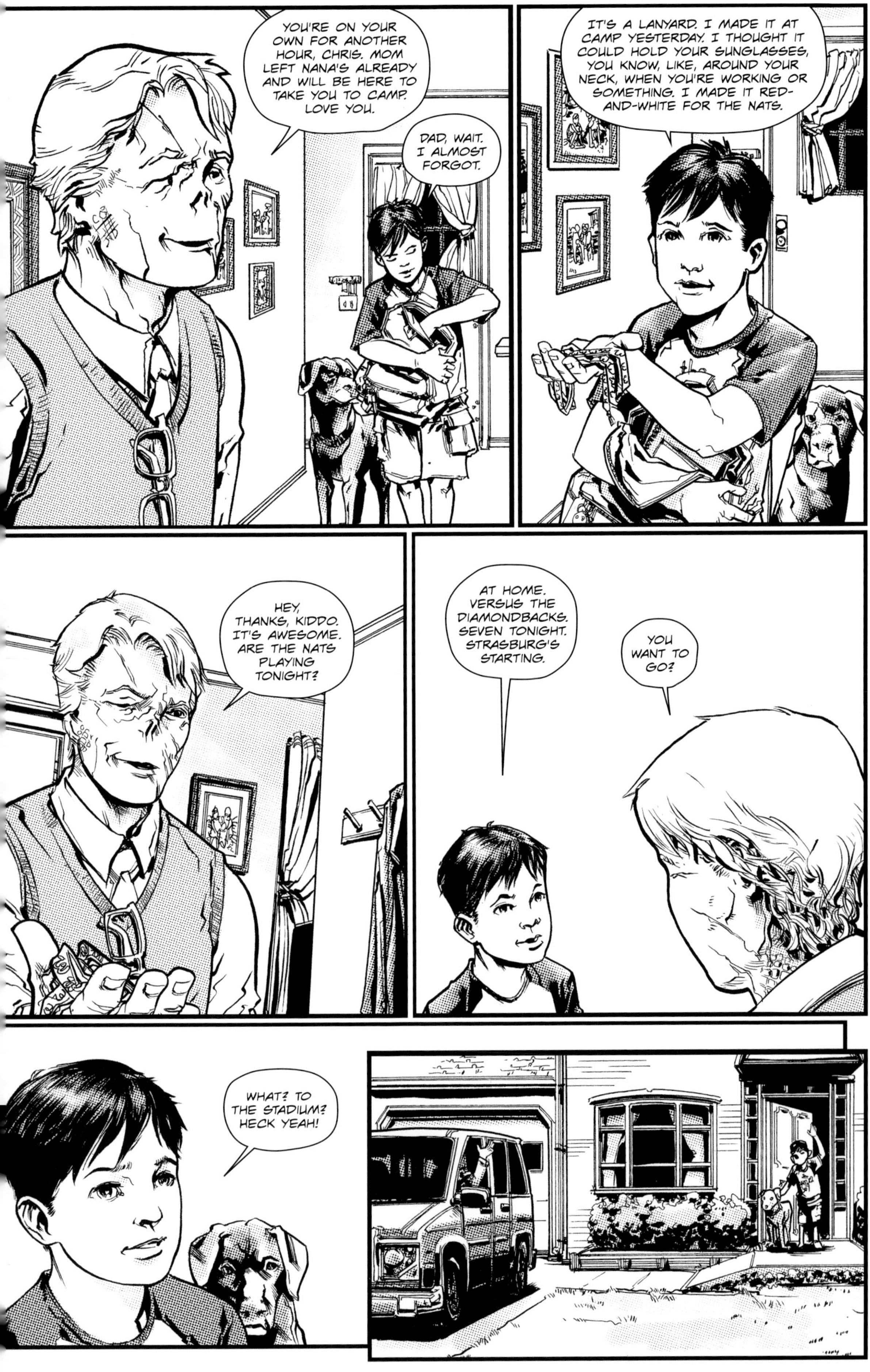
YOU'RE ON YOUR OWN FOR ANOTHER HOUR, CHRIS. MOM LEFT NANA'S ALREADY AND WILL BE HERE TO TAKE YOU TO CAMP. LOVE YOU.
DAD, WAIT. I ALMOST FORGOT.
IT'S A LANYARD. I MADE IT AT CAMP YESTERDAY. I THOUGHT IT COULD HOLD YOUR SUNGLASSES, YOU KNOW, LIKE, AROUND YOUR NECK, WHEN YOU'RE WORKING OR SOMETHING. I MADE IT RED-AND-WHITE FOR THE NATS.
HEY, THANKS, KIDDO. IT'S AWESOME. ARE THE NATS PLAYING TONIGHT?
AT HOME. VERSUS THE DIAMONDBACKS. SEVEN TONIGHT. STRASBURG'S STARTING.
YOU WANT TO GO?
WHAT? TO THE STADIUM? HECK YEAH!

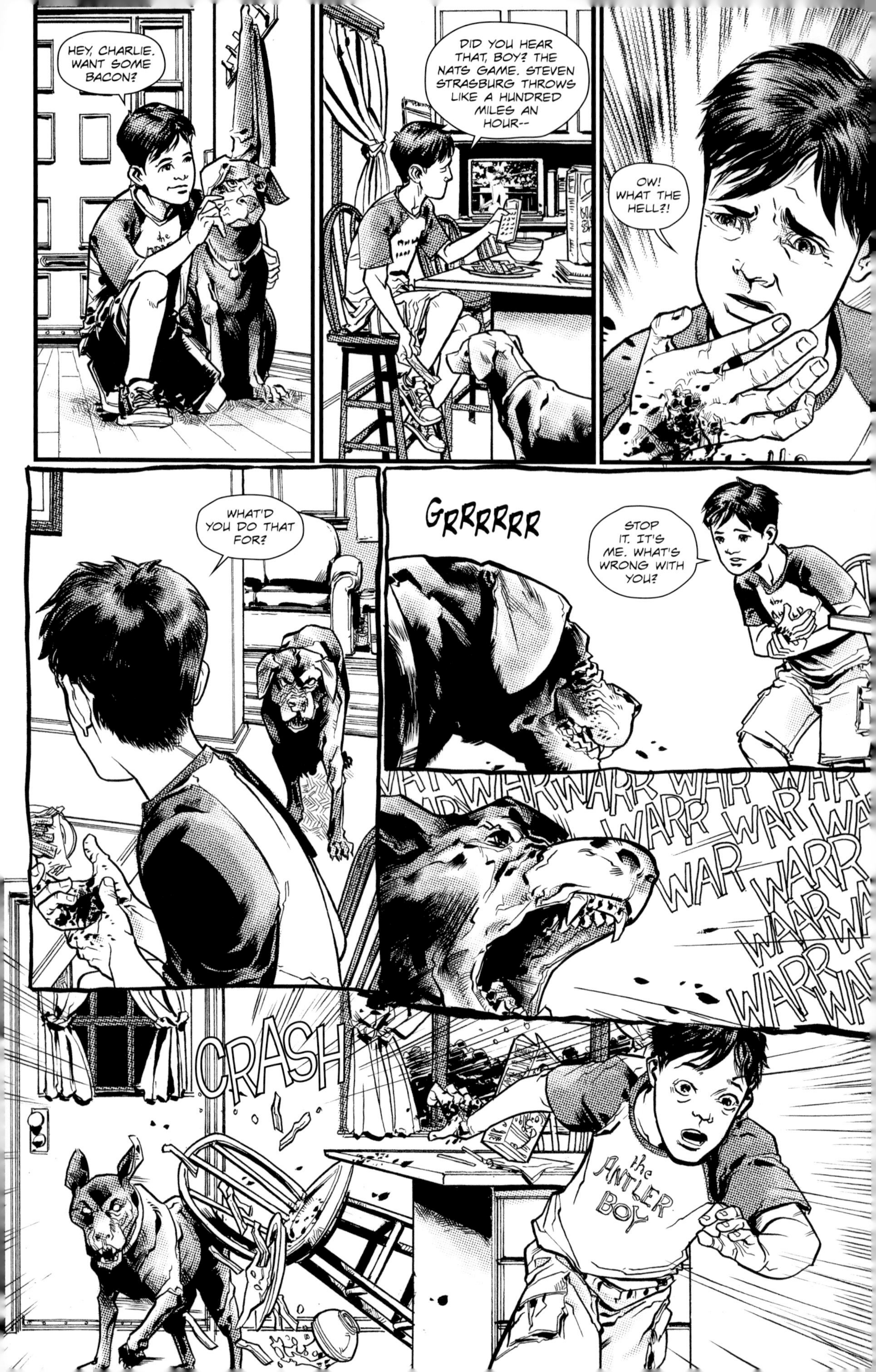

HEY, CHARLIE. WANT SOME BACON?
DID YOU HEAR THAT, BOY? THE NATS GAME. STEVEN STRASBURG THROWS LIKE A HUNDRED MILES AN HOUR--
OW! WHAT THE HELL?!
WHAT'D YOU DO THAT FOR?
GRRRRRR
STOP IT. IT'S ME. WHAT'S WRONG WITH YOU?
WARR WAR WARR
CRASH
the ANTLER BOY

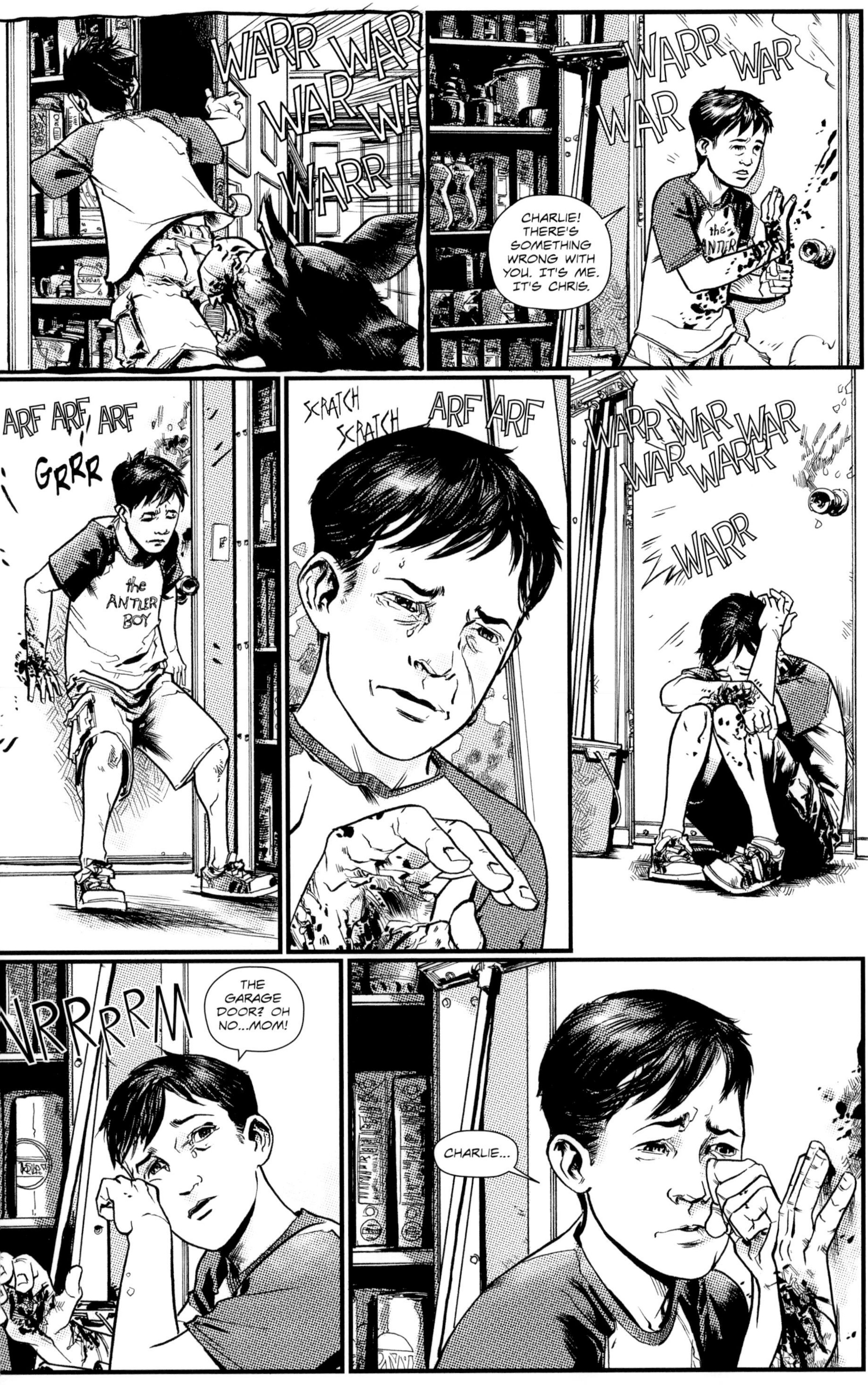

WARR WAR
WAR WA
WARR
WARR WAR
WAR
CHARLIE! THERE'S SOMETHING WRONG WITH YOU. IT'S ME. IT'S CHRIS.
the ANTLER
ARF ARF, ARF
GRRR
the ANTLER BOY
SCRATCH SCRATCH
ARF ARF
WARR WAR WAR
WAR WARR
WARR
VRRRRRM
THE GARAGE DOOR? OH NO...MOM!
CHARLIE...

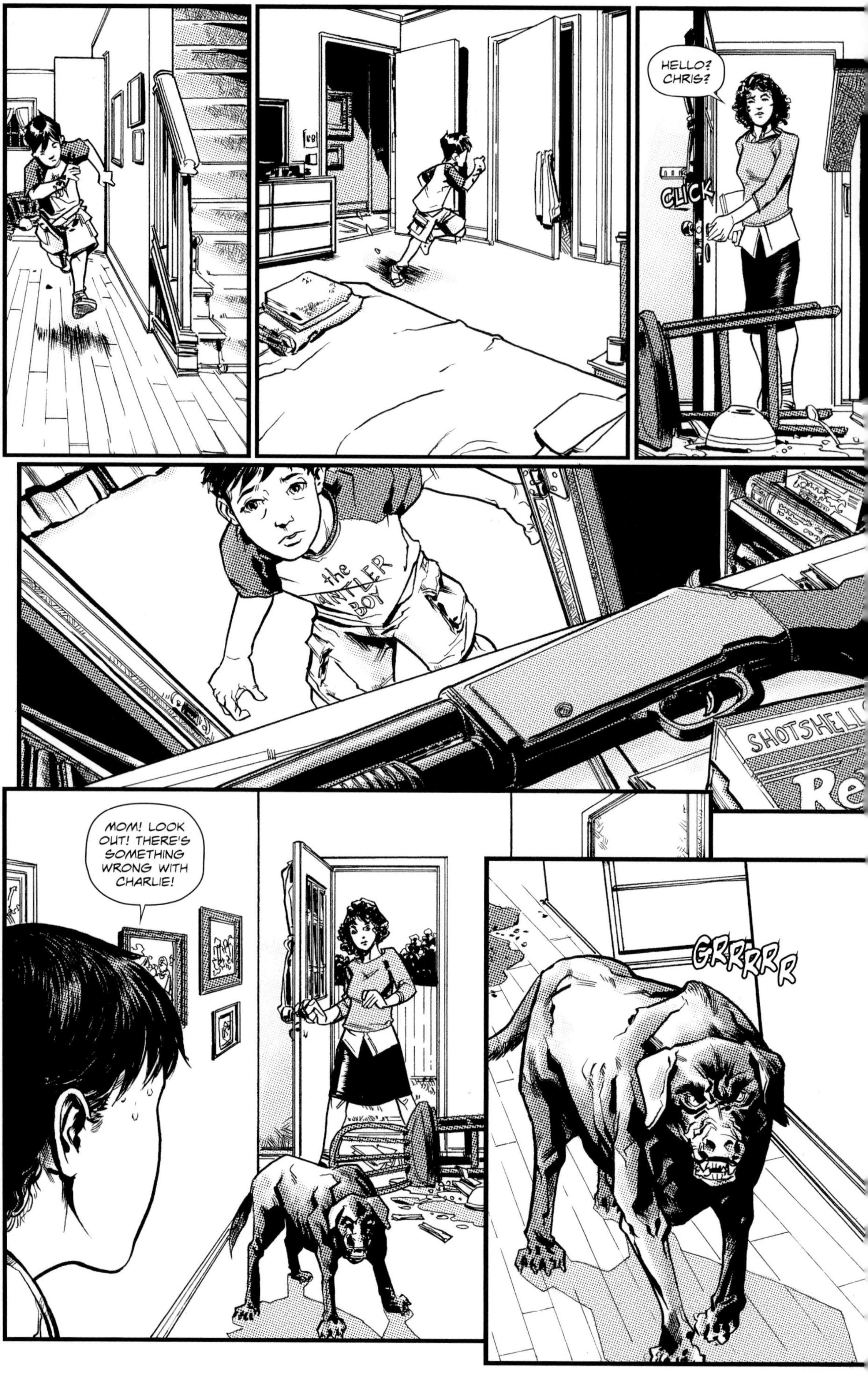
HELLO? CHRIS?
CLICK
the ANTLER BOY
SHOTSHELL
MOM! LOOK OUT! THERE'S SOMETHING WRONG WITH CHARLIE!
GRRRRR

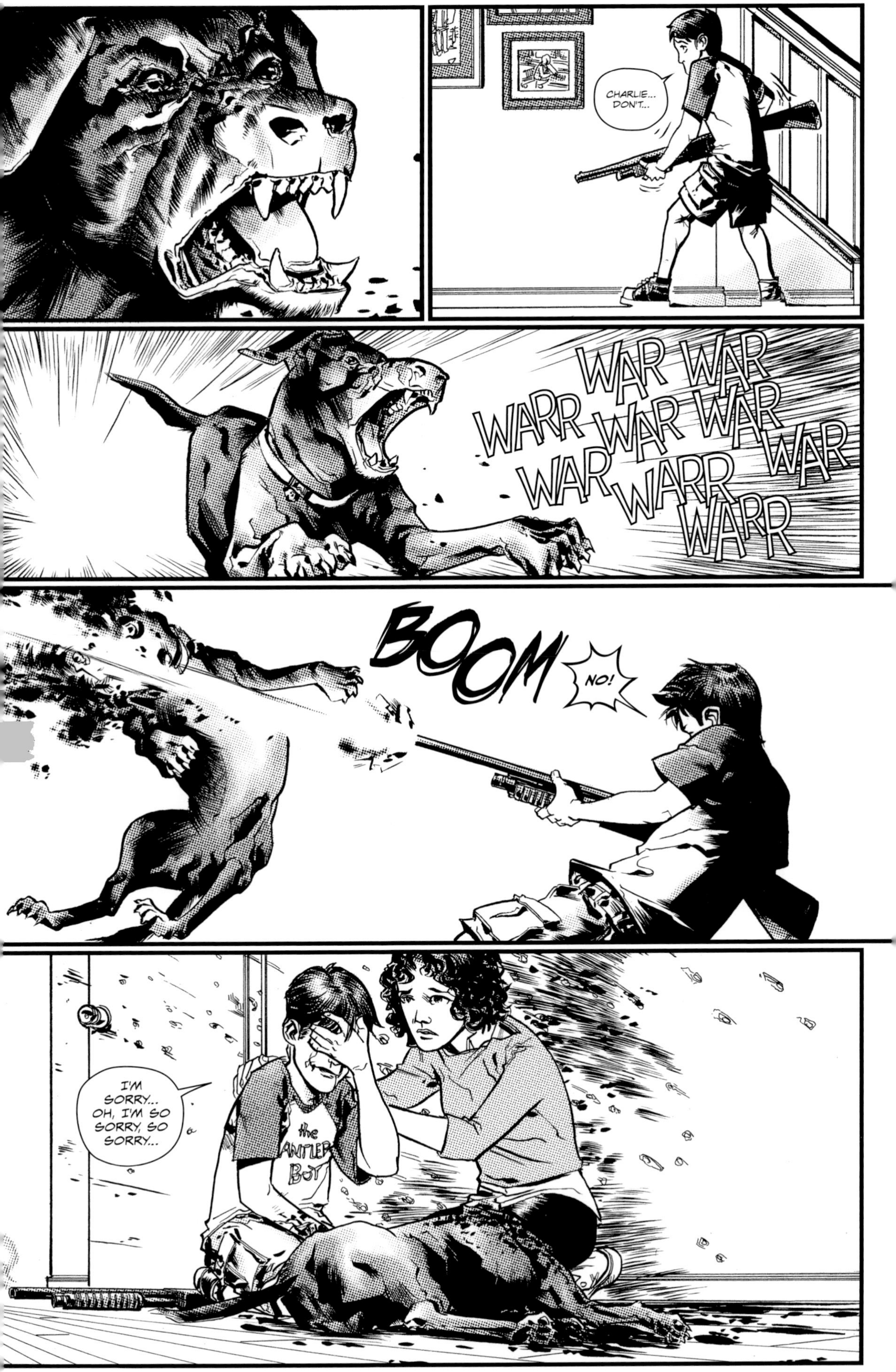
CHARLIE... DON'T...
WAR WAR WARR WAR WAR WAR WAR WARR WAR WARR
BOOM
NO!
I'M SORRY... OH, I'M SO SORRY, SO SORRY...
the ANTLER BOY

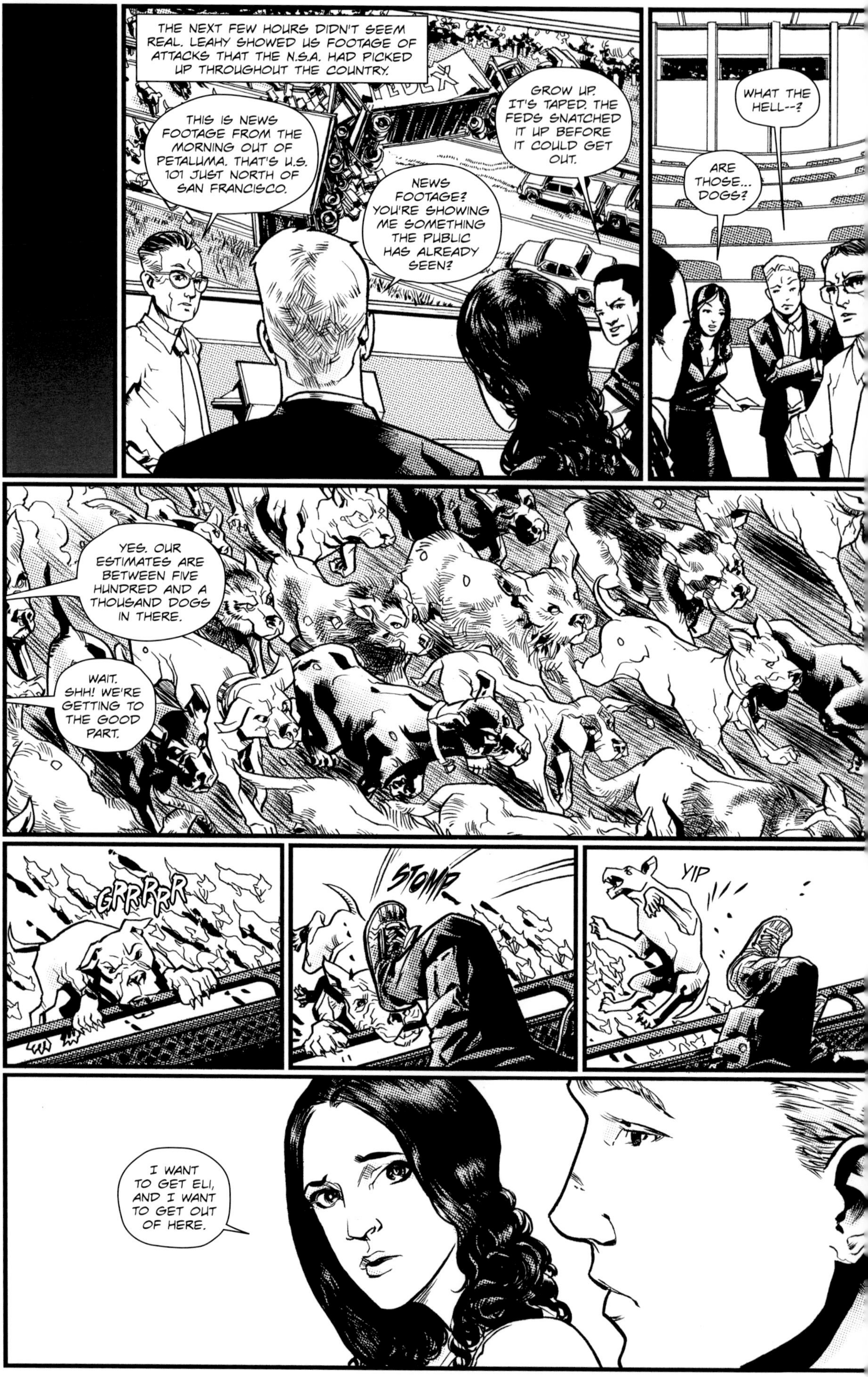
THE NEXT FEW HOURS DIDN'T SEEM REAL. LEAHY SHOWED US FOOTAGE OF ATTACKS THAT THE N.S.A. HAD PICKED UP THROUGHOUT THE COUNTRY.
THIS IS NEWS FOOTAGE FROM THE MORNING OUT OF PETALUMA. THAT'S U.S. 101 JUST NORTH OF SAN FRANCISCO.
NEWS FOOTAGE? YOU'RE SHOWING ME SOMETHING THE PUBLIC HAS ALREADY SEEN?
GROW UP. IT'S TAPED. THE FEDS SNATCHED IT UP BEFORE IT COULD GET OUT.
WHAT THE HELL--?
ARE THOSE... DOGS?
YES. OUR ESTIMATES ARE BETWEEN FIVE HUNDRED AND A THOUSAND DOGS IN THERE.
WAIT. SHH! WE'RE GETTING TO THE GOOD PART.
GRRRRR
STOMP
YIP
I WANT TO GET ELI, AND I WANT TO GET OUT OF HERE.

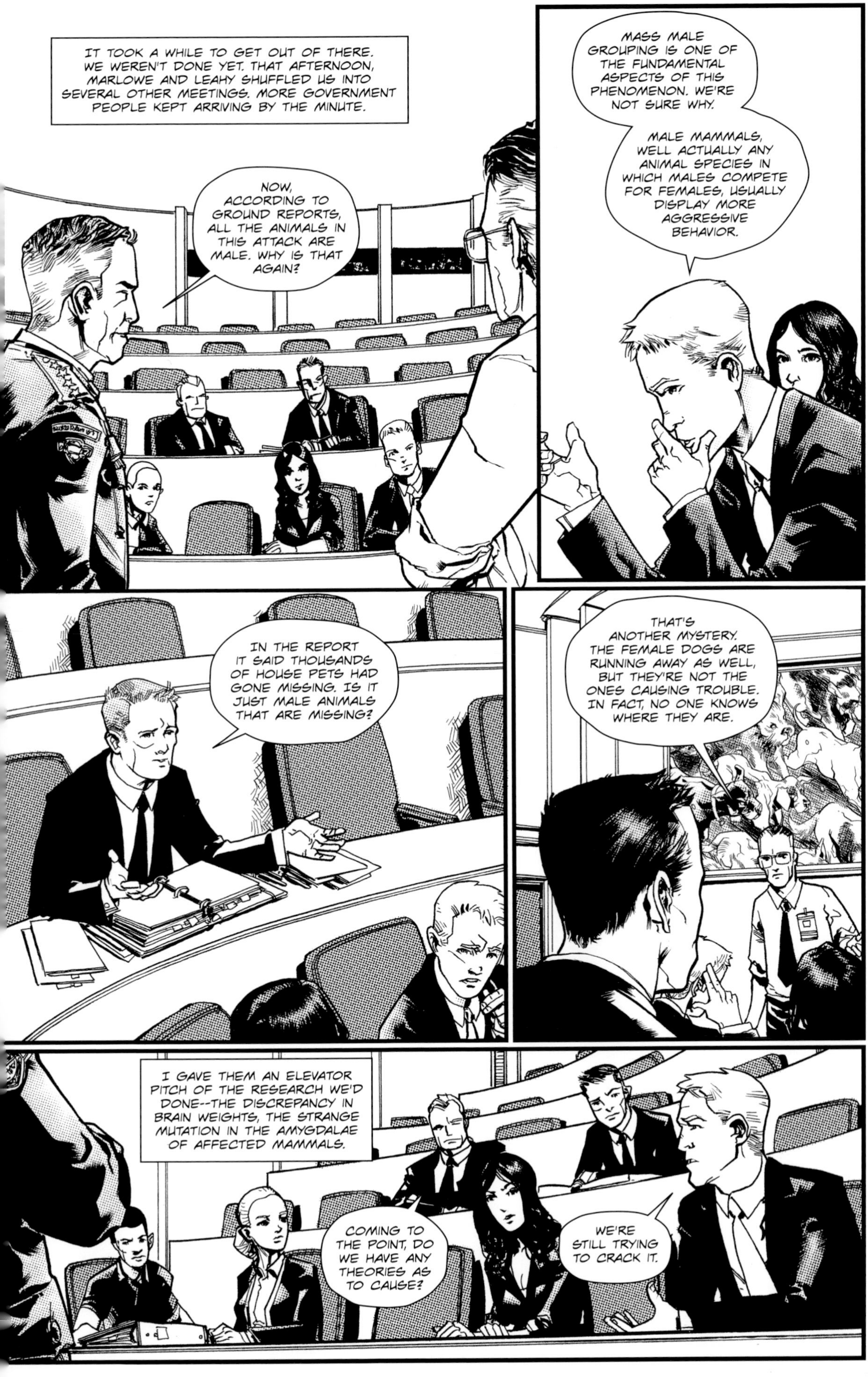
IT TOOK A WHILE TO GET OUT OF THERE. WE WEREN'T DONE YET. THAT AFTERNOON, MARLOWE AND LEAHY SHUFFLED US INTO SEVERAL OTHER MEETINGS. MORE GOVERNMENT PEOPLE KEPT ARRIVING BY THE MINUTE.
NOW, ACCORDING TO GROUND REPORTS, ALL THE ANIMALS IN THIS ATTACK ARE MALE. WHY IS THAT AGAIN?
MASS MALE GROUPING IS ONE OF THE FUNDAMENTAL ASPECTS OF THIS PHENOMENON. WE'RE NOT SURE WHY.
MALE MAMMALS, WELL ACTUALLY ANY ANIMAL SPECIES IN WHICH MALES COMPETE FOR FEMALES, USUALLY DISPLAY MORE AGGRESSIVE BEHAVIOR.
IN THE REPORT IT SAID THOUSANDS OF HOUSE PETS HAD GONE MISSING. IS IT JUST MALE ANIMALS THAT ARE MISSING?
THAT'S ANOTHER MYSTERY. THE FEMALE DOGS ARE RUNNING AWAY AS WELL, BUT THEY'RE NOT THE ONES CAUSING TROUBLE. IN FACT, NO ONE KNOWS WHERE THEY ARE.
I GAVE THEM AN ELEVATOR PITCH OF THE RESEARCH WE'D DONE--THE DISCREPANCY IN BRAIN WEIGHTS, THE STRANGE MUTATION IN THE AMYGDALAE OF AFFECTED MAMMALS.
COMING TO THE POINT, DO WE HAVE ANY THEORIES AS TO CAUSE?
WE'RE STILL TRYING TO CRACK IT.

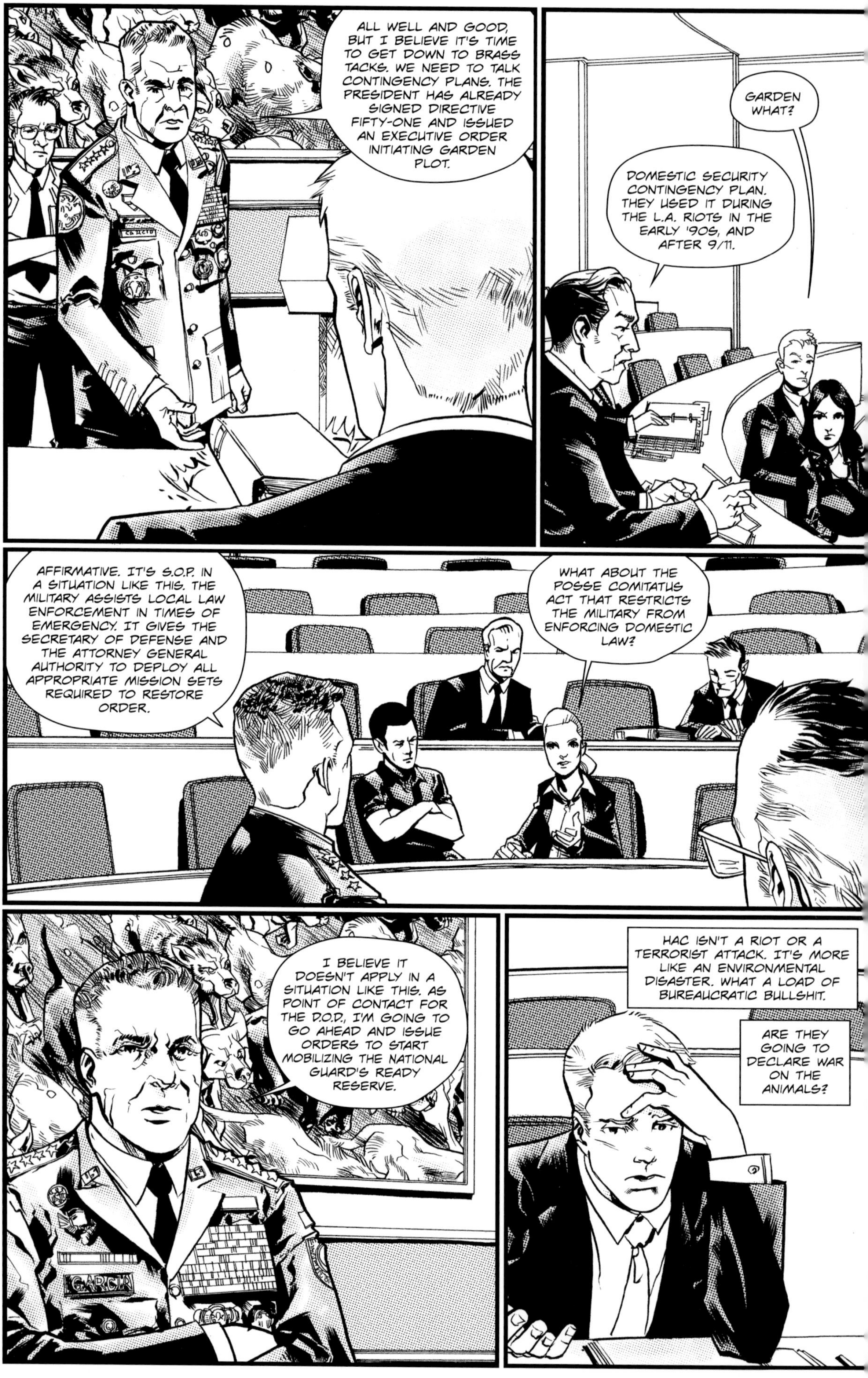
ALL WELL AND GOOD, BUT I BELIEVE IT'S TIME TO GET DOWN TO BRASS TACKS. WE NEED TO TALK CONTINGENCY PLANS. THE PRESIDENT HAS ALREADY SIGNED DIRECTIVE FIFTY-ONE AND ISSUED AN EXECUTIVE ORDER INITIATING GARDEN PLOT.
GARDEN WHAT?
DOMESTIC SECURITY CONTINGENCY PLAN. THEY USED IT DURING THE L.A. RIOTS IN THE EARLY '90S, AND AFTER 9/11.
AFFIRMATIVE. IT'S S.O.P. IN A SITUATION LIKE THIS. THE MILITARY ASSISTS LOCAL LAW ENFORCEMENT IN TIMES OF EMERGENCY. IT GIVES THE SECRETARY OF DEFENSE AND THE ATTORNEY GENERAL AUTHORITY TO DEPLOY ALL APPROPRIATE MISSION SETS REQUIRED TO RESTORE ORDER.
WHAT ABOUT THE POSSE COMITATUS ACT THAT RESTRICTS THE MILITARY FROM ENFORCING DOMESTIC LAW?
I BELIEVE IT DOESN'T APPLY IN A SITUATION LIKE THIS. AS POINT OF CONTACT FOR THE D.O.D., I'M GOING TO GO AHEAD AND ISSUE ORDERS TO START MOBILIZING THE NATIONAL GUARD'S READY RESERVE.
GARCIA
HAC ISN'T A RIOT OR A TERRORIST ATTACK. IT'S MORE LIKE AN ENVIRONMENTAL DISASTER. WHAT A LOAD OF BUREAUCRATIC BULLSHIT.
ARE THEY GOING TO DECLARE WAR ON THE ANIMALS?

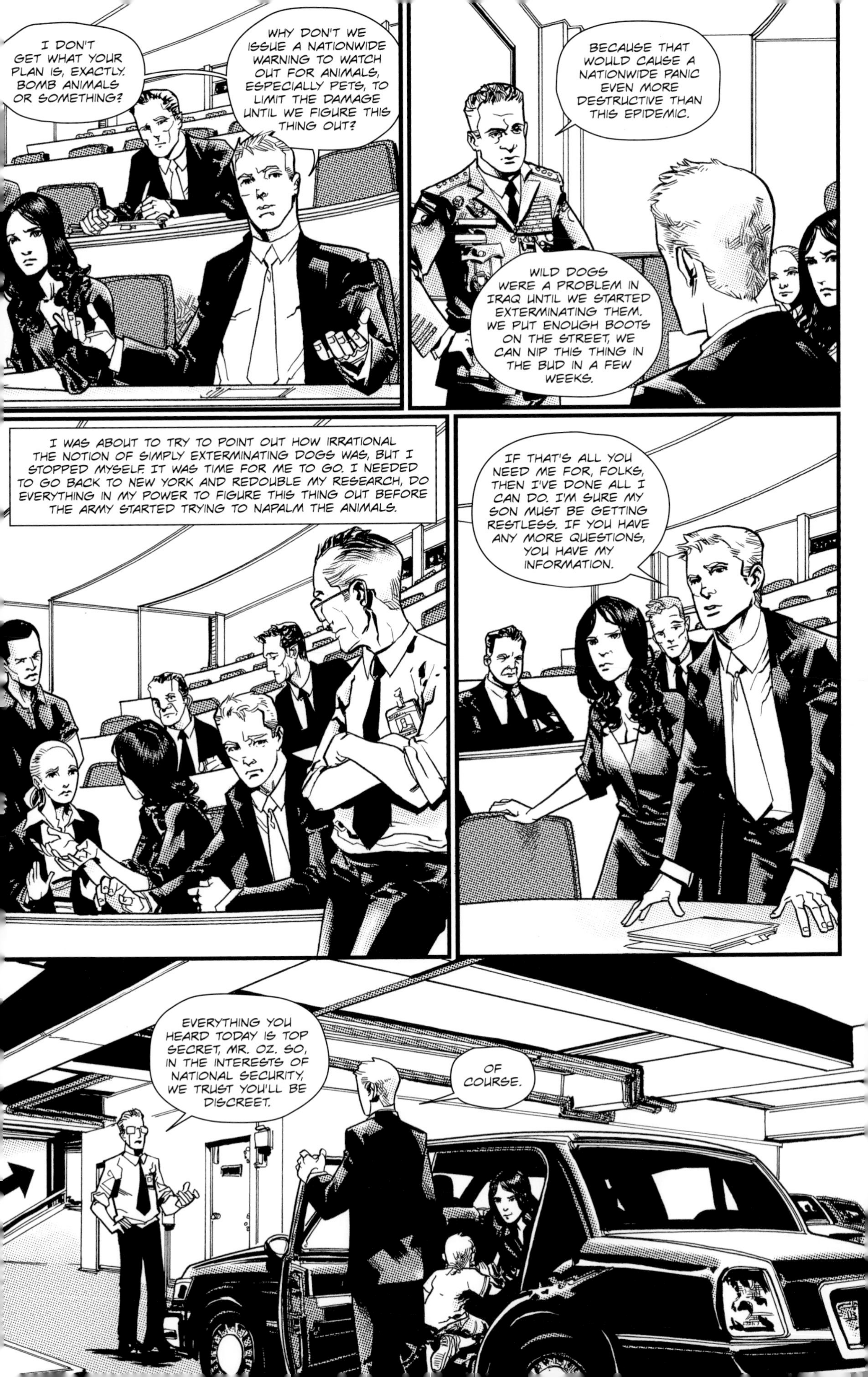

I DON'T GET WHAT YOUR PLAN IS, EXACTLY. BOMB ANIMALS OR SOMETHING?
WHY DON'T WE ISSUE A NATIONWIDE WARNING TO WATCH OUT FOR ANIMALS, ESPECIALLY PETS, TO LIMIT THE DAMAGE UNTIL WE FIGURE THIS THING OUT?
BECAUSE THAT WOULD CAUSE A NATIONWIDE PANIC EVEN MORE DESTRUCTIVE THAN THIS EPIDEMIC.
WILD DOGS WERE A PROBLEM IN IRAQ UNTIL WE STARTED EXTERMINATING THEM. WE PUT ENOUGH BOOTS ON THE STREET, WE CAN NIP THIS THING IN THE BUD IN A FEW WEEKS.
I WAS ABOUT TO TRY TO POINT OUT HOW IRRATIONAL THE NOTION OF SIMPLY EXTERMINATING DOGS WAS, BUT I STOPPED MYSELF. IT WAS TIME FOR ME TO GO. I NEEDED TO GO BACK TO NEW YORK AND REDOUBLE MY RESEARCH, DO EVERYTHING IN MY POWER TO FIGURE THIS THING OUT BEFORE THE ARMY STARTED TRYING TO NAPALM THE ANIMALS.
IF THAT'S ALL YOU NEED ME FOR, FOLKS, THEN I'VE DONE ALL I CAN DO. I'M SURE MY SON MUST BE GETTING RESTLESS. IF YOU HAVE ANY MORE QUESTIONS, YOU HAVE MY INFORMATION.
EVERYTHING YOU HEARD TODAY IS TOP SECRET, MR. OZ. SO, IN THE INTERESTS OF NATIONAL SECURITY, WE TRUST YOU'LL BE DISCREET.
OF COURSE.

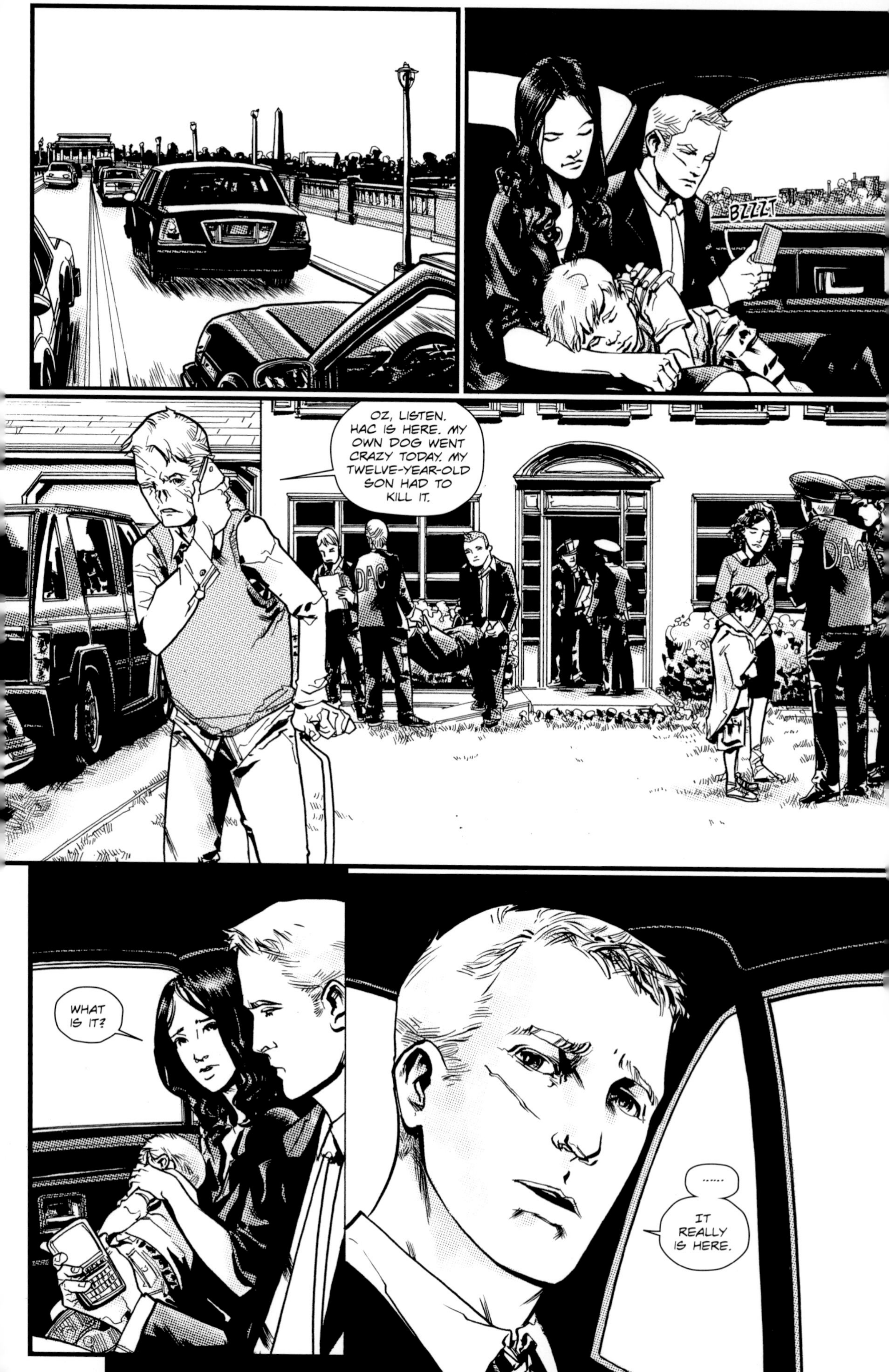
BZZZT
OZ, LISTEN. HAC IS HERE. MY OWN DOG WENT CRAZY TODAY. MY TWELVE-YEAR-OLD SON HAD TO KILL IT.
DAC
DAC
WHAT IS IT?
......
IT REALLY IS HERE.

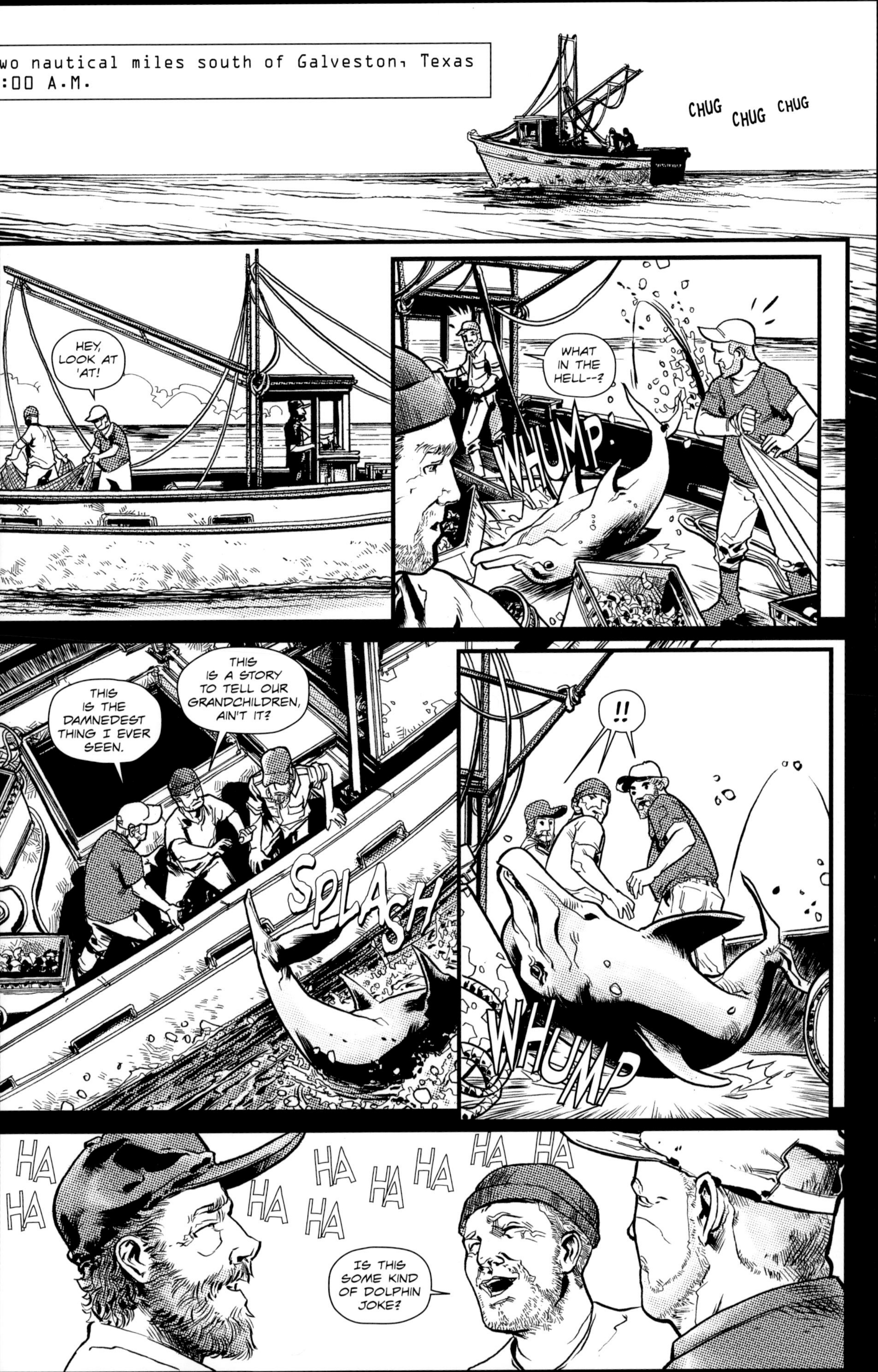
wo nautical miles south of Galveston, Texas
:00 A.M.
CHUG CHUG CHUG
HEY, LOOK AT 'AT!
WHAT IN THE HELL--?
WHUMP
THIS IS THE DAMNEDEST THING I EVER SEEN.
THIS IS A STORY TO TELL OUR GRANDCHILDREN, AIN'T IT?
SPLASH
!!
WHUMP
HA HA HA HA HA HA HA HA HA HA
IS THIS SOME KIND OF DOLPHIN JOKE?

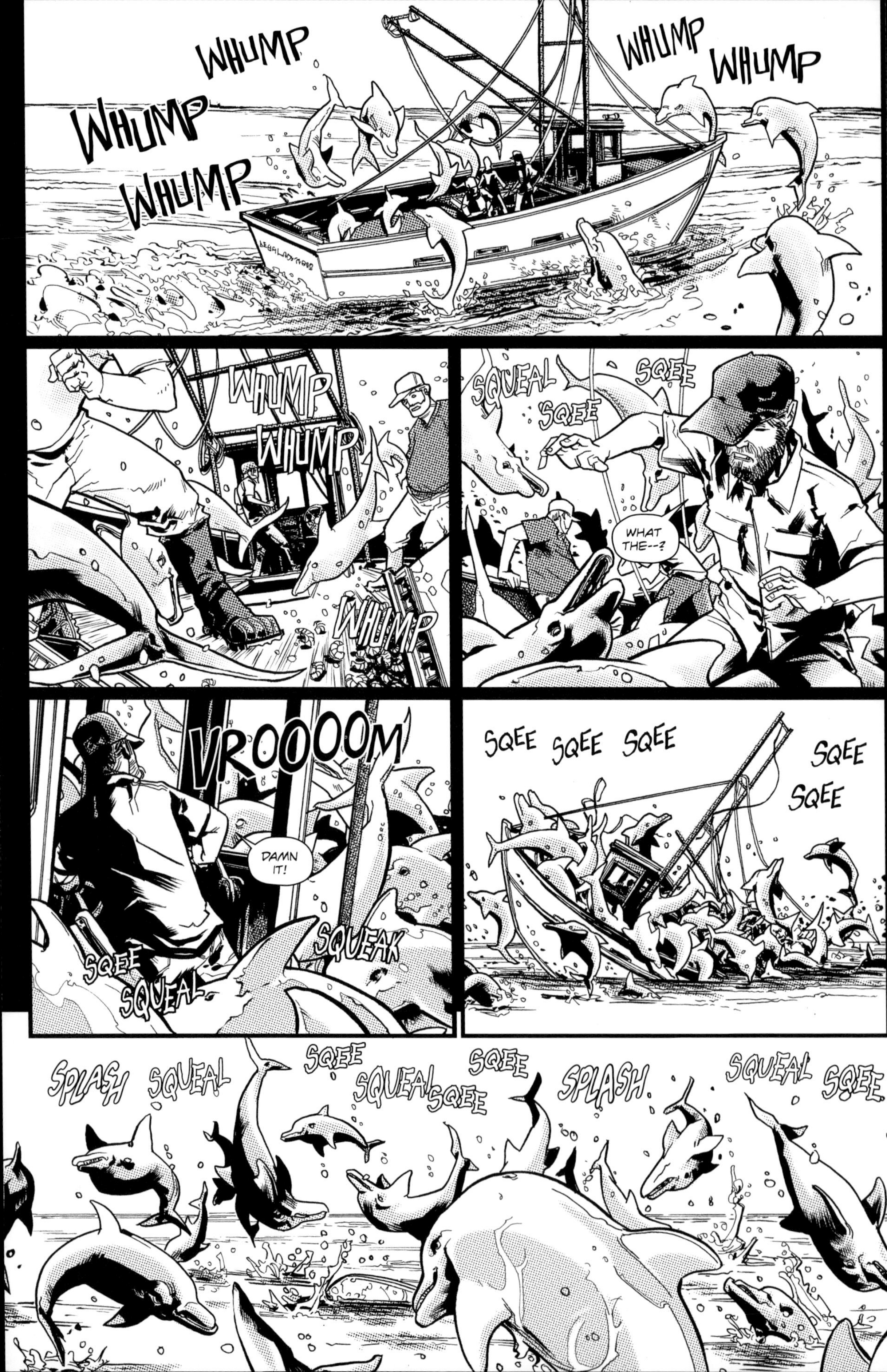
WHUMP
WHUMP
WHUMP
WHUMP
WHUMP
WHUMP
WHUMP
WHUMP
SQUEAL
SQEE
SQEE
WHAT THE--?
VROOOOM
DAMN IT!
SQUEAK
SQEE
SQUEAL
SQEE
SQEE
SQEE
SQEE
SQEE
SPLASH
SQUEAL
SQEE
SQUEAL
SQEE
SQEE
SPLASH
SQUEAL
SQEE

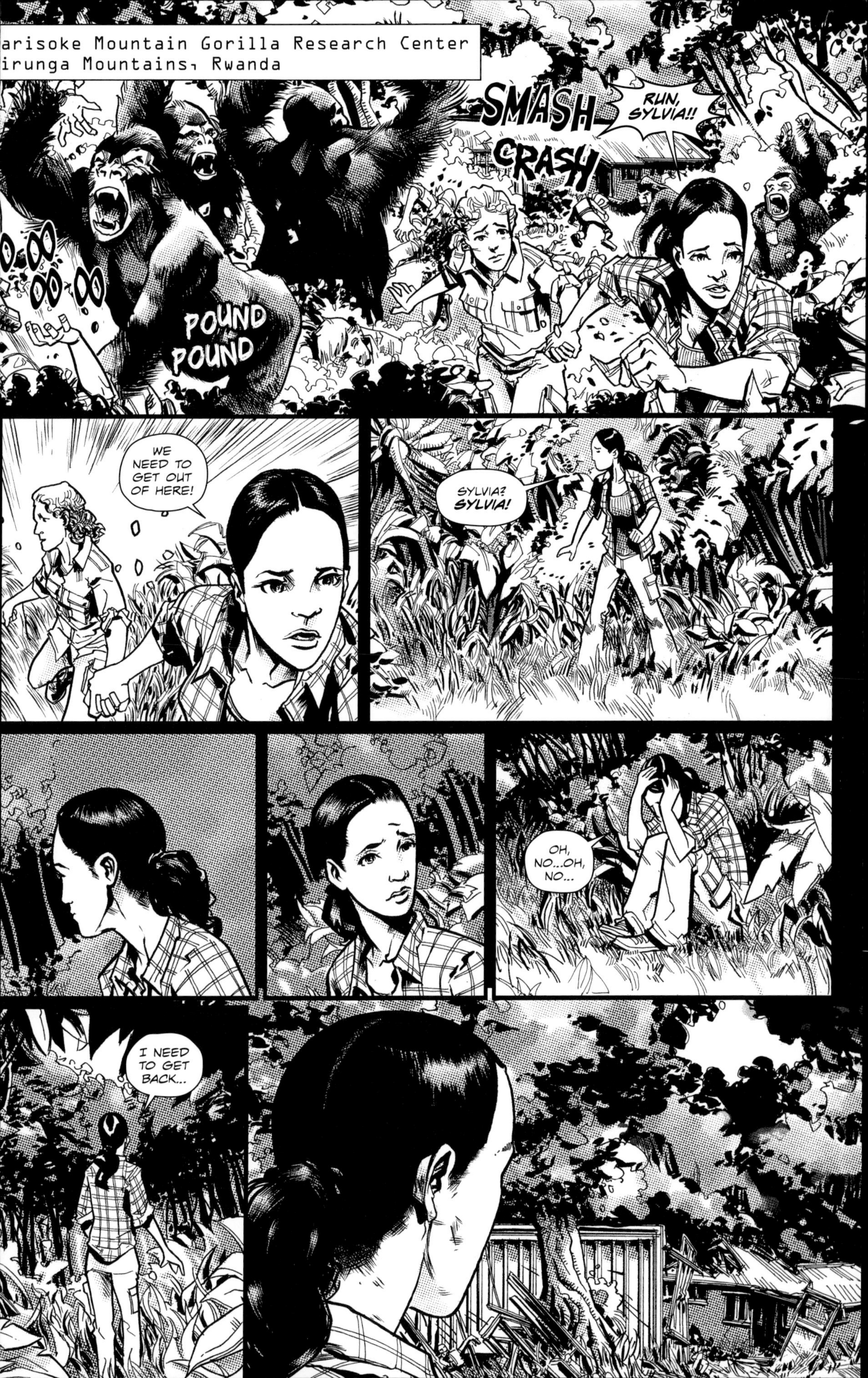
arisoke Mountain Gorilla Research Center
irunga Mountains, Rwanda
SMASH
CRASH
RUN, SYLVIA!!
POUND POUND
WE NEED TO GET OUT OF HERE!
SYLVIA? SYLVIA!
OH, NO...OH, NO...
I NEED TO GET BACK...

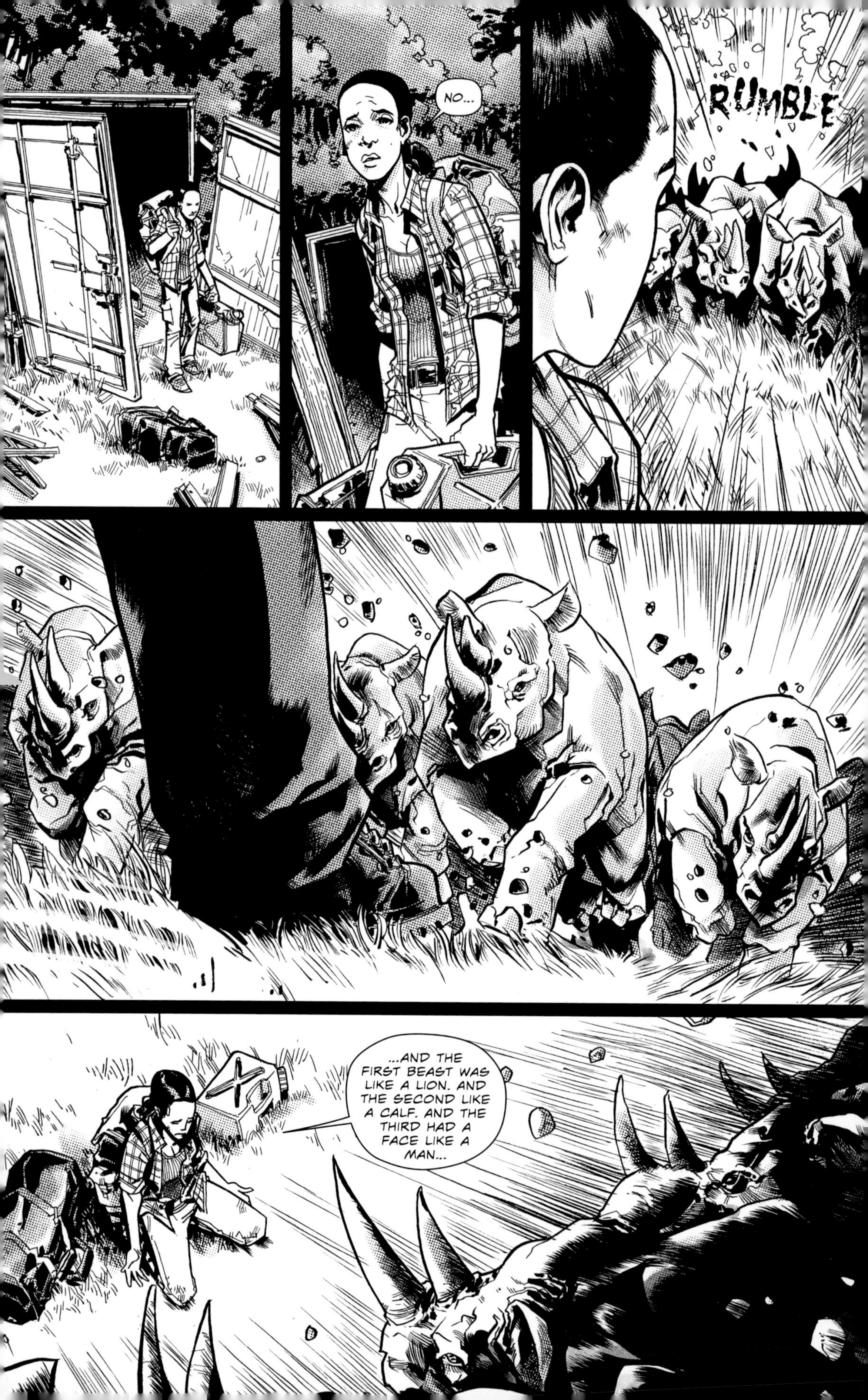
NO...
RUMBLE
...AND THE FIRST BEAST WAS LIKE A LION. AND THE SECOND LIKE A CALF. AND THE THIRD HAD A FACE LIKE A MAN...

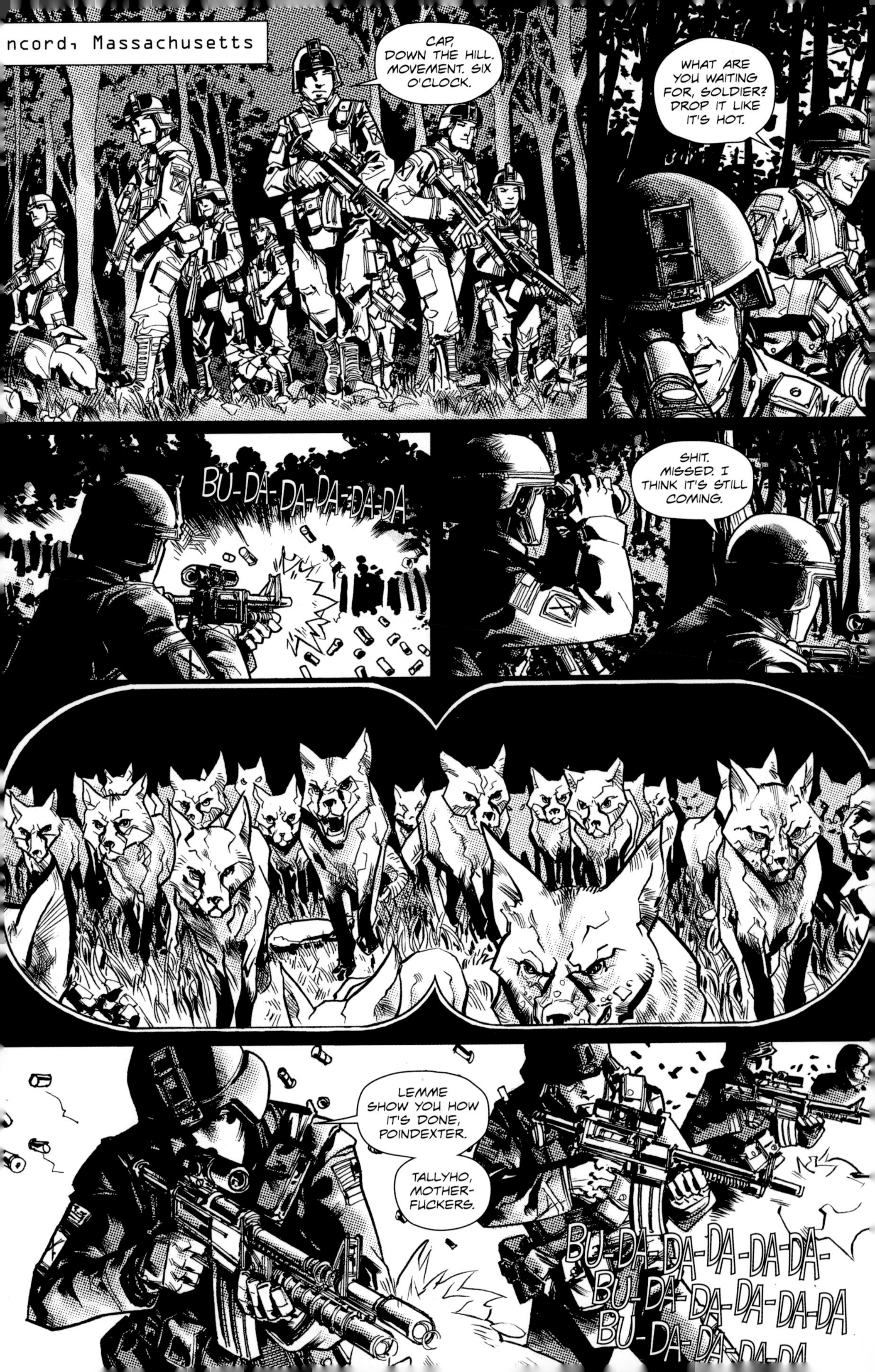
ncord, Massachusetts
CAP, DOWN THE HILL. MOVEMENT. SIX O'CLOCK.
WHAT ARE YOU WAITING FOR, SOLDIER? DROP IT LIKE IT'S HOT.
BU-DA-DA-DA-DA-DA
SHIT. MISSED. I THINK IT'S STILL COMING.
LEMME SHOW YOU HOW IT'S DONE, POINDEXTER.
TALLYHO, MOTHER-FUCKERS.
BU-DA-DA-DA-DA-DA-
BU-DA-DA-DA-DA-DA
BU-DA-DA-DA-DA

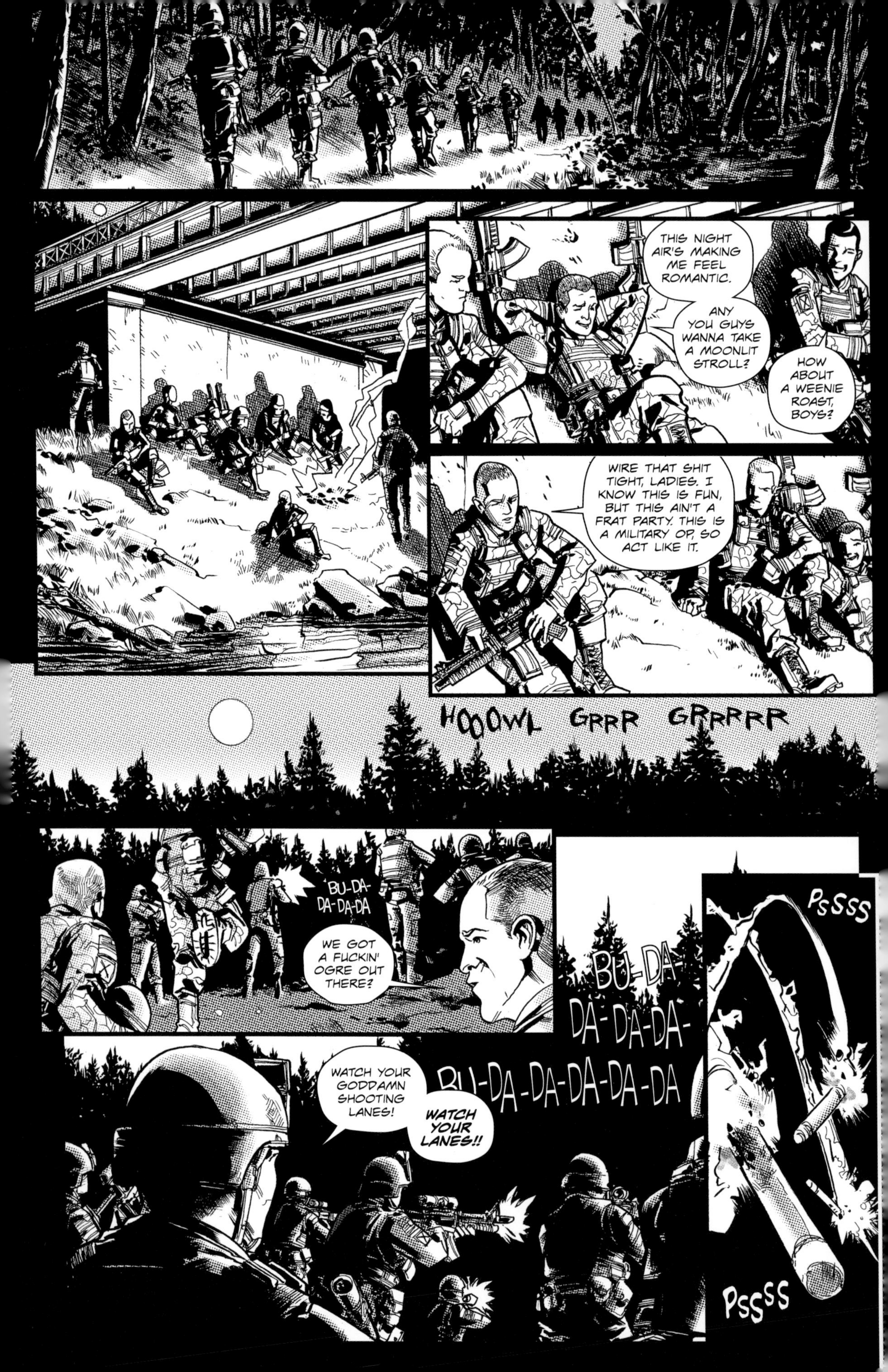

THIS NIGHT AIR'S MAKING ME FEEL ROMANTIC.
ANY YOU GUYS WANNA TAKE A MOONLIT STROLL?
HOW ABOUT A WEENIE ROAST, BOYS?
WIRE THAT SHIT TIGHT, LADIES. I KNOW THIS IS FUN, BUT THIS AIN'T A FRAT PARTY. THIS IS A MILITARY OP, SO ACT LIKE IT.
HOOOWL GRRR GRRRRR
BU-DA-DA-DA-DA
WE GOT A FUCKIN' OGRE OUT THERE?
BU-DA-DA-DA-DA-
PSSSS
WATCH YOUR GODDAMN SHOOTING LANES!
WATCH YOUR LANES!!
BU-DA-DA-DA-DA-DA
PSSSS

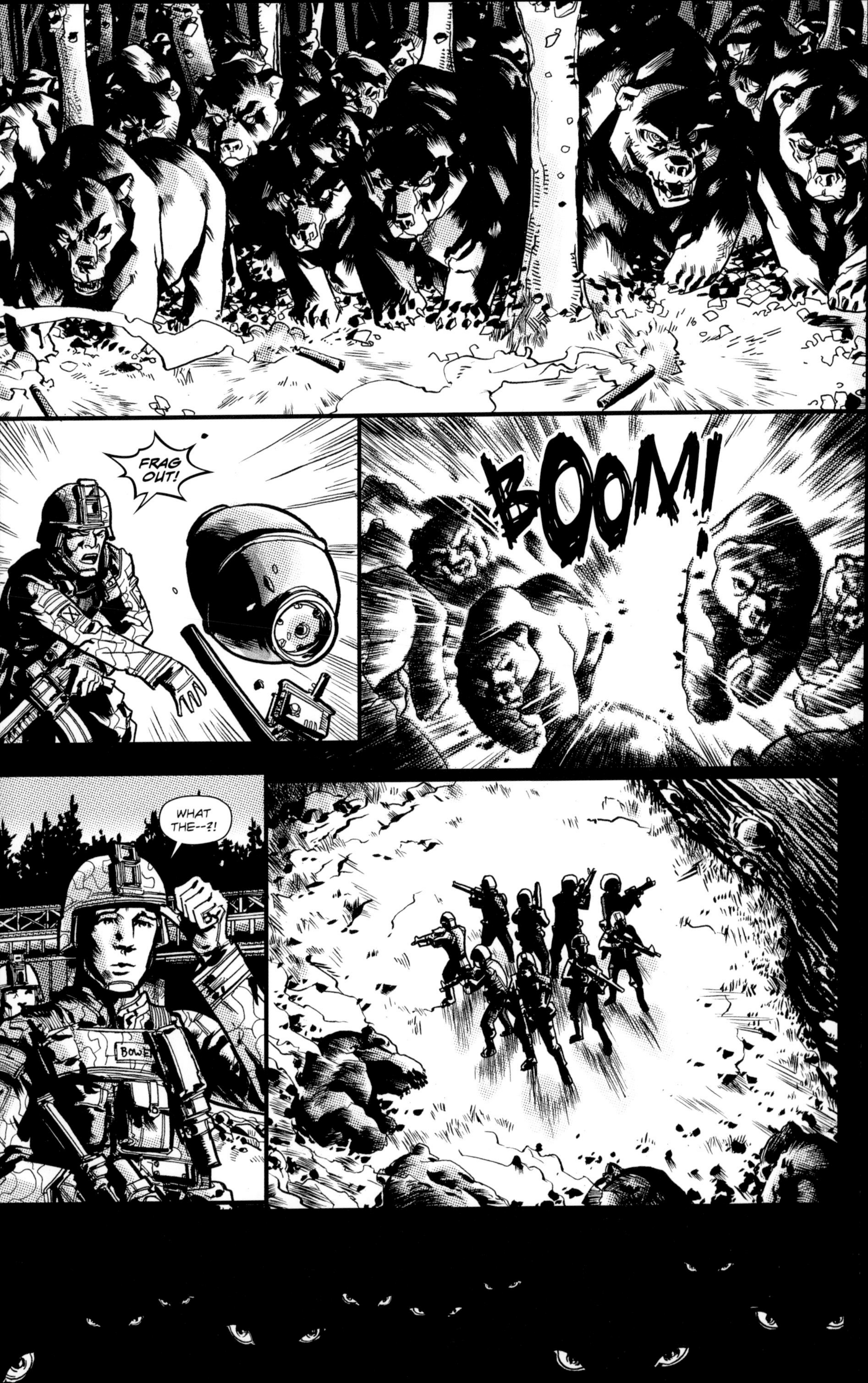
FRAG OUT!
BOOM!
WHAT THE--?!
BOWE

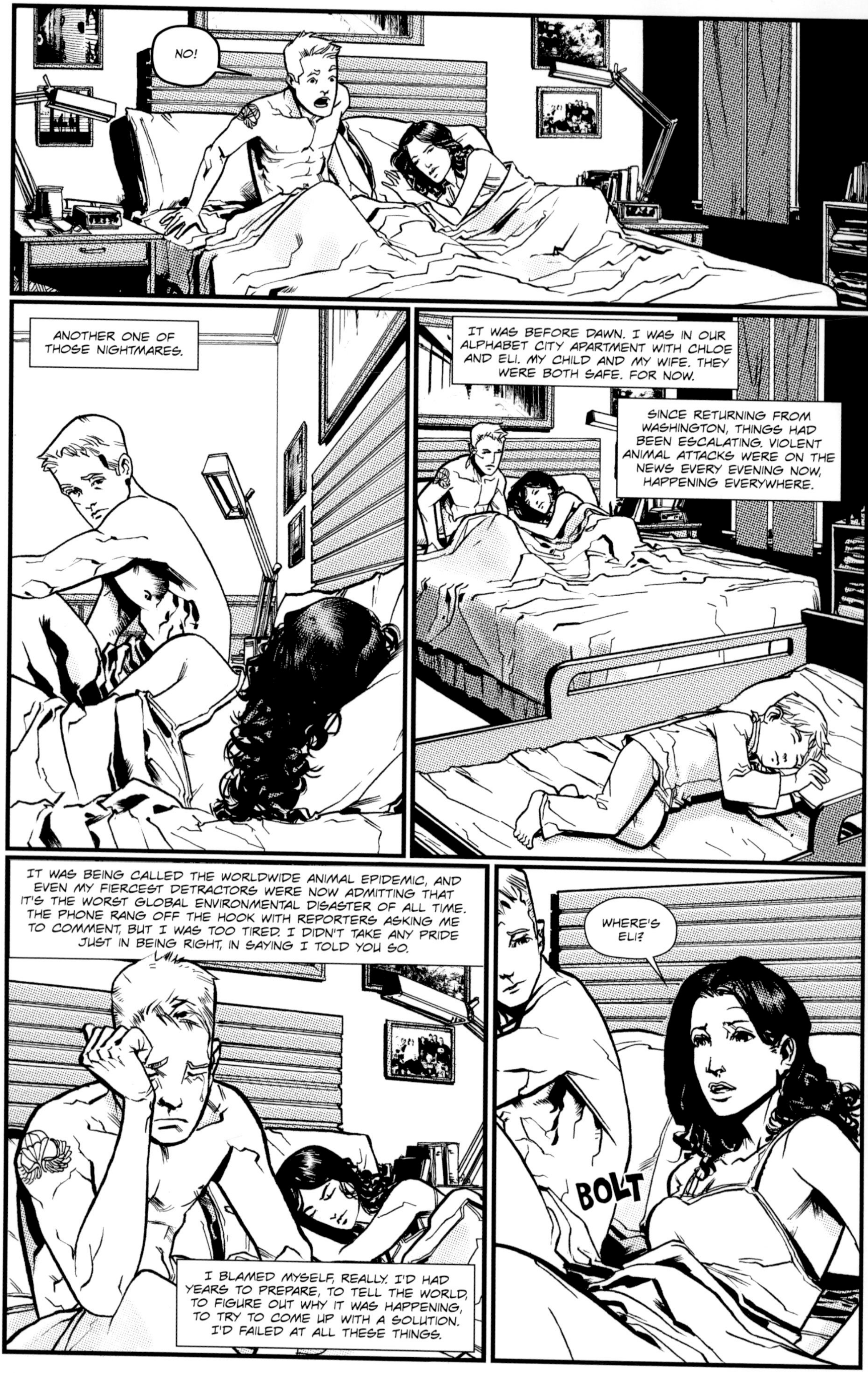

NO!
ANOTHER ONE OF THOSE NIGHTMARES.
IT WAS BEFORE DAWN. I WAS IN OUR ALPHABET CITY APARTMENT WITH CHLOE AND ELI. MY CHILD AND MY WIFE. THEY WERE BOTH SAFE. FOR NOW.
SINCE RETURNING FROM WASHINGTON, THINGS HAD BEEN ESCALATING. VIOLENT ANIMAL ATTACKS WERE ON THE NEWS EVERY EVENING NOW, HAPPENING EVERYWHERE.
IT WAS BEING CALLED THE WORLDWIDE ANIMAL EPIDEMIC, AND EVEN MY FIERCEST DETRACTORS WERE NOW ADMITTING THAT IT'S THE WORST GLOBAL ENVIRONMENTAL DISASTER OF ALL TIME. THE PHONE RANG OFF THE HOOK WITH REPORTERS ASKING ME TO COMMENT, BUT I WAS TOO TIRED. I DIDN'T TAKE ANY PRIDE JUST IN BEING RIGHT, IN SAYING I TOLD YOU SO.
I BLAMED MYSELF, REALLY. I'D HAD YEARS TO PREPARE, TO TELL THE WORLD, TO FIGURE OUT WHY IT WAS HAPPENING, TO TRY TO COME UP WITH A SOLUTION. I'D FAILED AT ALL THESE THINGS.
WHERE'S ELI?
BOLT

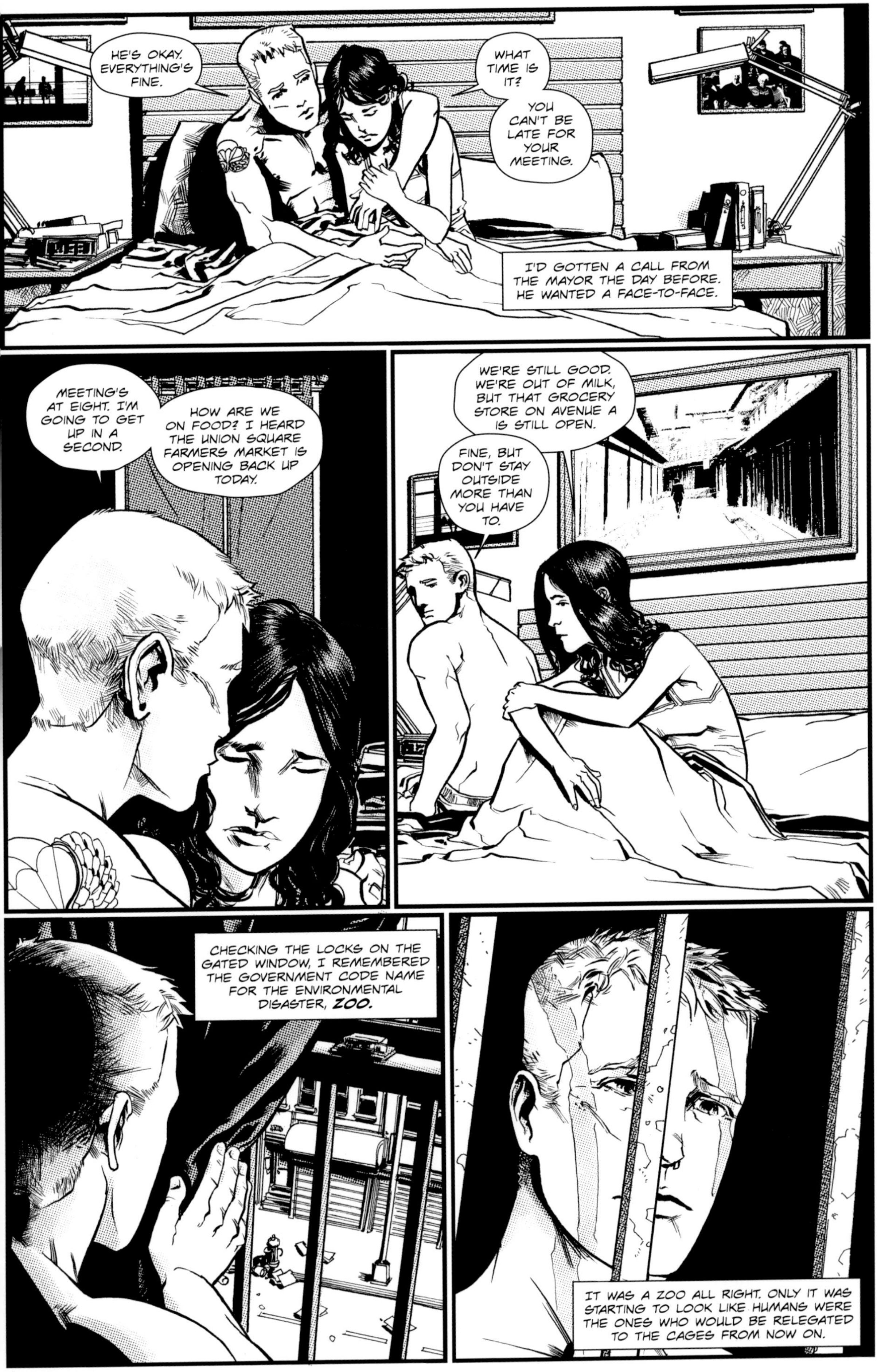

HE'S OKAY. EVERYTHING'S FINE.
WHAT TIME IS IT?
YOU CAN'T BE LATE FOR YOUR MEETING.
I'D GOTTEN A CALL FROM THE MAYOR THE DAY BEFORE. HE WANTED A FACE-TO-FACE.
MEETING'S AT EIGHT. I'M GOING TO GET UP IN A SECOND.
HOW ARE WE ON FOOD? I HEARD THE UNION SQUARE FARMERS MARKET IS OPENING BACK UP TODAY.
WE'RE STILL GOOD. WE'RE OUT OF MILK, BUT THAT GROCERY STORE ON AVENUE A IS STILL OPEN.
FINE, BUT DON'T STAY OUTSIDE MORE THAN YOU HAVE TO.
CHECKING THE LOCKS ON THE GATED WINDOW, I REMEMBERED THE GOVERNMENT CODE NAME FOR THE ENVIRONMENTAL DISASTER, ZOO.
IT WAS A ZOO ALL RIGHT. ONLY IT WAS STARTING TO LOOK LIKE HUMANS WERE THE ONES WHO WOULD BE RELEGATED TO THE CAGES FROM NOW ON.

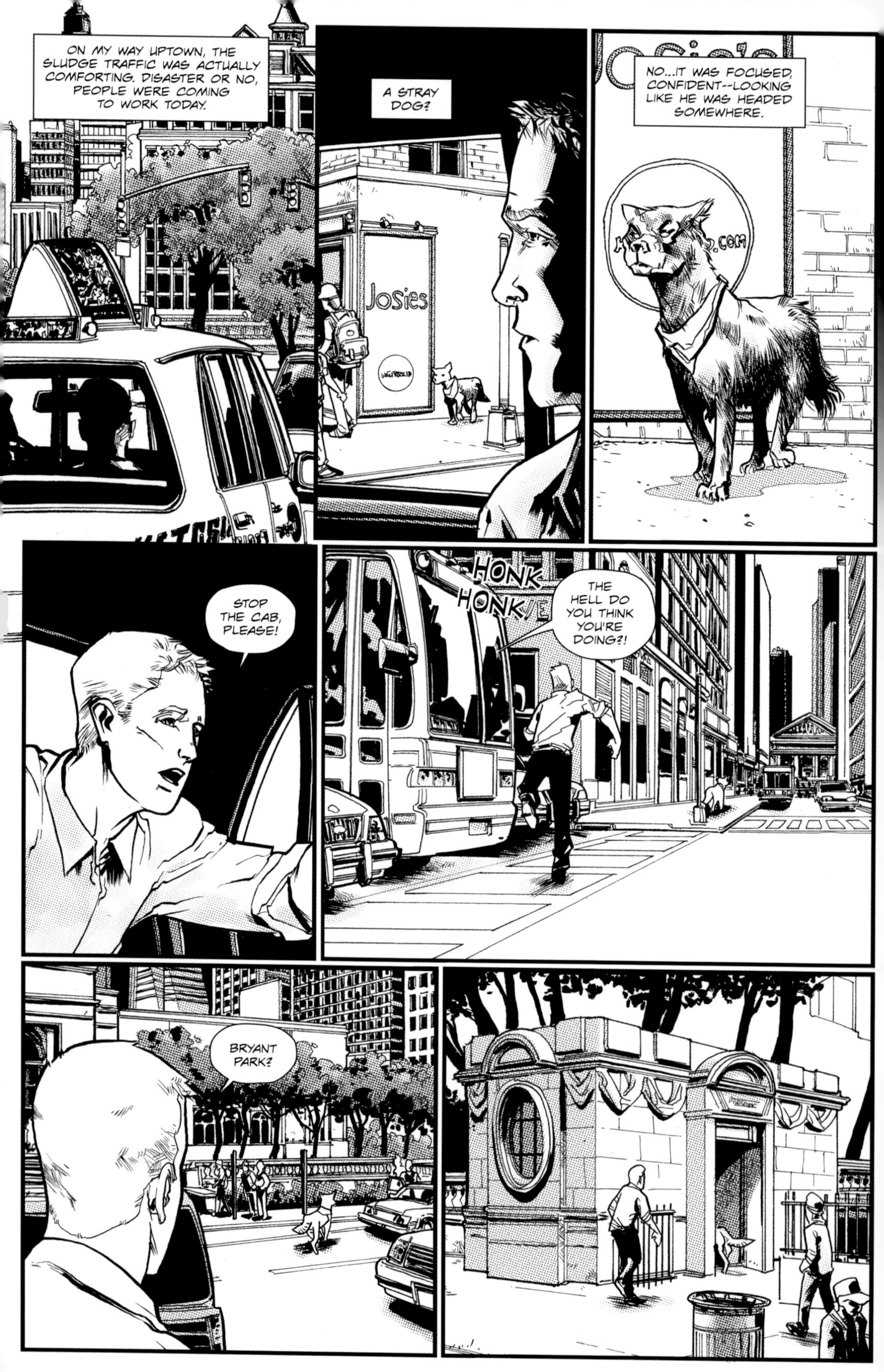
ON MY WAY UPTOWN, THE SLUDGE TRAFFIC WAS ACTUALLY COMFORTING. DISASTER OR NO, PEOPLE WERE COMING TO WORK TODAY.
A STRAY DOG?
Josies
NO...IT WAS FOCUSED, CONFIDENT--LOOKING LIKE HE WAS HEADED SOMEWHERE.
STOP THE CAB, PLEASE!
HONK
HONK
THE HELL DO YOU THINK YOU'RE DOING?!
BRYANT PARK?

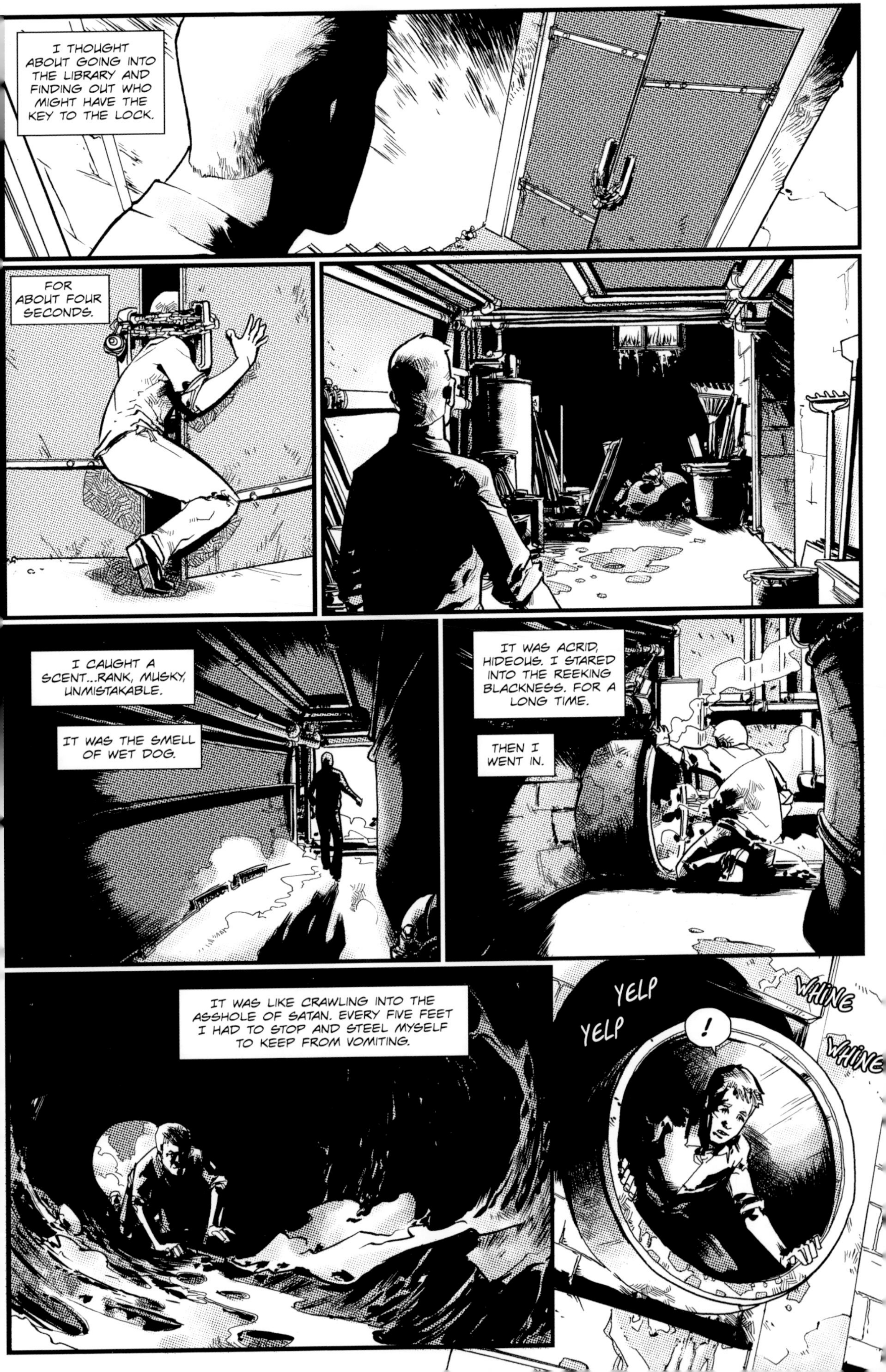
I THOUGHT ABOUT GOING INTO THE LIBRARY AND FINDING OUT WHO MIGHT HAVE THE KEY TO THE LOCK.
FOR ABOUT FOUR SECONDS.
I CAUGHT A SCENT...RANK, MUSKY, UNMISTAKABLE.
IT WAS THE SMELL OF WET DOG.
IT WAS ACRID, HIDEOUS. I STARED INTO THE REEKING BLACKNESS. FOR A LONG TIME.
THEN I WENT IN.
IT WAS LIKE CRAWLING INTO THE ASSHOLE OF SATAN. EVERY FIVE FEET I HAD TO STOP AND STEEL MYSELF TO KEEP FROM VOMITING.
YELP
YELP
!
WHINE
WHINE

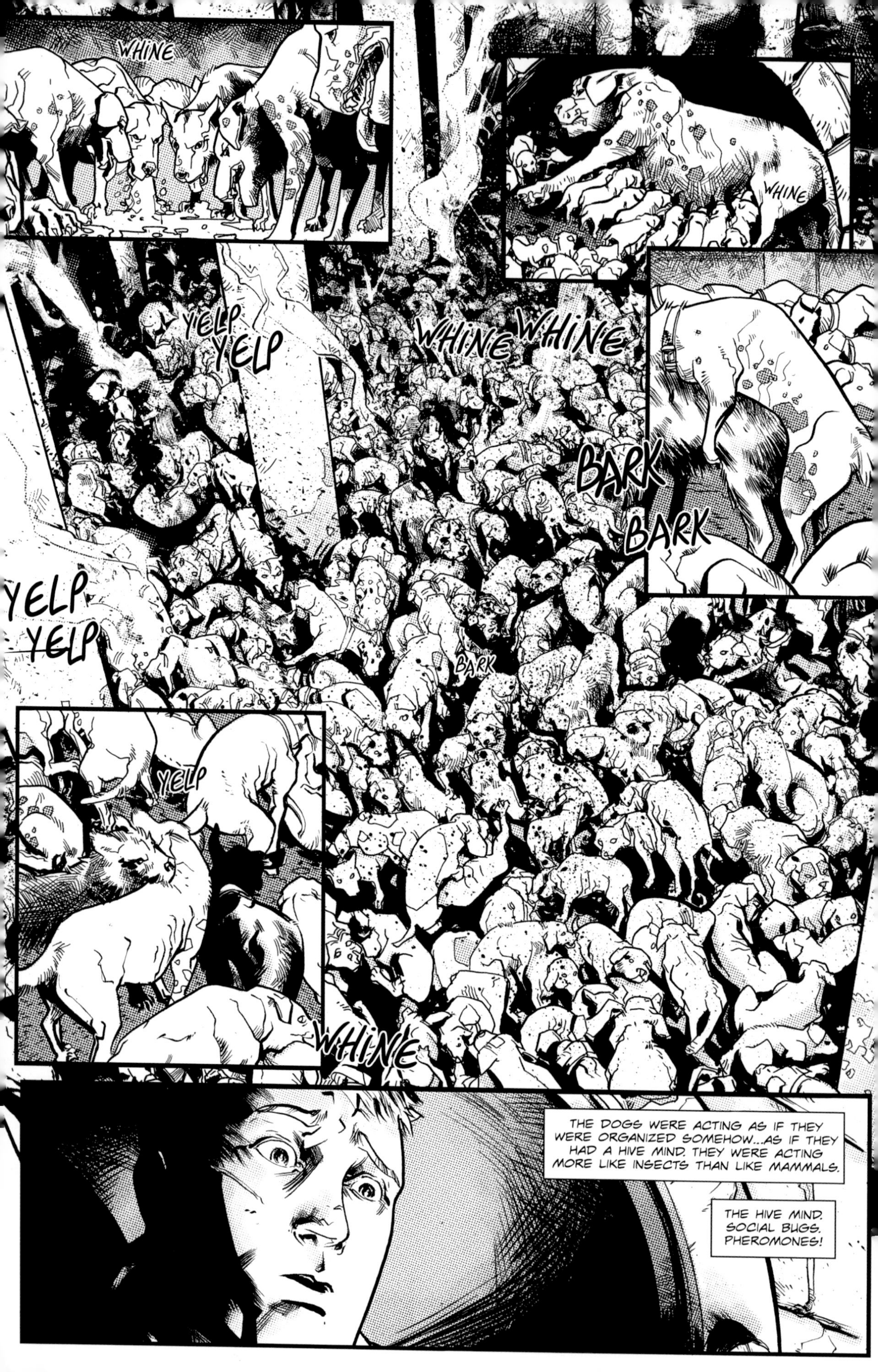
WHINE
WHINE
YELP
YELP
WHINE
WHINE
BARK
BARK
YELP
YELP
BARK
YELP
WHINE
THE DOGS WERE ACTING AS IF THEY WERE ORGANIZED SOMEHOW...AS IF THEY HAD A HIVE MIND. THEY WERE ACTING MORE LIKE INSECTS THAN LIKE MAMMALS.
THE HIVE MIND. SOCIAL BUGS. PHEROMONES!

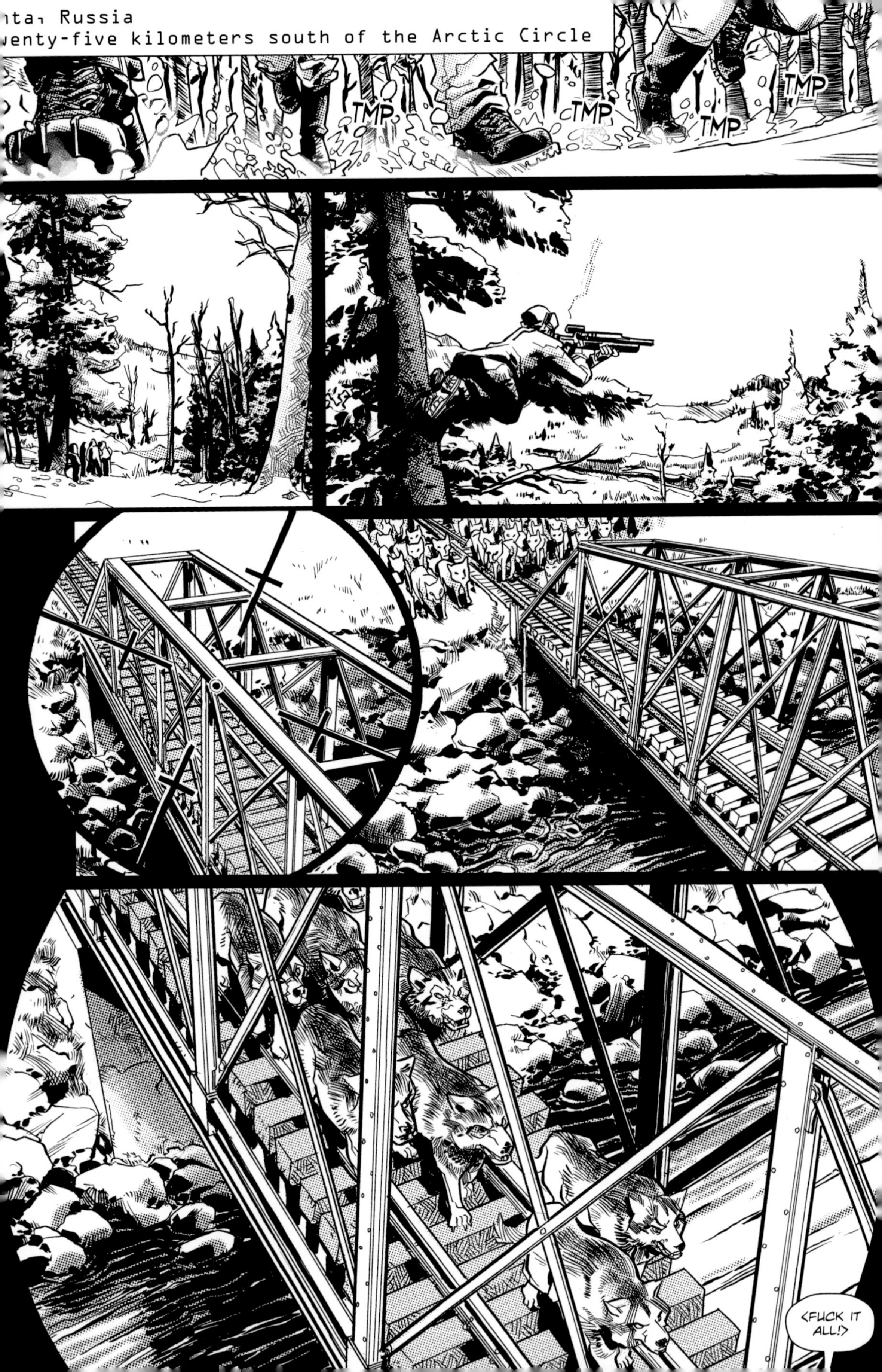
nta, Russia
wenty-five kilometers south of the Arctic Circle
TMP
TMP
TMP
TMP
<FUCK IT ALL!>

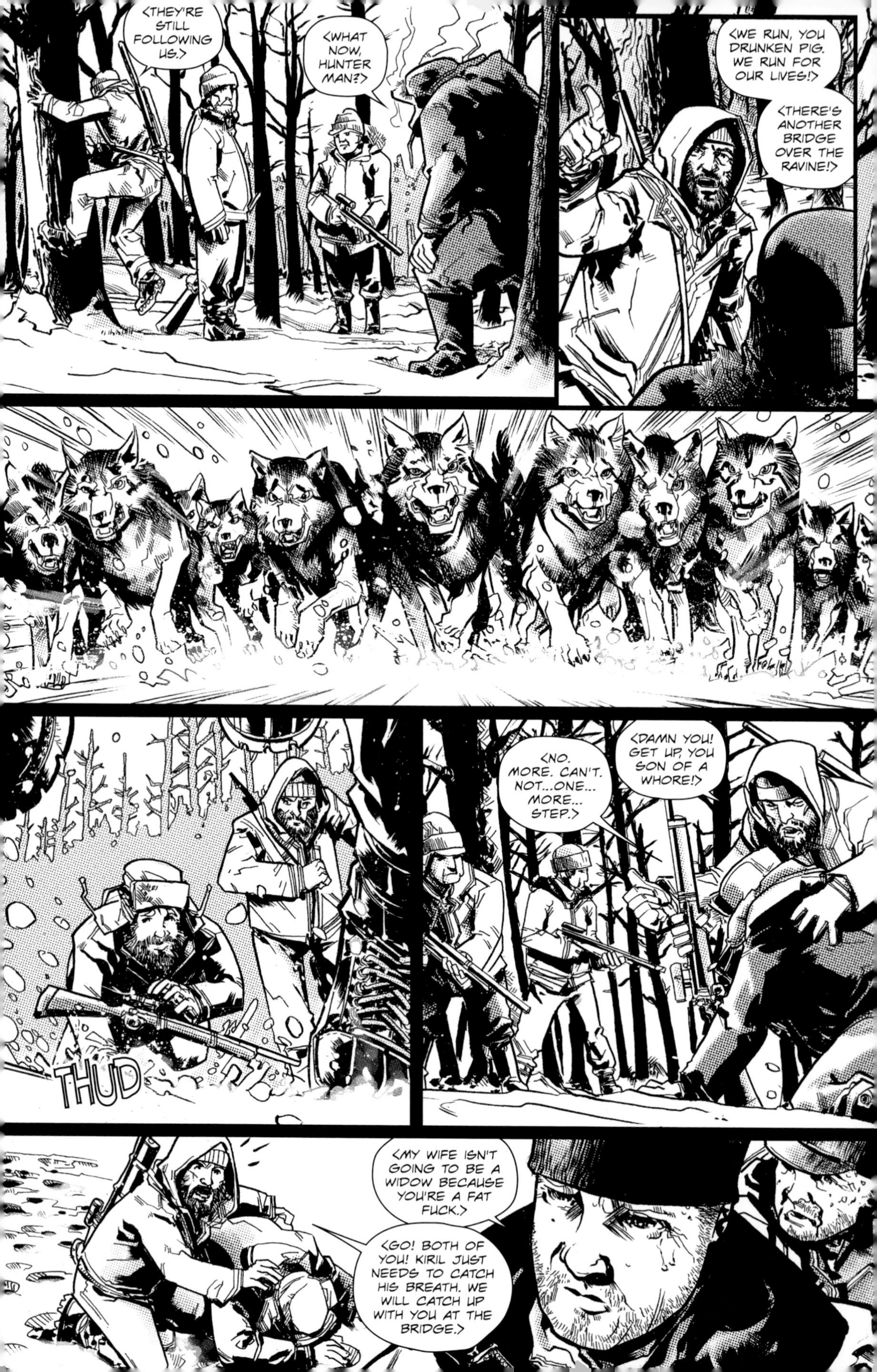

<THEY'RE STILL FOLLOWING US.>
<WHAT NOW, HUNTER MAN?>
<WE RUN, YOU DRUNKEN PIG. WE RUN FOR OUR LIVES!>
<THERE'S ANOTHER BRIDGE OVER THE RAVINE!>
THUD
<NO. MORE. CAN'T. NOT...ONE... MORE... STEP.>
<DAMN YOU! GET UP, YOU SON OF A WHORE!>
<MY WIFE ISN'T GOING TO BE A WIDOW BECAUSE YOU'RE A FAT FUCK.>
<GO! BOTH OF YOU! KIRIL JUST NEEDS TO CATCH HIS BREATH. WE WILL CATCH UP WITH YOU AT THE BRIDGE.>

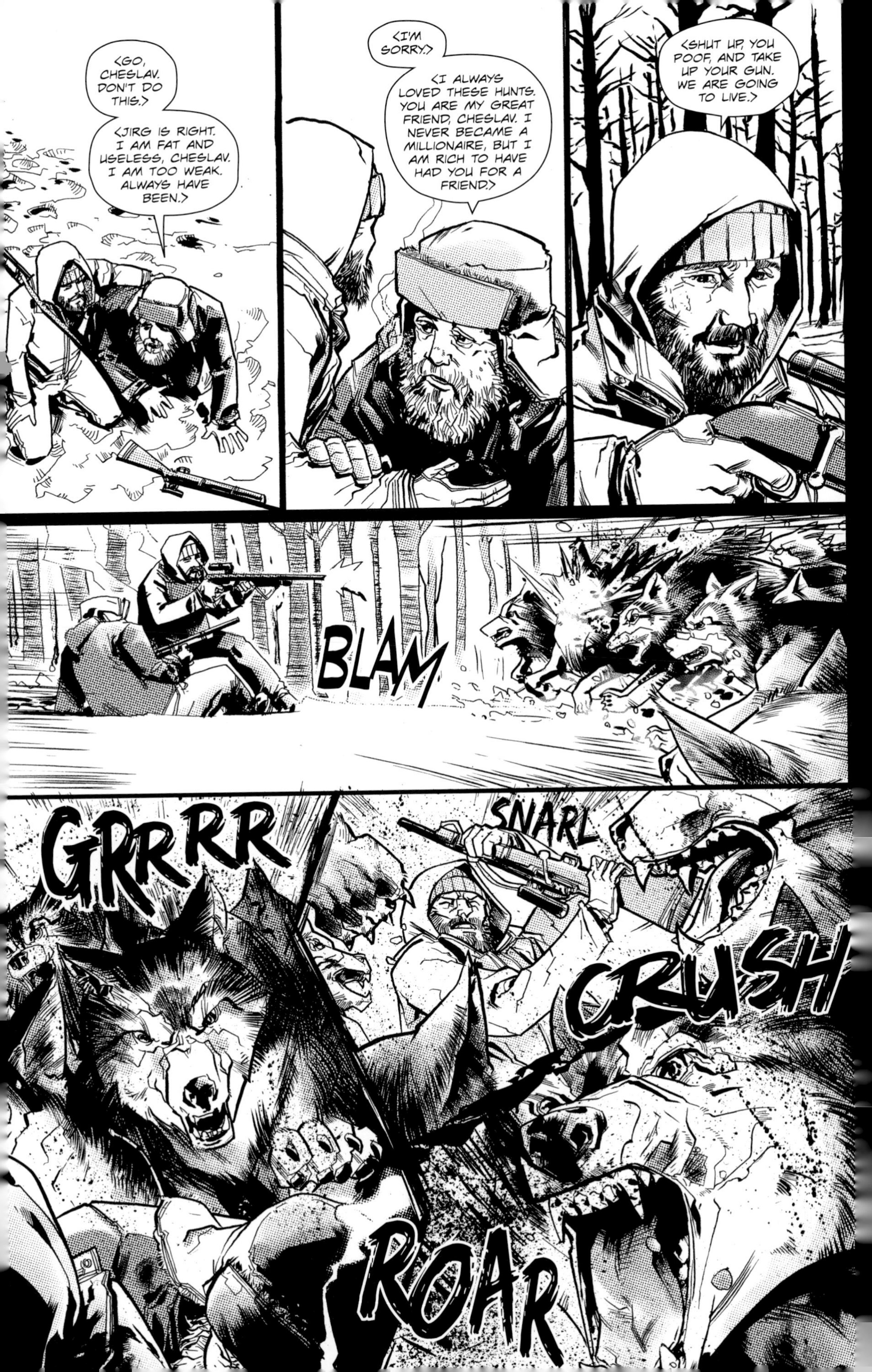

<GO, CHESLAV. DON'T DO THIS.>
<JIRG IS RIGHT. I AM FAT AND USELESS, CHESLAV. I AM TOO WEAK. ALWAYS HAVE BEEN.>
<I'M SORRY.>
<I ALWAYS LOVED THESE HUNTS. YOU ARE MY GREAT FRIEND, CHESLAV. I NEVER BECAME A MILLIONAIRE, BUT I AM RICH TO HAVE HAD YOU FOR A FRIEND.>
<SHUT UP, YOU POOF, AND TAKE UP YOUR GUN. WE ARE GOING TO LIVE.>
BLAM
GRRRR
SNARL
CRUSH
ROAR

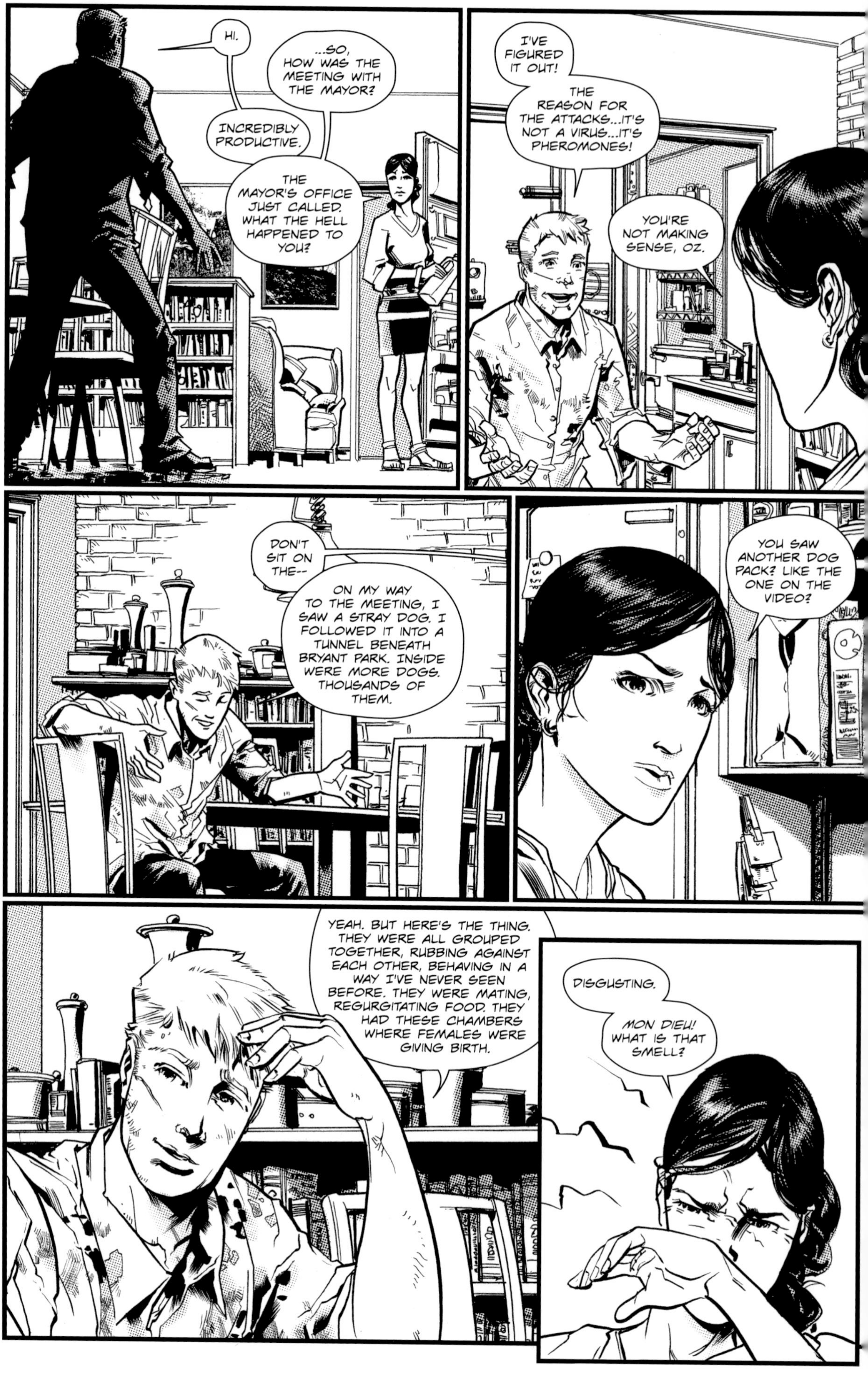
HI.
...SO, HOW WAS THE MEETING WITH THE MAYOR?
INCREDIBLY PRODUCTIVE.
THE MAYOR'S OFFICE JUST CALLED. WHAT THE HELL HAPPENED TO YOU?
I'VE FIGURED IT OUT!
THE REASON FOR THE ATTACKS...IT'S NOT A VIRUS...IT'S PHEROMONES!
YOU'RE NOT MAKING SENSE, OZ.
DON'T SIT ON THE--
ON MY WAY TO THE MEETING, I SAW A STRAY DOG. I FOLLOWED IT INTO A TUNNEL BENEATH BRYANT PARK. INSIDE WERE MORE DOGS. THOUSANDS OF THEM.
YOU SAW ANOTHER DOG PACK? LIKE THE ONE ON THE VIDEO?
YEAH. BUT HERE'S THE THING. THEY WERE ALL GROUPED TOGETHER, RUBBING AGAINST EACH OTHER, BEHAVING IN A WAY I'VE NEVER SEEN BEFORE. THEY WERE MATING, REGURGITATING FOOD. THEY HAD THESE CHAMBERS WHERE FEMALES WERE GIVING BIRTH.
DISGUSTING.
MON DIEU! WHAT IS THAT SMELL?

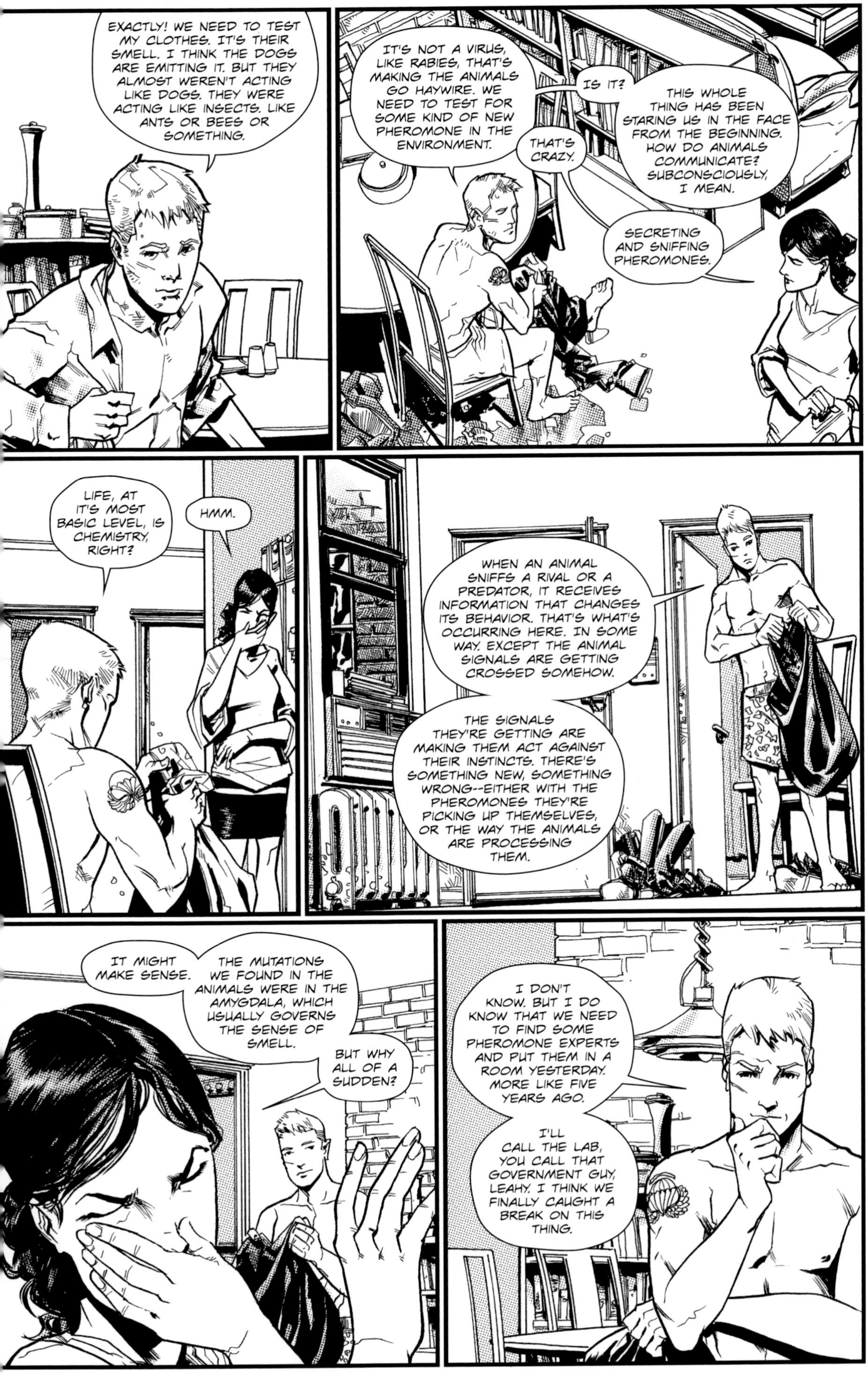
EXACTLY! WE NEED TO TEST MY CLOTHES. IT'S THEIR SMELL. I THINK THE DOGS ARE EMITTING IT. BUT THEY ALMOST WEREN'T ACTING LIKE DOGS. THEY WERE ACTING LIKE INSECTS. LIKE ANTS OR BEES OR SOMETHING.
IT'S NOT A VIRUS, LIKE RABIES, THAT'S MAKING THE ANIMALS GO HAYWIRE. WE NEED TO TEST FOR SOME KIND OF NEW PHEROMONE IN THE ENVIRONMENT.
IS IT?
THAT'S CRAZY.
THIS WHOLE THING HAS BEEN STARING US IN THE FACE FROM THE BEGINNING. HOW DO ANIMALS COMMUNICATE? SUBCONSCIOUSLY, I MEAN.
SECRETING AND SNIFFING PHEROMONES.
LIFE, AT IT'S MOST BASIC LEVEL, IS CHEMISTRY, RIGHT?
HMM.
WHEN AN ANIMAL SNIFFS A RIVAL OR A PREDATOR, IT RECEIVES INFORMATION THAT CHANGES ITS BEHAVIOR. THAT'S WHAT'S OCCURRING HERE. IN SOME WAY. EXCEPT THE ANIMAL SIGNALS ARE GETTING CROSSED SOMEHOW.
THE SIGNALS THEY'RE GETTING ARE MAKING THEM ACT AGAINST THEIR INSTINCTS. THERE'S SOMETHING NEW, SOMETHING WRONG--EITHER WITH THE PHEROMONES THEY'RE PICKING UP THEMSELVES, OR THE WAY THE ANIMALS ARE PROCESSING THEM.
IT MIGHT MAKE SENSE.
THE MUTATIONS WE FOUND IN THE ANIMALS WERE IN THE AMYGDALA, WHICH USUALLY GOVERNS THE SENSE OF SMELL.
BUT WHY ALL OF A SUDDEN?
I DON'T KNOW. BUT I DO KNOW THAT WE NEED TO FIND SOME PHEROMONE EXPERTS AND PUT THEM IN A ROOM YESTERDAY. MORE LIKE FIVE YEARS AGO.
I'LL CALL THE LAB, YOU CALL THAT GOVERNMENT GUY, LEAHY. I THINK WE FINALLY CAUGHT A BREAK ON THIS THING.

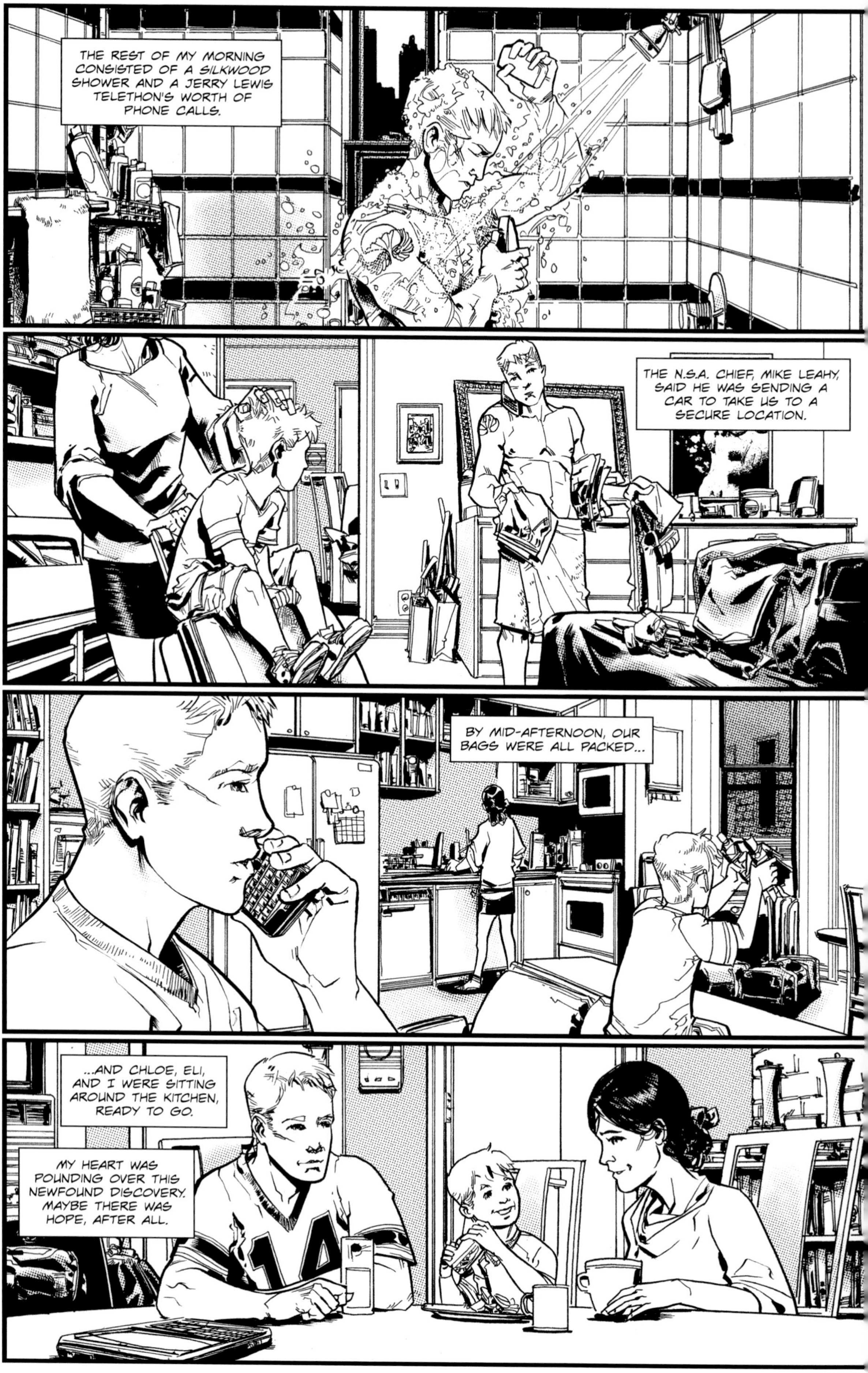
THE REST OF MY MORNING CONSISTED OF A SILKWOOD SHOWER AND A JERRY LEWIS TELETHON'S WORTH OF PHONE CALLS.
THE N.S.A. CHIEF, MIKE LEAHY, SAID HE WAS SENDING A CAR TO TAKE US TO A SECURE LOCATION.
BY MID-AFTERNOON, OUR BAGS WERE ALL PACKED...
...AND CHLOE, ELI, AND I WERE SITTING AROUND THE KITCHEN, READY TO GO.
MY HEART WAS POUNDING OVER THIS NEWFOUND DISCOVERY. MAYBE THERE WAS HOPE, AFTER ALL.
14

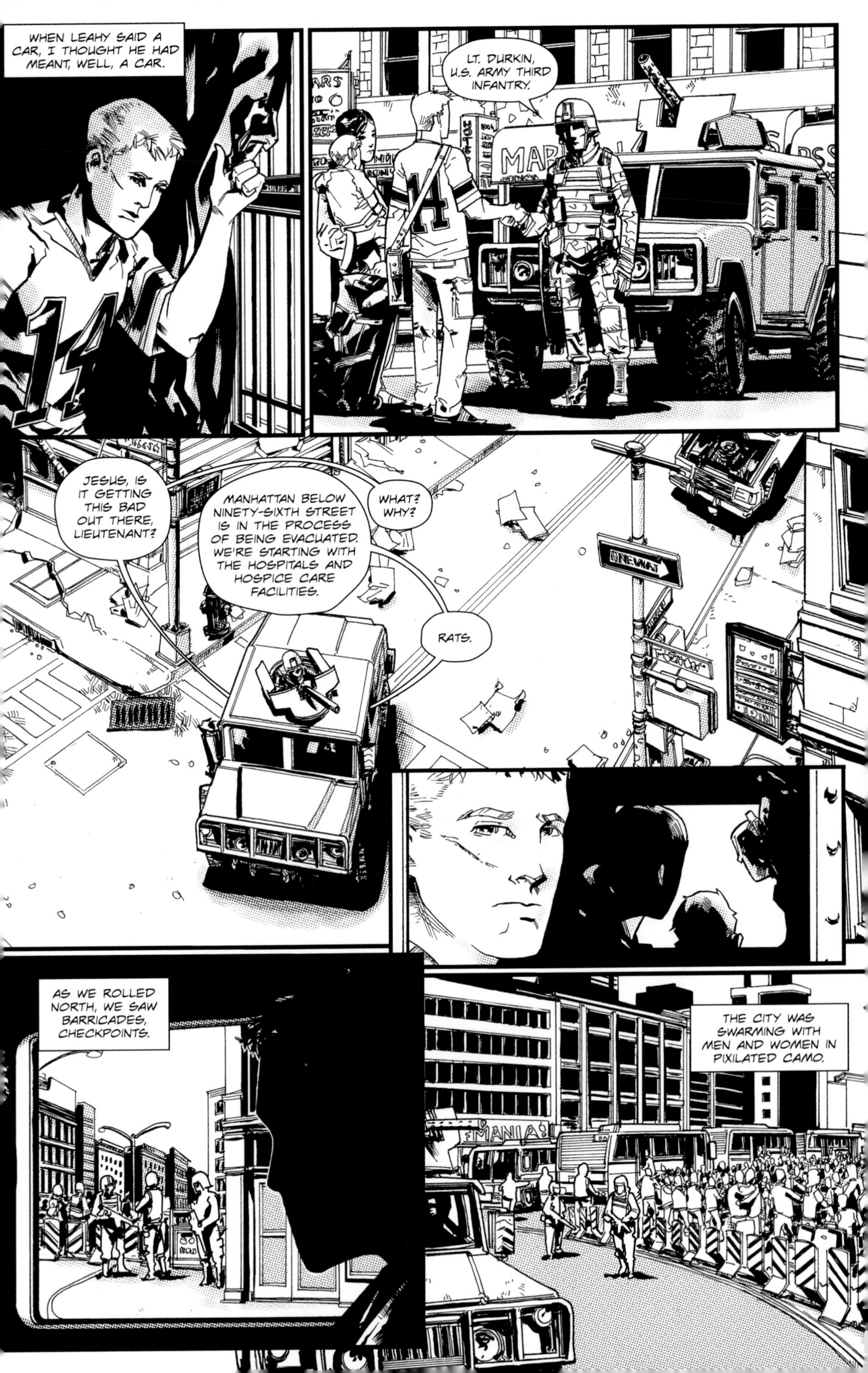
WHEN LEAHY SAID A CAR, I THOUGHT HE HAD MEANT, WELL, A CAR.
LT. DURKIN, U.S. ARMY THIRD INFANTRY.
JESUS, IS IT GETTING THIS BAD OUT THERE, LIEUTENANT?
MANHATTAN BELOW NINETY-SIXTH STREET IS IN THE PROCESS OF BEING EVACUATED. WE'RE STARTING WITH THE HOSPITALS AND HOSPICE CARE FACILITIES.
WHAT? WHY?
RATS.
ONE WAY
AS WE ROLLED NORTH, WE SAW BARRICADES, CHECKPOINTS.
THE CITY WAS SWARMING WITH MEN AND WOMEN IN PIXILATED CAMO.
MANIA

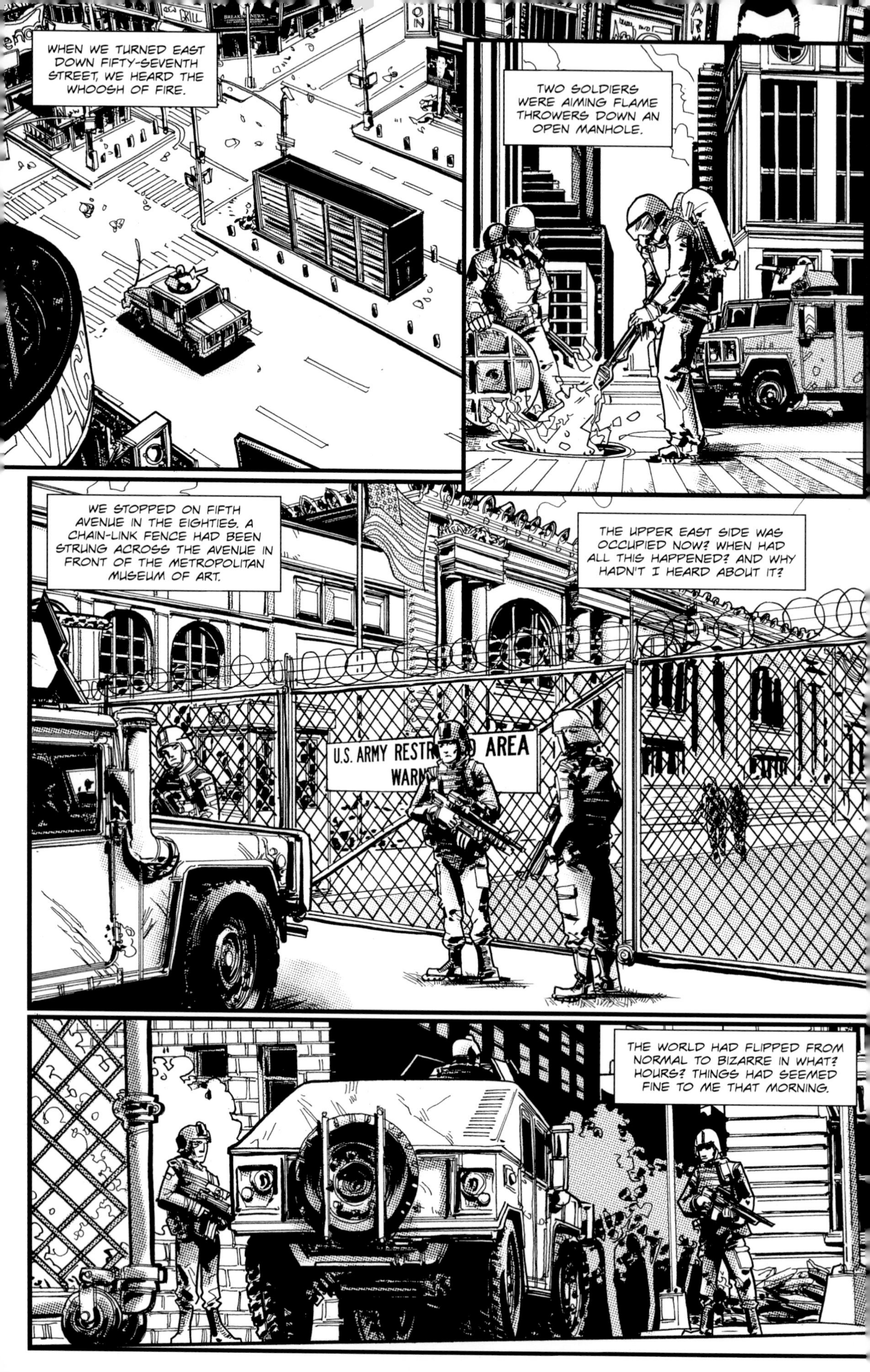
WHEN WE TURNED EAST DOWN FIFTY-SEVENTH STREET, WE HEARD THE WHOOSH OF FIRE.
TWO SOLDIERS WERE AIMING FLAME THROWERS DOWN AN OPEN MANHOLE.
WE STOPPED ON FIFTH AVENUE IN THE EIGHTIES. A CHAIN-LINK FENCE HAD BEEN STRUNG ACROSS THE AVENUE IN FRONT OF THE METROPOLITAN MUSEUM OF ART.
THE UPPER EAST SIDE WAS OCCUPIED NOW? WHEN HAD ALL THIS HAPPENED? AND WHY HADN'T I HEARD ABOUT IT?
U.S. ARMY RESTR D AREA
WARN
THE WORLD HAD FLIPPED FROM NORMAL TO BIZARRE IN WHAT? HOURS? THINGS HAD SEEMED FINE TO ME THAT MORNING.

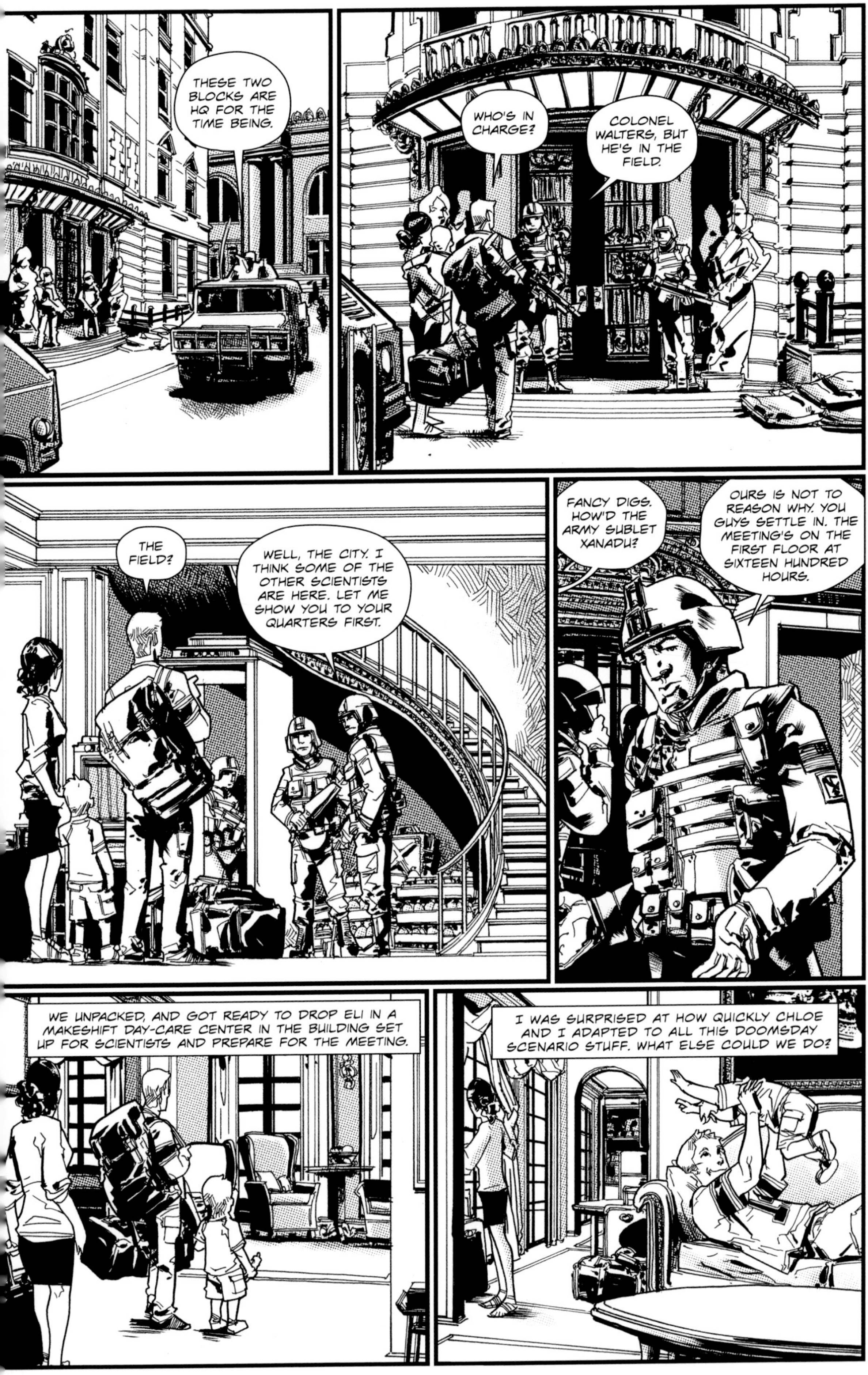
THESE TWO BLOCKS ARE HQ FOR THE TIME BEING.
WHO'S IN CHARGE?
COLONEL WALTERS, BUT HE'S IN THE FIELD.
THE FIELD?
WELL, THE CITY. I THINK SOME OF THE OTHER SCIENTISTS ARE HERE. LET ME SHOW YOU TO YOUR QUARTERS FIRST.
FANCY DIGS. HOW'D THE ARMY SUBLET XANADU?
OURS IS NOT TO REASON WHY. YOU GUYS SETTLE IN. THE MEETING'S ON THE FIRST FLOOR AT SIXTEEN HUNDRED HOURS.
WE UNPACKED, AND GOT READY TO DROP ELI IN A MAKESHIFT DAY-CARE CENTER IN THE BUILDING SET UP FOR SCIENTISTS AND PREPARE FOR THE MEETING.
I WAS SURPRISED AT HOW QUICKLY CHLOE AND I ADAPTED TO ALL THIS DOOMSDAY SCENARIO STUFF. WHAT ELSE COULD WE DO?

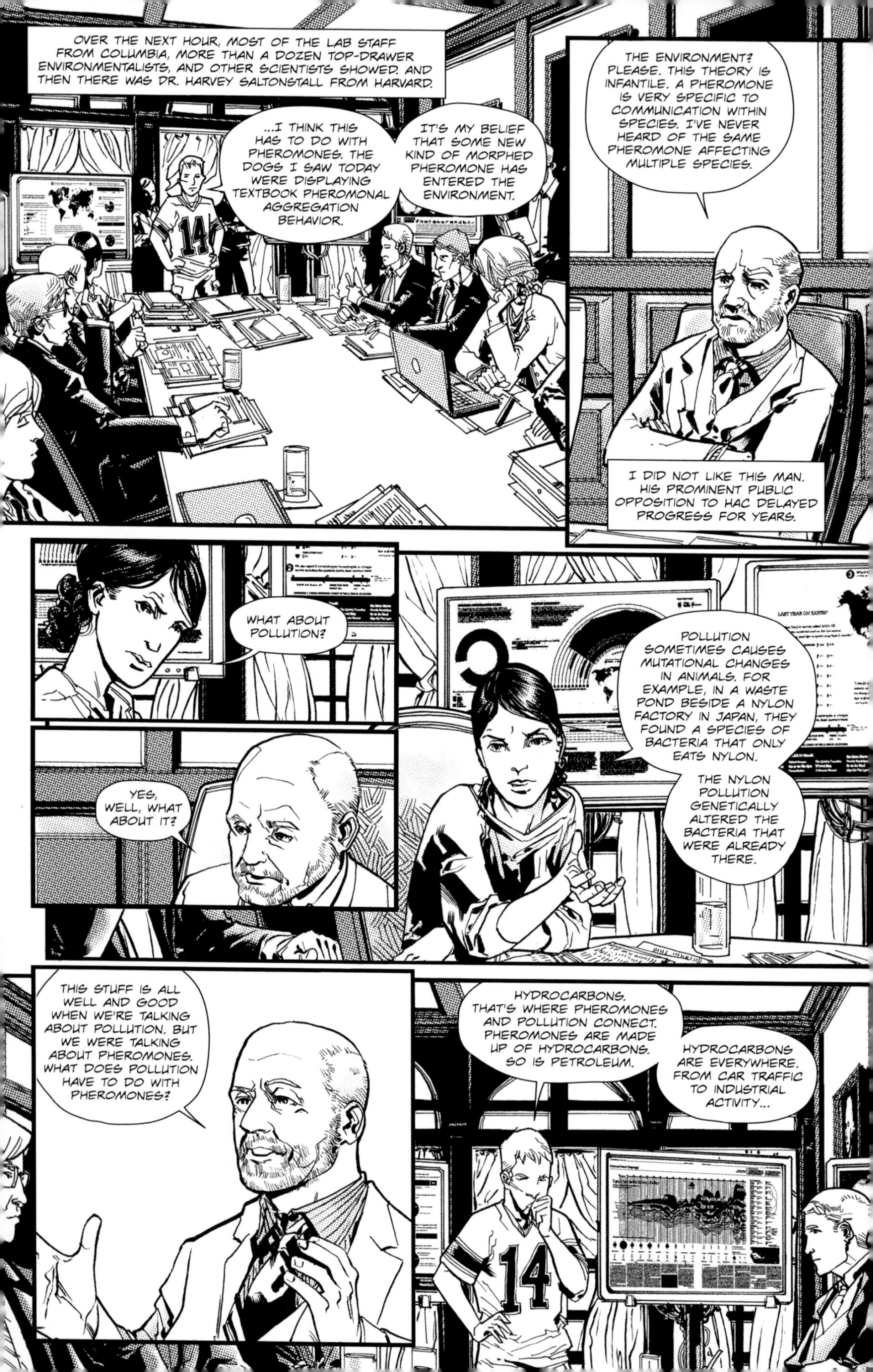

OVER THE NEXT HOUR, MOST OF THE LAB STAFF FROM COLUMBIA, MORE THAN A DOZEN TOP-DRAWER ENVIRONMENTALISTS, AND OTHER SCIENTISTS SHOWED. AND THEN THERE WAS DR. HARVEY SALTONSTALL FROM HARVARD.
...I THINK THIS HAS TO DO WITH PHEROMONES. THE DOGS I SAW TODAY WERE DISPLAYING TEXTBOOK PHEROMONAL AGGREGATION BEHAVIOR.
IT'S MY BELIEF THAT SOME NEW KIND OF MORPHED PHEROMONE HAS ENTERED THE ENVIRONMENT.
THE ENVIRONMENT? PLEASE. THIS THEORY IS INFANTILE. A PHEROMONE IS VERY SPECIFIC TO COMMUNICATION WITHIN SPECIES. I'VE NEVER HEARD OF THE SAME PHEROMONE AFFECTING MULTIPLE SPECIES.
I DID NOT LIKE THIS MAN. HIS PROMINENT PUBLIC OPPOSITION TO HAC DELAYED PROGRESS FOR YEARS.
WHAT ABOUT POLLUTION?
YES, WELL, WHAT ABOUT IT?
POLLUTION SOMETIMES CAUSES MUTATIONAL CHANGES IN ANIMALS. FOR EXAMPLE, IN A WASTE POND BESIDE A NYLON FACTORY IN JAPAN, THEY FOUND A SPECIES OF BACTERIA THAT ONLY EATS NYLON.
THE NYLON POLLUTION GENETICALLY ALTERED THE BACTERIA THAT WERE ALREADY THERE.
THIS STUFF IS ALL WELL AND GOOD WHEN WE'RE TALKING ABOUT POLLUTION. BUT WE WERE TALKING ABOUT PHEROMONES. WHAT DOES POLLUTION HAVE TO DO WITH PHEROMONES?
HYDROCARBONS. THAT'S WHERE PHEROMONES AND POLLUTION CONNECT. PHEROMONES ARE MADE UP OF HYDROCARBONS. SO IS PETROLEUM.
HYDROCARBONS ARE EVERYWHERE. FROM CAR TRAFFIC TO INDUSTRIAL ACTIVITY...

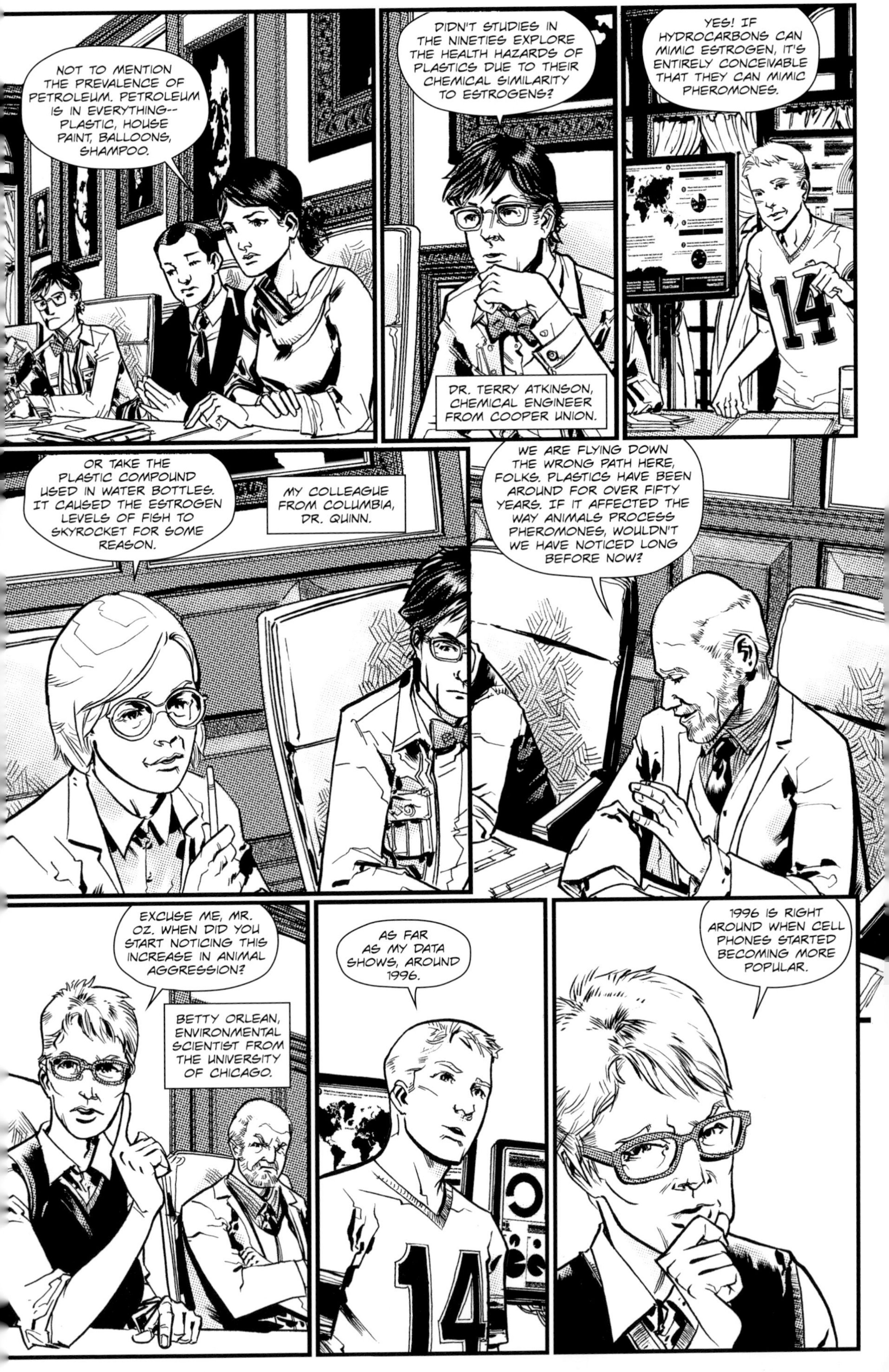
NOT TO MENTION THE PREVALENCE OF PETROLEUM. PETROLEUM IS IN EVERYTHING-- PLASTIC, HOUSE PAINT, BALLOONS, SHAMPOO.
DIDN'T STUDIES IN THE NINETIES EXPLORE THE HEALTH HAZARDS OF PLASTICS DUE TO THEIR CHEMICAL SIMILARITY TO ESTROGENS?
DR. TERRY ATKINSON, CHEMICAL ENGINEER FROM COOPER UNION.
YES! IF HYDROCARBONS CAN MIMIC ESTROGEN, IT'S ENTIRELY CONCEIVABLE THAT THEY CAN MIMIC PHEROMONES.
OR TAKE THE PLASTIC COMPOUND USED IN WATER BOTTLES. IT CAUSED THE ESTROGEN LEVELS OF FISH TO SKYROCKET FOR SOME REASON.
MY COLLEAGUE FROM COLUMBIA, DR. QUINN.
WE ARE FLYING DOWN THE WRONG PATH HERE, FOLKS. PLASTICS HAVE BEEN AROUND FOR OVER FIFTY YEARS. IF IT AFFECTED THE WAY ANIMALS PROCESS PHEROMONES, WOULDN'T WE HAVE NOTICED LONG BEFORE NOW?
EXCUSE ME, MR. OZ. WHEN DID YOU START NOTICING THIS INCREASE IN ANIMAL AGGRESSION?
BETTY ORLEAN, ENVIRONMENTAL SCIENTIST FROM THE UNIVERSITY OF CHICAGO.
AS FAR AS MY DATA SHOWS, AROUND 1996.
1996 IS RIGHT AROUND WHEN CELL PHONES STARTED BECOMING MORE POPULAR.

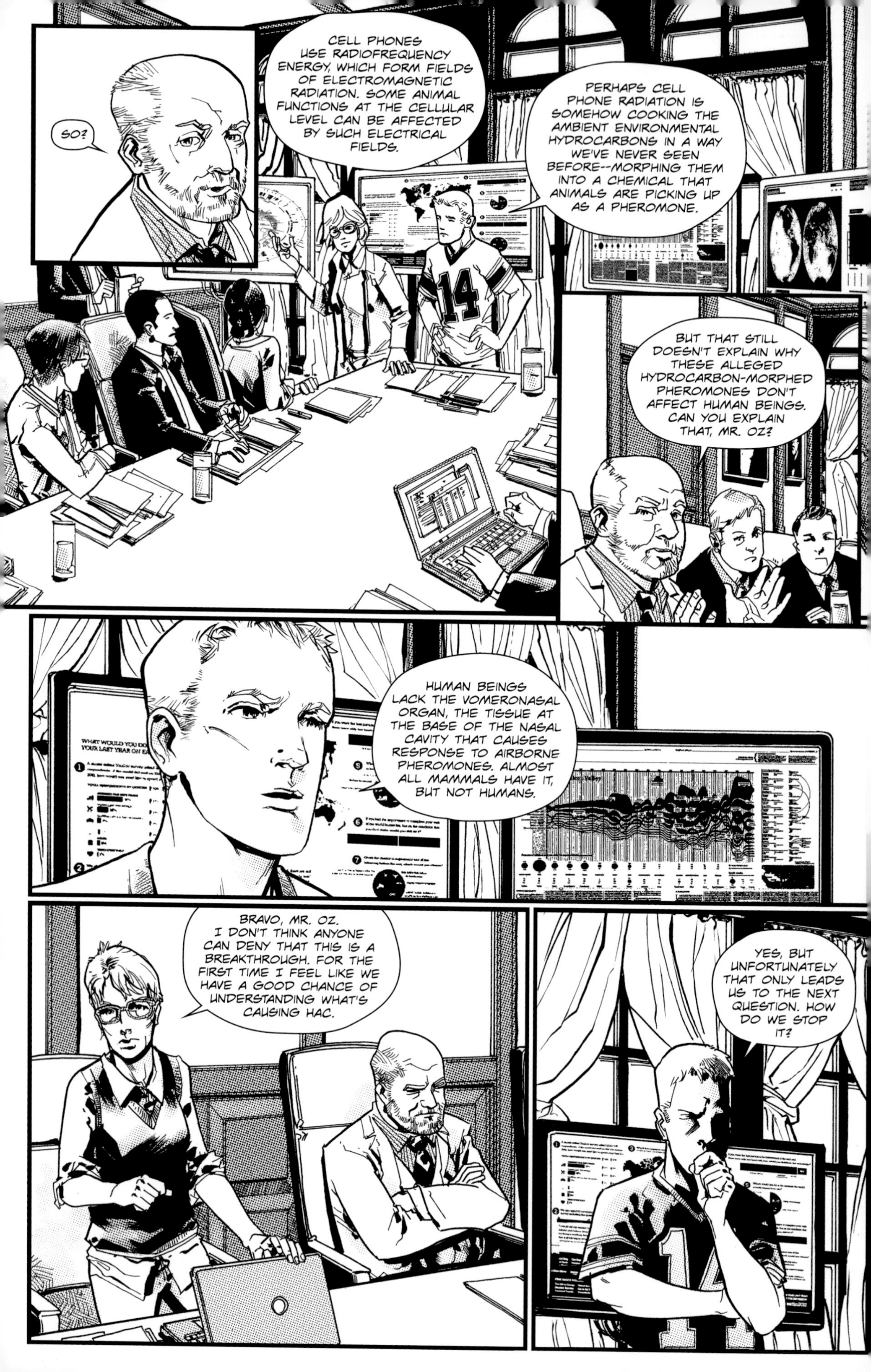
SO?
CELL PHONES USE RADIOFREQUENCY ENERGY, WHICH FORM FIELDS OF ELECTROMAGNETIC RADIATION. SOME ANIMAL FUNCTIONS AT THE CELLULAR LEVEL CAN BE AFFECTED BY SUCH ELECTRICAL FIELDS.
PERHAPS CELL PHONE RADIATION IS SOMEHOW COOKING THE AMBIENT ENVIRONMENTAL HYDROCARBONS IN A WAY WE'VE NEVER SEEN BEFORE--MORPHING THEM INTO A CHEMICAL THAT ANIMALS ARE PICKING UP AS A PHEROMONE.
BUT THAT STILL DOESN'T EXPLAIN WHY THESE ALLEGED HYDROCARBON-MORPHED PHEROMONES DON'T AFFECT HUMAN BEINGS. CAN YOU EXPLAIN THAT, MR. OZ?
HUMAN BEINGS LACK THE VOMERONASAL ORGAN, THE TISSUE AT THE BASE OF THE NASAL CAVITY THAT CAUSES RESPONSE TO AIRBORNE PHEROMONES. ALMOST ALL MAMMALS HAVE IT, BUT NOT HUMANS.
BRAVO, MR. OZ. I DON'T THINK ANYONE CAN DENY THAT THIS IS A BREAKTHROUGH. FOR THE FIRST TIME I FEEL LIKE WE HAVE A GOOD CHANCE OF UNDERSTANDING WHAT'S CAUSING HAC.
YES, BUT UNFORTUNATELY THAT ONLY LEADS US TO THE NEXT QUESTION. HOW DO WE STOP IT?

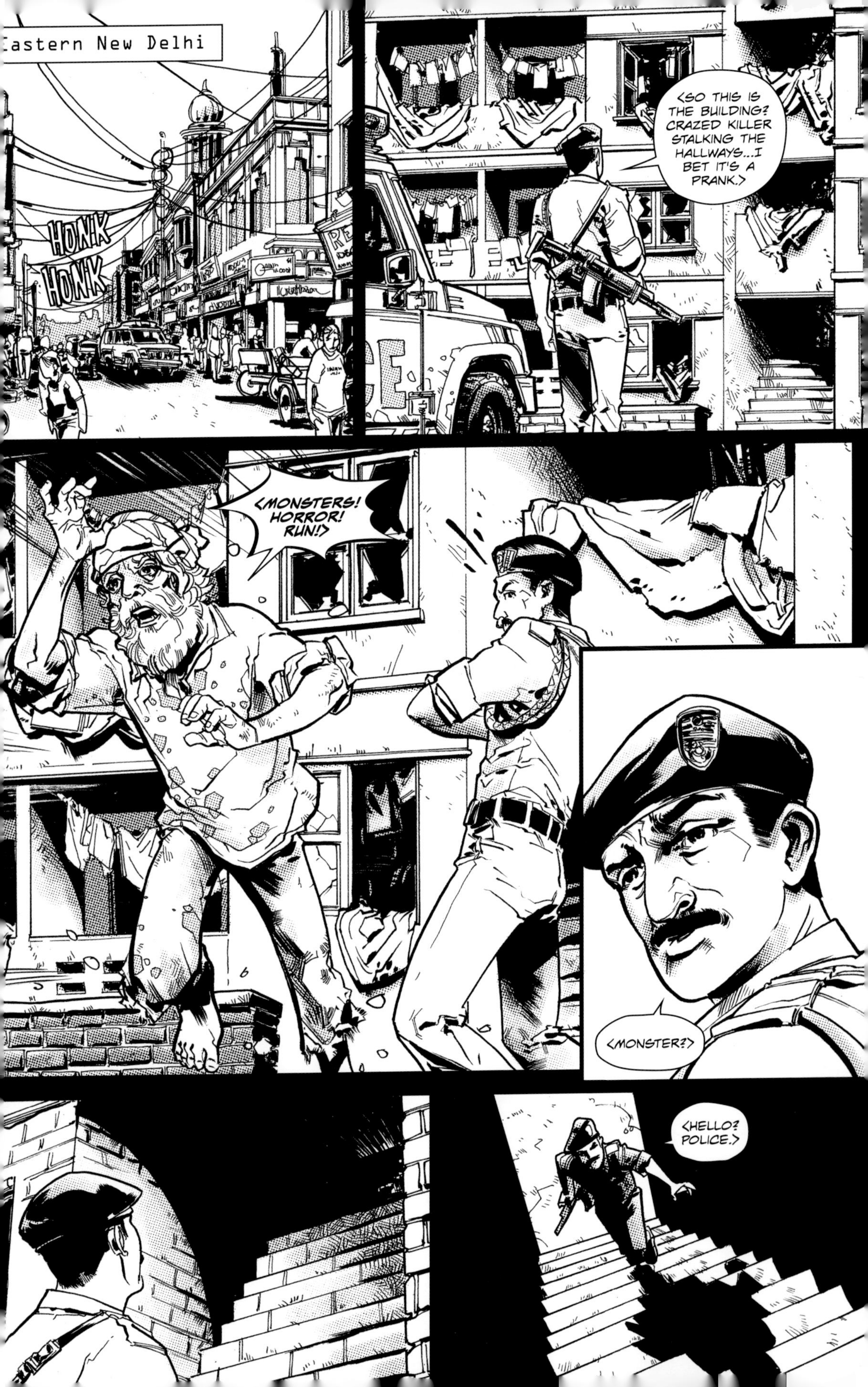
Eastern New Delhi
HONK HONK
<SO THIS IS THE BUILDING? CRAZED KILLER STALKING THE HALLWAYS...I BET IT'S A PRANK.>
<MONSTERS! HORROR! RUN!>
<MONSTER?>
<HELLO? POLICE.>

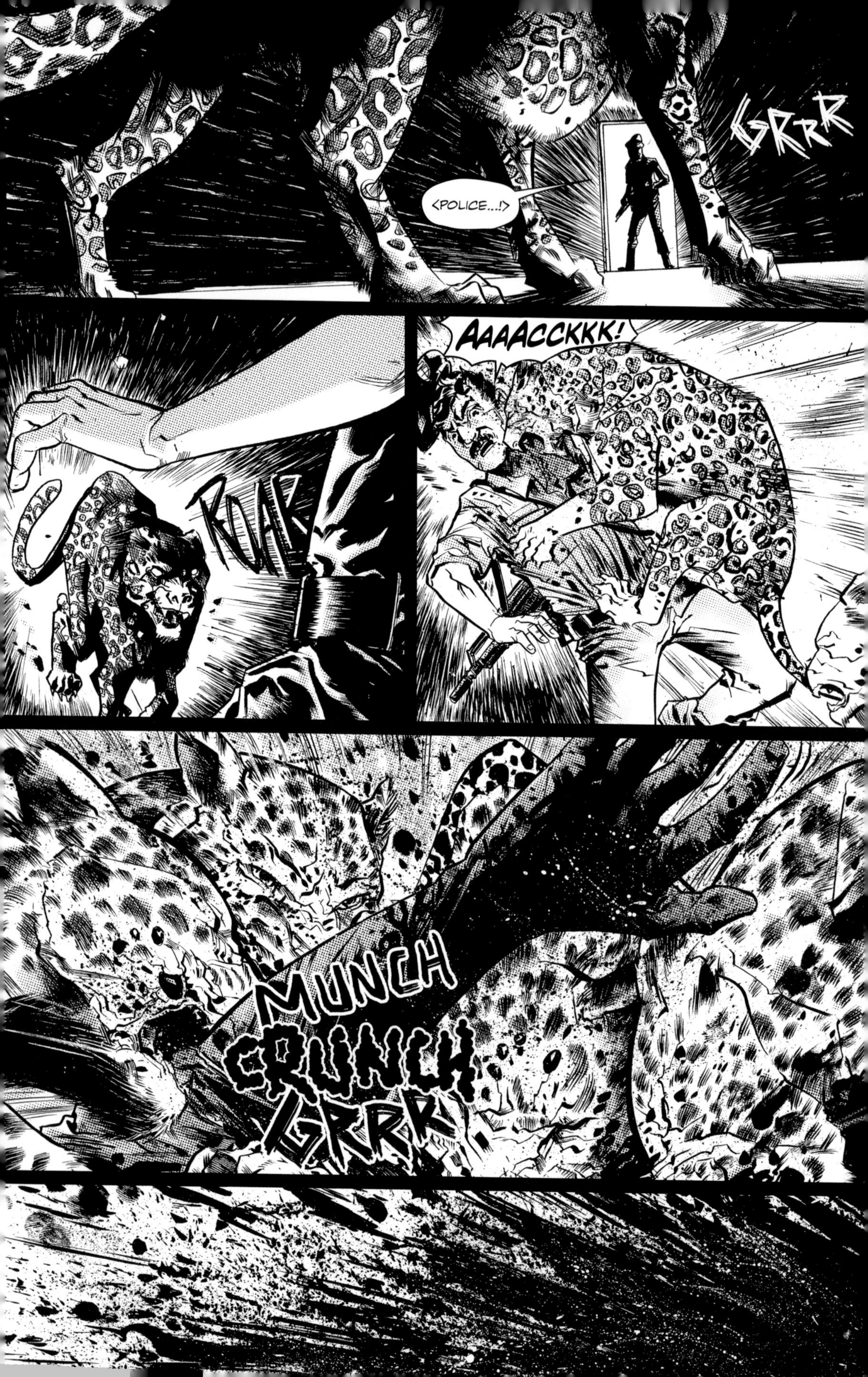
GRRR
<POLICE...!>
ROAR
AAAACCKKK!
MUNCH
CRUNCH
GRRR

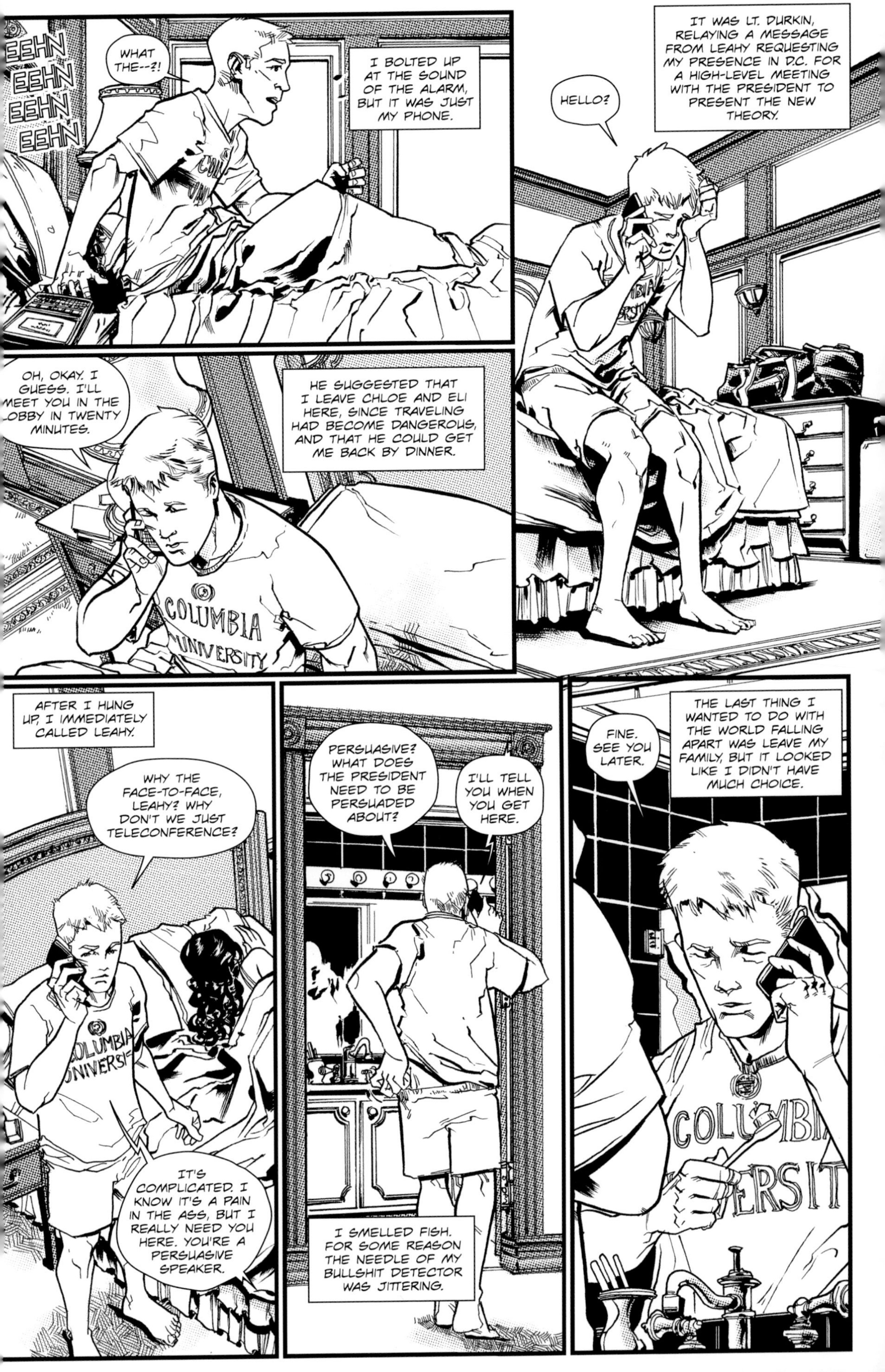
EEHN EEHN EEHN EEHN
WHAT THE--?!
I BOLTED UP AT THE SOUND OF THE ALARM, BUT IT WAS JUST MY PHONE.
HELLO?
IT WAS LT. DURKIN, RELAYING A MESSAGE FROM LEAHY REQUESTING MY PRESENCE IN D.C. FOR A HIGH-LEVEL MEETING WITH THE PRESIDENT TO PRESENT THE NEW THEORY.
OH, OKAY. I GUESS. I'LL MEET YOU IN THE LOBBY IN TWENTY MINUTES.
HE SUGGESTED THAT I LEAVE CHLOE AND ELI HERE, SINCE TRAVELING HAD BECOME DANGEROUS, AND THAT HE COULD GET ME BACK BY DINNER.
COLUMBIA UNIVERSITY
AFTER I HUNG UP, I IMMEDIATELY CALLED LEAHY.
WHY THE FACE-TO-FACE, LEAHY? WHY DON'T WE JUST TELECONFERENCE?
IT'S COMPLICATED. I KNOW IT'S A PAIN IN THE ASS, BUT I REALLY NEED YOU HERE. YOU'RE A PERSUASIVE SPEAKER.
PERSUASIVE? WHAT DOES THE PRESIDENT NEED TO BE PERSUADED ABOUT?
I'LL TELL YOU WHEN YOU GET HERE.
I SMELLED FISH. FOR SOME REASON THE NEEDLE OF MY BULLSHIT DETECTOR WAS JITTERING.
FINE. SEE YOU LATER.
THE LAST THING I WANTED TO DO WITH THE WORLD FALLING APART WAS LEAVE MY FAMILY, BUT IT LOOKED LIKE I DIDN'T HAVE MUCH CHOICE.

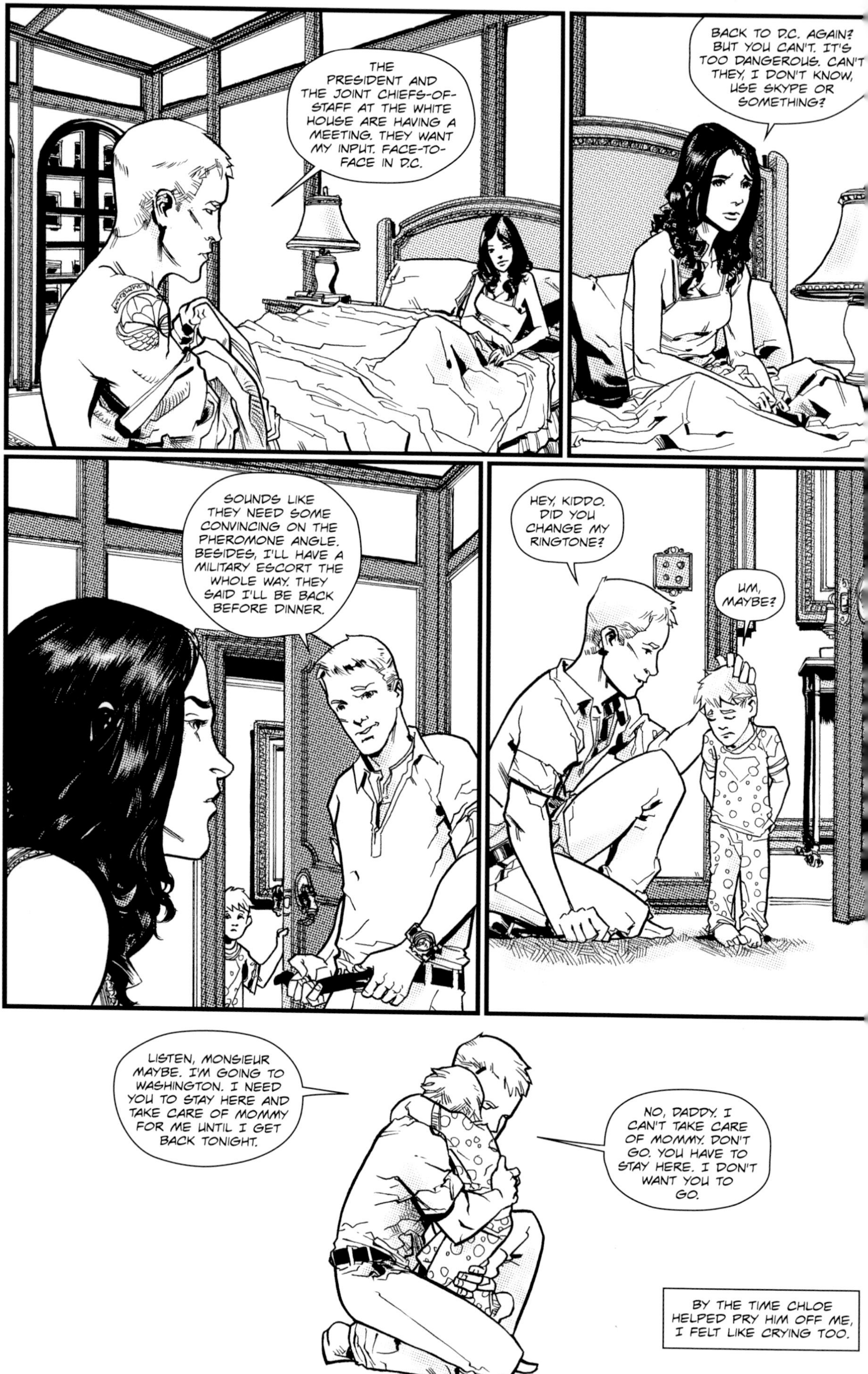

THE PRESIDENT AND THE JOINT CHIEFS-OF-STAFF AT THE WHITE HOUSE ARE HAVING A MEETING. THEY WANT MY INPUT. FACE-TO-FACE IN D.C.
BACK TO D.C. AGAIN? BUT YOU CAN'T. IT'S TOO DANGEROUS. CAN'T THEY, I DON'T KNOW, USE SKYPE OR SOMETHING?
SOUNDS LIKE THEY NEED SOME CONVINCING ON THE PHEROMONE ANGLE. BESIDES, I'LL HAVE A MILITARY ESCORT THE WHOLE WAY. THEY SAID I'LL BE BACK BEFORE DINNER.
HEY, KIDDO. DID YOU CHANGE MY RINGTONE?
UM, MAYBE?
LISTEN, MONSIEUR MAYBE. I'M GOING TO WASHINGTON. I NEED YOU TO STAY HERE AND TAKE CARE OF MOMMY FOR ME UNTIL I GET BACK TONIGHT.
NO, DADDY. I CAN'T TAKE CARE OF MOMMY. DON'T GO. YOU HAVE TO STAY HERE. I DON'T WANT YOU TO GO.
BY THE TIME CHLOE HELPED PRY HIM OFF ME, I FELT LIKE CRYING TOO.

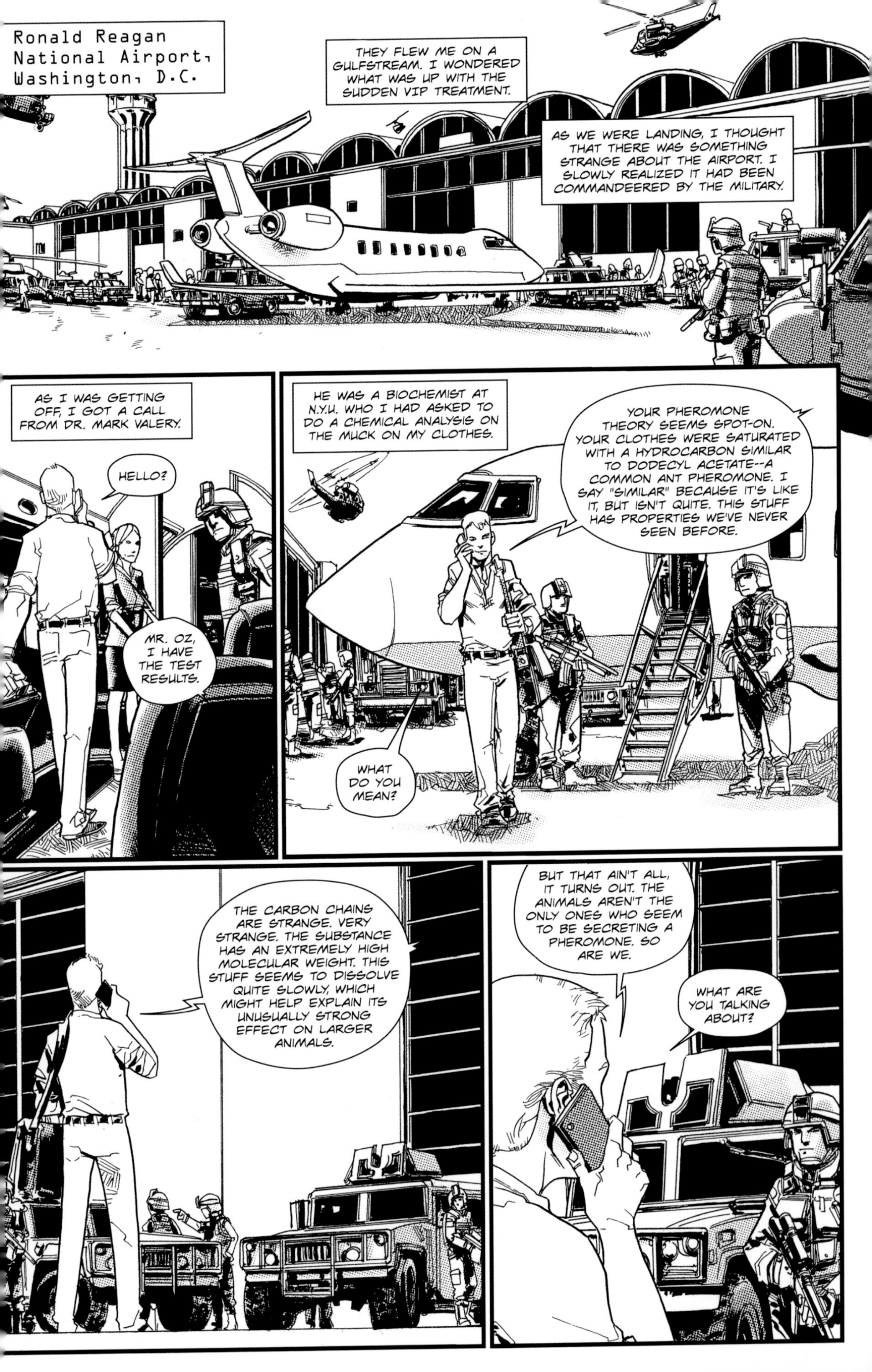
Ronald Reagan National Airport, Washington, D.C.
THEY FLEW ME ON A GULFSTREAM. I WONDERED WHAT WAS UP WITH THE SUDDEN VIP TREATMENT.
AS WE WERE LANDING, I THOUGHT THAT THERE WAS SOMETHING STRANGE ABOUT THE AIRPORT. I SLOWLY REALIZED IT HAD BEEN COMMANDEERED BY THE MILITARY.
AS I WAS GETTING OFF, I GOT A CALL FROM DR. MARK VALERY.
HELLO?
MR. OZ, I HAVE THE TEST RESULTS.
HE WAS A BIOCHEMIST AT N.Y.U. WHO I HAD ASKED TO DO A CHEMICAL ANALYSIS ON THE MUCK ON MY CLOTHES.
YOUR PHEROMONE THEORY SEEMS SPOT-ON. YOUR CLOTHES WERE SATURATED WITH A HYDROCARBON SIMILAR TO DODECYL ACETATE--A COMMON ANT PHEROMONE. I SAY "SIMILAR" BECAUSE IT'S LIKE IT, BUT ISN'T QUITE. THIS STUFF HAS PROPERTIES WE'VE NEVER SEEN BEFORE.
WHAT DO YOU MEAN?
THE CARBON CHAINS ARE STRANGE. VERY STRANGE. THE SUBSTANCE HAS AN EXTREMELY HIGH MOLECULAR WEIGHT. THIS STUFF SEEMS TO DISSOLVE QUITE SLOWLY, WHICH MIGHT HELP EXPLAIN ITS UNUSUALLY STRONG EFFECT ON LARGER ANIMALS.
BUT THAT AIN'T ALL, IT TURNS OUT. THE ANIMALS AREN'T THE ONLY ONES WHO SEEM TO BE SECRETING A PHEROMONE. SO ARE WE.
WHAT ARE YOU TALKING ABOUT?

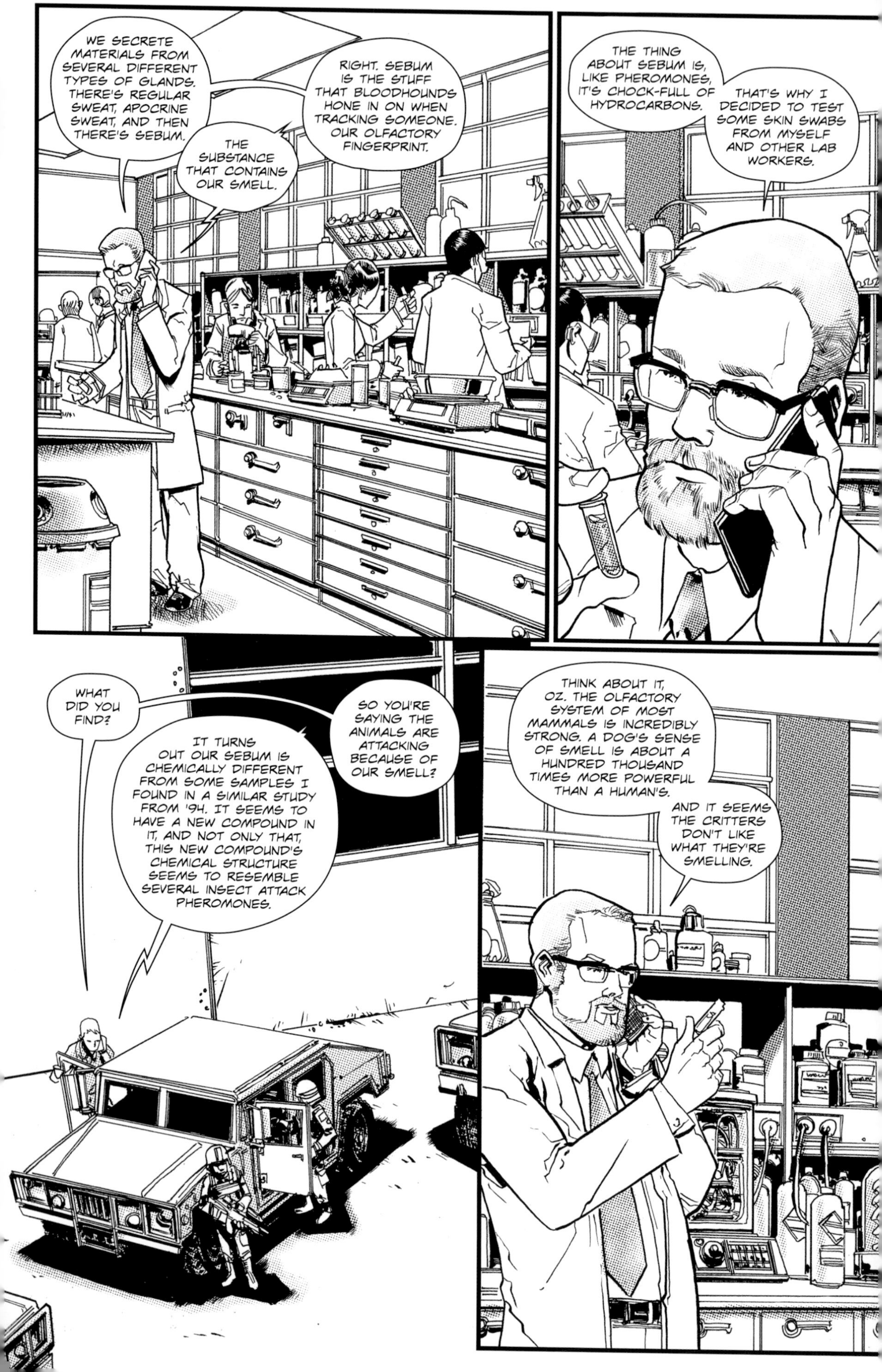
WE SECRETE MATERIALS FROM SEVERAL DIFFERENT TYPES OF GLANDS. THERE'S REGULAR SWEAT, APOCRINE SWEAT, AND THEN THERE'S SEBUM.
THE SUBSTANCE THAT CONTAINS OUR SMELL.
RIGHT. SEBUM IS THE STUFF THAT BLOODHOUNDS HONE IN ON WHEN TRACKING SOMEONE. OUR OLFACTORY FINGERPRINT.
THE THING ABOUT SEBUM IS, LIKE PHEROMONES, IT'S CHOCK-FULL OF HYDROCARBONS.
THAT'S WHY I DECIDED TO TEST SOME SKIN SWABS FROM MYSELF AND OTHER LAB WORKERS.
WHAT DID YOU FIND?
IT TURNS OUT OUR SEBUM IS CHEMICALLY DIFFERENT FROM SOME SAMPLES I FOUND IN A SIMILAR STUDY FROM '94. IT SEEMS TO HAVE A NEW COMPOUND IN IT, AND NOT ONLY THAT, THIS NEW COMPOUND'S CHEMICAL STRUCTURE SEEMS TO RESEMBLE SEVERAL INSECT ATTACK PHEROMONES.
SO YOU'RE SAYING THE ANIMALS ARE ATTACKING BECAUSE OF OUR SMELL?
THINK ABOUT IT, OZ. THE OLFACTORY SYSTEM OF MOST MAMMALS IS INCREDIBLY STRONG. A DOG'S SENSE OF SMELL IS ABOUT A HUNDRED THOUSAND TIMES MORE POWERFUL THAN A HUMAN'S.
AND IT SEEMS THE CRITTERS DON'T LIKE WHAT THEY'RE SMELLING.

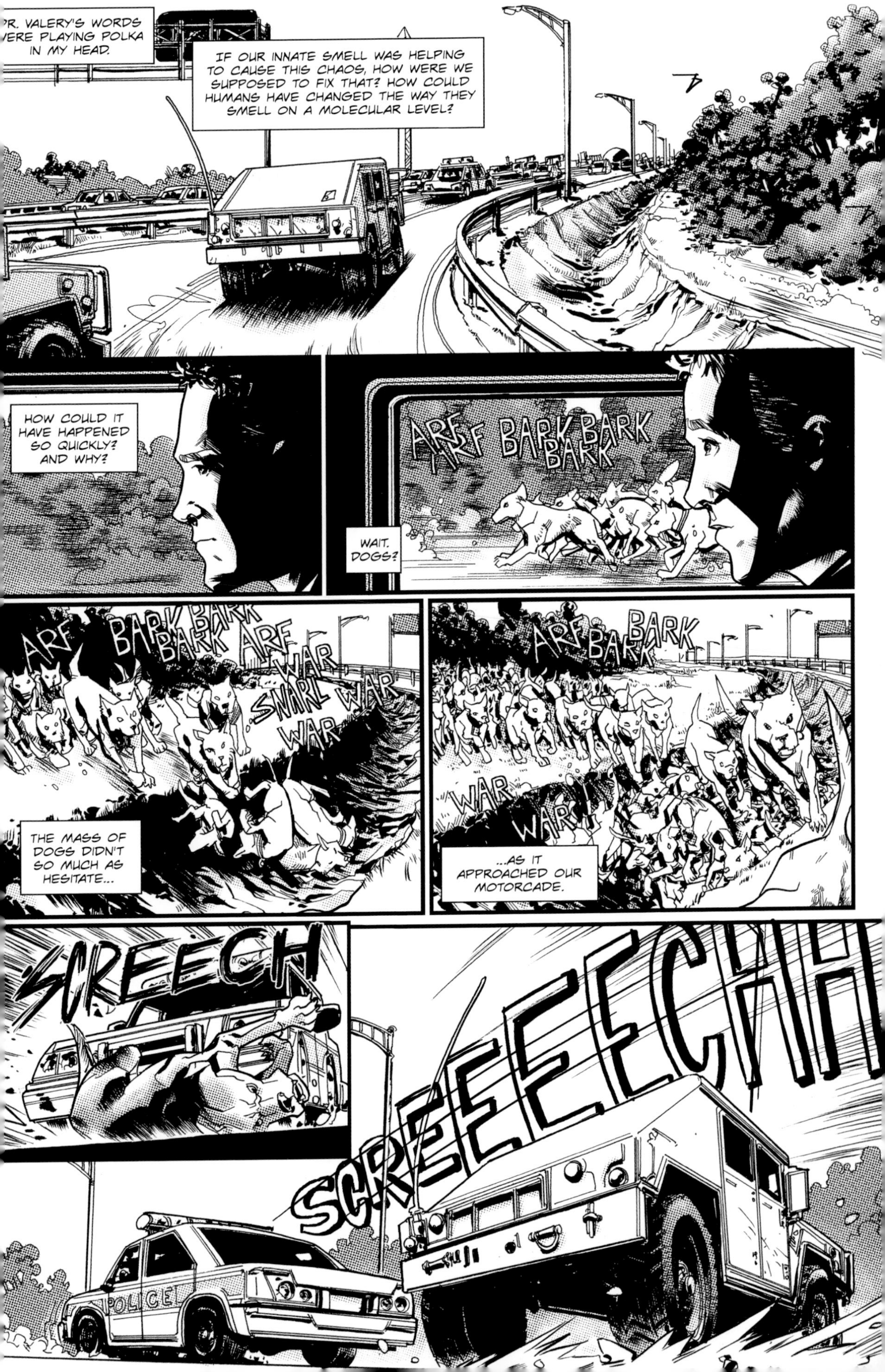

DR. VALERY'S WORDS WERE PLAYING POLKA IN MY HEAD.
IF OUR INNATE SMELL WAS HELPING TO CAUSE THIS CHAOS, HOW WERE WE SUPPOSED TO FIX THAT? HOW COULD HUMANS HAVE CHANGED THE WAY THEY SMELL ON A MOLECULAR LEVEL?
HOW COULD IT HAVE HAPPENED SO QUICKLY? AND WHY?
ARF ARF BARK BARK BARK
WAIT. DOGS?
ARF BARK BARK BARK ARF
WAR SNARL WAR WAR
THE MASS OF DOGS DIDN'T SO MUCH AS HESITATE...
ARF BARK BARK
WAR WAR
...AS IT APPROACHED OUR MOTORCADE.
SCREECH
SCREEEECHH
POLICE

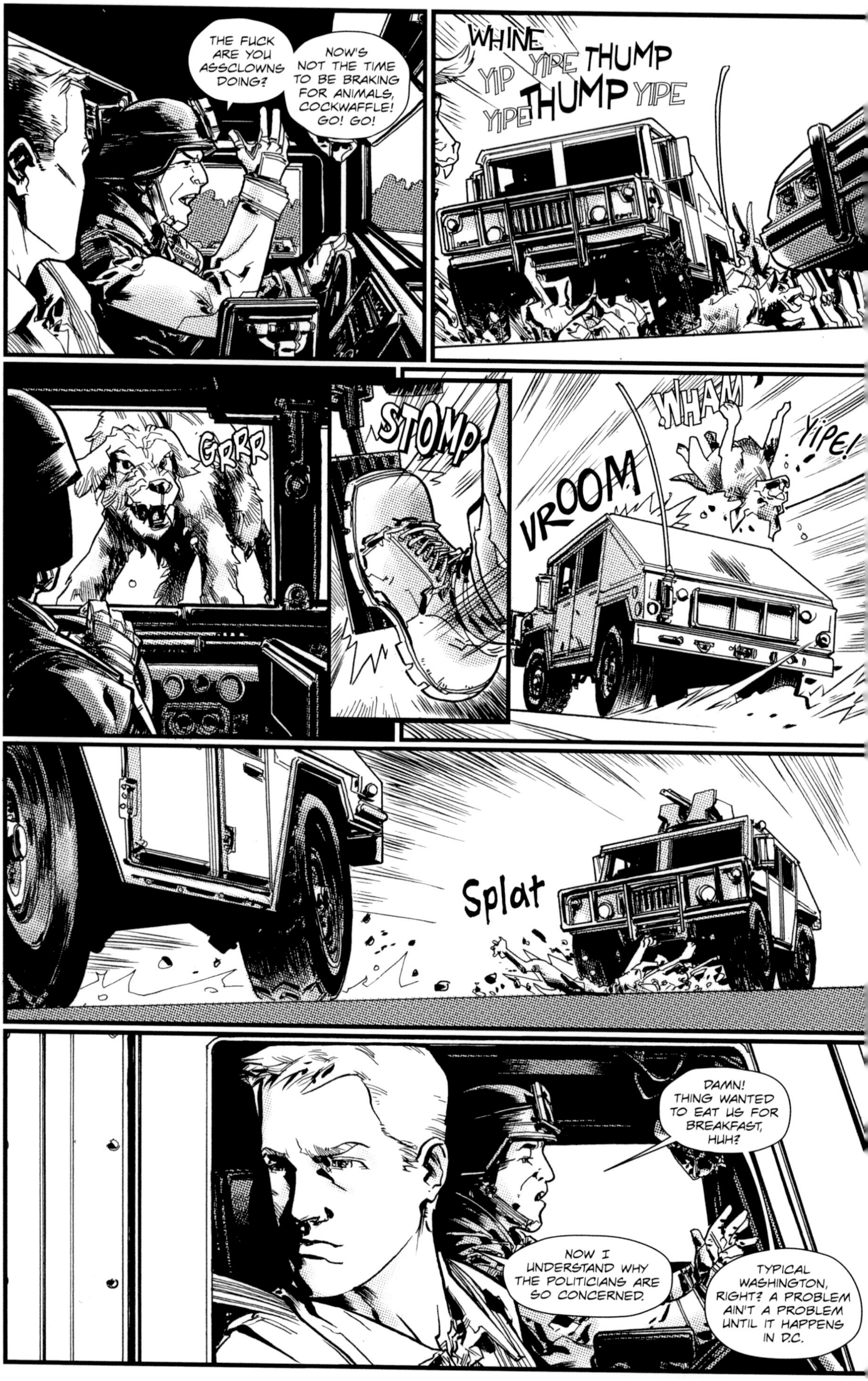
THE FUCK ARE YOU ASSCLOWNS DOING?
NOW'S NOT THE TIME TO BE BRAKING FOR ANIMALS, COCKWAFFLE! GO! GO!
WHINE
YIP
YIPE
THUMP
YIPE
THUMP
YIPE
GRRR
STOMP
WHAM
YIPE!
VROOM
Splat
DAMN! THING WANTED TO EAT US FOR BREAKFAST, HUH?
NOW I UNDERSTAND WHY THE POLITICIANS ARE SO CONCERNED.
TYPICAL WASHINGTON, RIGHT? A PROBLEM AIN'T A PROBLEM UNTIL IT HAPPENS IN D.C.

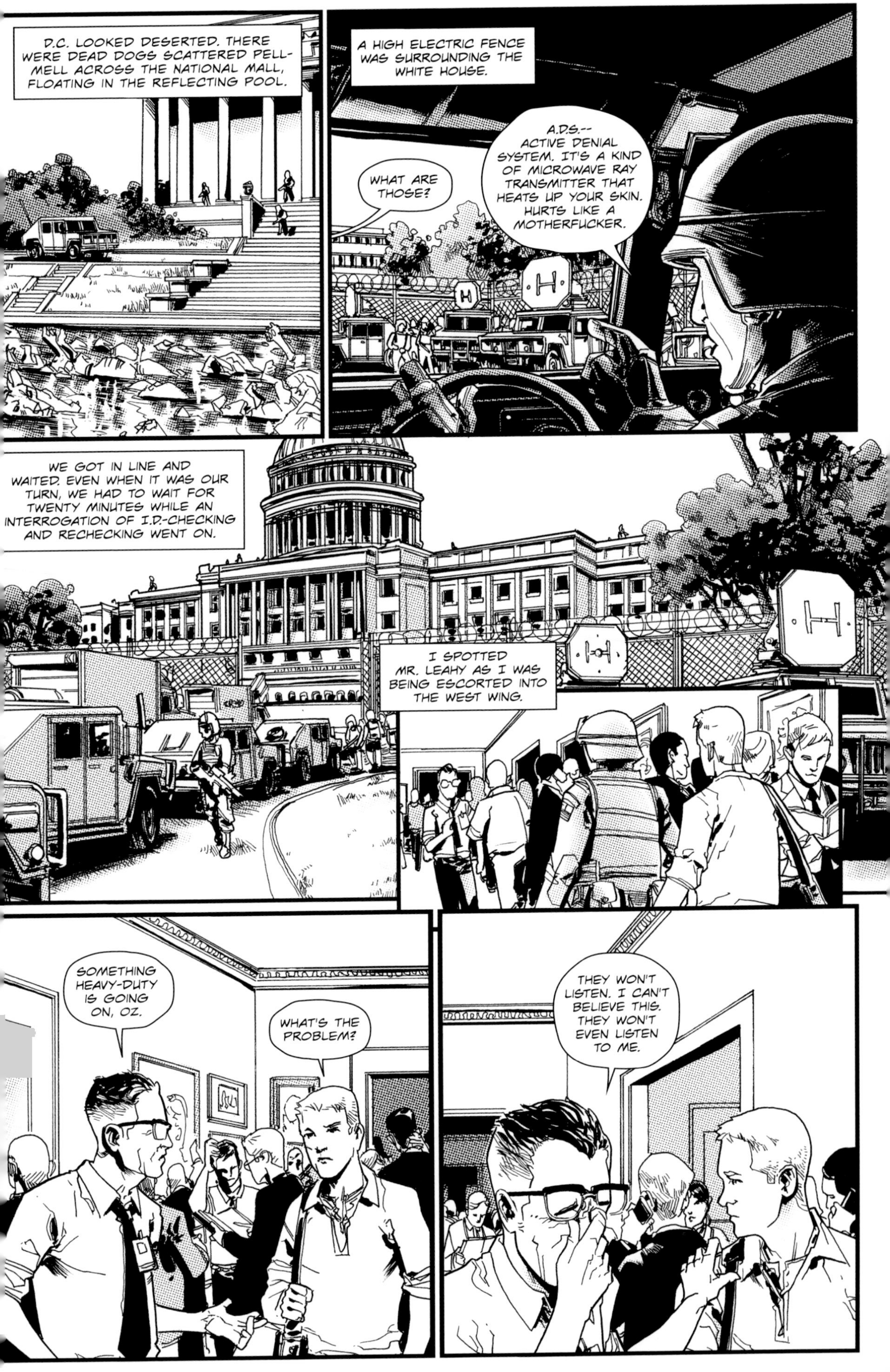
D.C. LOOKED DESERTED. THERE WERE DEAD DOGS SCATTERED PELL-MELL ACROSS THE NATIONAL MALL, FLOATING IN THE REFLECTING POOL.
A HIGH ELECTRIC FENCE WAS SURROUNDING THE WHITE HOUSE.
WHAT ARE THOSE?
A.D.S.-- ACTIVE DENIAL SYSTEM. IT'S A KIND OF MICROWAVE RAY TRANSMITTER THAT HEATS UP YOUR SKIN. HURTS LIKE A MOTHERFUCKER.
WE GOT IN LINE AND WAITED. EVEN WHEN IT WAS OUR TURN, WE HAD TO WAIT FOR TWENTY MINUTES WHILE AN INTERROGATION OF I.D.-CHECKING AND RECHECKING WENT ON.
I SPOTTED MR. LEAHY AS I WAS BEING ESCORTED INTO THE WEST WING.
SOMETHING HEAVY-DUTY IS GOING ON, OZ.
WHAT'S THE PROBLEM?
THEY WON'T LISTEN. I CAN'T BELIEVE THIS. THEY WON'T EVEN LISTEN TO ME.

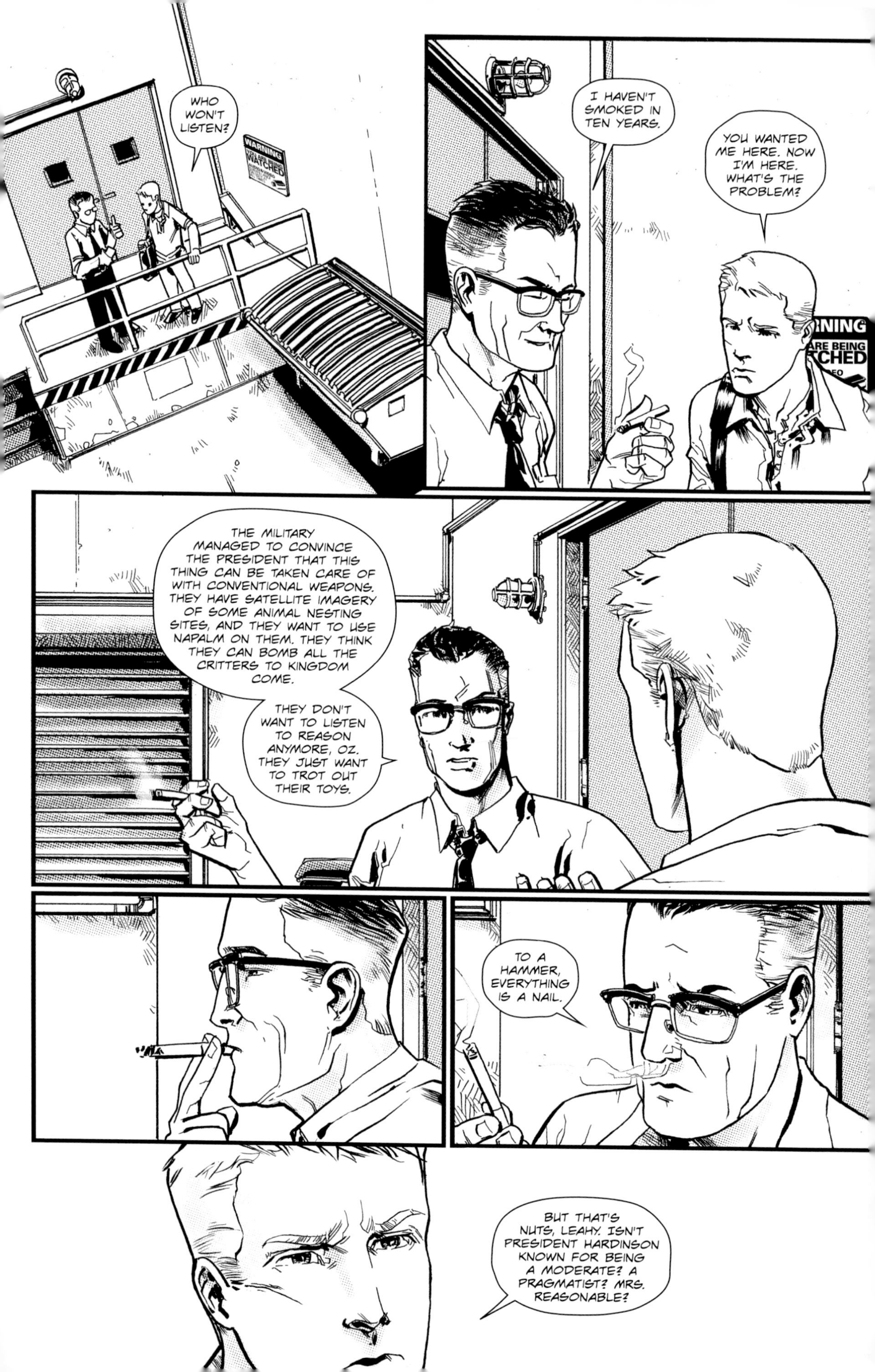
WHO WON'T LISTEN?
WARNING
WATCHED
I HAVEN'T SMOKED IN TEN YEARS.
YOU WANTED ME HERE. NOW I'M HERE. WHAT'S THE PROBLEM?
THE MILITARY MANAGED TO CONVINCE THE PRESIDENT THAT THIS THING CAN BE TAKEN CARE OF WITH CONVENTIONAL WEAPONS. THEY HAVE SATELLITE IMAGERY OF SOME ANIMAL NESTING SITES, AND THEY WANT TO USE NAPALM ON THEM. THEY THINK THEY CAN BOMB ALL THE CRITTERS TO KINGDOM COME.
THEY DON'T WANT TO LISTEN TO REASON ANYMORE, OZ. THEY JUST WANT TO TROT OUT THEIR TOYS.
TO A HAMMER, EVERYTHING IS A NAIL.
BUT THAT'S NUTS, LEAHY. ISN'T PRESIDENT HARDINSON KNOWN FOR BEING A MODERATE? A PRAGMATIST? MRS. REASONABLE?

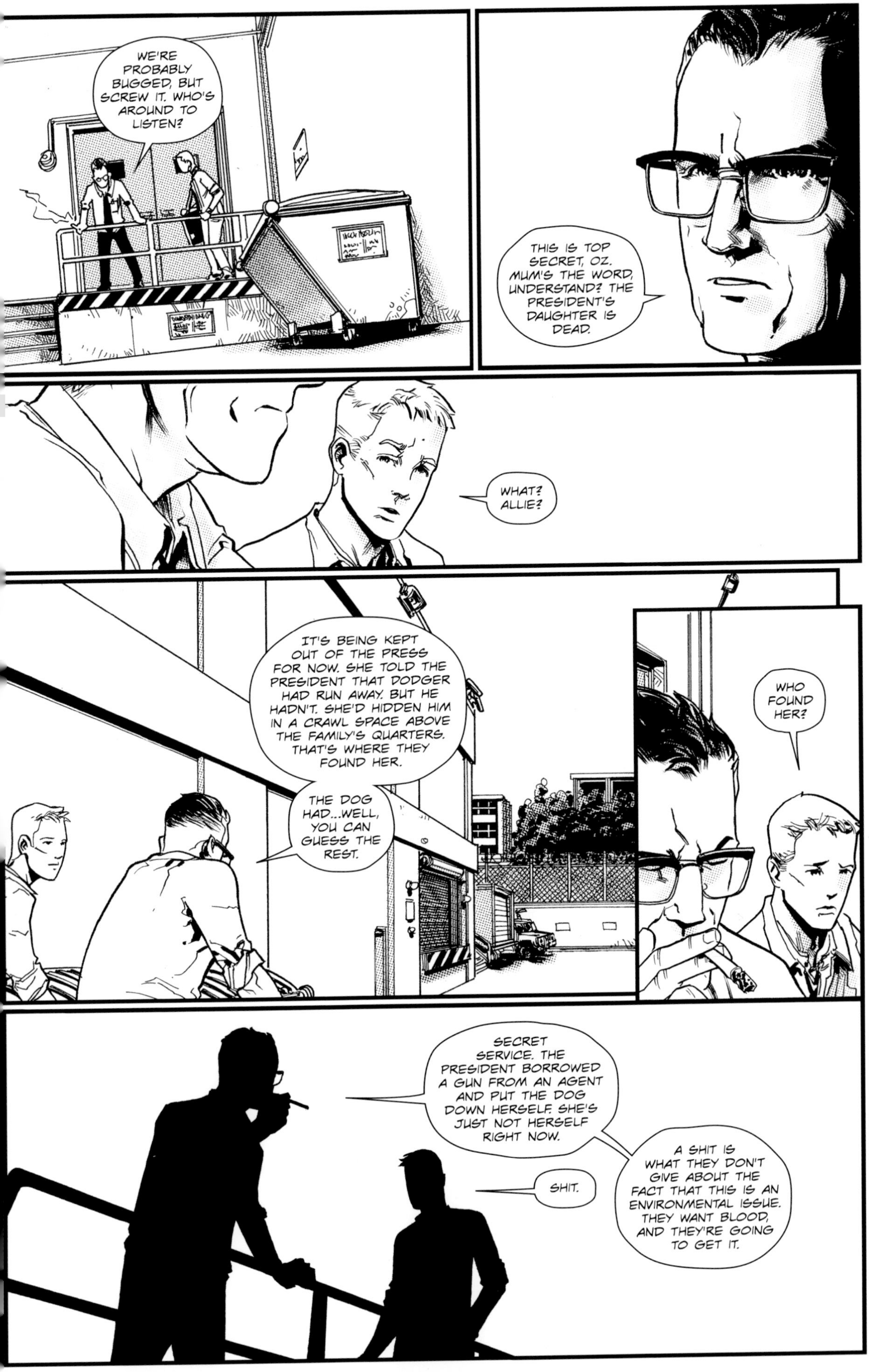
WE'RE PROBABLY BUGGED, BUT SCREW IT. WHO'S AROUND TO LISTEN?
THIS IS TOP SECRET, OZ. MUM'S THE WORD, UNDERSTAND? THE PRESIDENT'S DAUGHTER IS DEAD.
WHAT? ALLIE?
IT'S BEING KEPT OUT OF THE PRESS FOR NOW. SHE TOLD THE PRESIDENT THAT DODGER HAD RUN AWAY. BUT HE HADN'T. SHE'D HIDDEN HIM IN A CRAWL SPACE ABOVE THE FAMILY'S QUARTERS. THAT'S WHERE THEY FOUND HER.
THE DOG HAD...WELL, YOU CAN GUESS THE REST.
WHO FOUND HER?
SECRET SERVICE. THE PRESIDENT BORROWED A GUN FROM AN AGENT AND PUT THE DOG DOWN HERSELF. SHE'S JUST NOT HERSELF RIGHT NOW.
SHIT.
A SHIT IS WHAT THEY DON'T GIVE ABOUT THE FACT THAT THIS IS AN ENVIRONMENTAL ISSUE. THEY WANT BLOOD, AND THEY'RE GOING TO GET IT.

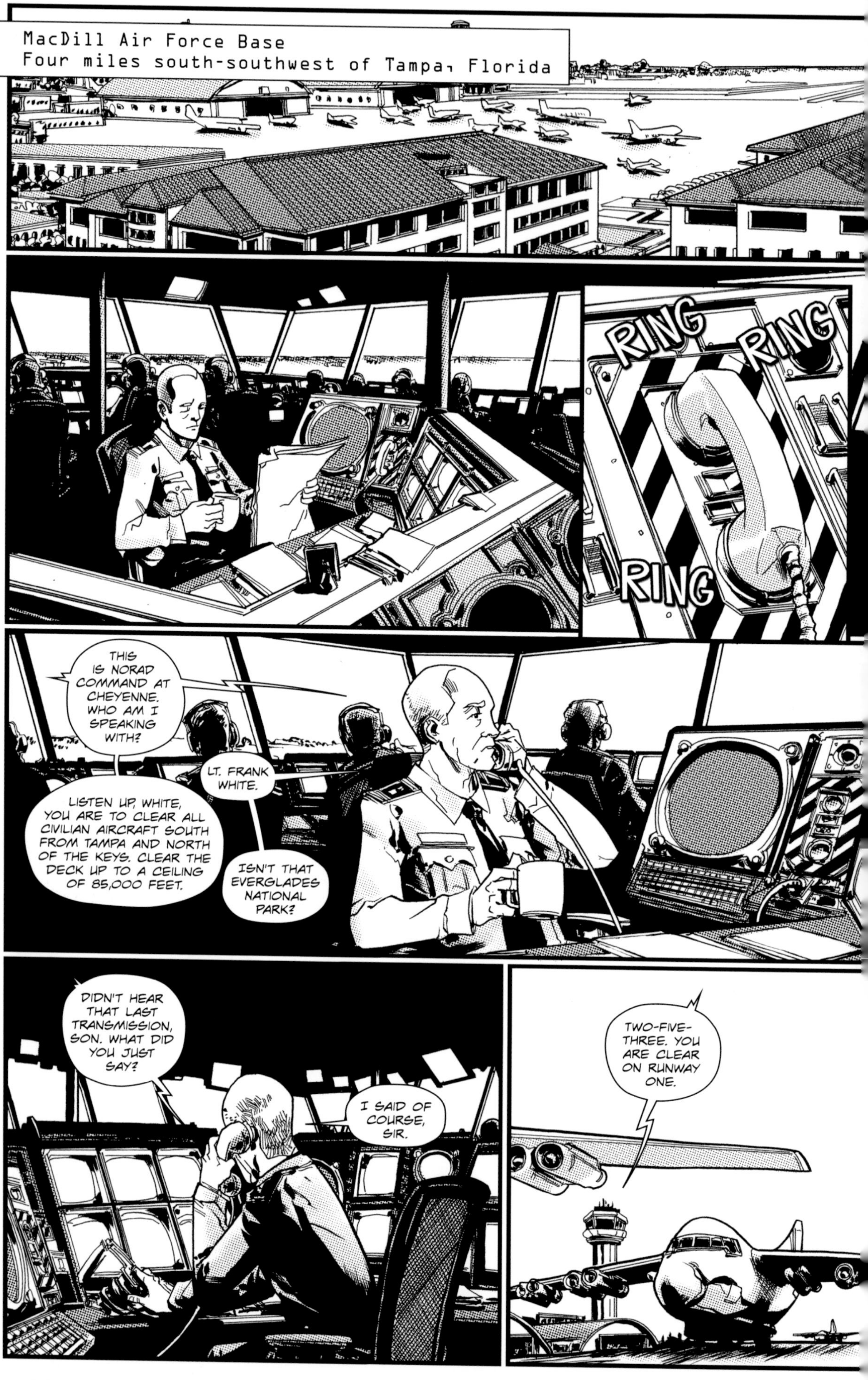
MacDill Air Force Base
Four miles south-southwest of Tampa, Florida
RING RING
RING
THIS IS NORAD COMMAND AT CHEYENNE. WHO AM I SPEAKING WITH?
LT. FRANK WHITE.
LISTEN UP, WHITE, YOU ARE TO CLEAR ALL CIVILIAN AIRCRAFT SOUTH FROM TAMPA AND NORTH OF THE KEYS. CLEAR THE DECK UP TO A CEILING OF 85,000 FEET.
ISN'T THAT EVERGLADES NATIONAL PARK?
DIDN'T HEAR THAT LAST TRANSMISSION, SON. WHAT DID YOU JUST SAY?
I SAID OF COURSE, SIR.
TWO-FIVE-THREE. YOU ARE CLEAR ON RUNWAY ONE.

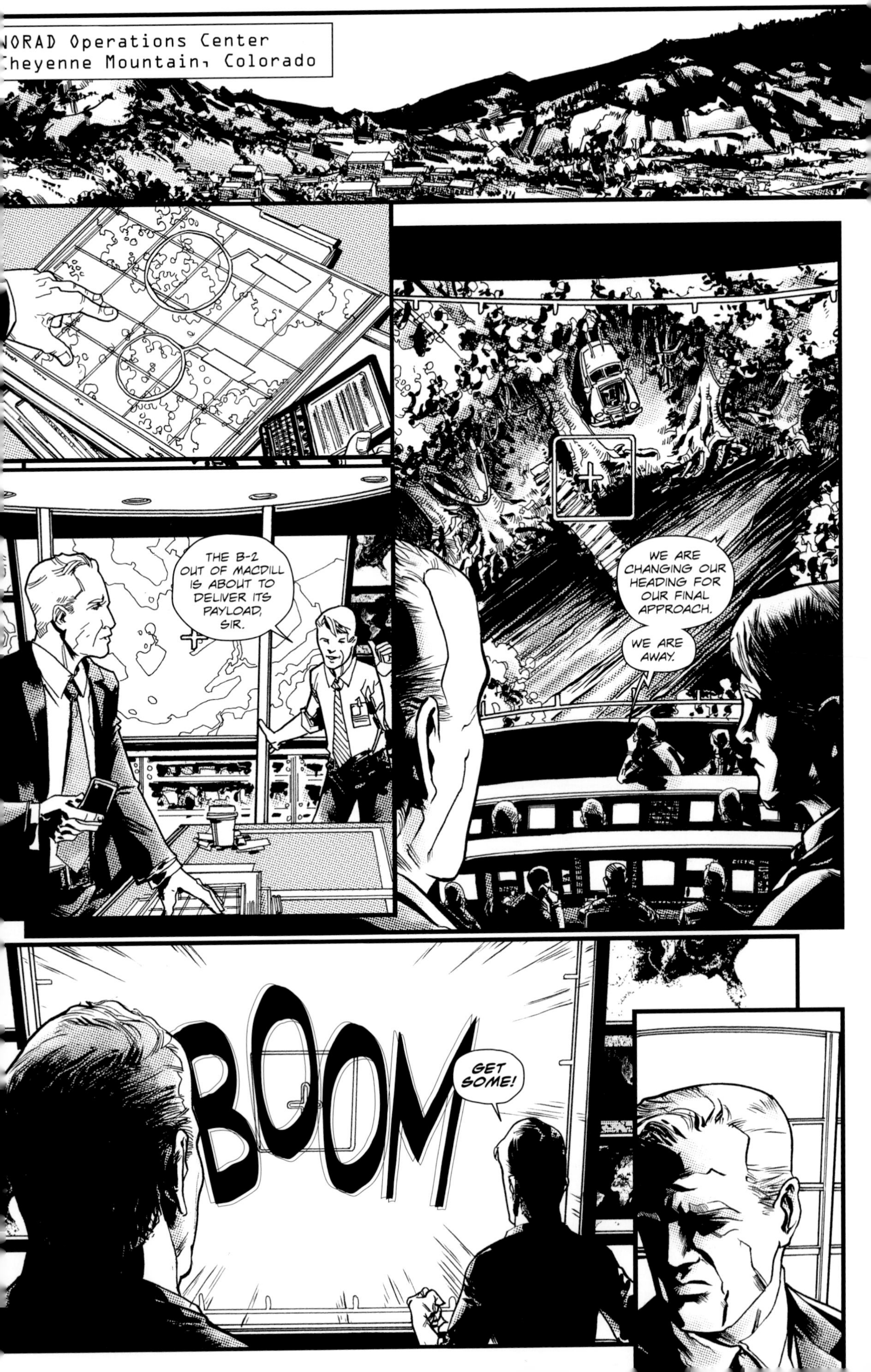
NORAD Operations Center
Cheyenne Mountain, Colorado
THE B-2 OUT OF MACDILL IS ABOUT TO DELIVER ITS PAYLOAD, SIR.
WE ARE CHANGING OUR HEADING FOR OUR FINAL APPROACH.
WE ARE AWAY.
BOOM
GET SOME!

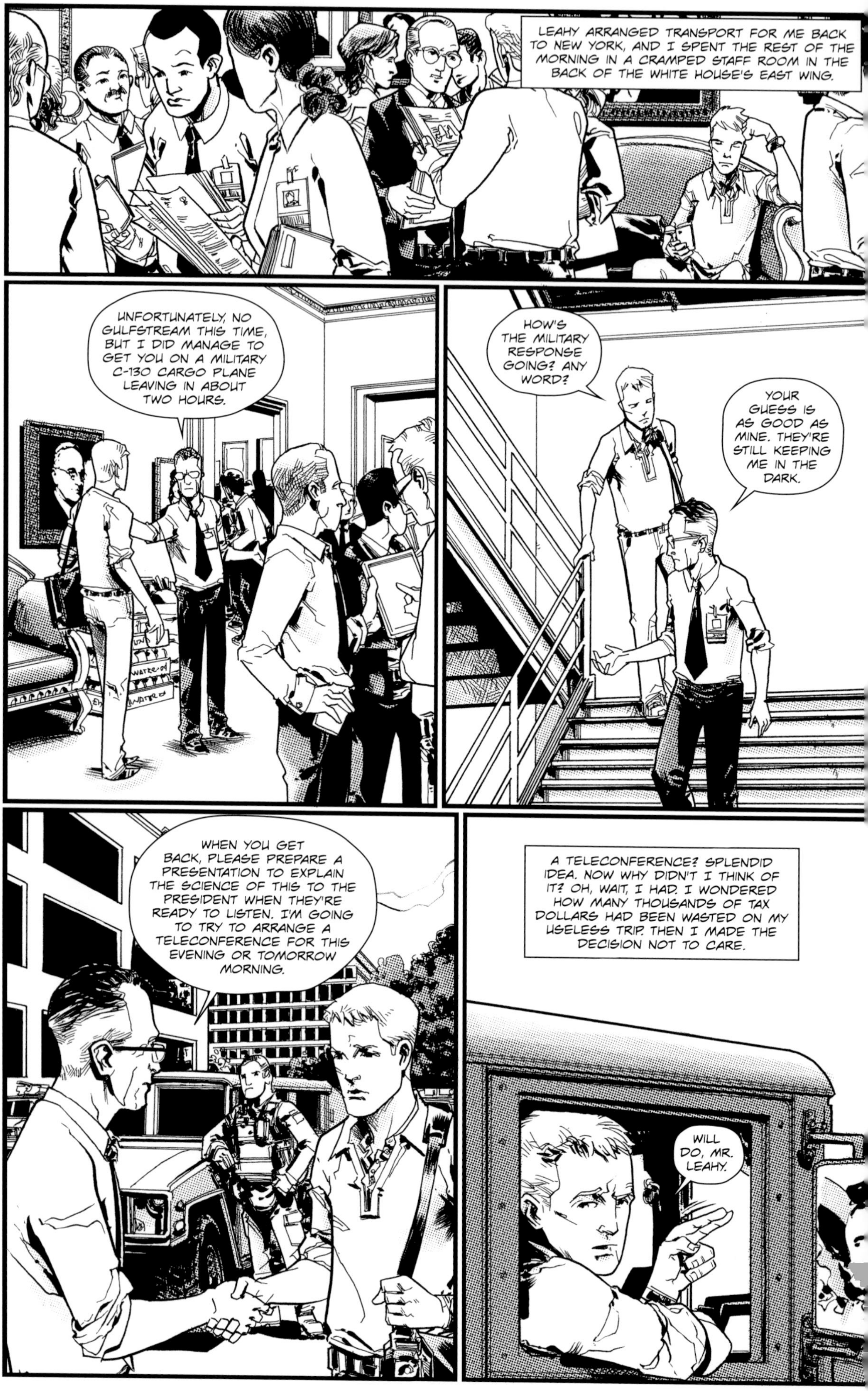
LEAHY ARRANGED TRANSPORT FOR ME BACK TO NEW YORK, AND I SPENT THE REST OF THE MORNING IN A CRAMPED STAFF ROOM IN THE BACK OF THE WHITE HOUSE'S EAST WING.
UNFORTUNATELY, NO GULFSTREAM THIS TIME, BUT I DID MANAGE TO GET YOU ON A MILITARY C-130 CARGO PLANE LEAVING IN ABOUT TWO HOURS.
HOW'S THE MILITARY RESPONSE GOING? ANY WORD?
YOUR GUESS IS AS GOOD AS MINE. THEY'RE STILL KEEPING ME IN THE DARK.
WHEN YOU GET BACK, PLEASE PREPARE A PRESENTATION TO EXPLAIN THE SCIENCE OF THIS TO THE PRESIDENT WHEN THEY'RE READY TO LISTEN. I'M GOING TO TRY TO ARRANGE A TELECONFERENCE FOR THIS EVENING OR TOMORROW MORNING.
A TELECONFERENCE? SPLENDID IDEA. NOW WHY DIDN'T I THINK OF IT? OH, WAIT, I HAD. I WONDERED HOW MANY THOUSANDS OF TAX DOLLARS HAD BEEN WASTED ON MY USELESS TRIP. THEN I MADE THE DECISION NOT TO CARE.
WILL DO, MR. LEAHY.

THINGS WERE EVEN WORSE ON THE STREETS OF D.C. I WISHED I WAS ALREADY AIRBORNE.

SOME KIDS WERE ON THE STREET, DRINKING BEER, WITH HANDMADE SIGNS. I SMELLED POT.

AIN'T PAY BACK A BITCH!?

MEAT IS MURDER

HO HO HO

MEAT IS MURDER

IT'S TIME FOR PAYBACK

MEAT

EVERYTHING HAS GONE NUTS, I THOUGHT. ANIMALS, THE PRESIDENT, COLLEGE KIDS.

THERE WERE MORE PROTESTORS ON THE ARLINGTON BRIDGE. THEY LOOKED MORE SINISTER WITH SKI MASKS AND BANDANAS.

CRASH

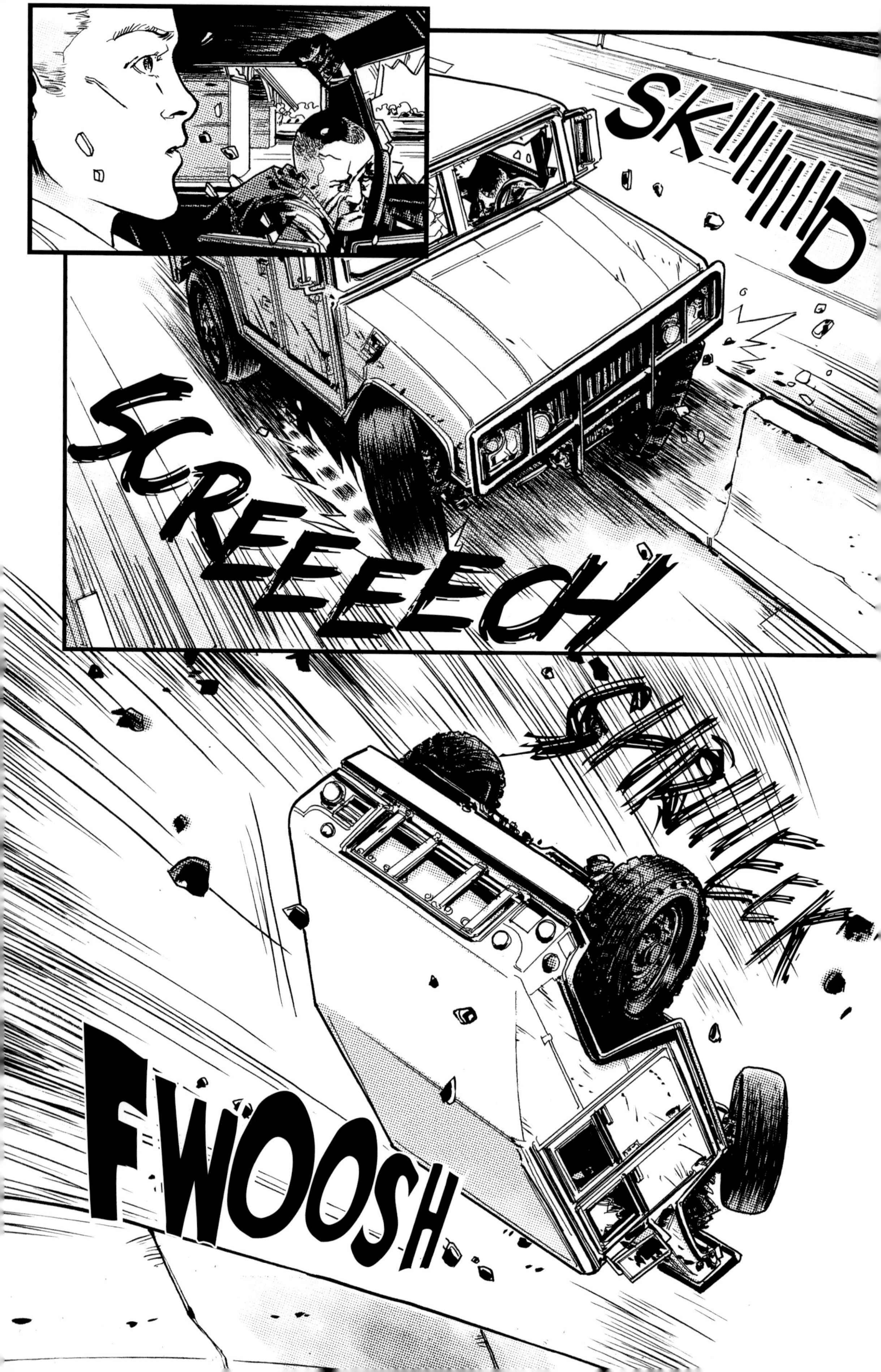
SKIIIIID
SCREEEECH
SKRIIEEK
FWOOSH

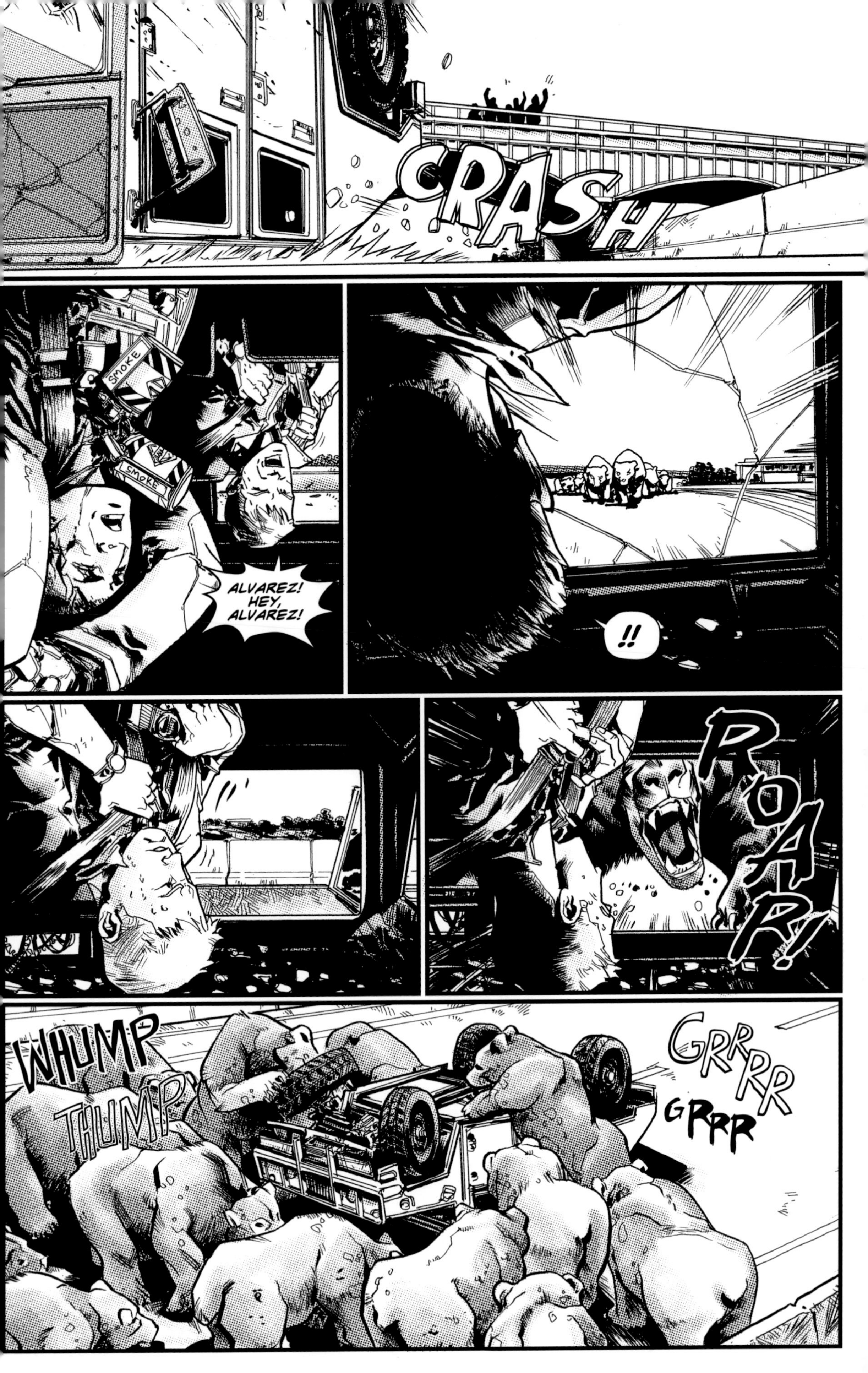
CRASH
SMOKE
SMOKE
ALVAREZ! HEY, ALVAREZ!
!!
ROAR!
WHUMP
THUMP
GRRRR
GRRR

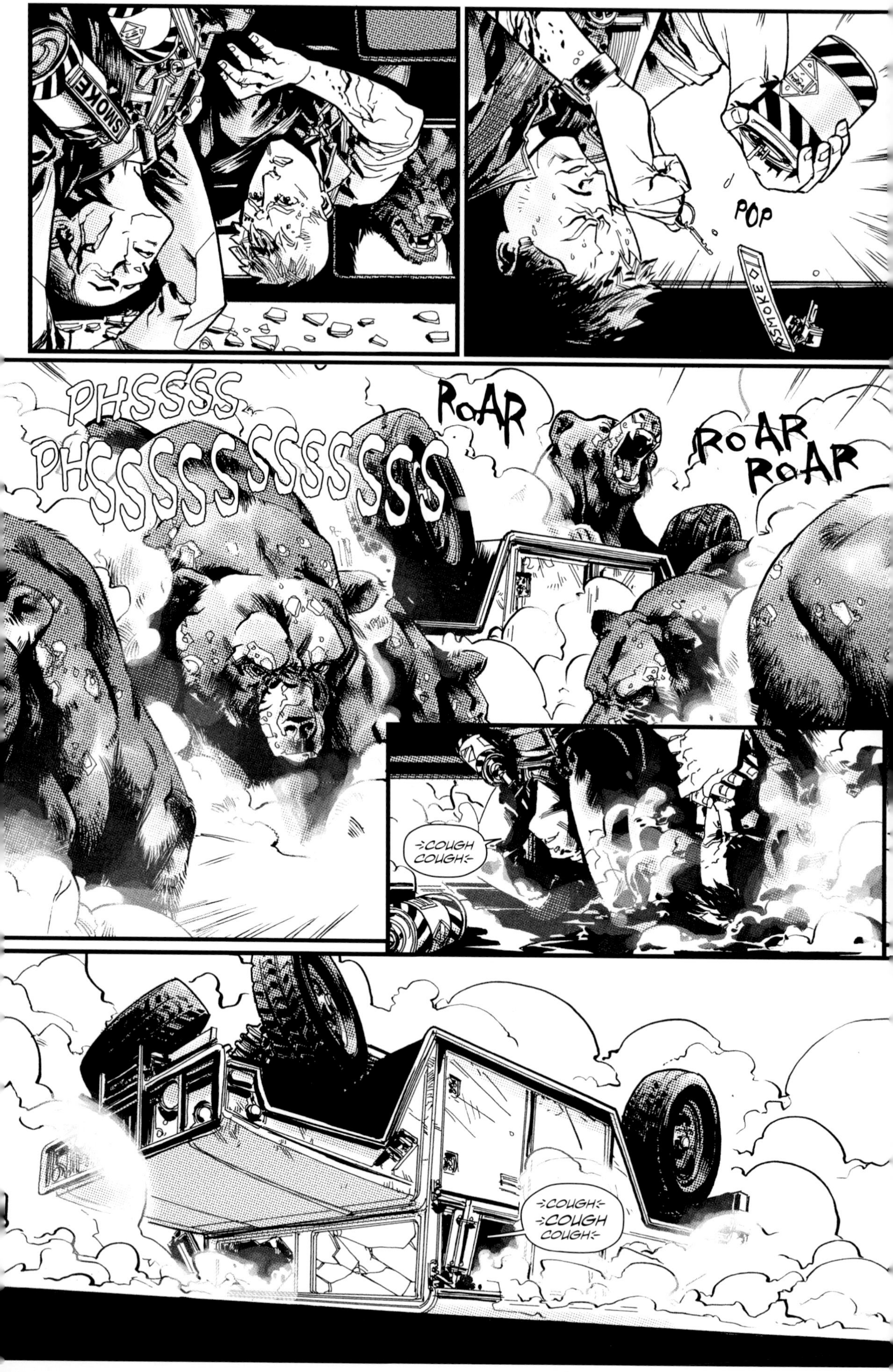
SMOKE
POP
SMOKE
PHSSSS
PHSSSSSSSSSSSSS
ROAR
ROAR
ROAR
COUGH
COUGH
COUGH
COUGH
COUGH

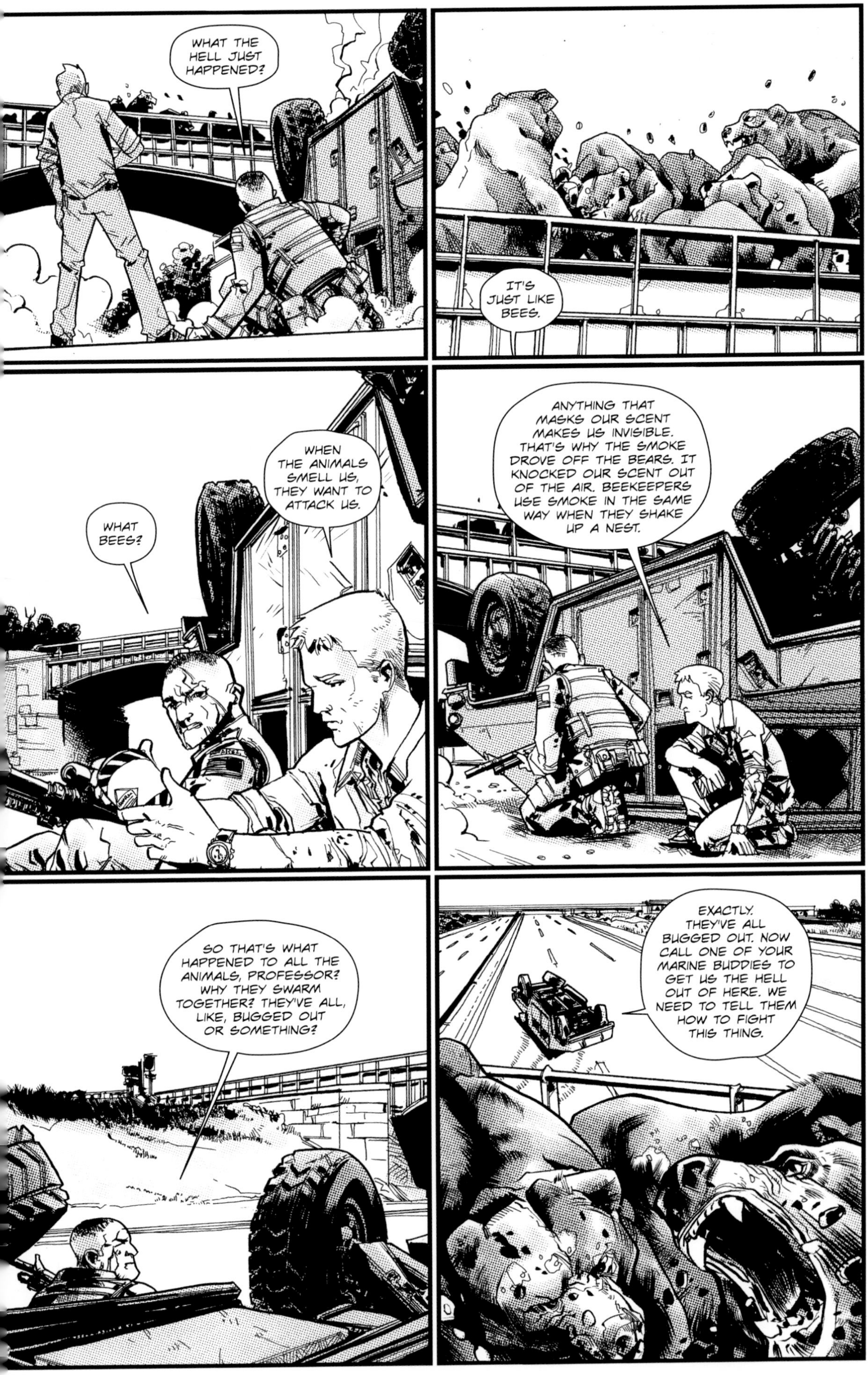
WHAT THE HELL JUST HAPPENED?
IT'S JUST LIKE BEES.
WHAT BEES?
WHEN THE ANIMALS SMELL US, THEY WANT TO ATTACK US.
ANYTHING THAT MASKS OUR SCENT MAKES US INVISIBLE. THAT'S WHY THE SMOKE DROVE OFF THE BEARS. IT KNOCKED OUR SCENT OUT OF THE AIR. BEEKEEPERS USE SMOKE IN THE SAME WAY WHEN THEY SHAKE UP A NEST.
SO THAT'S WHAT HAPPENED TO ALL THE ANIMALS, PROFESSOR? WHY THEY SWARM TOGETHER? THEY'VE ALL, LIKE, BUGGED OUT OR SOMETHING?
EXACTLY. THEY'VE ALL BUGGED OUT. NOW CALL ONE OF YOUR MARINE BUDDIES TO GET US THE HELL OUT OF HERE. WE NEED TO TELL THEM HOW TO FIGHT THIS THING.

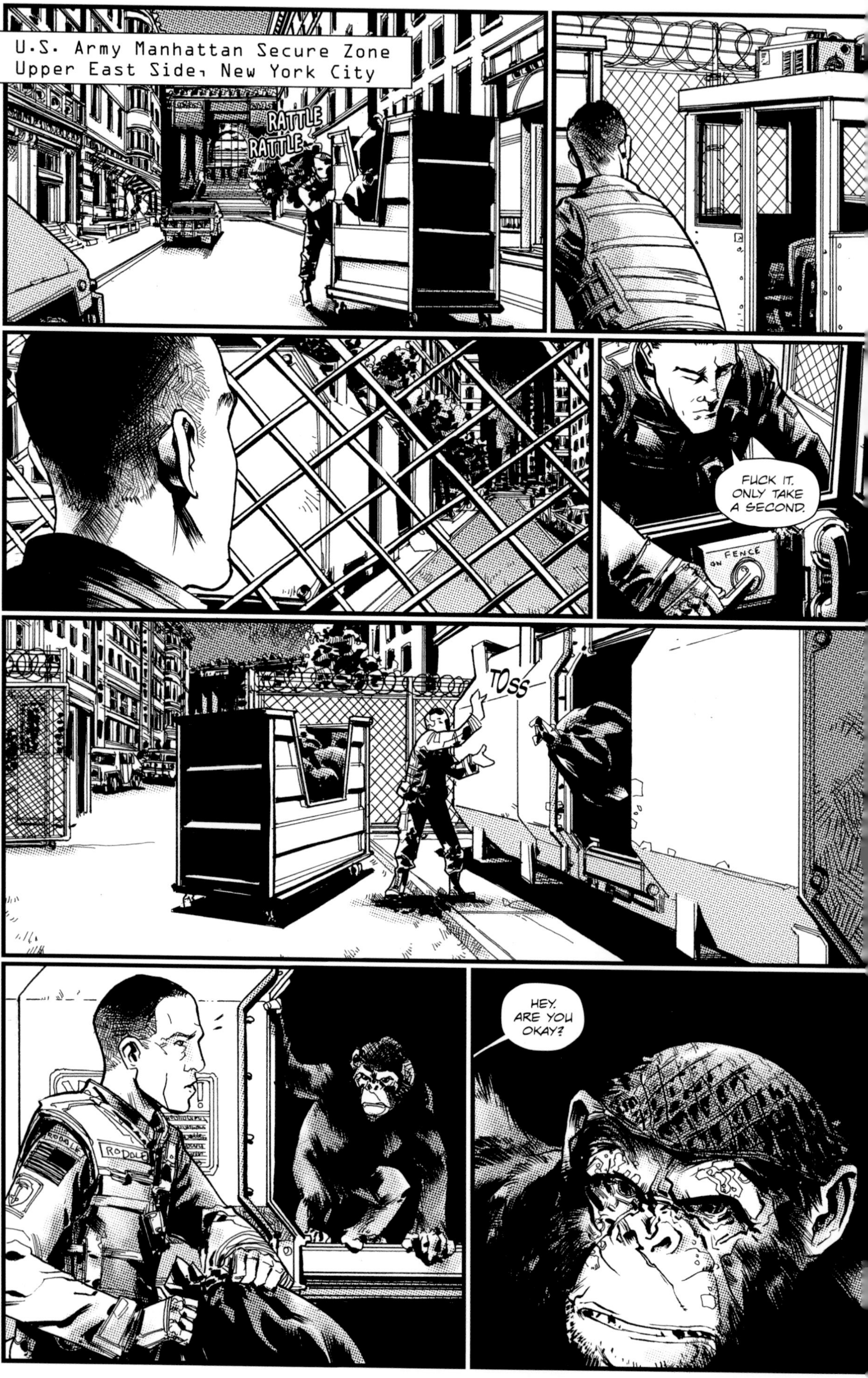
U.S. Army Manhattan Secure Zone
Upper East Side, New York City
RATTLE
RATTLE
FUCK IT. ONLY TAKE A SECOND.
ON FENCE
TOSS
RODDLE
HEY. ARE YOU OKAY?

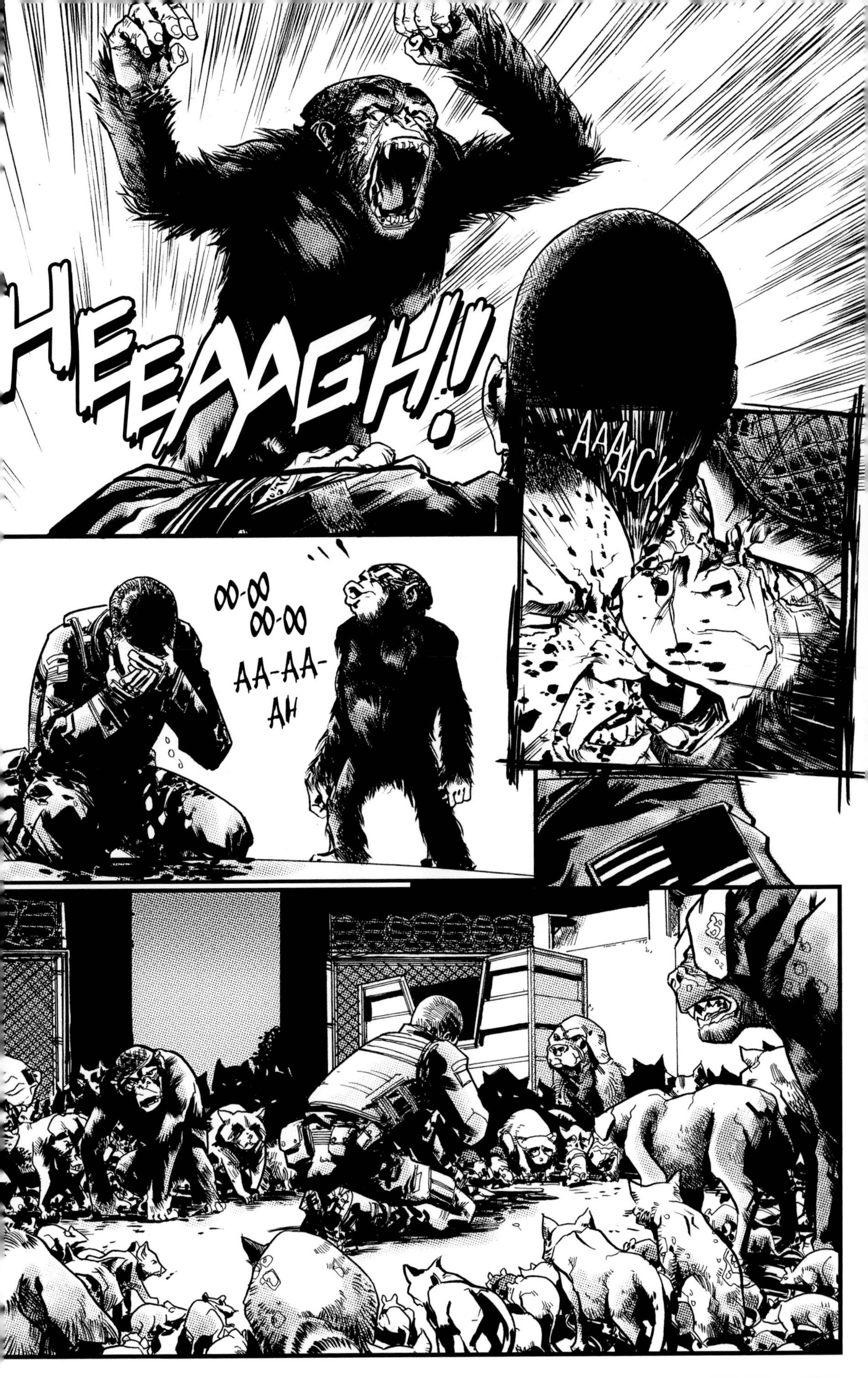
HEEAAGH!!
AAAACK!
OO-OO
OO-OO
AA-AA-
AH

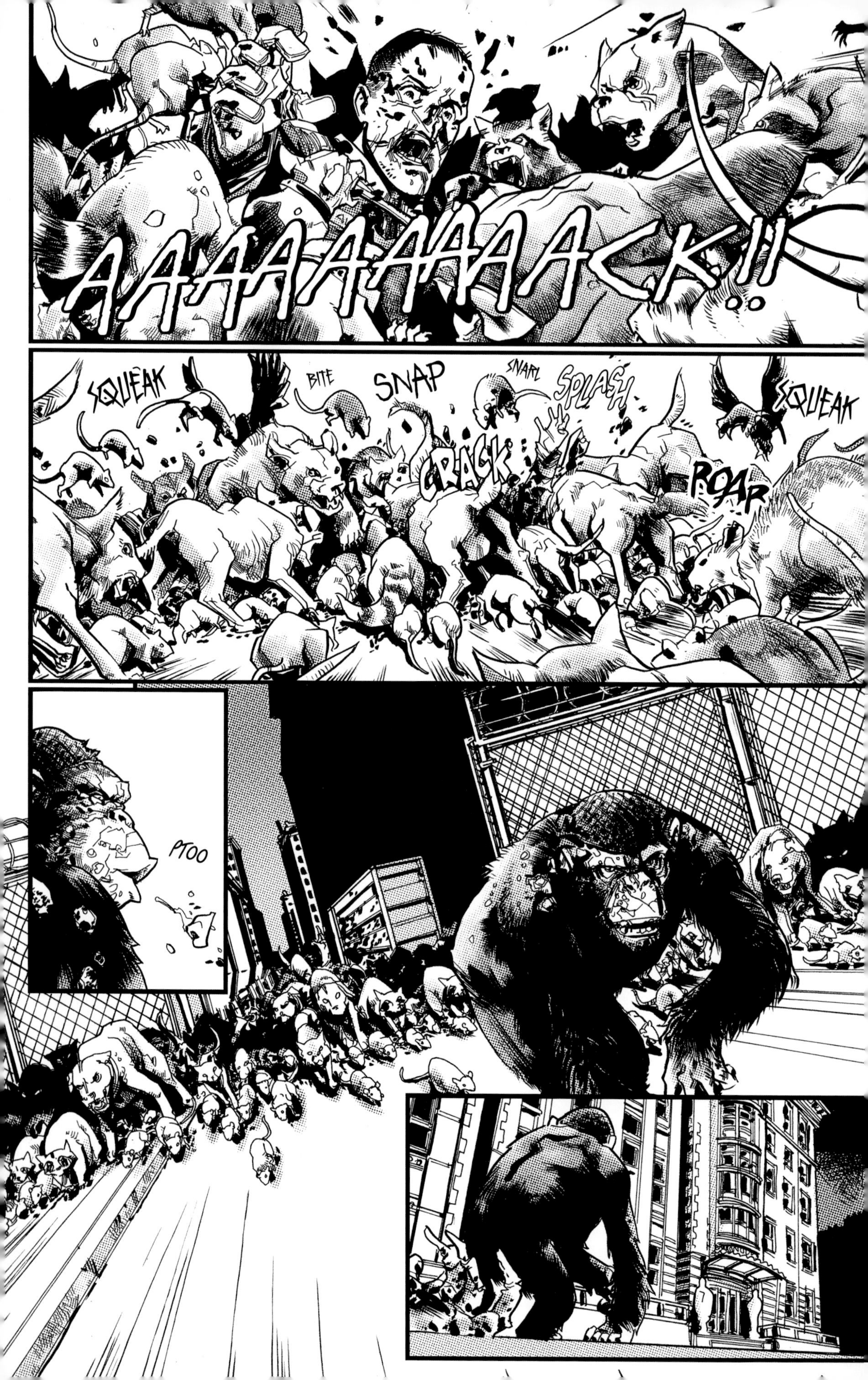
AAAAAAAACK!!
SQUEAK
BITE
SNAP
SNARL
SPLASH
SQUEAK
CRACK
ROAR
PTOO

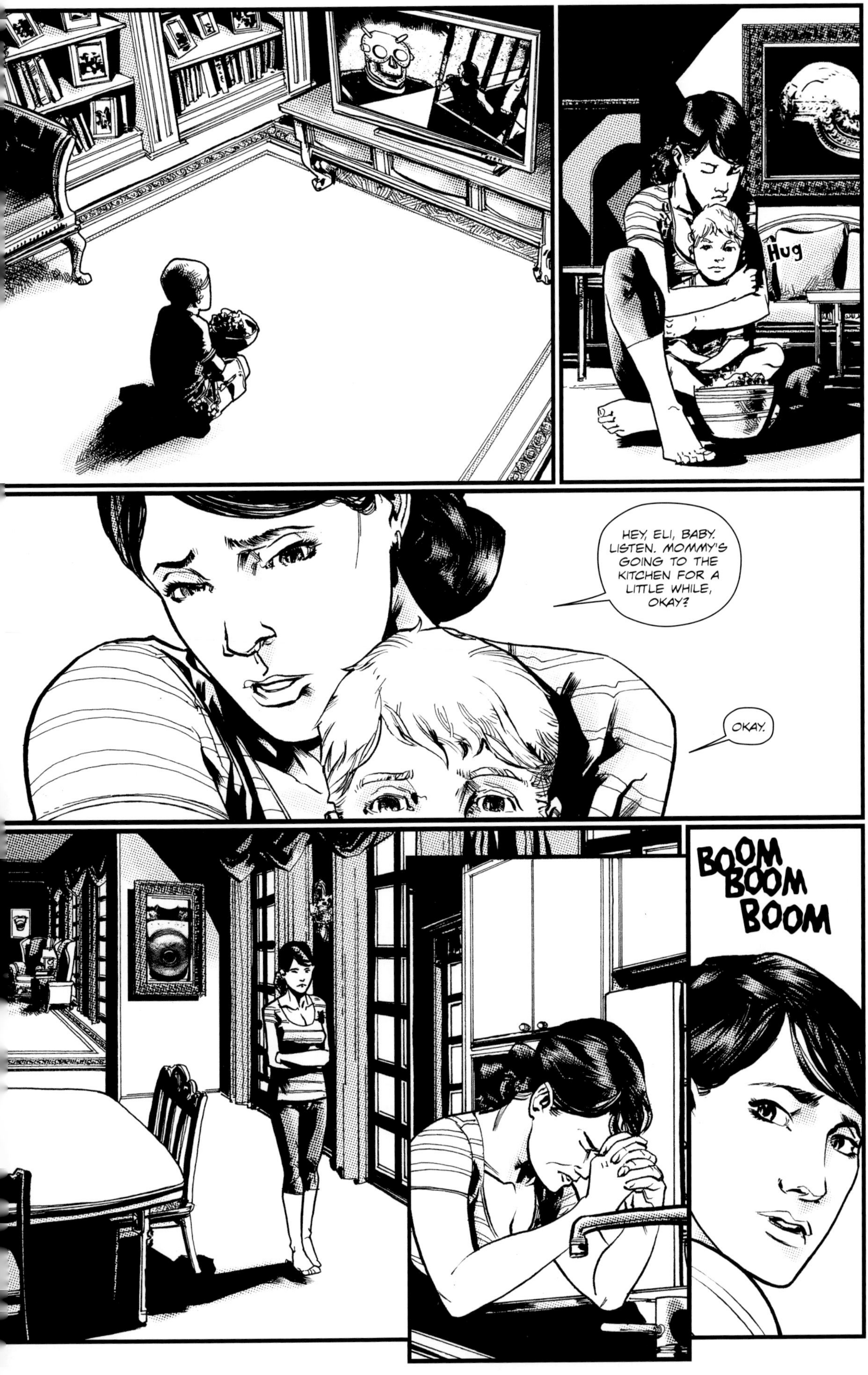
Hug
HEY, ELI, BABY. LISTEN. MOMMY'S GOING TO THE KITCHEN FOR A LITTLE WHILE, OKAY?
OKAY.
BOOM BOOM BOOM

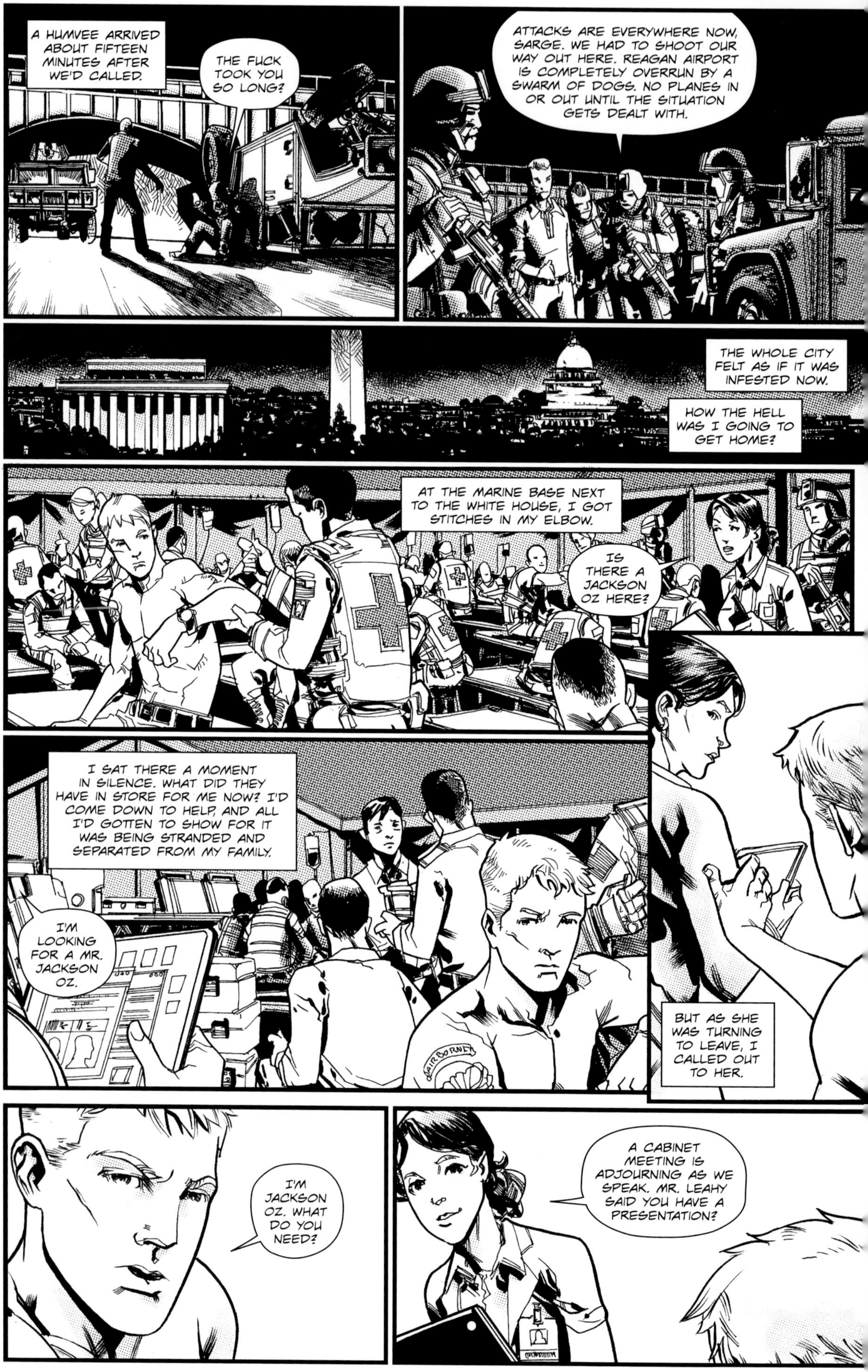
A HUMVEE ARRIVED ABOUT FIFTEEN MINUTES AFTER WE'D CALLED.
THE FUCK TOOK YOU SO LONG?
ATTACKS ARE EVERYWHERE NOW, SARGE. WE HAD TO SHOOT OUR WAY OUT HERE. REAGAN AIRPORT IS COMPLETELY OVERRUN BY A SWARM OF DOGS. NO PLANES IN OR OUT UNTIL THE SITUATION GETS DEALT WITH.
THE WHOLE CITY FELT AS IF IT WAS INFESTED NOW.
HOW THE HELL WAS I GOING TO GET HOME?
AT THE MARINE BASE NEXT TO THE WHITE HOUSE, I GOT STITCHES IN MY ELBOW.
IS THERE A JACKSON OZ HERE?
I SAT THERE A MOMENT IN SILENCE. WHAT DID THEY HAVE IN STORE FOR ME NOW? I'D COME DOWN TO HELP, AND ALL I'D GOTTEN TO SHOW FOR IT WAS BEING STRANDED AND SEPARATED FROM MY FAMILY.
I'M LOOKING FOR A MR. JACKSON OZ.
BUT AS SHE WAS TURNING TO LEAVE, I CALLED OUT TO HER.
I'M JACKSON OZ. WHAT DO YOU NEED?
A CABINET MEETING IS ADJOURNING AS WE SPEAK. MR. LEAHY SAID YOU HAVE A PRESENTATION?

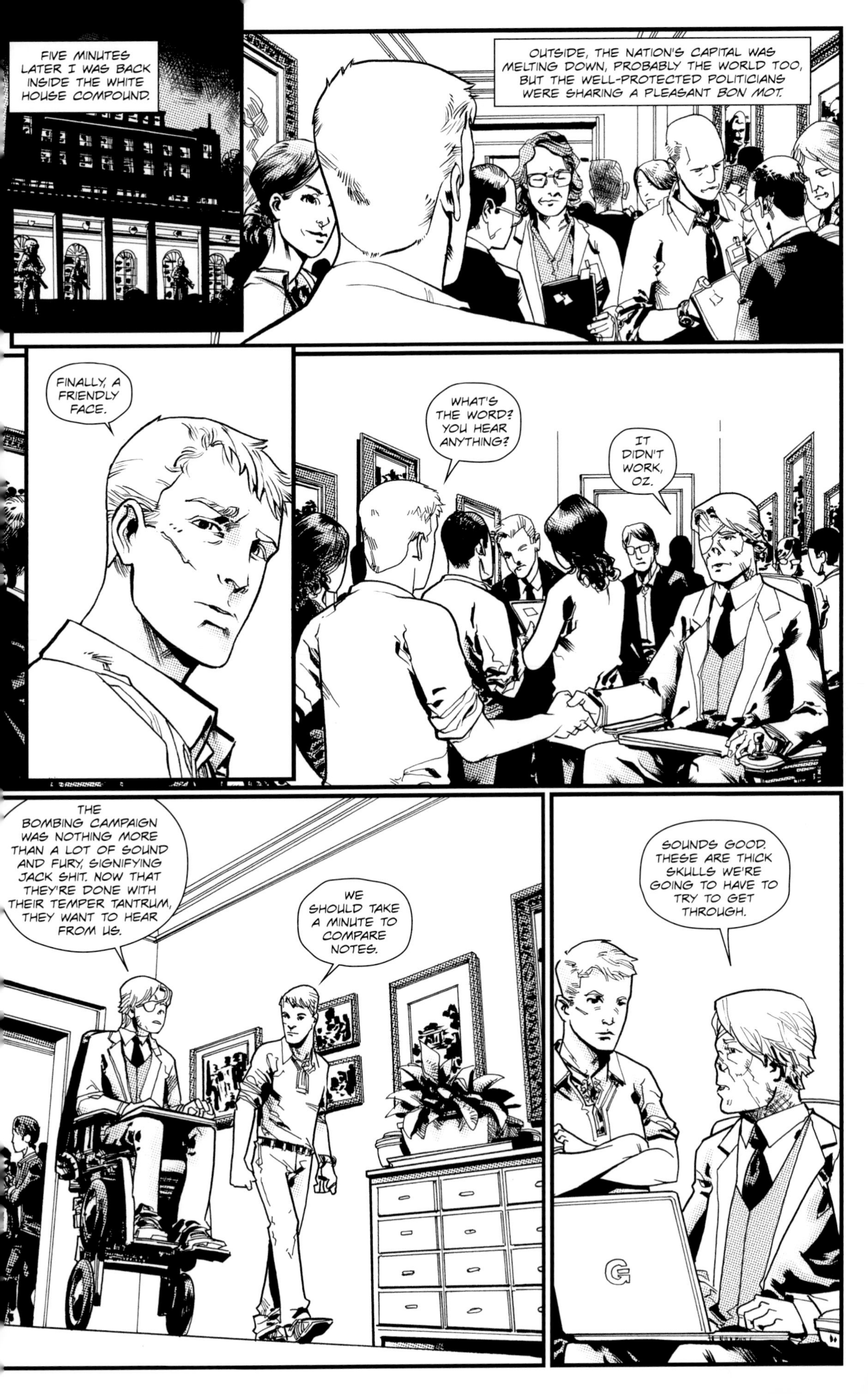
FIVE MINUTES LATER I WAS BACK INSIDE THE WHITE HOUSE COMPOUND.
OUTSIDE, THE NATION'S CAPITAL WAS MELTING DOWN, PROBABLY THE WORLD TOO, BUT THE WELL-PROTECTED POLITICIANS WERE SHARING A PLEASANT BON MOT.
FINALLY, A FRIENDLY FACE.
WHAT'S THE WORD? YOU HEAR ANYTHING?
IT DIDN'T WORK, OZ.
THE BOMBING CAMPAIGN WAS NOTHING MORE THAN A LOT OF SOUND AND FURY, SIGNIFYING JACK SHIT. NOW THAT THEY'RE DONE WITH THEIR TEMPER TANTRUM, THEY WANT TO HEAR FROM US.
WE SHOULD TAKE A MINUTE TO COMPARE NOTES.
SOUNDS GOOD. THESE ARE THICK SKULLS WE'RE GOING TO HAVE TO TRY TO GET THROUGH.

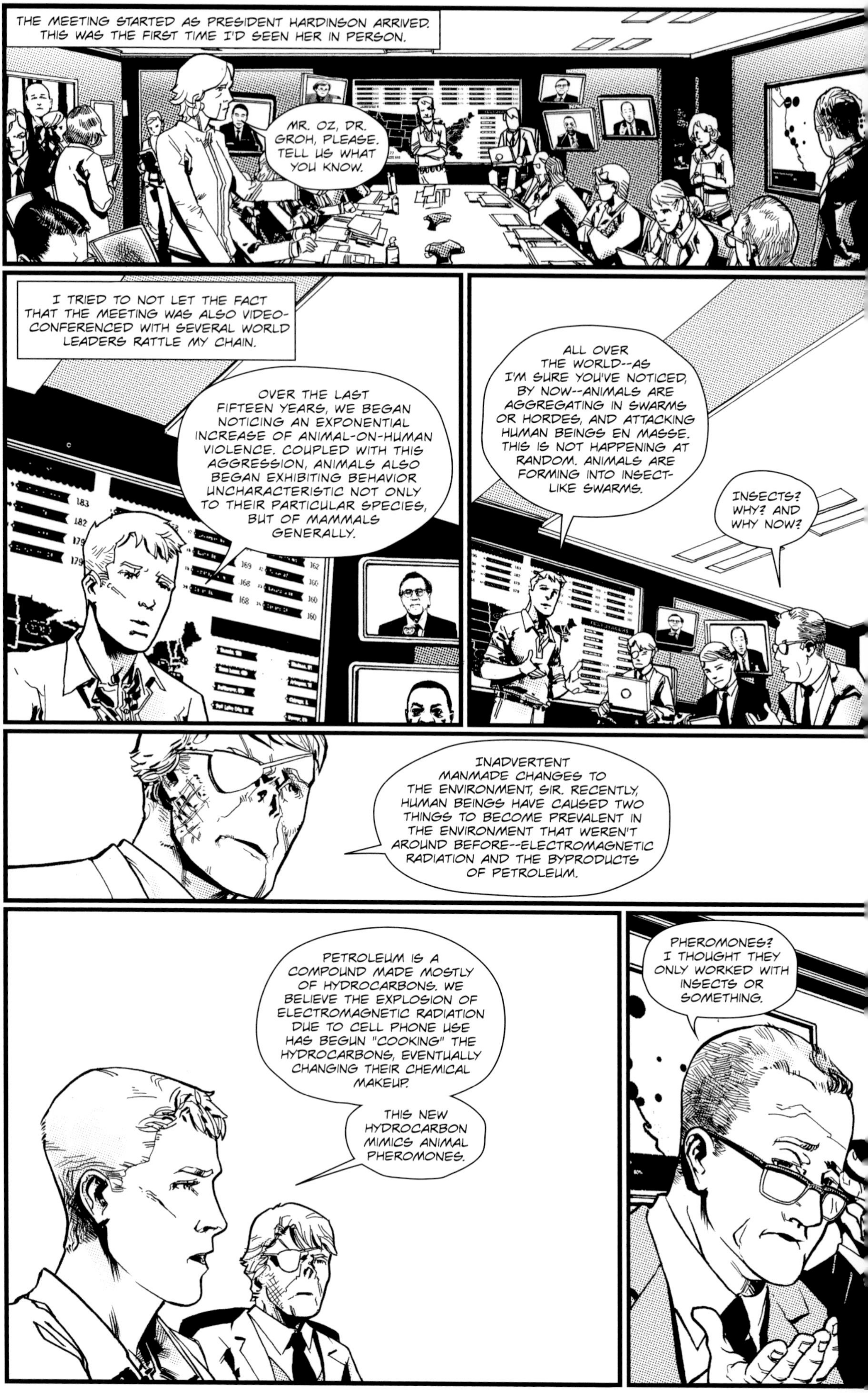
THE MEETING STARTED AS PRESIDENT HARDINSON ARRIVED. THIS WAS THE FIRST TIME I'D SEEN HER IN PERSON.
MR. OZ, DR. GROH, PLEASE. TELL US WHAT YOU KNOW.
I TRIED TO NOT LET THE FACT THAT THE MEETING WAS ALSO VIDEO-CONFERENCED WITH SEVERAL WORLD LEADERS RATTLE MY CHAIN.
OVER THE LAST FIFTEEN YEARS, WE BEGAN NOTICING AN EXPONENTIAL INCREASE OF ANIMAL-ON-HUMAN VIOLENCE. COUPLED WITH THIS AGGRESSION, ANIMALS ALSO BEGAN EXHIBITING BEHAVIOR UNCHARACTERISTIC NOT ONLY TO THEIR PARTICULAR SPECIES, BUT OF MAMMALS GENERALLY.
ALL OVER THE WORLD--AS I'M SURE YOU'VE NOTICED, BY NOW--ANIMALS ARE AGGREGATING IN SWARMS OR HORDES, AND ATTACKING HUMAN BEINGS EN MASSE. THIS IS NOT HAPPENING AT RANDOM. ANIMALS ARE FORMING INTO INSECT-LIKE SWARMS.
INSECTS? WHY? AND WHY NOW?
INADVERTENT MANMADE CHANGES TO THE ENVIRONMENT, SIR. RECENTLY, HUMAN BEINGS HAVE CAUSED TWO THINGS TO BECOME PREVALENT IN THE ENVIRONMENT THAT WEREN'T AROUND BEFORE--ELECTROMAGNETIC RADIATION AND THE BYPRODUCTS OF PETROLEUM.
PETROLEUM IS A COMPOUND MADE MOSTLY OF HYDROCARBONS. WE BELIEVE THE EXPLOSION OF ELECTROMAGNETIC RADIATION DUE TO CELL PHONE USE HAS BEGUN "COOKING" THE HYDROCARBONS, EVENTUALLY CHANGING THEIR CHEMICAL MAKEUP.
THIS NEW HYDROCARBON MIMICS ANIMAL PHEROMONES.
PHEROMONES? I THOUGHT THEY ONLY WORKED WITH INSECTS OR SOMETHING.

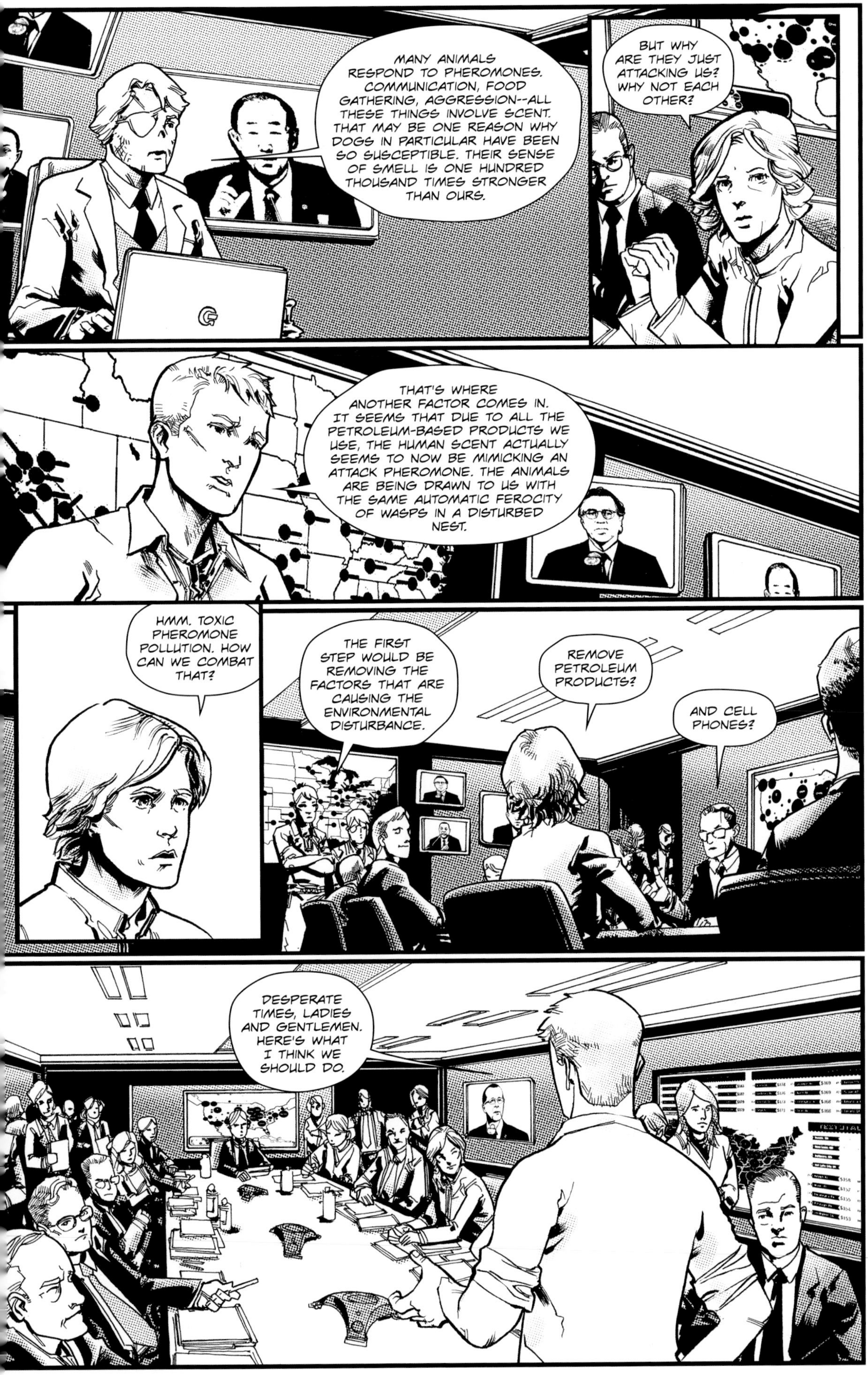
MANY ANIMALS RESPOND TO PHEROMONES. COMMUNICATION, FOOD GATHERING, AGGRESSION--ALL THESE THINGS INVOLVE SCENT. THAT MAY BE ONE REASON WHY DOGS IN PARTICULAR HAVE BEEN SO SUSCEPTIBLE. THEIR SENSE OF SMELL IS ONE HUNDRED THOUSAND TIMES STRONGER THAN OURS.
BUT WHY ARE THEY JUST ATTACKING US? WHY NOT EACH OTHER?
THAT'S WHERE ANOTHER FACTOR COMES IN. IT SEEMS THAT DUE TO ALL THE PETROLEUM-BASED PRODUCTS WE USE, THE HUMAN SCENT ACTUALLY SEEMS TO NOW BE MIMICKING AN ATTACK PHEROMONE. THE ANIMALS ARE BEING DRAWN TO US WITH THE SAME AUTOMATIC FEROCITY OF WASPS IN A DISTURBED NEST.
HMM. TOXIC PHEROMONE POLLUTION. HOW CAN WE COMBAT THAT?
THE FIRST STEP WOULD BE REMOVING THE FACTORS THAT ARE CAUSING THE ENVIRONMENTAL DISTURBANCE.
REMOVE PETROLEUM PRODUCTS?
AND CELL PHONES?
DESPERATE TIMES, LADIES AND GENTLEMEN. HERE'S WHAT I THINK WE SHOULD DO.

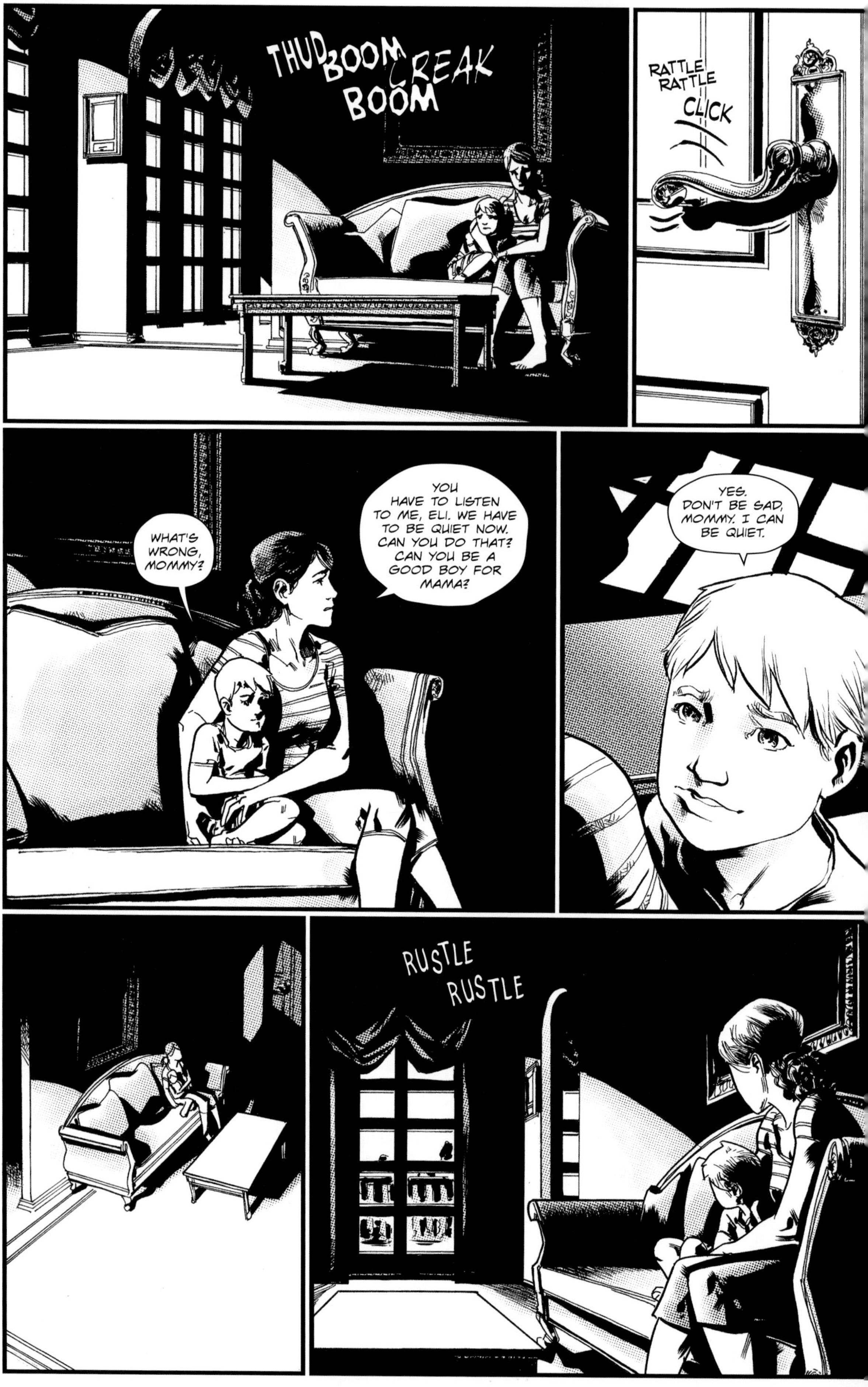
THUD BOOM CREAK BOOM
RATTLE RATTLE CLICK
WHAT'S WRONG, MOMMY?
YOU HAVE TO LISTEN TO ME, ELI. WE HAVE TO BE QUIET NOW. CAN YOU DO THAT? CAN YOU BE A GOOD BOY FOR MAMA?
YES. DON'T BE SAD, MOMMY. I CAN BE QUIET.
RUSTLE RUSTLE

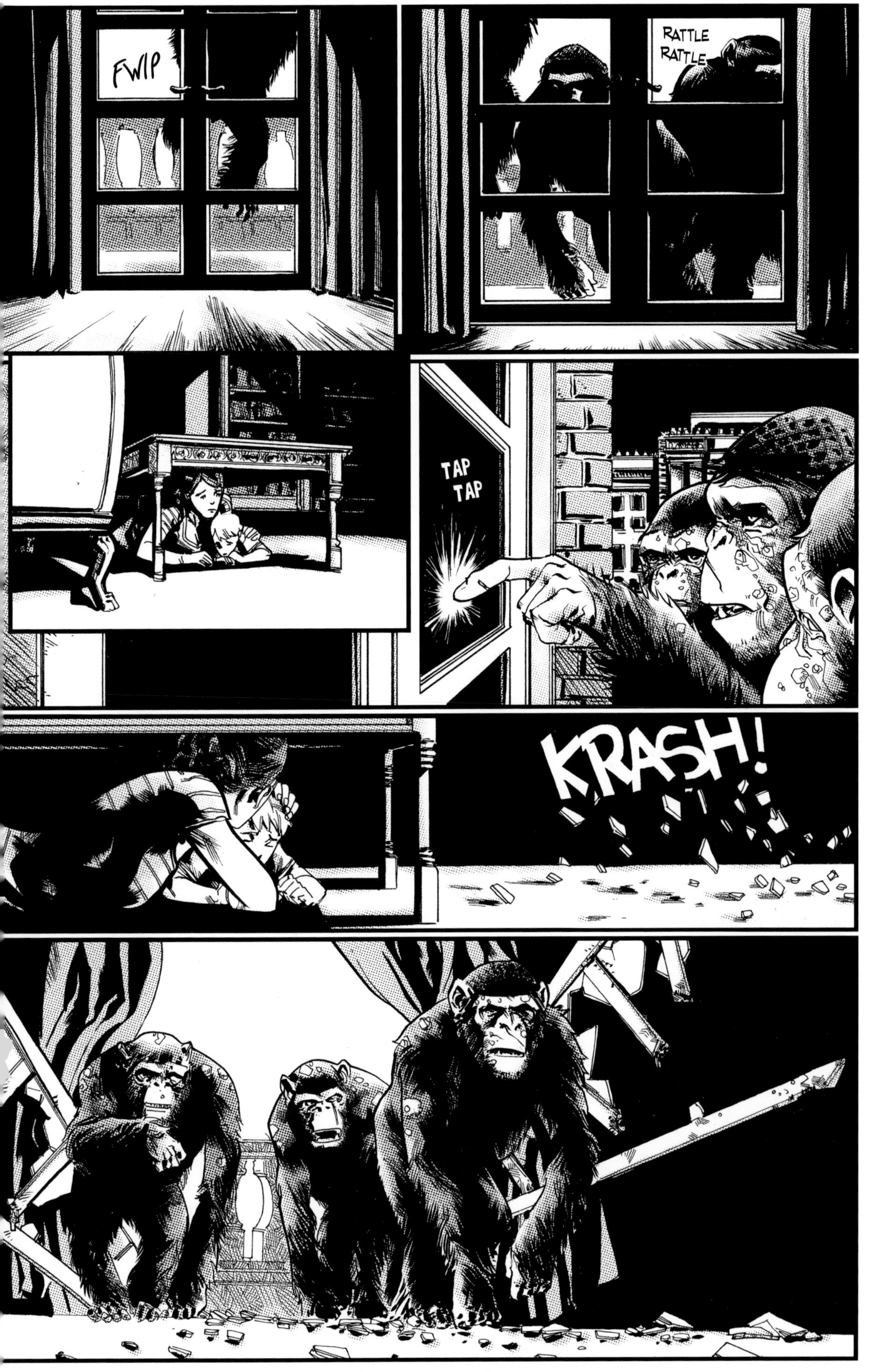
FWIP
RATTLE
RATTLE
TAP
TAP
KRASH!

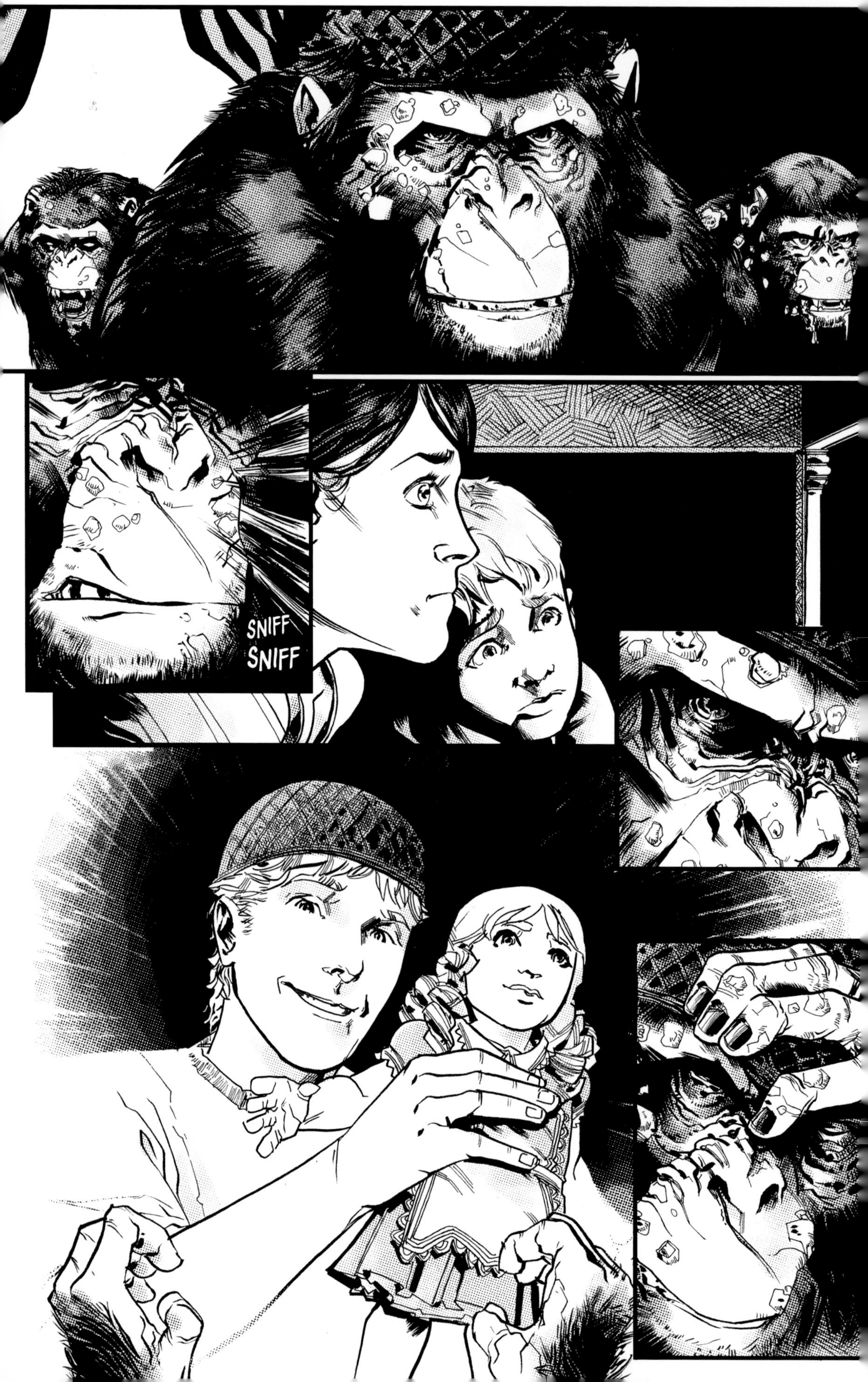
SNIFF
SNIFF

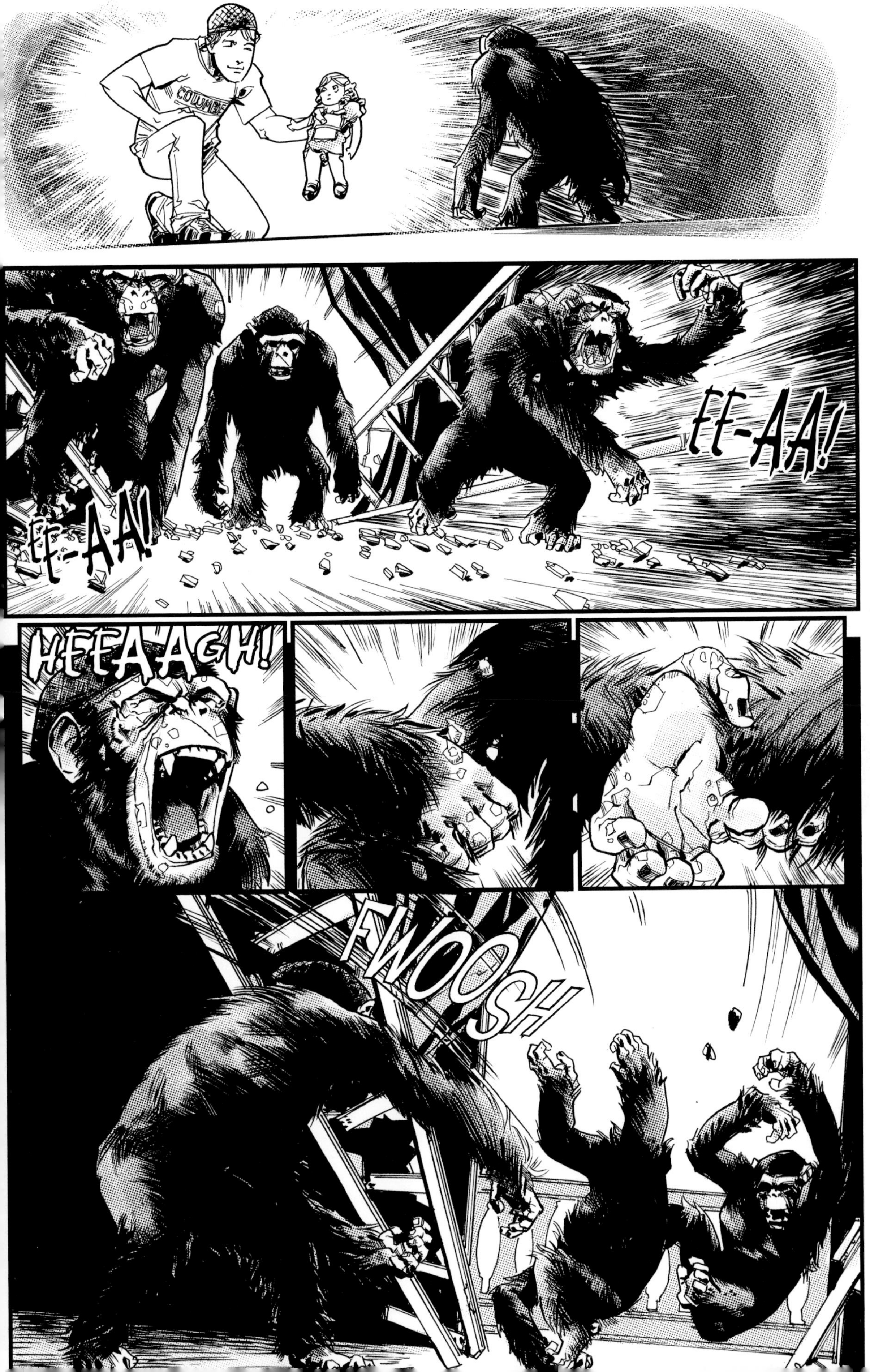

COLUMBIA
EE-AA!
EE-AA!
HEEAAAGH!
FWOOSH

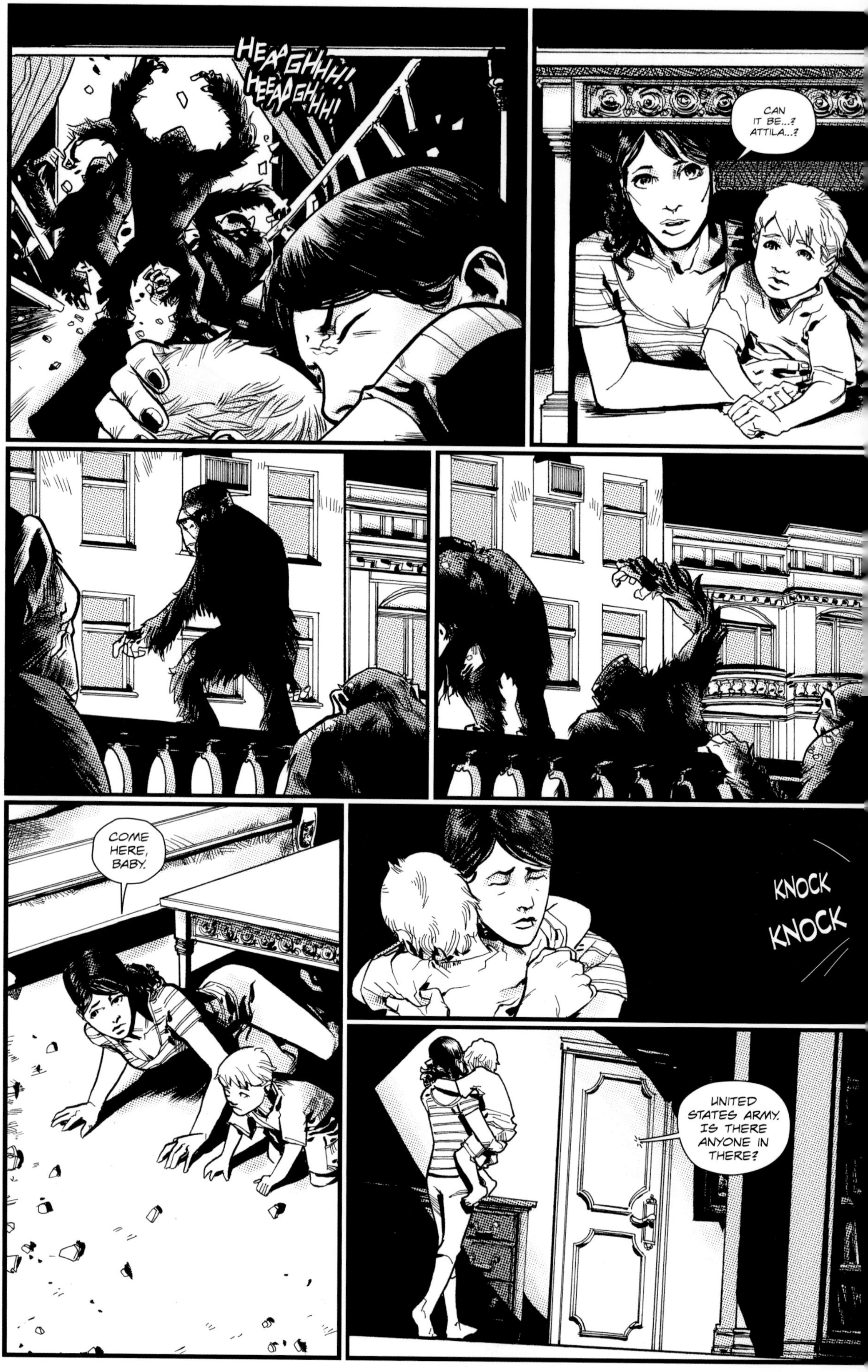
HEAAGHHH!
HEEAAGHHH!
CAN IT BE...? ATTILA...?
COME HERE, BABY.
KNOCK
KNOCK
UNITED STATES ARMY. IS THERE ANYONE IN THERE?

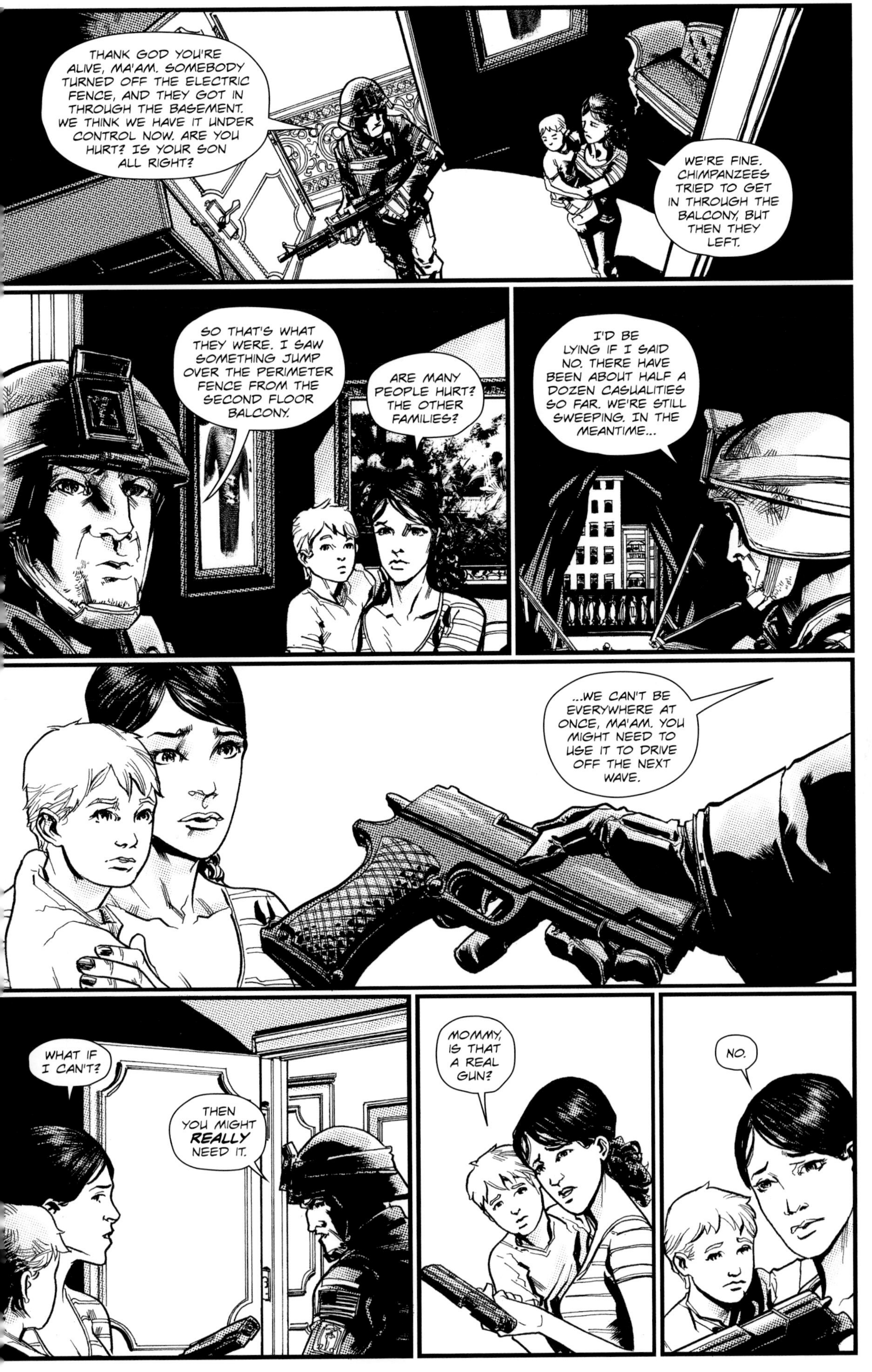
THANK GOD YOU'RE ALIVE, MA'AM. SOMEBODY TURNED OFF THE ELECTRIC FENCE, AND THEY GOT IN THROUGH THE BASEMENT. WE THINK WE HAVE IT UNDER CONTROL NOW. ARE YOU HURT? IS YOUR SON ALL RIGHT?
WE'RE FINE. CHIMPANZEES TRIED TO GET IN THROUGH THE BALCONY, BUT THEN THEY LEFT.
SO THAT'S WHAT THEY WERE. I SAW SOMETHING JUMP OVER THE PERIMETER FENCE FROM THE SECOND FLOOR BALCONY.
ARE MANY PEOPLE HURT? THE OTHER FAMILIES?
I'D BE LYING IF I SAID NO. THERE HAVE BEEN ABOUT HALF A DOZEN CASUALITIES SO FAR. WE'RE STILL SWEEPING. IN THE MEANTIME...
...WE CAN'T BE EVERYWHERE AT ONCE, MA'AM. YOU MIGHT NEED TO USE IT TO DRIVE OFF THE NEXT WAVE.
WHAT IF I CAN'T?
THEN YOU MIGHT REALLY NEED IT.
MOMMY, IS THAT A REAL GUN?
NO.

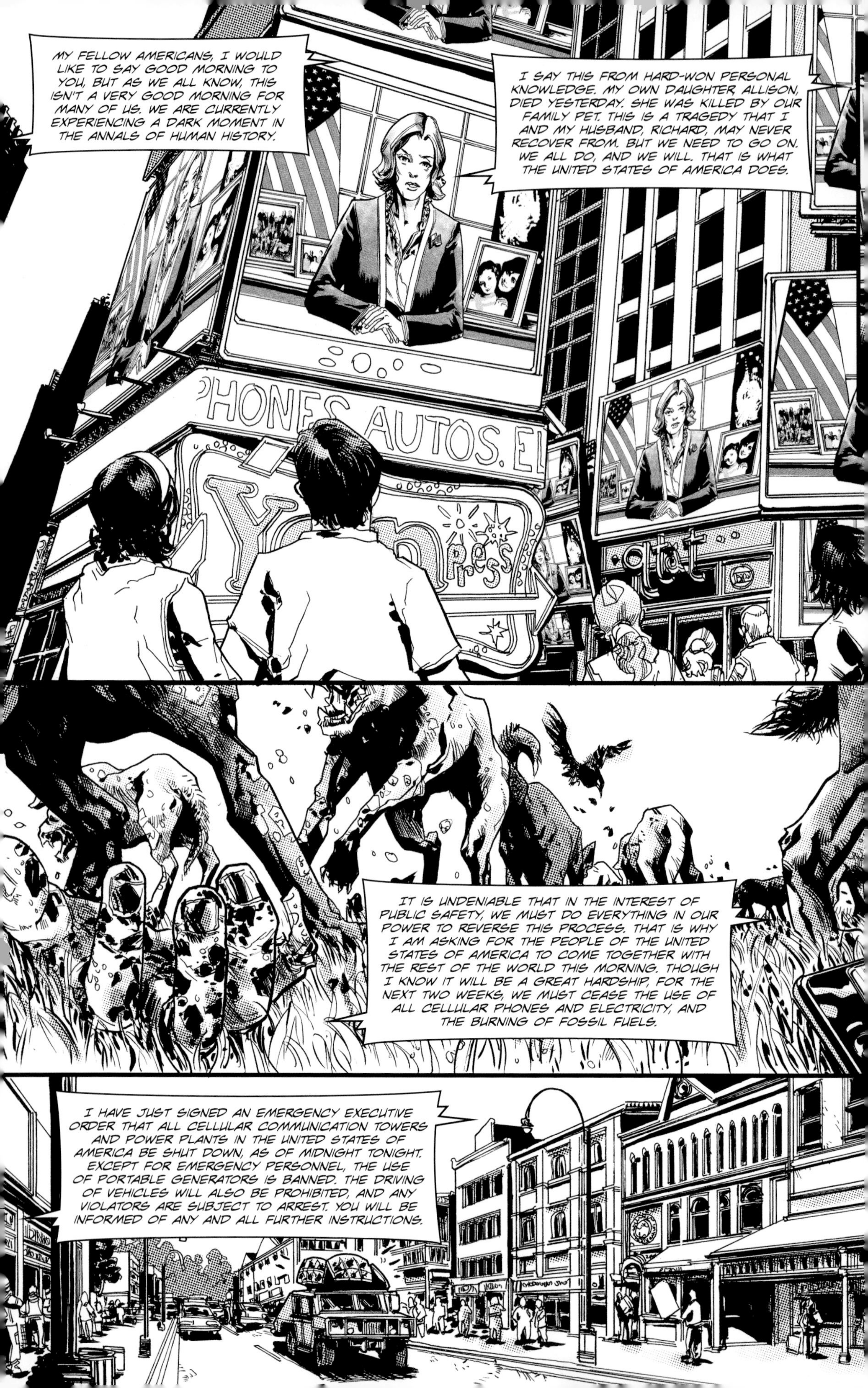

MY FELLOW AMERICANS, I WOULD LIKE TO SAY GOOD MORNING TO YOU, BUT AS WE ALL KNOW, THIS ISN'T A VERY GOOD MORNING FOR MANY OF US. WE ARE CURRENTLY EXPERIENCING A DARK MOMENT IN THE ANNALS OF HUMAN HISTORY.
I SAY THIS FROM HARD-WON PERSONAL KNOWLEDGE. MY OWN DAUGHTER, ALLISON, DIED YESTERDAY. SHE WAS KILLED BY OUR FAMILY PET. THIS IS A TRAGEDY THAT I AND MY HUSBAND, RICHARD, MAY NEVER RECOVER FROM. BUT WE NEED TO GO ON. WE ALL DO, AND WE WILL. THAT IS WHAT THE UNITED STATES OF AMERICA DOES.
PHONES AUTOS. EL
IT IS UNDENIABLE THAT IN THE INTEREST OF PUBLIC SAFETY, WE MUST DO EVERYTHING IN OUR POWER TO REVERSE THIS PROCESS. THAT IS WHY I AM ASKING FOR THE PEOPLE OF THE UNITED STATES OF AMERICA TO COME TOGETHER WITH THE REST OF THE WORLD THIS MORNING. THOUGH I KNOW IT WILL BE A GREAT HARDSHIP, FOR THE NEXT TWO WEEKS, WE MUST CEASE THE USE OF ALL CELLULAR PHONES AND ELECTRICITY, AND THE BURNING OF FOSSIL FUELS.
I HAVE JUST SIGNED AN EMERGENCY EXECUTIVE ORDER THAT ALL CELLULAR COMMUNICATION TOWERS AND POWER PLANTS IN THE UNITED STATES OF AMERICA BE SHUT DOWN, AS OF MIDNIGHT TONIGHT. EXCEPT FOR EMERGENCY PERSONNEL, THE USE OF PORTABLE GENERATORS IS BANNED. THE DRIVING OF VEHICLES WILL ALSO BE PROHIBITED, AND ANY VIOLATORS ARE SUBJECT TO ARREST. YOU WILL BE INFORMED OF ANY AND ALL FURTHER INSTRUCTIONS.

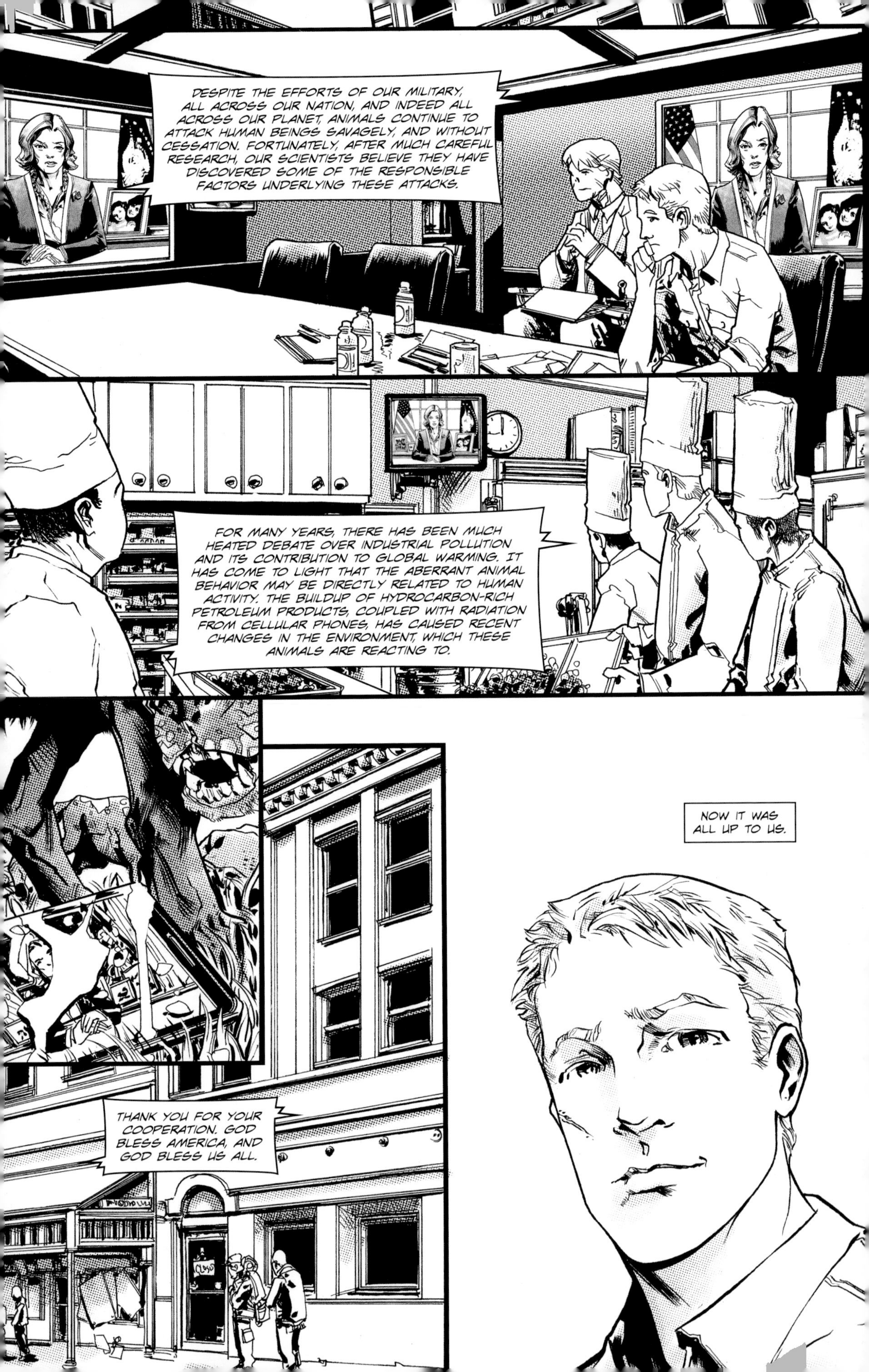
DESPITE THE EFFORTS OF OUR MILITARY, ALL ACROSS OUR NATION, AND INDEED ALL ACROSS OUR PLANET, ANIMALS CONTINUE TO ATTACK HUMAN BEINGS SAVAGELY, AND WITHOUT CESSATION. FORTUNATELY, AFTER MUCH CAREFUL RESEARCH, OUR SCIENTISTS BELIEVE THEY HAVE DISCOVERED SOME OF THE RESPONSIBLE FACTORS UNDERLYING THESE ATTACKS.
FOR MANY YEARS, THERE HAS BEEN MUCH HEATED DEBATE OVER INDUSTRIAL POLLUTION AND ITS CONTRIBUTION TO GLOBAL WARMING. IT HAS COME TO LIGHT THAT THE ABERRANT ANIMAL BEHAVIOR MAY BE DIRECTLY RELATED TO HUMAN ACTIVITY. THE BUILDUP OF HYDROCARBON-RICH PETROLEUM PRODUCTS, COUPLED WITH RADIATION FROM CELLULAR PHONES, HAS CAUSED RECENT CHANGES IN THE ENVIRONMENT, WHICH THESE ANIMALS ARE REACTING TO.
THANK YOU FOR YOUR COOPERATION. GOD BLESS AMERICA, AND GOD BLESS US ALL.
NOW IT WAS ALL UP TO US.

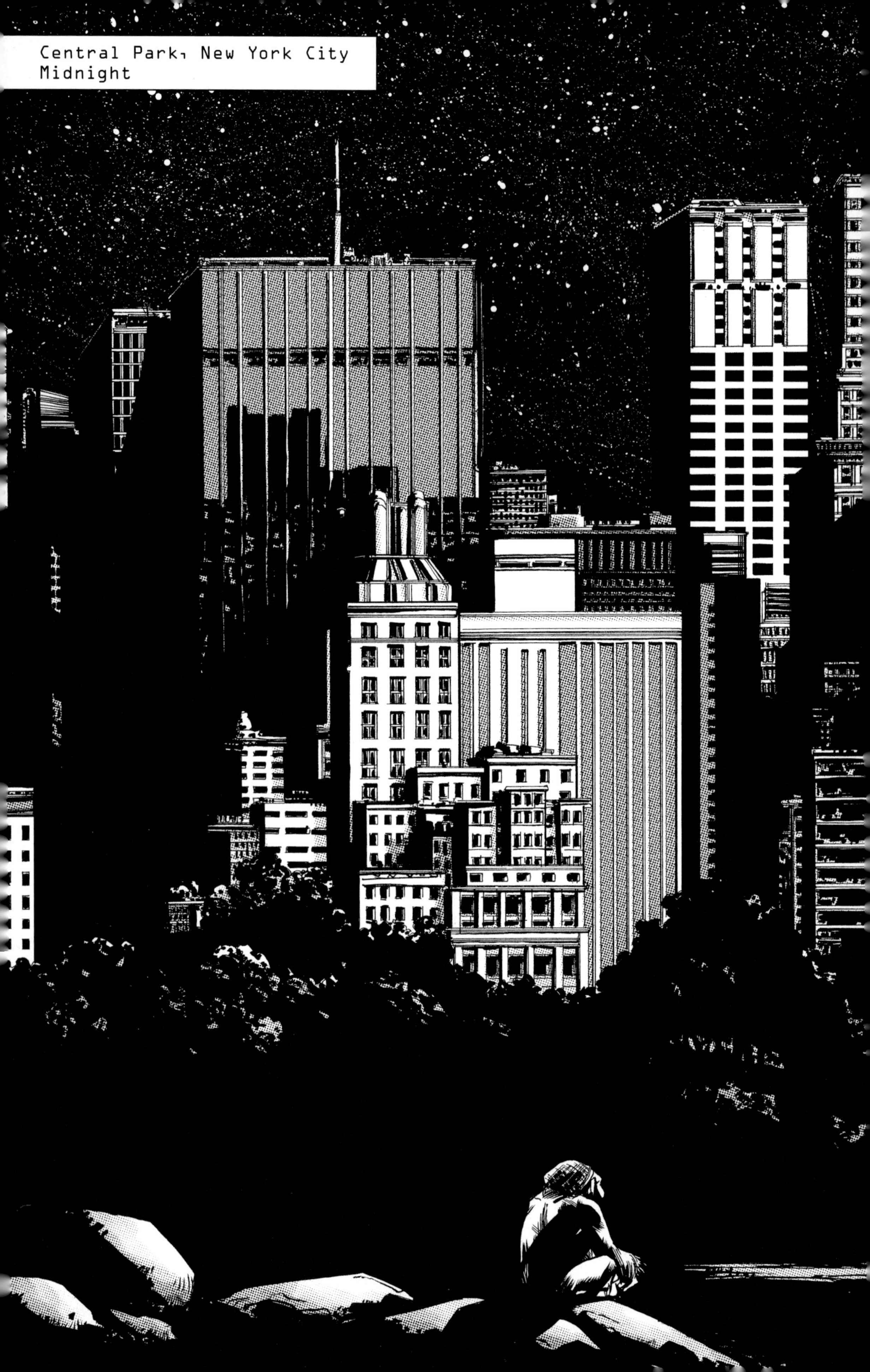
Central Park, New York City
Midnight

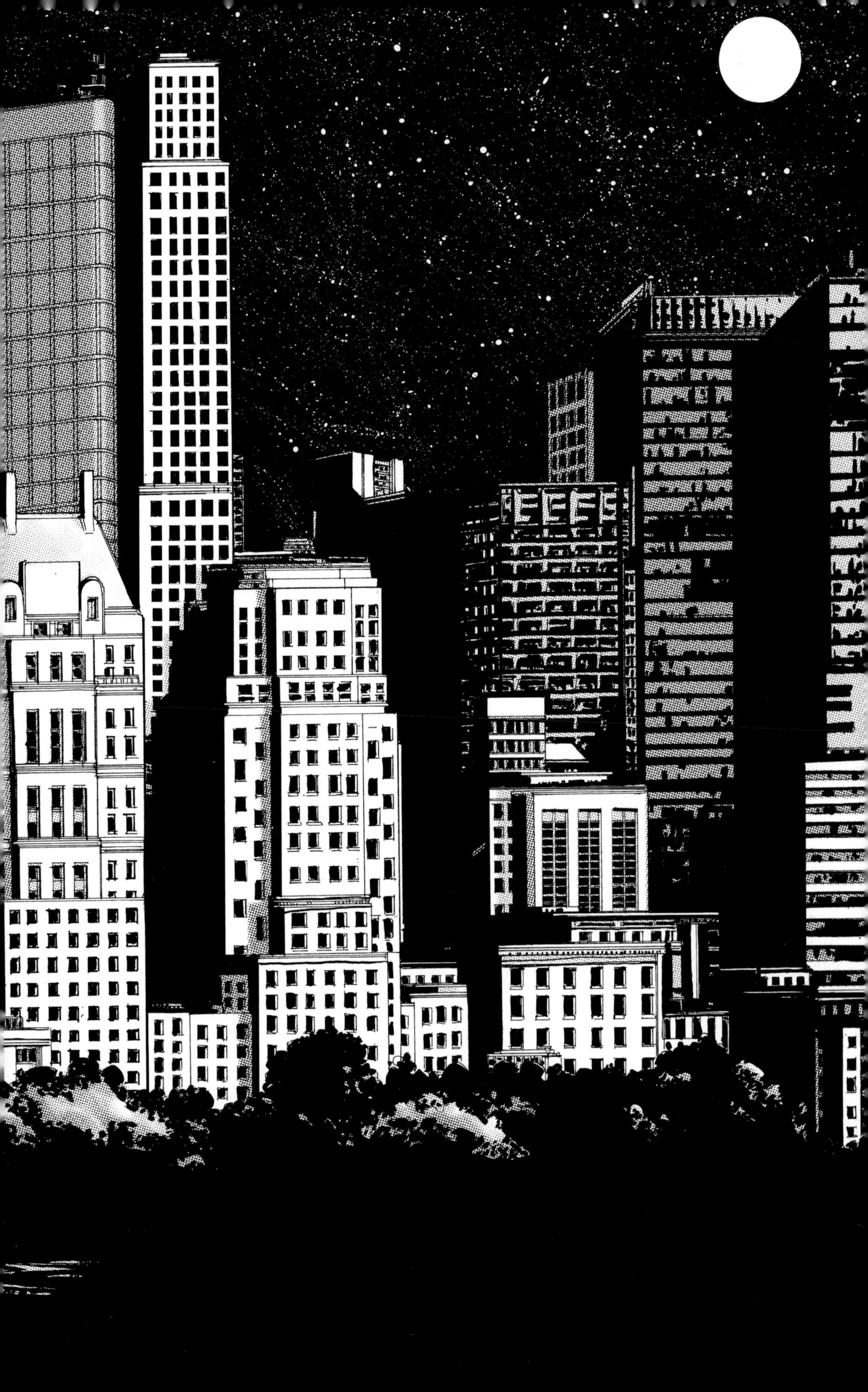

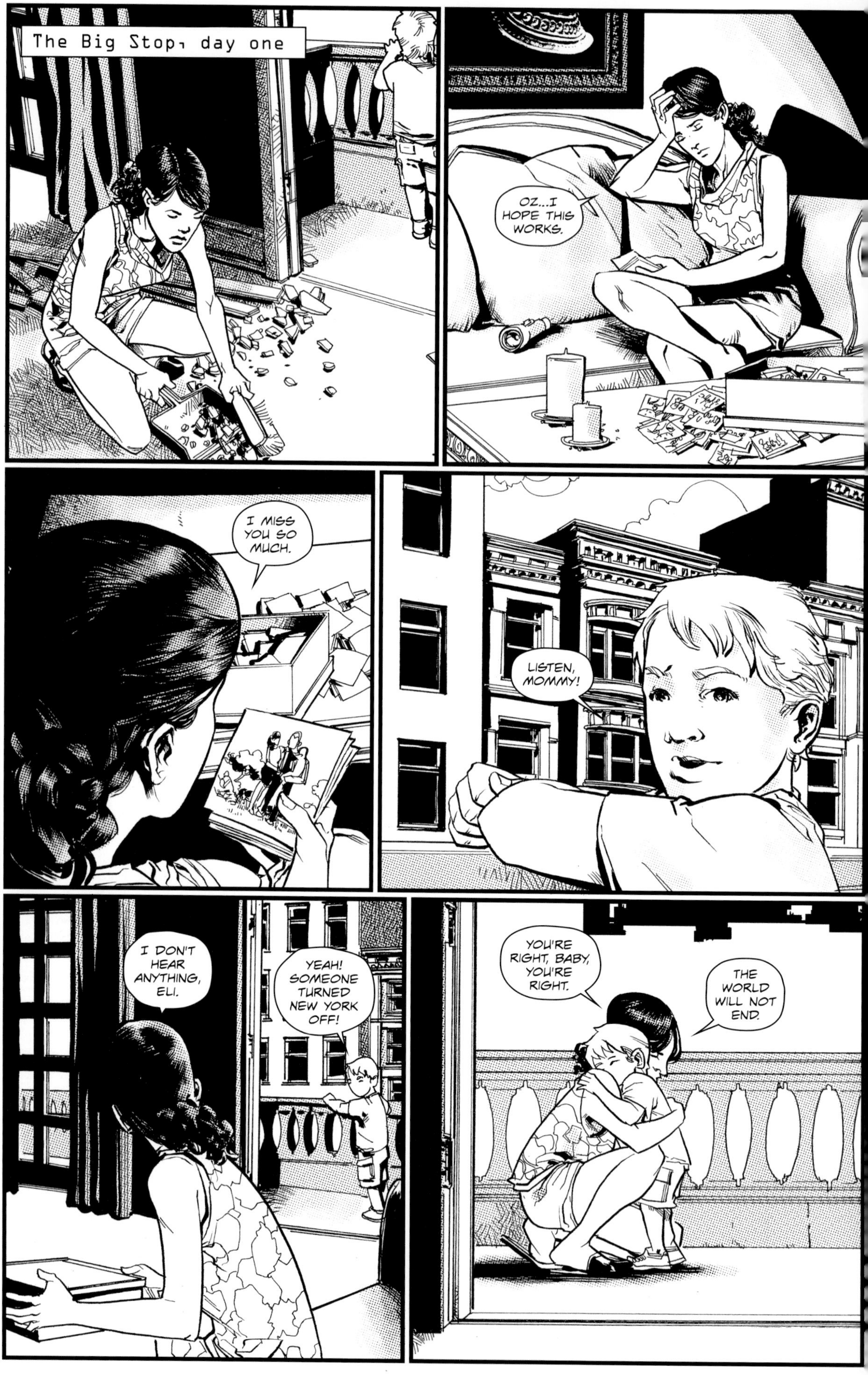
The Big Stop, day one
OZ...I HOPE THIS WORKS.
I MISS YOU SO MUCH.
LISTEN, MOMMY!
I DON'T HEAR ANYTHING, ELI.
YEAH! SOMEONE TURNED NEW YORK OFF!
YOU'RE RIGHT, BABY, YOU'RE RIGHT.
THE WORLD WILL NOT END.

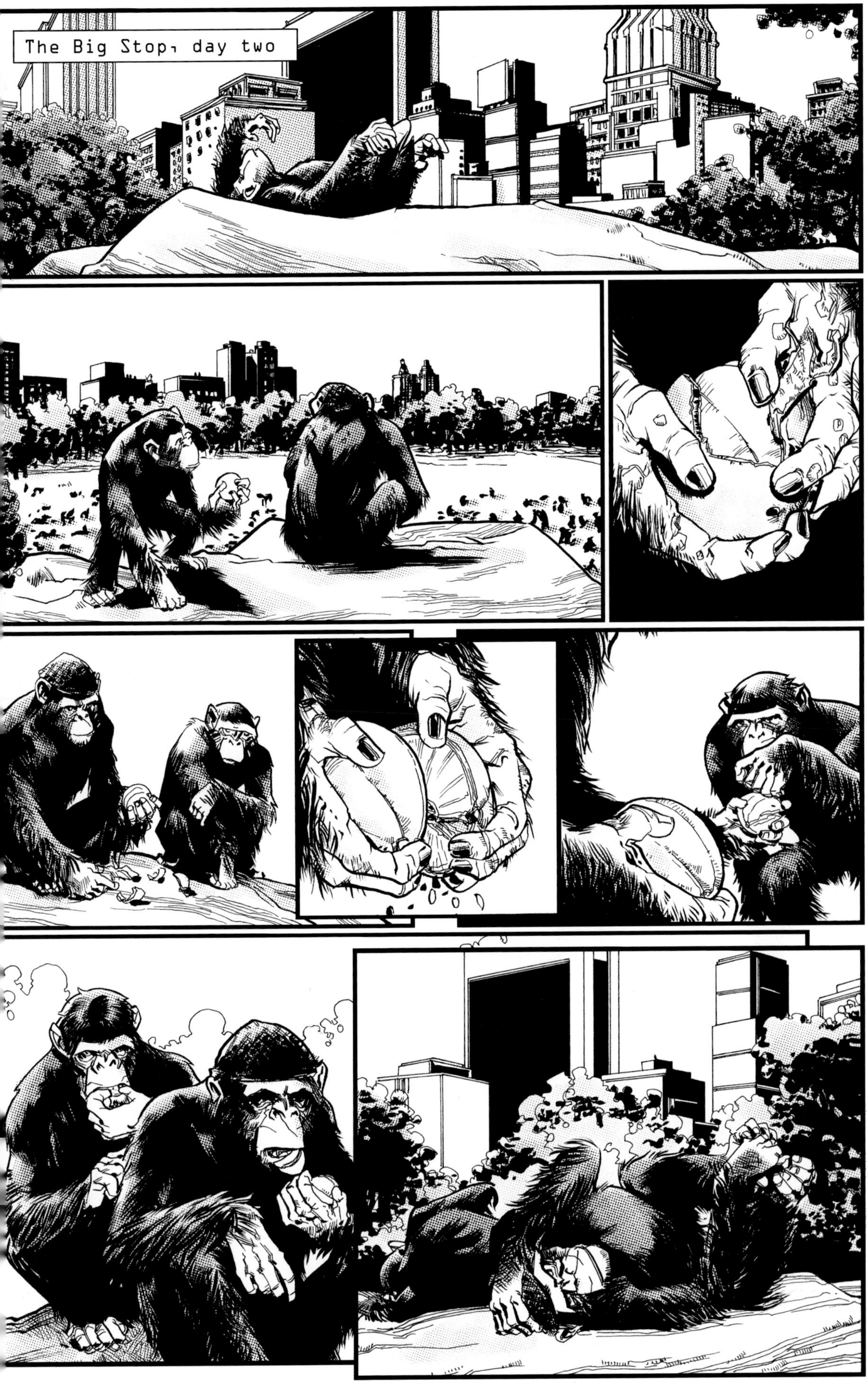
The Big Stop, day two

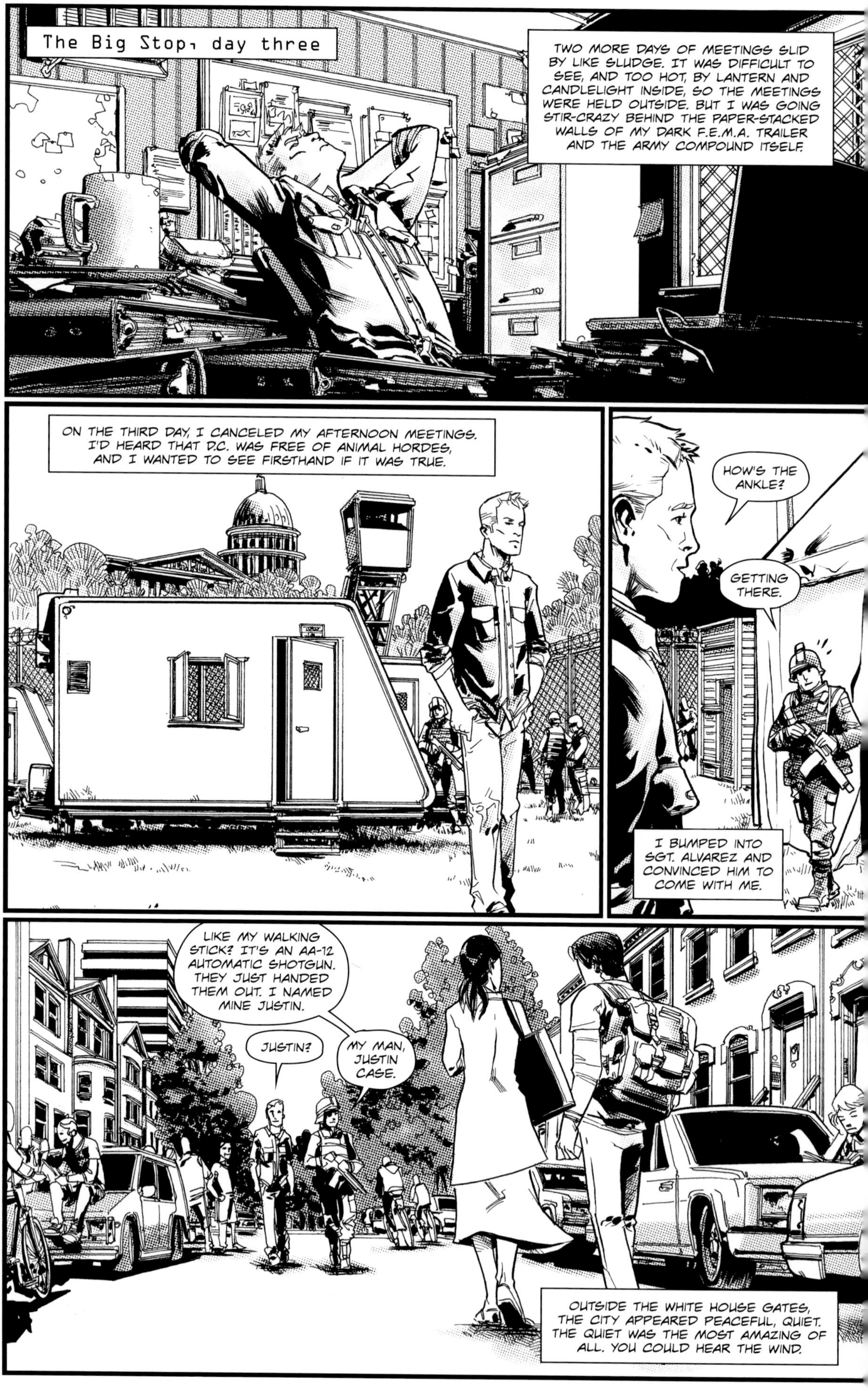
The Big Stop, day three
TWO MORE DAYS OF MEETINGS SLID BY LIKE SLUDGE. IT WAS DIFFICULT TO SEE, AND TOO HOT, BY LANTERN AND CANDLELIGHT INSIDE, SO THE MEETINGS WERE HELD OUTSIDE. BUT I WAS GOING STIR-CRAZY BEHIND THE PAPER-STACKED WALLS OF MY DARK F.E.M.A. TRAILER AND THE ARMY COMPOUND ITSELF.
ON THE THIRD DAY, I CANCELED MY AFTERNOON MEETINGS. I'D HEARD THAT D.C. WAS FREE OF ANIMAL HORDES, AND I WANTED TO SEE FIRSTHAND IF IT WAS TRUE.
HOW'S THE ANKLE?
GETTING THERE.
I BUMPED INTO SGT. ALVAREZ AND CONVINCED HIM TO COME WITH ME.
LIKE MY WALKING STICK? IT'S AN AA-12 AUTOMATIC SHOTGUN. THEY JUST HANDED THEM OUT. I NAMED MINE JUSTIN.
JUSTIN?
MY MAN, JUSTIN CASE.
OUTSIDE THE WHITE HOUSE GATES, THE CITY APPEARED PEACEFUL, QUIET. THE QUIET WAS THE MOST AMAZING OF ALL. YOU COULD HEAR THE WIND.

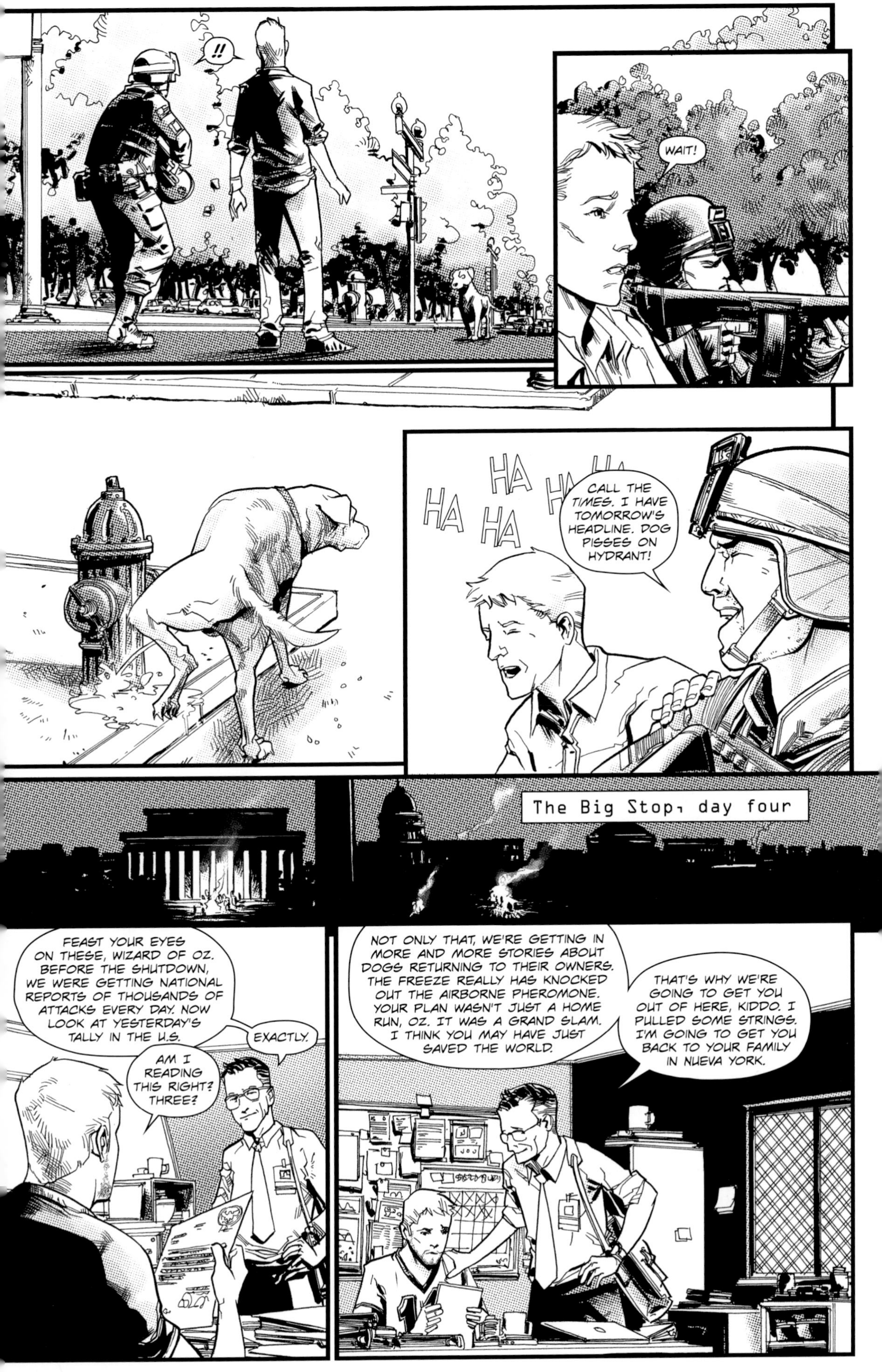
!!
WAIT!
HA HA HA HA HA
CALL THE TIMES. I HAVE TOMORROW'S HEADLINE. DOG PISSES ON HYDRANT!
The Big Stop, day four
FEAST YOUR EYES ON THESE, WIZARD OF OZ. BEFORE THE SHUTDOWN, WE WERE GETTING NATIONAL REPORTS OF THOUSANDS OF ATTACKS EVERY DAY. NOW LOOK AT YESTERDAY'S TALLY IN THE U.S.
AM I READING THIS RIGHT? THREE?
EXACTLY.
NOT ONLY THAT, WE'RE GETTING IN MORE AND MORE STORIES ABOUT DOGS RETURNING TO THEIR OWNERS. THE FREEZE REALLY HAS KNOCKED OUT THE AIRBORNE PHEROMONE. YOUR PLAN WASN'T JUST A HOME RUN, OZ. IT WAS A GRAND SLAM. I THINK YOU MAY HAVE JUST SAVED THE WORLD.
THAT'S WHY WE'RE GOING TO GET YOU OUT OF HERE, KIDDO. I PULLED SOME STRINGS. I'M GOING TO GET YOU BACK TO YOUR FAMILY IN NUEVA YORK.

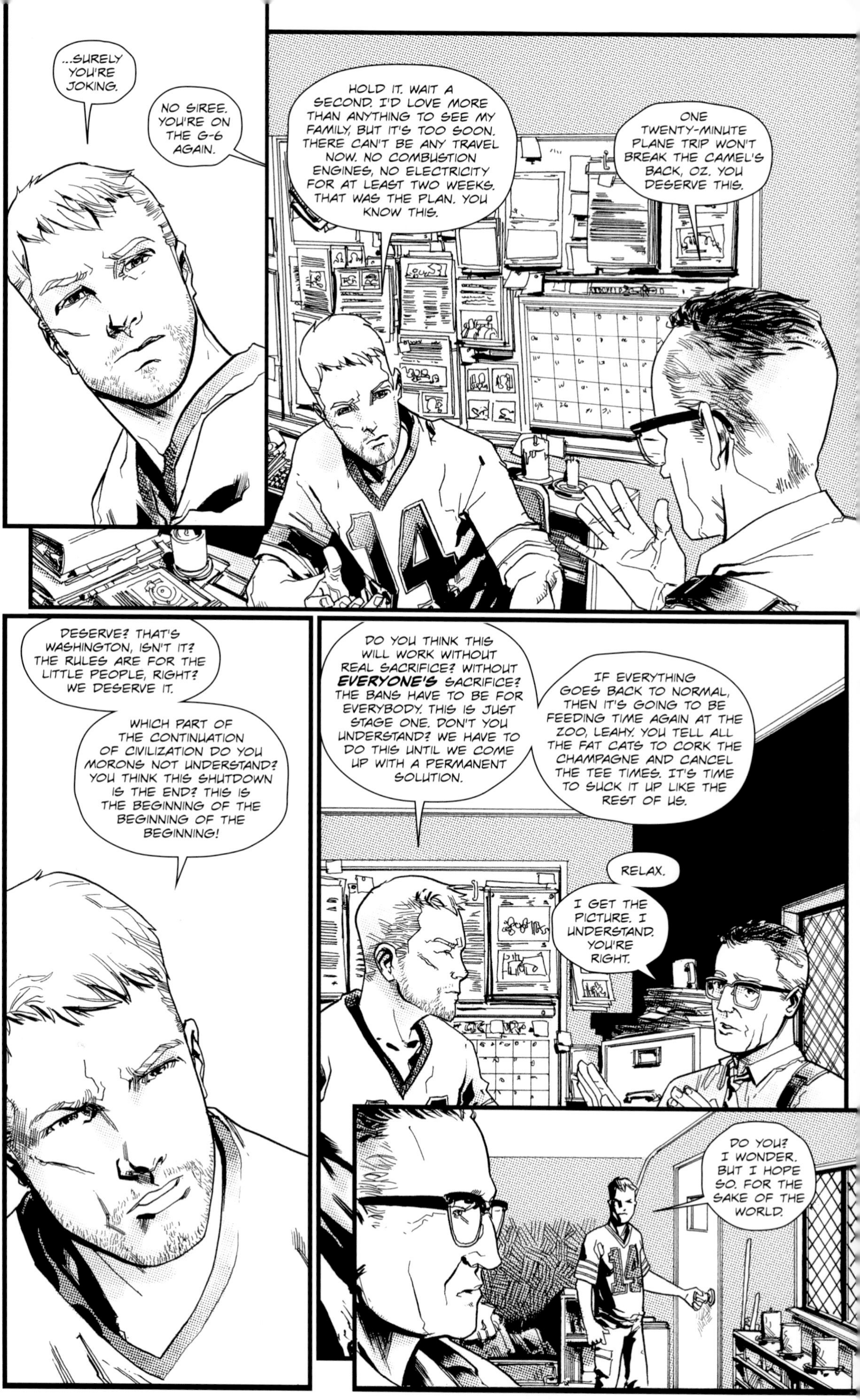
...SURELY YOU'RE JOKING.
NO SIREE. YOU'RE ON THE G-6 AGAIN.
HOLD IT. WAIT A SECOND. I'D LOVE MORE THAN ANYTHING TO SEE MY FAMILY, BUT IT'S TOO SOON. THERE CAN'T BE ANY TRAVEL NOW. NO COMBUSTION ENGINES, NO ELECTRICITY FOR AT LEAST TWO WEEKS. THAT WAS THE PLAN. YOU KNOW THIS.
ONE TWENTY-MINUTE PLANE TRIP WON'T BREAK THE CAMEL'S BACK, OZ. YOU DESERVE THIS.
DESERVE? THAT'S WASHINGTON, ISN'T IT? THE RULES ARE FOR THE LITTLE PEOPLE, RIGHT? WE DESERVE IT.
WHICH PART OF THE CONTINUATION OF CIVILIZATION DO YOU MORONS NOT UNDERSTAND? YOU THINK THIS SHUTDOWN IS THE END? THIS IS THE BEGINNING OF THE BEGINNING OF THE BEGINNING!
DO YOU THINK THIS WILL WORK WITHOUT REAL SACRIFICE? WITHOUT **EVERYONE'S** SACRIFICE? THE BANS HAVE TO BE FOR EVERYBODY. THIS IS JUST STAGE ONE. DON'T YOU UNDERSTAND? WE HAVE TO DO THIS UNTIL WE COME UP WITH A PERMANENT SOLUTION.
IF EVERYTHING GOES BACK TO NORMAL, THEN IT'S GOING TO BE FEEDING TIME AGAIN AT THE ZOO, LEAHY. YOU TELL ALL THE FAT CATS TO CORK THE CHAMPAGNE AND CANCEL THE TEE TIMES. IT'S TIME TO SUCK IT UP LIKE THE REST OF US.
RELAX.
I GET THE PICTURE. I UNDERSTAND. YOU'RE RIGHT.
DO YOU? I WONDER. BUT I HOPE SO. FOR THE SAKE OF THE WORLD.

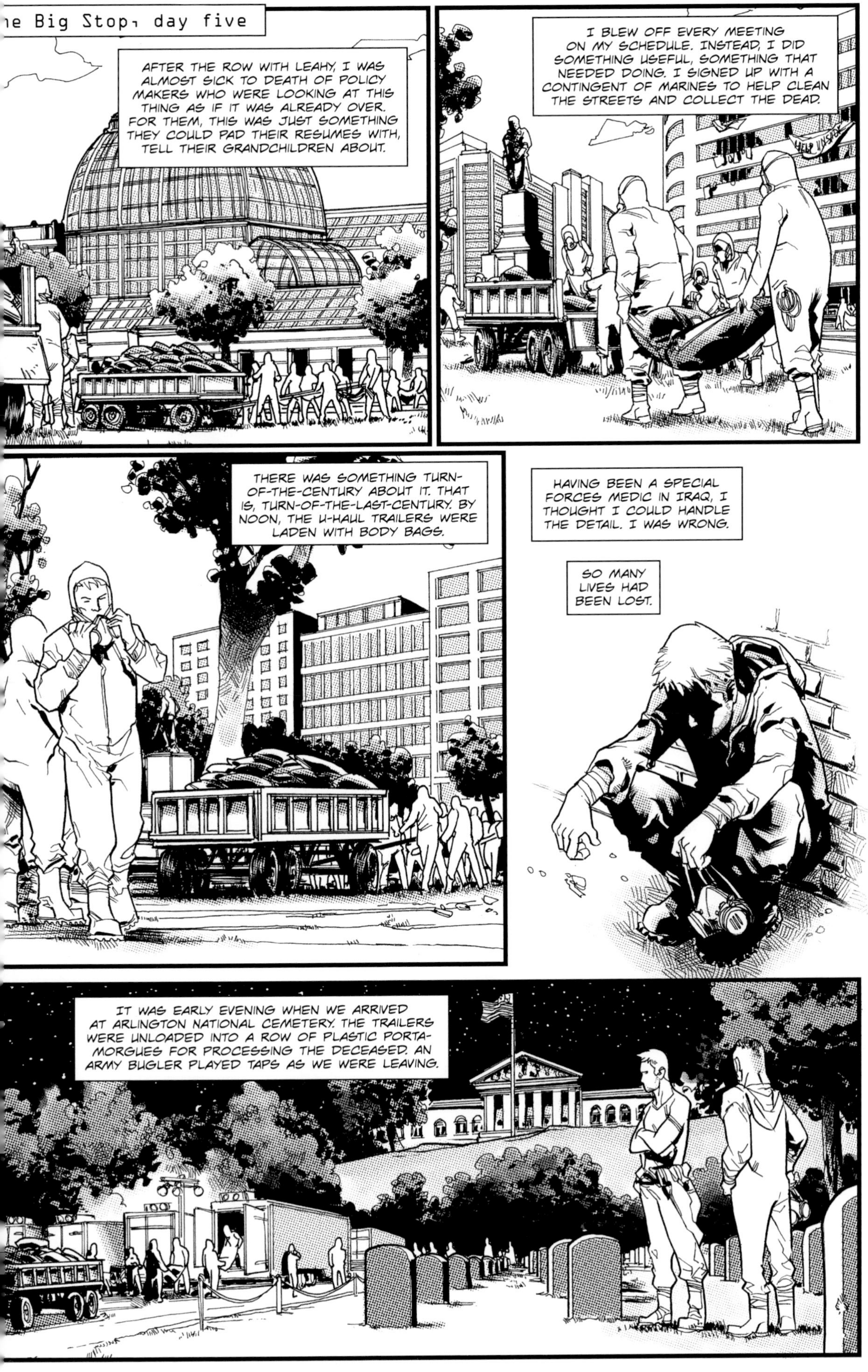

e Big Stop, day five
AFTER THE ROW WITH LEAHY, I WAS ALMOST SICK TO DEATH OF POLICY MAKERS WHO WERE LOOKING AT THIS THING AS IF IT WAS ALREADY OVER. FOR THEM, THIS WAS JUST SOMETHING THEY COULD PAD THEIR RESUMES WITH, TELL THEIR GRANDCHILDREN ABOUT.
I BLEW OFF EVERY MEETING ON MY SCHEDULE. INSTEAD, I DID SOMETHING USEFUL, SOMETHING THAT NEEDED DOING. I SIGNED UP WITH A CONTINGENT OF MARINES TO HELP CLEAN THE STREETS AND COLLECT THE DEAD.
THERE WAS SOMETHING TURN-OF-THE-CENTURY ABOUT IT. THAT IS, TURN-OF-THE-LAST-CENTURY. BY NOON, THE U-HAUL TRAILERS WERE LADEN WITH BODY BAGS.
HAVING BEEN A SPECIAL FORCES MEDIC IN IRAQ, I THOUGHT I COULD HANDLE THE DETAIL. I WAS WRONG.
SO MANY LIVES HAD BEEN LOST.
IT WAS EARLY EVENING WHEN WE ARRIVED AT ARLINGTON NATIONAL CEMETERY. THE TRAILERS WERE UNLOADED INTO A ROW OF PLASTIC PORTA-MORGUES FOR PROCESSING THE DECEASED. AN ARMY BUGLER PLAYED TAPS AS WE WERE LEAVING.

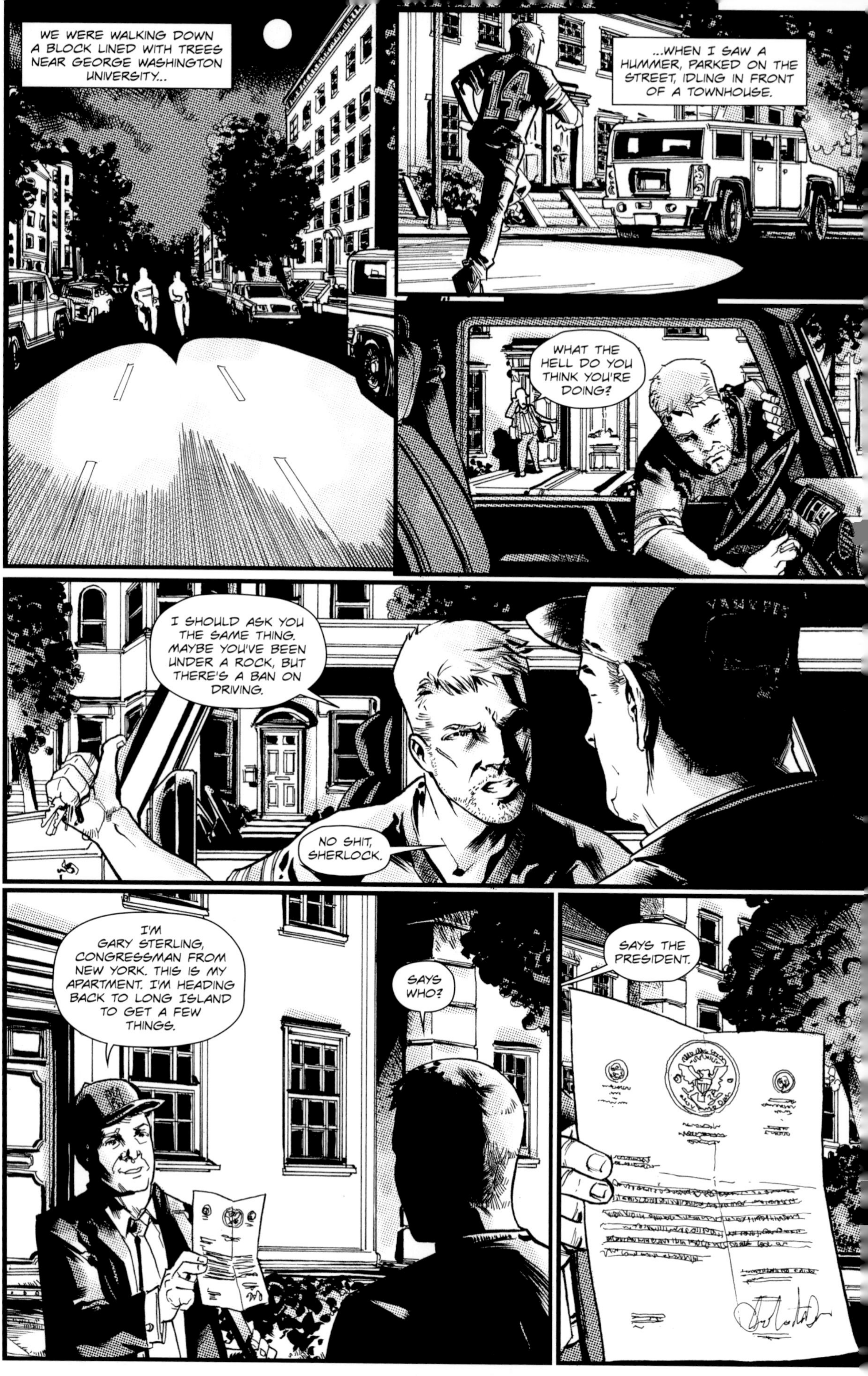
WE WERE WALKING DOWN A BLOCK LINED WITH TREES NEAR GEORGE WASHINGTON UNIVERSITY...
...WHEN I SAW A HUMMER, PARKED ON THE STREET, IDLING IN FRONT OF A TOWNHOUSE.
WHAT THE HELL DO YOU THINK YOU'RE DOING?
I SHOULD ASK YOU THE SAME THING. MAYBE YOU'VE BEEN UNDER A ROCK, BUT THERE'S A BAN ON DRIVING.
NO SHIT, SHERLOCK.
I'M GARY STERLING, CONGRESSMAN FROM NEW YORK. THIS IS MY APARTMENT. I'M HEADING BACK TO LONG ISLAND TO GET A FEW THINGS.
SAYS WHO?
SAYS THE PRESIDENT.

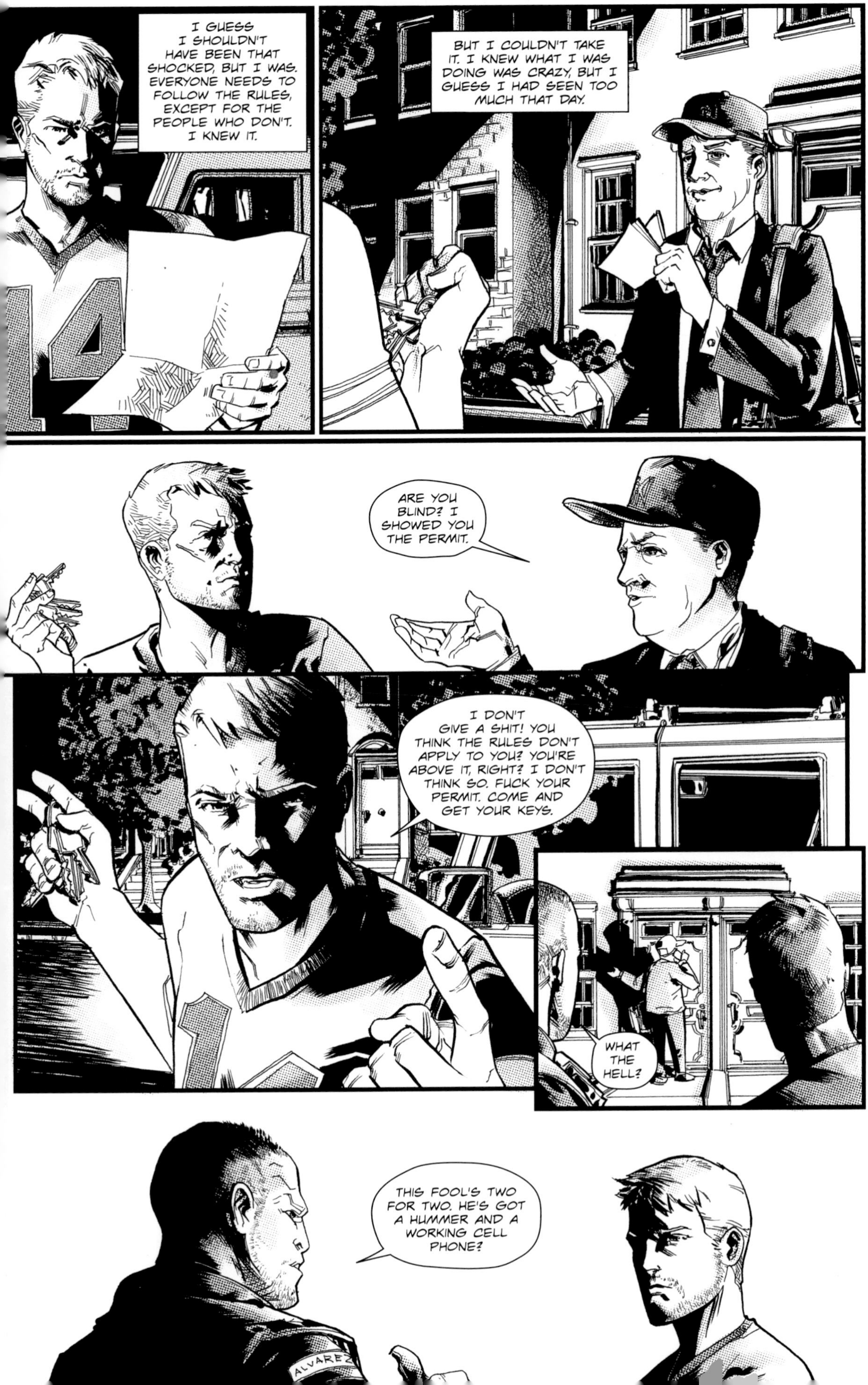
I GUESS I SHOULDN'T HAVE BEEN THAT SHOCKED, BUT I WAS. EVERYONE NEEDS TO FOLLOW THE RULES, EXCEPT FOR THE PEOPLE WHO DON'T. I KNEW IT.
BUT I COULDN'T TAKE IT. I KNEW WHAT I WAS DOING WAS CRAZY, BUT I GUESS I HAD SEEN TOO MUCH THAT DAY.
ARE YOU BLIND? I SHOWED YOU THE PERMIT.
I DON'T GIVE A SHIT! YOU THINK THE RULES DON'T APPLY TO YOU? YOU'RE ABOVE IT, RIGHT? I DON'T THINK SO. FUCK YOUR PERMIT. COME AND GET YOUR KEYS.
WHAT THE HELL?
THIS FOOL'S TWO FOR TWO. HE'S GOT A HUMMER AND A WORKING CELL PHONE?
ALVAREZ

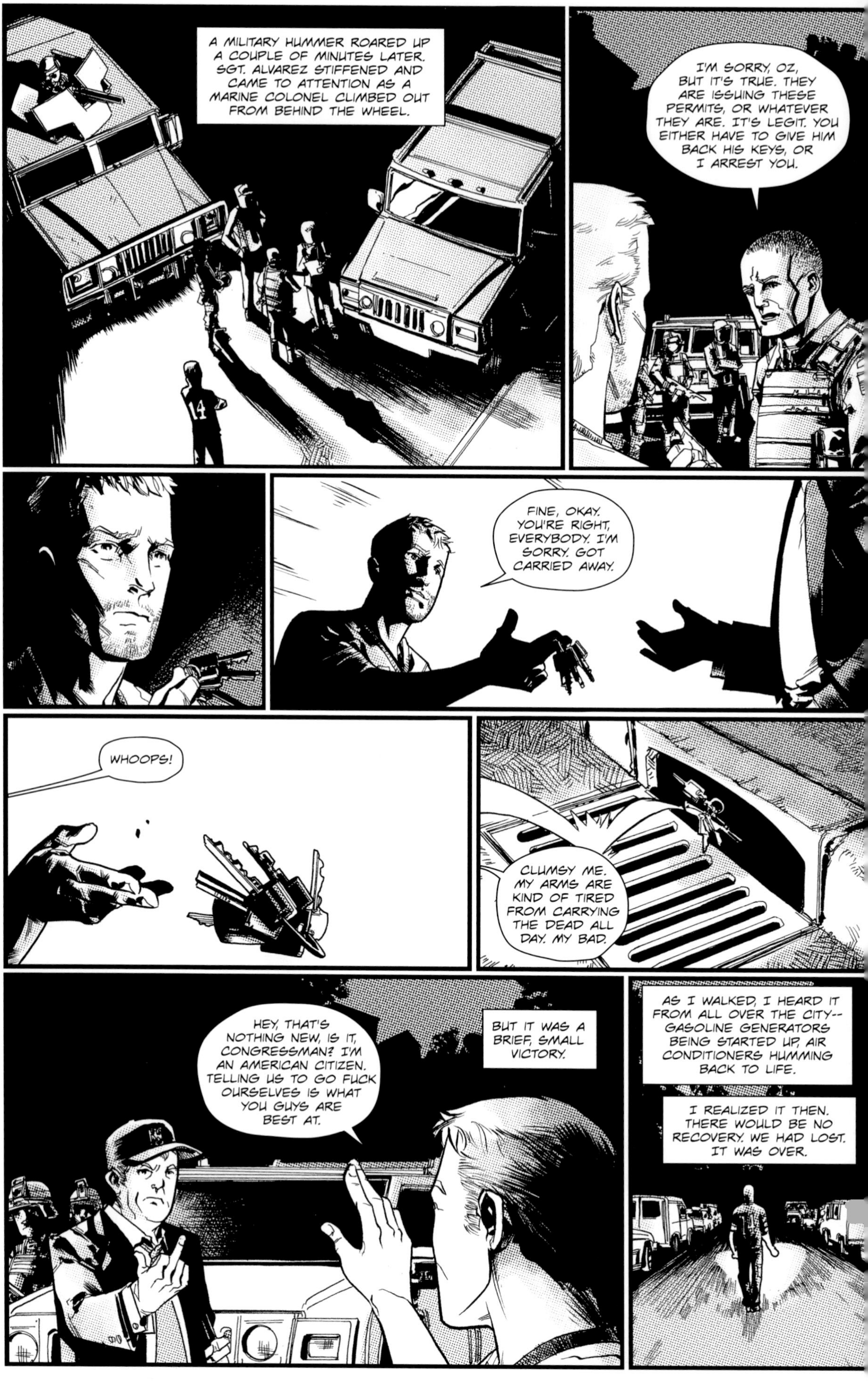
A MILITARY HUMMER ROARED UP A COUPLE OF MINUTES LATER. SGT. ALVAREZ STIFFENED AND CAME TO ATTENTION AS A MARINE COLONEL CLIMBED OUT FROM BEHIND THE WHEEL.
I'M SORRY, OZ, BUT IT'S TRUE. THEY ARE ISSUING THESE PERMITS, OR WHATEVER THEY ARE. IT'S LEGIT. YOU EITHER HAVE TO GIVE HIM BACK HIS KEYS, OR I ARREST YOU.
FINE, OKAY. YOU'RE RIGHT, EVERYBODY. I'M SORRY. GOT CARRIED AWAY.
WHOOPS!
CLUMSY ME. MY ARMS ARE KIND OF TIRED FROM CARRYING THE DEAD ALL DAY. MY BAD.
HEY, THAT'S NOTHING NEW, IS IT, CONGRESSMAN? I'M AN AMERICAN CITIZEN. TELLING US TO GO FUCK OURSELVES IS WHAT YOU GUYS ARE BEST AT.
BUT IT WAS A BRIEF, SMALL VICTORY.
AS I WALKED, I HEARD IT FROM ALL OVER THE CITY-- GASOLINE GENERATORS BEING STARTED UP, AIR CONDITIONERS HUMMING BACK TO LIFE.
I REALIZED IT THEN. THERE WOULD BE NO RECOVERY. WE HAD LOST. IT WAS OVER.

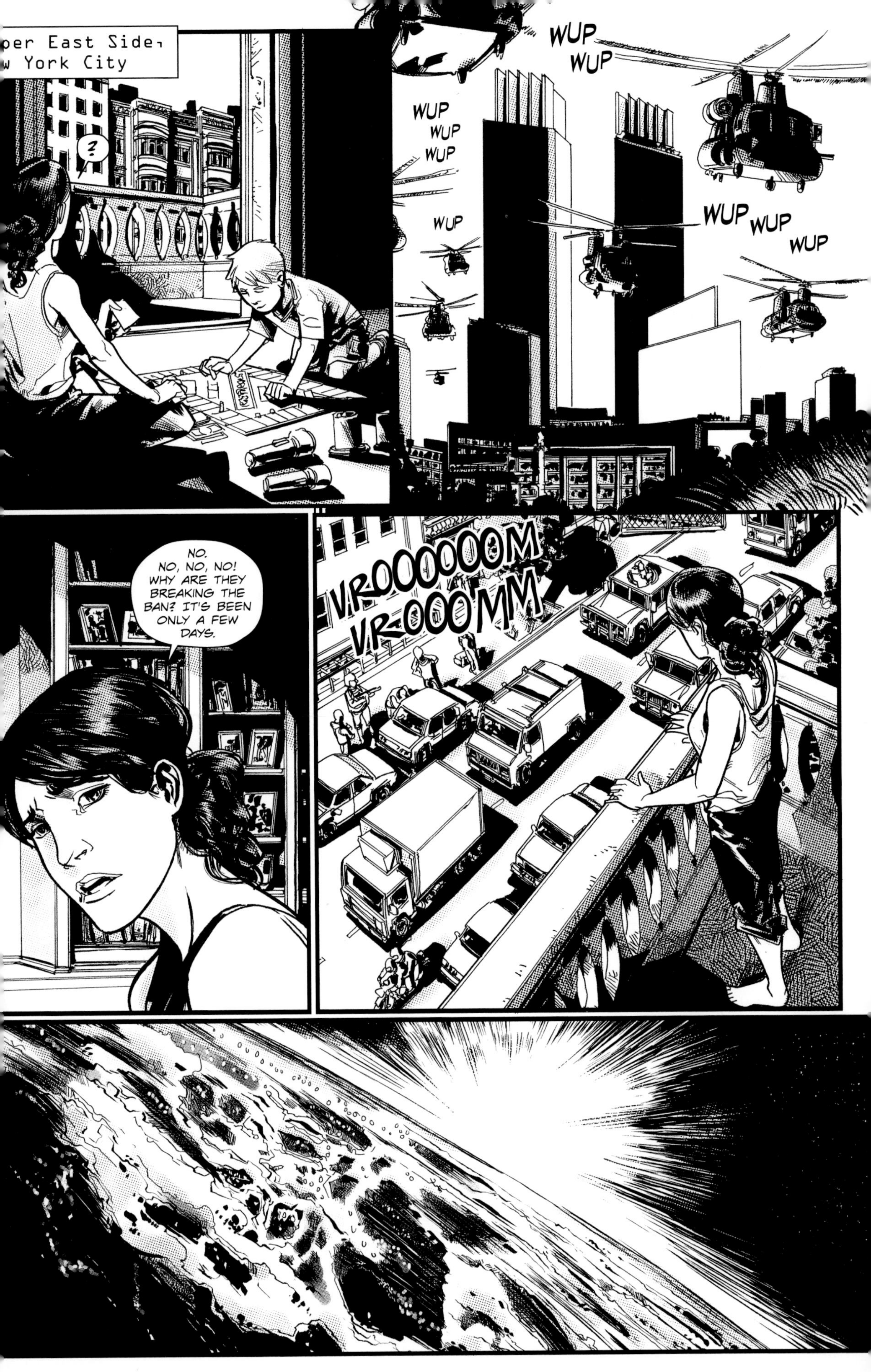
per East Side,
w York City
?
WUP
WUP
WUP
WUP
WUP
WUP
WUP
WUP
WUP
WUP
NO.
NO, NO, NO!
WHY ARE THEY
BREAKING THE
BAN? IT'S BEEN
ONLY A FEW
DAYS.
VROOOOOOM
VROOOMM

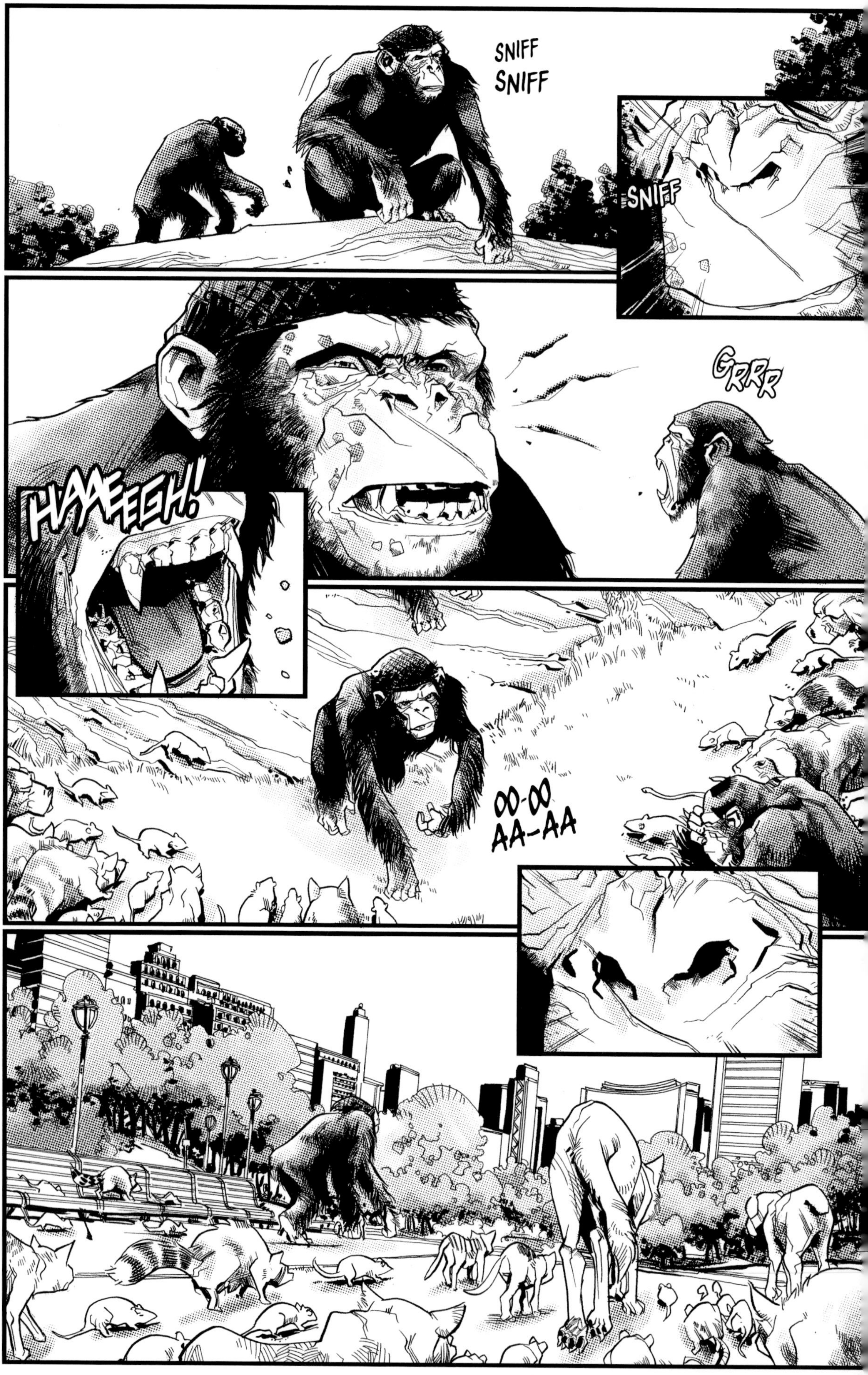
SNIFF
SNIFF
SNIFF
GRRR
HAAAEEGH!
OO-OO
AA-AA

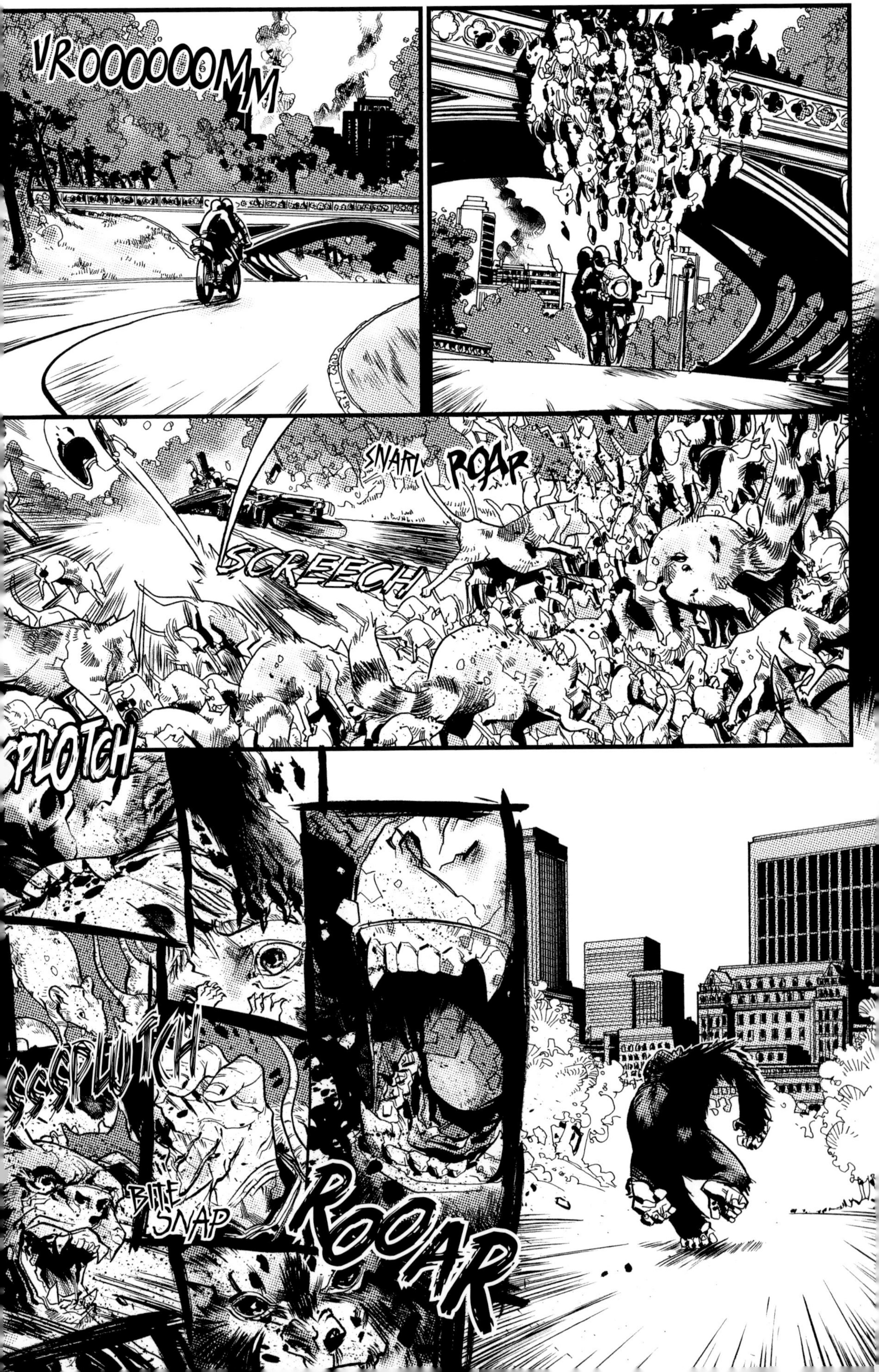
VROOOOOOMM
SNARL
ROAR
SCREECH
SPLOTCH
SSSPLUTCH
BITE
SNAP
ROOAR

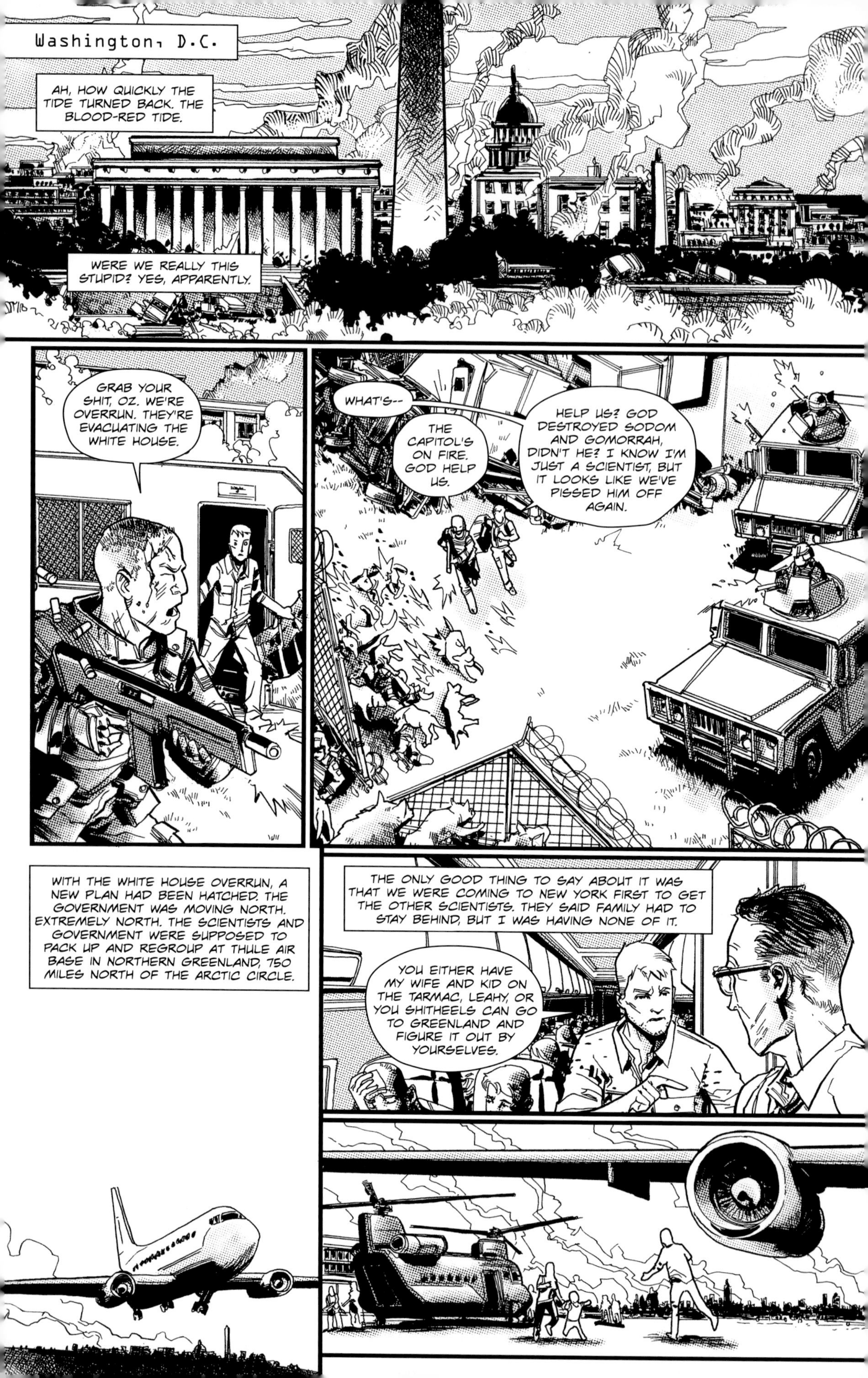
Washington, D.C.
AH, HOW QUICKLY THE TIDE TURNED BACK. THE BLOOD-RED TIDE.
WERE WE REALLY THIS STUPID? YES, APPARENTLY.
GRAB YOUR SHIT, OZ. WE'RE OVERRUN. THEY'RE EVACUATING THE WHITE HOUSE.
WHAT'S--
THE CAPITOL'S ON FIRE. GOD HELP US.
HELP US? GOD DESTROYED SODOM AND GOMORRAH, DIDN'T HE? I KNOW I'M JUST A SCIENTIST, BUT IT LOOKS LIKE WE'VE PISSED HIM OFF AGAIN.
WITH THE WHITE HOUSE OVERRUN, A NEW PLAN HAD BEEN HATCHED. THE GOVERNMENT WAS MOVING NORTH. EXTREMELY NORTH. THE SCIENTISTS AND GOVERNMENT WERE SUPPOSED TO PACK UP AND REGROUP AT THULE AIR BASE IN NORTHERN GREENLAND, 750 MILES NORTH OF THE ARCTIC CIRCLE.
THE ONLY GOOD THING TO SAY ABOUT IT WAS THAT WE WERE COMING TO NEW YORK FIRST TO GET THE OTHER SCIENTISTS. THEY SAID FAMILY HAD TO STAY BEHIND, BUT I WAS HAVING NONE OF IT.
YOU EITHER HAVE MY WIFE AND KID ON THE TARMAC, LEAHY, OR YOU SHITHEELS CAN GO TO GREENLAND AND FIGURE IT OUT BY YOURSELVES.

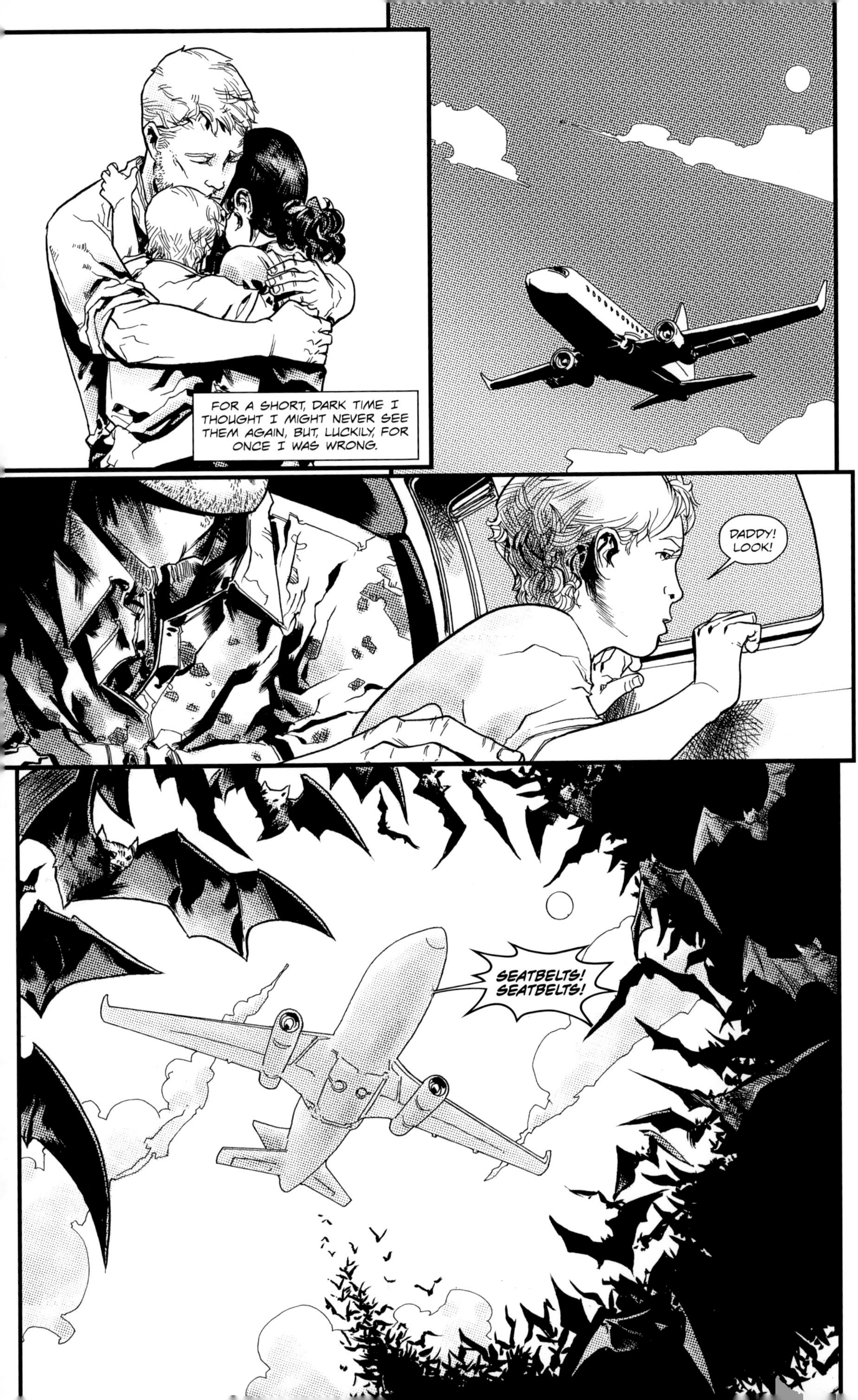
FOR A SHORT, DARK TIME I THOUGHT I MIGHT NEVER SEE THEM AGAIN, BUT, LUCKILY, FOR ONCE I WAS WRONG.
DADDY! LOOK!
SEATBELTS! SEATBELTS!

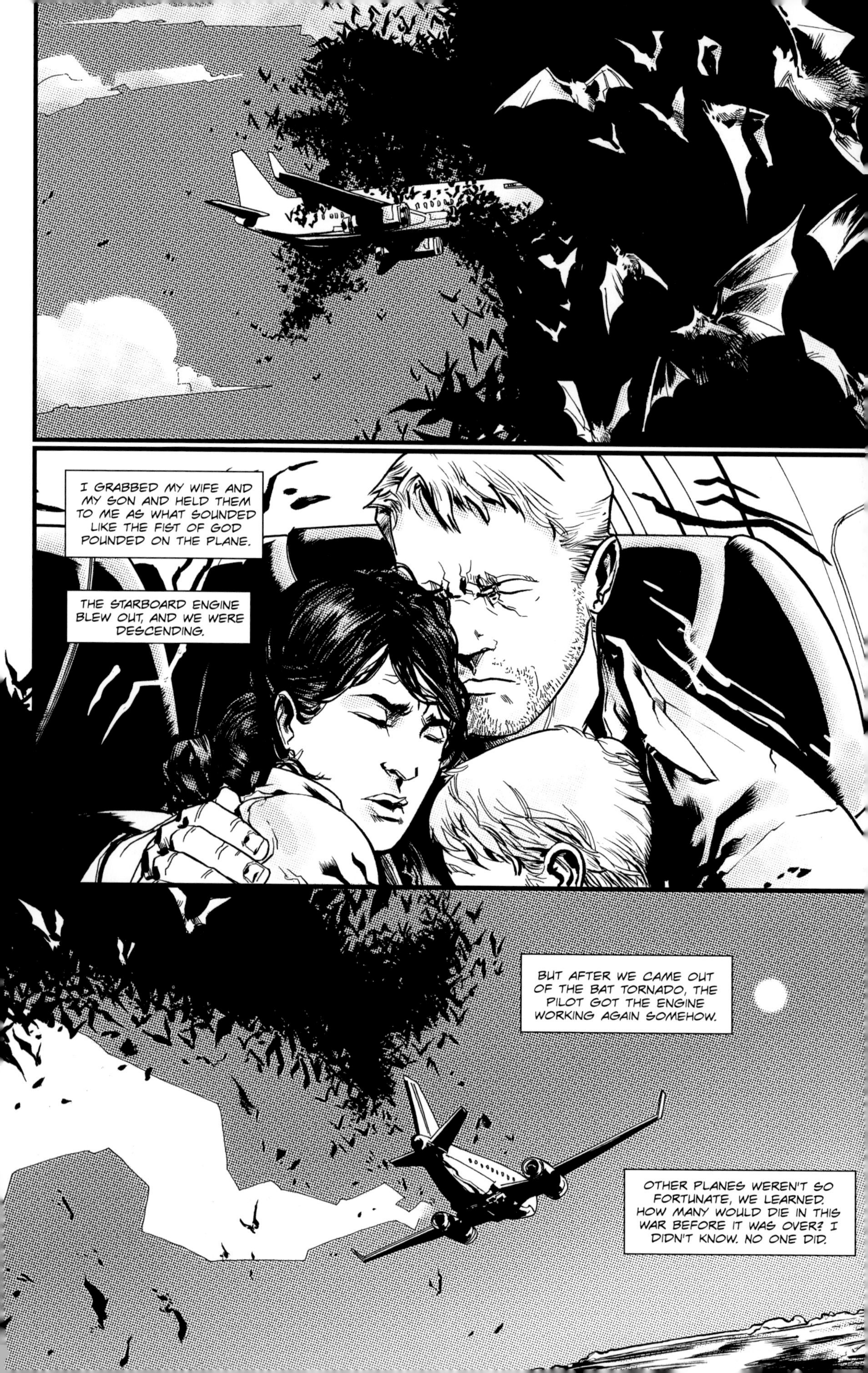
I GRABBED MY WIFE AND MY SON AND HELD THEM TO ME AS WHAT SOUNDED LIKE THE FIST OF GOD POUNDED ON THE PLANE.
THE STARBOARD ENGINE BLEW OUT, AND WE WERE DESCENDING.
BUT AFTER WE CAME OUT OF THE BAT TORNADO, THE PILOT GOT THE ENGINE WORKING AGAIN SOMEHOW.
OTHER PLANES WEREN'T SO FORTUNATE, WE LEARNED. HOW MANY WOULD DIE IN THIS WAR BEFORE IT WAS OVER? I DIDN'T KNOW. NO ONE DID.

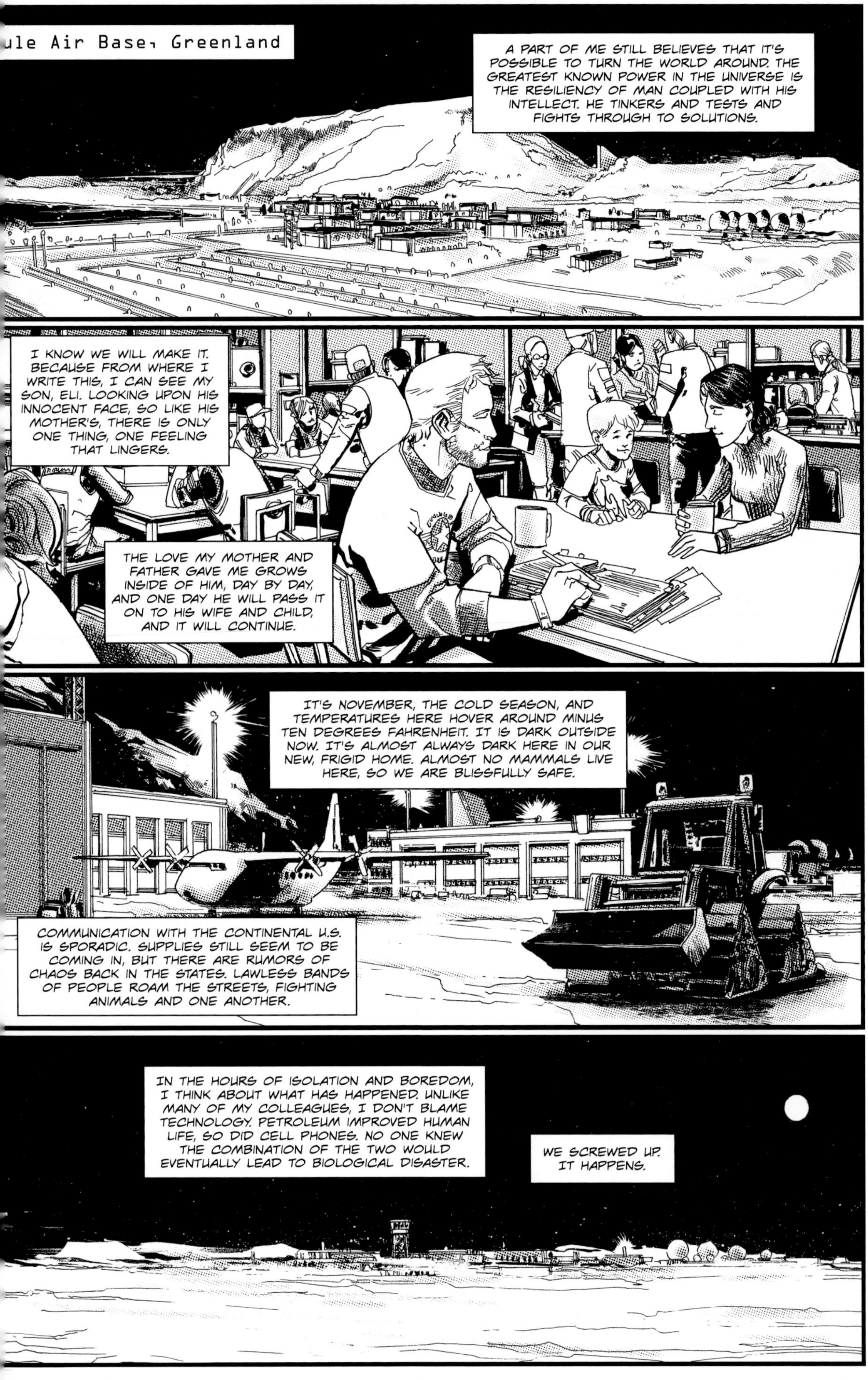
ule Air Base, Greenland
A PART OF ME STILL BELIEVES THAT IT'S POSSIBLE TO TURN THE WORLD AROUND. THE GREATEST KNOWN POWER IN THE UNIVERSE IS THE RESILIENCY OF MAN COUPLED WITH HIS INTELLECT. HE TINKERS AND TESTS AND FIGHTS THROUGH TO SOLUTIONS.
I KNOW WE WILL MAKE IT. BECAUSE FROM WHERE I WRITE THIS, I CAN SEE MY SON, ELI. LOOKING UPON HIS INNOCENT FACE, SO LIKE HIS MOTHER'S, THERE IS ONLY ONE THING, ONE FEELING THAT LINGERS.
THE LOVE MY MOTHER AND FATHER GAVE ME GROWS INSIDE OF HIM, DAY BY DAY, AND ONE DAY HE WILL PASS IT ON TO HIS WIFE AND CHILD, AND IT WILL CONTINUE.
IT'S NOVEMBER, THE COLD SEASON, AND TEMPERATURES HERE HOVER AROUND MINUS TEN DEGREES FAHRENHEIT. IT IS DARK OUTSIDE NOW. IT'S ALMOST ALWAYS DARK HERE IN OUR NEW, FRIGID HOME. ALMOST NO MAMMALS LIVE HERE, SO WE ARE BLISSFULLY SAFE.
COMMUNICATION WITH THE CONTINENTAL U.S. IS SPORADIC. SUPPLIES STILL SEEM TO BE COMING IN, BUT THERE ARE RUMORS OF CHAOS BACK IN THE STATES. LAWLESS BANDS OF PEOPLE ROAM THE STREETS, FIGHTING ANIMALS AND ONE ANOTHER.
IN THE HOURS OF ISOLATION AND BOREDOM, I THINK ABOUT WHAT HAS HAPPENED. UNLIKE MANY OF MY COLLEAGUES, I DON'T BLAME TECHNOLOGY. PETROLEUM IMPROVED HUMAN LIFE, SO DID CELL PHONES. NO ONE KNEW THE COMBINATION OF THE TWO WOULD EVENTUALLY LEAD TO BIOLOGICAL DISASTER.
WE SCREWED UP. IT HAPPENS.

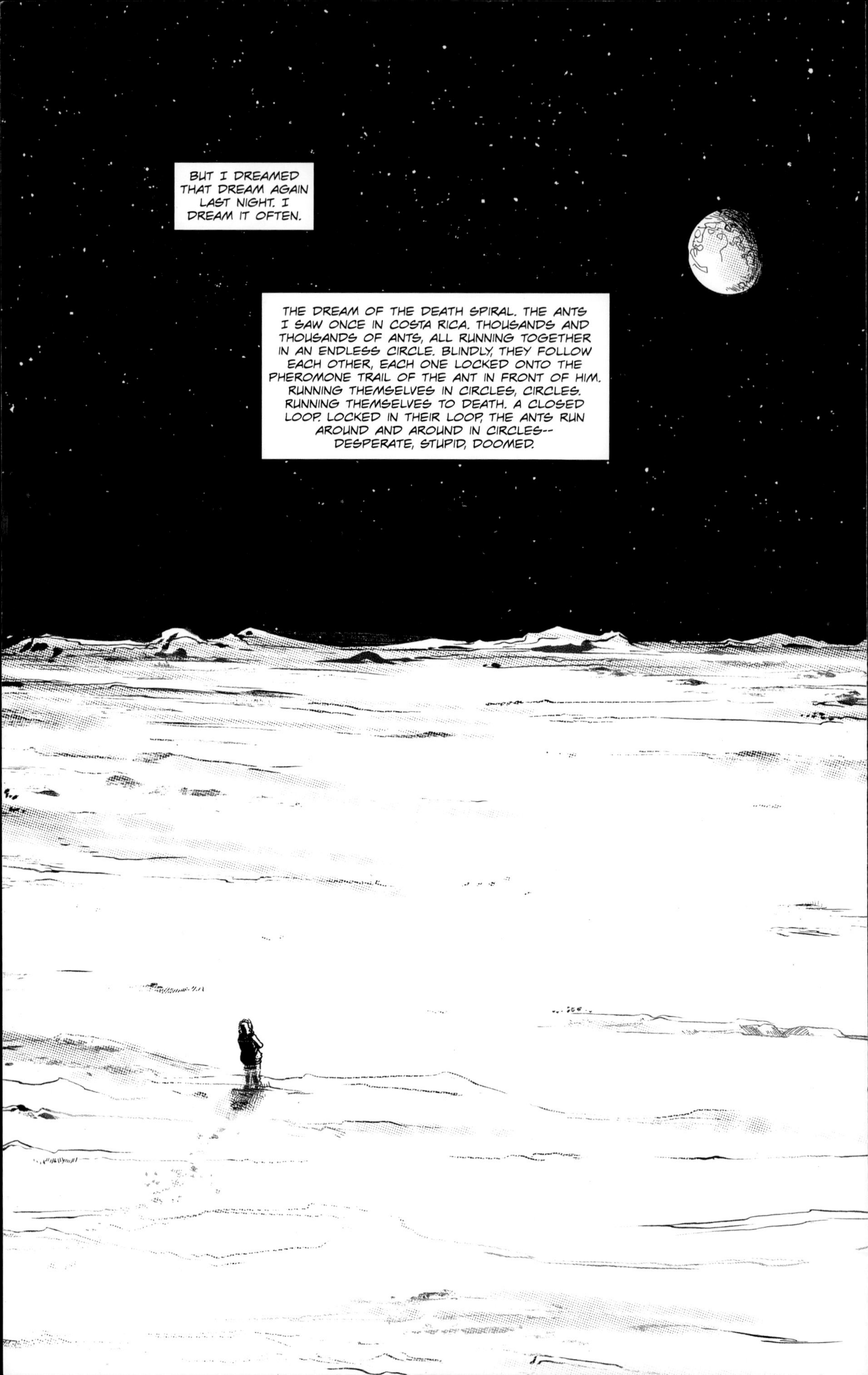
BUT I DREAMED THAT DREAM AGAIN LAST NIGHT. I DREAM IT OFTEN.
THE DREAM OF THE DEATH SPIRAL. THE ANTS I SAW ONCE IN COSTA RICA. THOUSANDS AND THOUSANDS OF ANTS, ALL RUNNING TOGETHER IN AN ENDLESS CIRCLE. BLINDLY, THEY FOLLOW EACH OTHER, EACH ONE LOCKED ONTO THE PHEROMONE TRAIL OF THE ANT IN FRONT OF HIM. RUNNING THEMSELVES IN CIRCLES, CIRCLES. RUNNING THEMSELVES TO DEATH. A CLOSED LOOP. LOCKED IN THEIR LOOP, THE ANTS RUN AROUND AND AROUND IN CIRCLES--DESPERATE, STUPID, DOOMED.